China in Africa

"The relationship between Africa and China is based on equality, mutual respect, and a commitment to a shared well-being."

Paul Kagame, Chairman of African Union

"A lot of developments in Botswana are a result of the sheer hard work of the Chinese people in our country,"

Mokgweetsi Masisi, President of Botswana

"No country in the world has added so much value to our products as China has. China has done a lot of technology transfer and job creation,"

Hage Geingob, President of Namibia

"We embrace China's 'Belt and Road' initiative. We are confident that this initiative will reduce the costs and increase the volume of trade between Africa and China. It will encourage the development of Africa's infrastructure, a critical requirement for meaningful regional and continental integration."

Cyril Ramaphosa, President of South Africa

"Togo intends to be the anchor point in West Africa for the New Silk Road initiative supported by China and which is based on ties between countries through land and maritime infrastructures."

Faure Gnassingbe, President of Togo

"When I think about Africa, I think about a continent with infinite resources, and beauty, diverse identities, ambitious, and cultivated youth, and also tremendous potential that the World envy."

Jilles Djon, African Chamber of Commerce in China

Lorenzo Riccardi · Giorgio Riccardi

China in Africa

FDI, Tax and Trends of the New African Geo-economics

Springer

Lorenzo Riccardi
Shanghai Jiao Tong University
Shanghai, China

Giorgio Riccardi
RsA Asia Tax Advisors
Shanghai, China

ISBN 978-981-16-1147-6 ISBN 978-981-16-1148-3 (eBook)
https://doi.org/10.1007/978-981-16-1148-3

This Springer imprint is published by the registered company Springer Nature Singapore Pte Ltd.
The registered company address is: 152 Beach Road, #21-01/04 Gateway East, Singapore 189721, Singapore

Introduction

The trade between China and Africa has a long history and can be traced back to the Chinese Tang and Song Dynasties in the ninth and tenth centuries. In the fifteenth century, the Ming Dynasty's fleet of Zheng He's voyages to the West Coast reached the east coast of Africa three times. For more than half a century since 1949, the Chinese leadership has put great importance on economic and trade cooperation between China and African countries. Through the joint efforts of the governments and enterprises of China and Africa, the economic cooperation between China and African countries has been fruitful. The economic and trade exchanges between the two sides have grown from nothing to small and to thrive.

China's engagement in Africa has been growing in many aspects, such as trade, investment, and aid. China's engagement with Africa is marked by close linkages between trade, investment, and finance. Chinese trade has undoubtedly contributed to economic growth in Africa. According to statistics from the General Administration of Customs of China, in 2018, China's total import and export volume with Africa was US$204.19 billion, a year-on-year increase of 19.7%, exceeding the overall growth rate of foreign trade in the same period by 7.1 percentage points. Among these, China's exports to Africa were US$104.91 billion, up 10.8%, and China's imports from Africa were US$99.28 billion, up 30.8%; the surplus was US$5.63 billion, down 70.0% year on year.[1] Commodity exporters in **the** diversification of exports in particular have benefited from high demand and associated price rises, and the competitiveness of Africa's non-oil natural resources has increased over the past decade. As China–Africa trade cooperation moves into its next phase, there is significant scope for, particularly, agriculture and manufactures. Based on its own experience, China could help African countries to address structural and logistical constraints that limit the competitiveness of these exports.

All African countries are benefiting from Chinese Foreign Direct Investment (FDI), which extends across the continent, and are increasingly diversified. Over the last decade, although the traditional partners of the African countries, namely, the European Union and the United States, continue to dominate Foreign Direct Investment (FDI) in Africa, the rise of China is highly noticeable. Statistics show

[1] http://english.mofcom.gov.cn/article/statistic/lanmubb/AsiaAfrica/201901/20190102831255.shtml.

Chapter 1
Algeria

1.1 Country Profile

1.1.1 Introduction

Official Name	People's Democratic Republic of Algeria
Capital	Algiers
Government	Presidential republic
Population	42,972,878
Area	2,381,741 sq. km
Official language(s)	Arabic, Berber and French

(continued)

L. Riccardi and G. Riccardi, *China in Africa*,
https://doi.org/10.1007/978-981-16-1148-3_1

(continued)

Official Name	People's Democratic Republic of Algeria
Main religion(s)	Islam
Currency	Dinar
GDP	$630 billion
GDP per capita	$15,200
Life expectancy	77.5

Source CIA Factbook, 2020

1.2 History

Algerians fought during the 1950s to achieve independence from France, achieving it in 1962. More than a million Algerians were killed during this fight for independence. The National Liberation Front (FLN), Algeria's primary political party, was established in 1954 as part of the effort for independence and has since dominated politics. In response to public disorder, the Government of Algeria instituted a multi-party system in 1988. However, the primary victory of the Islamic Salvation Front (FIS), in the December 1991 vote, prompted the Algerian army to intervene and postpone the second round of elections. The authorities feared Algeria would become an extremist-led government. After a ban of the Islamic Salvation Front party, FIS supporters began to attack the government officials. The fighting escalated into an insurrection, which leads to intense violence from 1992 to 1998, in which more than 100,000 people are thought to have died. The government gained the upper hand at the end of the 1990s, and consequently, FIS's militia and the Islamic Salvation Army were disbanded in January 2000.

Abdelaziz Bouteflika, with the support of the military, won the presidency in 1999. Bouteflika also won re-election in 2004, 2009, and 2014. However, elections are often criticized by opposition bodies as unfair, and international human rights groups say that media censorship and harassment of political opponents continues.

World view	1990	2000	2010	2020
Population, total (millions)	25.022	30.506	35.978	44.227
GDP (current US$) (billions)	61.892	54.749	161.207	178.637
GDP (% change)	0.800	3.8	3.616	2.406
GDP per capita (current $)	2,473.51	1,794.69	4,480.71	4,039.10
Inflation (%)	9.2	0.3	3.9	4.1

Source IMF World Economic Outlook database/RsA Asia 2020

1.2.1 Geography

Algeria is bordered by Morocco and Western Sahara to the west, by Tunisia and Libya to the east, Niger and Mali to the south and the Mediterranean Sea to the north. The Sahara covers over 90% of Algeria's territory. The high plateaus stretch for more than 600 km and consist of steppe-like plains, which average at 1,100–1,300 m high and drop to 400 m in the east.

The Atlas Mountains sit to the north, and the Ahaggar Massif is situated in the southeast. The highest point of Algeria is Mount Tahat at 3,003 m; the lowest point is Lake Chott Melrhir at −40 m. Lake Chott Melrhir is a salt lake that varies in size throughout the year. It is the largest lake in Algeria, with a maximum area of about 6,700 sq. km.

Algeria's territory is often assumed to be arid and semiarid, although the accuracy of this assumption depends on the location being referred to within the country. The coastal areas experience mild, wet winters (rainfall measure around 1000 mm annually) and hot, dry summers. Temperatures in the Sahara Desert can exceed 55 °C, and precipitation is highly irregular. Three years may pass without precipitation in the Tademaït region, and as many as five years on the Ahaggar Plateau.

Algeria's natural resources are comprised of petroleum, iron ore, zinc, lead, natural gas, and uranium. Algeria's most important agricultural outputs, which are grown in the more fertile regions, are barley, sorghum, wheat, oats, and maize. Tobacco plantations and vineyards export their products. Other grown goods are figs, dates, vegetables, olives, and fruits. Algeria also exports large quantities of cork. However, Algeria is currently facing some environmental issues such as soil erosion from overgrazing, poor farming practices, and desertification. Dumping of raw sewage, petroleum refining wastes, and other industrial sewages trigger the pollution of rivers and coastal waters. The Mediterranean Sea is becoming polluted from soil erosion, oil wastes, and fertilizer runoff.

Most populated cities

City	Population
Algiers	2,988,145
Oran	1,224,540
Constantine	943,112
Sétif	609,499
Annaba	317,206

Source Office National des Statistiques (ONS)

1.2.2 Government

The People's Democratic Republic of Algeria (Al Jaza'ir in the local form) is a presidential republic which was founded in 1962. The latest constitution was approved on 23rd February 1989. Amendments to the constitution are proposed by the President of the Republic or through the President with the support of three-fourths of the member of both houses of Parliament in joint sessions. Passage requires approval by both houses, approval by referendum, and promulgation by the President. The President can forego a referendum if the Constitutional Council determines the proposed amendment does not conflict with basic constitutional principles. Moreover, articles, including the republican form of government, the integrity and unity of the country, and the fundamental citizen's liberties and rights cannot be amended.

In 2014, Abdelaziz Bouteflika was re-elected as president for his fourth term (81.5% of the vote). The President of Algeria is directly elected by absolute majority popular vote for a 5-year term. A constitutional amendment reinstated a two-term limit in February 2016 after a constitutional amendment passed by the Parliament in November 2008 removed the limitation. The Prime Minister (Ahmed Ouyahia since August 2017) was nominated by the president of the majority party in Parliament. The cabinet of Ministers is appointed by the President.

Abdelkader Bensalah, the speaker of the upper house of parliament, became interim head of state on 9 April, a week after the resignation of President Bouteflika on 2 April 2019. Bensalah remained in office exceeding the 90-day constitutional limit until Algerians elected the country's new president in December 2019, former Prime Minister Abdelmadjid Tebboune.

Key political figures	
Title	Name
President	Abdelmadjid Tebboune
Prime Minister	Abdelaziz Djerad
President of the Council of the Nation	Salah Goudjil
President of the Constitutional Council	Kamel Feniche

Source The World Factbook—CIA, 2020

1.2.3 Culture

Algeria's Radio has three national stations, two thematic stations, and 32 regional stations. This organization, which claims 20 million listeners in Algeria, is owned by the Algerian State, which has kept a monopoly of the media since 1962. It broadcasts in Arabic, Berber, and French, although the written press only includes Arabic and French.

More global than Algerian media is Algeria's influence in the world of sports. Several Algerians participated in various sports events in the twentieth century, such as the Olympic Games, the Pan-African Games, the Pan-Arab Games, and the Mediterranean Games. Today, football is the most popular sport in Algeria with the famous national team called "The Green" or "The Fennecs."

Furthermore, another important component of Algerian culture is its cuisine, which is characterized by a variety of ingredients derived from land and marine production. Out of all the specialties present in Algeria, the most famous is couscous. This is recognized as the national dish along with traditional pastries, which are described as "oriental" in Western countries.

1.2.4 Economy

Global links	1990	2000	2010	2018
Merchandise trade (% of GDP)	37	57	60	48
Net barter of trade index (2000 = 100)	74	100	225	216
External debt stocks, total (DOD, current US$) (billion)	28.692	23.359	3.63	1.72
Net migration (thousands)	−129	−205	−143	–
Personal remittances, received (current US$) (million)	352	790	197	1792
Foreign direct investment, net inflows (BoP, current US$ (million)	335	280	2,300	1,506
Net official development assistance received (current US$) (million)	331.6	200	201.3	144

Source World Development Indicators database/RsA Asia 2020

Economy	1990	2000	2010	2018
GDP (current US$) (billions)	62.05	54.79	161.21	173.76
GDP growth (annual %)	0.8	3.8	3.6	1.4
Inflation, GDP deflator (annual %)	30.3	22.7	16.1	7.6
Agriculture, value added (% of GDP)	11	8.4	8.5	12
Industry, value added (% of GDP)	48	54.4	50.5	39.6
Services, etc., value added (% of GDP)	40	32.2	38.2	44
Exports of goods and services (% of GDP)	23.4	42.1	38.4	25.6
Import of goods and services (% of GDP)	24.9	20.8	31.4	32.3
Gross capital formation (% of GDP)	28.6	23.6	41.4	47.1
Revenue, excluding grants (% of GDP)	...	38.3	37.1	...
Net lending (+)/ net borrowing (−) (% of GDP)	...	9.7	0.4	...

Source World Development Indicators database/RsA Asia 2020

The state controls Algeria's economy, a legacy of the country's socialist post-independence development model. In recent years, the Algerian government has halted the privatization of state-owned industries and has imposed restrictions on imports and foreign involvement. Hydrocarbons are the backbone of the economy, accounting for roughly 30% of GDP, 60% of budget revenues, and nearly 95% of export earnings. Algeria has the 10th largest natural gas reserves and the 16th largest oil reserves, ranking as the sixth-largest gas exporter. It was their hydrocarbon exports, which enabled Algeria to maintain macroeconomic stability and amass vast foreign currency reserves while oil prices were high.

Algeria's external debt is extremely low, at about 2% of GDP. However, Algeria has struggled to develop non-hydrocarbon industries because of heavy regulation and an emphasis on state-driven growth. Declining oil prices since 2014 have reduced the government's ability to use state-driven growth to distribute rents and fund generous public subsidies. Algeria's foreign exchange reserves have declined by more than 40% since late 2013, and its oil stabilization fund has decreased from about $75 billion at the end of 2013 to about $7 billion in 2017, which is the statutory minimum.

Main suppliers	
Import (% of import)	
China	17.9%
France	10.1%
Italy	9.9%
Spain	7.6%
Germany	6.4%
USA	4.9%
Turkey	4.1%
Argentine	2.8%
Brazil	2.6%
South Korea	2.3%

However, Algeria has strengthened protectionist measures since 2015, to limit its import bill and encourage domestic production of non-oil and gas industries. Since 2015, the government has imposed additional regulatory requirements on access to foreign exchange for imports and import quotas for specific products, such as cars, to limit their importation. Meanwhile, Algeria has not increased non-hydrocarbon exports and hydrocarbon exports, have declined because of field depletion and increased domestic demand.

Main Customers	
Export (% of export)	
Italy	17.4%
Spain	12.9%
USA	12.9%
France	11.4%
Brazil	5.4%
Netherlands	4.9%
Turkey	4.5%
Canada	4.3%
United Kingdom	3.5%
Belgium	3.3%

Source ComTrade, 2020

With declining revenues caused by falling oil prices, the government has been under pressure to reduce spending. A wave of economic protests in February and increased March 2011 prompted Algiers to offer more than $23 billion in public grants, and retroactive salary and benefit increases. These moves continue to weigh on public finances. In 2016, the government taxes on electricity and fuel, resulting in a modest increase in gasoline prices, and in 2017 they raised the value-added tax by 2% on nearly all products. Still, they refrained from directly reducing subsidies, particularly for education, healthcare, and housing programs. Long-term economic challenges include moving the economy away from its reliance on hydrocarbon exports, bolstering the private sector, attracting foreign investment, and providing adequate jobs for younger Algerians.

State and markets	1990	2000	2010	2018
Time required to start a business (days)	…	25	22	18
Domestic credit provided by financial (% of GDP)	78.4	28.3	−6.6	75.5
Tax revenue (% of GDP)	…	36.9	34.4	…
Military expenditure (%of GDP)	1.5	3.4	3.5	5.3
Mobile cellular subscriptions (per 100 people)	0	0.3	91.1	111.7
Individual using the Internet (% of population)	0	0.5	12.5	49
High-technology exports (% of manufactured exports)	1	4	1	0

Source World Development Indicators database / RsA Asia 2020

The Biggest Algerian Companies				
Name	Industry	Sector	Headquarters	State-Owned
Air Algérie	Consumer Services	Airlines	Algiers	Yes
Air Express Algeria	Industrials	Delivery Services	Hassi Messaoud	No

(continued)

(continued)

The Biggest Algerian Companies				
Name	Industry	Sector	Headquarters	State-Owned
Algerian Petroleum Institute	Industrials	Business Training & Employment	Algiers	Yes
Algérie Ferries	Industrials	Marine Transportation	Annaba	Yes
Asmidal	Basic Materials	Specialty Chemicals	Béjaïa	Yes
Cevital	Consumer Goods	Food Products	Algiers	No
Djezzy	Telecommunication	Mobile Telecommunication	Algiers	No
Echourouk	Consumer Services	Broadcasting & Entertainment	Algiers	No
El Khabar	Consumer Services	Publishing	Algiers	No
El Massa	Consumer Services	Publishing	Algiers	No
El Moudjahid	Consumer Services	Publishing	Algiers	No
El Watan	Consumer Services	Publishing	Algiers	No
ENRS	Consumer Services	Broadcasting & Entertainment	Algiers	Yes
Hamoud Boualem	Consumer Goods	Soft Drinks	Algiers	No
Naftal	Oil & Gas	Soft Drinks	Algiers	Yes
SNTF	Industrials	Railroads	Algiers	Yes
Public Establishment of Telecommunication	Consumer Services	Broadcasting & Entertainment	Algiers	Yes
Saidal	Health Care	Pharmaceuticals	Algiers	Yes
SNVI	Industrials	Commercial Vehicles & Trucks	Rouïba	Yes
Sonatrach	Oil & Gas	Exploration & Production	Algiers	Yes
Sonelgaz	Utilities	Conventional Electricity	Algiers	Yes
Star Aviation	Consumer Services	Airlines	Hassi Messaoud	No
Tassili Airlines	Consumer Services	Airlines	Algiers	Yes

Source RsA Asia 2020

1.2.5 Regulations

Indicator	Algeria	Middle East & North Africa	OECD members	Overall Best Performer
Starting a business				
Procedure–Man (number)	12	7.7	4.9	1.00 (New Zealand)
Time–Man (days)	20	18.6	8.5	0.5 (New Zealand)
Cost–Man (% of income per capita)	11.1	18.7	3.1	0 (UK)
Paid-in min. capital (% of income per capita)	0	9.9	8.7	0 (113 economies)
Dealing with construction permit				
Procedure–Men (number)	19	16.2	12.5	7 (Denmark)
Time–Men (days)	146	132.1	154.6	27.5 (The Republic of Korea)
Cost–Man (% of warehouse value)	8.1	4.3	1.6	0.1 (5 economies)
Building quality control index (0–15)	10	11.9	11.4	15 (3 economies)
Registering property				
Procedures (number)	10	5.7	4.803	1 (4 economies)
Time (days)	55	32.8	22.329	1 (3 economies)
Cost (% of property value)	−129	−205	−143	..
Getting credit				
Strength of legal rights index (0–12)	2	1.857	6.086	12 (4 economies)
Depth of credit information index (0–8)	0	4.8	6.6	8 (34 economies)
Credit registry coverage (% of adults)	2.9	14	18.3	100 (3 economies)
Credit bureau coverage (% of adults)	0	14.2	63.7	100 (23 economies)

Source World Development Indicators database/RsA Asia 2020

Algerian companies are increasingly interested in joint venture opportunities with foreign partners to modernize their factories and license technologies. However, foreign enterprises must comply with the 51% Algerian majority ownership requirement on all investments in Algeria. Besides the certificate of origin and the certificates of conformity and quality from an independent third party, the Government of Algeria also requires imported products to have transcripts in Arabic of the contents and the origin of the products.

Concerning trade barriers, getting goods cleared through Algerian customs represents the single most frequently reported problem facing foreign companies operating in Algeria, as delays can take weeks or months.

Tax or mandatory contribution	Payments (number)	Notes on Payments	Time (hour)	Statutory tax rate	Tax base	Total tax and contribution rate (% of profit)	Notes on TTR
Social security contributions	12		76	25.5%	Gross salaries	28.76	
Tax on professional activity	0	Jointly		1%	Turnover	26.52	
Corporate income tax	0	Jointly	122	19%	Taxable profit	8.27	
Apprenticeship tax and training tax	0	Jointly		2%	Net salaries	1.8	
Tax on interest	0			10%	Interest income	0.26	Included in other taxes
Tax on built land	0	Jointly		3%	Rental value of land	0.12	
Drainage tax	0	Jointly		DZD 10,000	Fixed fee	0.05	
Tax on built land	1			7%	Rental value of land	0.03	
Vehicle tax	1			DZD 1,000	Fixed fee	0.01	
Value added tax (VAT)	12			17%	Value added	0	Not included
Employee Labour Tax	0	Jointly	67			0	Withheld
Flue tax	1			DZD 1/litre	Value added	0	Small amount

Source World Development Indicators database/RsA Asia 2020

1.3 Double Tax Agreement

Agreement Between the Government of The People's Republic of China and the Government of the People's Democratic Republic of Algeria for the Avoidance of Double Taxation and the Prevention of Fiscal Evasion with Respect to Taxes on Income and on Capital

The Government of the People's Republic of China and the Government of the People's Democratic Republic of Algeria,

Desiring to conclude an Agreement for the avoidance of double taxation and the prevention of fiscal evasion with respect to taxes on income and on capital and with a view to promoting economic cooperation between the two countries,

Have agreed as follows:

Article 1: Personal Scope

This Agreement shall apply to persons who are residents of one or both of the Contracting States.

Article 2: Taxes Covered

1. This Agreement shall apply to taxes on income and on capital imposed on behalf of a Contracting State or of its local authorities, irrespective of the manner in which they are levied.
2. There shall be regarded as taxes on income and on capital all taxes imposed on total income, on total capital, or on elements of income, or of capital, including taxes on gains from the alienation of movable or immovable property, as well as taxes on capital appreciation.
3. The existing taxes to which the Agreement shall apply are in particular:
   a. in Algeria:
      i. the Tax on Global Income;
      ii. the Tax on Profits of Companies;
      iii. the Tax on Professional Activity;
      iv. the Patrimony tax;
      v. Royalties and taxes on results relating to activities of exploration, research, exploitation and transport of hydrocarbons by way of pipelines.(hereinafter referred to as "Algerian Tax").
   b. in China:
      i. the Individual Income Tax;
      ii. the Income Tax for enterprises with foreign investment and foreign enterprises. (hereinafter referred to as "Chinese Tax").
4. The Agreement shall also apply to any identical or substantially similar taxes which are imposed after the date of signature of the Agreement in addition to, or in place of, the existing taxes. The competent authorities of the Contracting States shall notify each other of any significant changes which have been made in their respective taxation laws.

Article 3: General Definitions

1. For the purposes of this Agreement, unless the context otherwise requires:
   a. the term "Algeria" means the People's Democratic Republic of Algeria and, when used in a geographical sense, means the territory of the People's Democratic Republic of Algeria, including the territorial sea and, beyond it, the zones in which, in accordance with international law and national legislation, the People's Democratic Republic of Algeria exercises its jurisdiction or its sovereign rights for the purposes of exploration and exploitation of natural resources, biological and non-biological, of the sea-bed, the subsoil and superjacent water;
   b. the term "China" means the People's Republic of China; when used in a geographical sense, means all the territory of the People's Republic of China, including its territorial sea, in which Chinese laws relating taxation apply, and any area beyond its territorial sea, within which the People's Republic of China has sovereign rights of exploration for and exploitation of resources of the sea-bed and its sub-soil and superjacent water resources in accordance with international law;
   c. the term "person" includes an individual, a company and any other body of persons;
   d. the term "company" means anybody corporate or any entity which is treated as a body corporate for tax purposes;
   e. the term "enterprise of a Contracting State" and "enterprise of the other Contracting State" mean, respectively, an enterprise carried on by a resident of a Contracting State and an enterprise carried on by a resident of the other Contracting State;
   f. the term "international traffic" means any transport by a ship or aircraft operated by an enterprise that has its place of effective management in a Contracting State, except when the ship or aircraft is operated solely between places in the other Contracting State;
   g. the term "competent authority" means:
      i. in the case of Algeria, the Minister in charge of finance or his authorized representative;
      ii. in the case of China, the State Administration of Taxation or its authorized representative;
   h. the term "national" means:
      i. any individual possessing the nationality of a Contracting State;
      ii. any legal person, partnership or association deriving its status as such from the laws in force in a Contracting State.

2. As regards the application of the Agreement at any time by a Contracting State, any term not defined therein shall, unless the context otherwise requires, have the meaning that it has at that time under the law of that State for the purposes of the taxes to which the Agreement applies, any meaning under the applicable

tax laws of that State prevailing over a meaning given to the term under other laws of that State.

Article 4: Resident

1. For the purposes of this Agreement, the term "resident of a Contracting State" means any person who, under the laws of that State, is liable to tax therein by reason of his domicile, residence, place of head office, place of management or any other criterion of a similar nature.
2. Whereby reason of the provisions of paragraph 1, an individual is a resident of both Contracting States, then his status shall be determined as follows:

   a. he shall be deemed to be a resident only of the State in which he has a permanent home available to him; if he has a permanent home available to him in both States, he shall be deemed to be a resident only of the State with which his personal and economic relations are closer (centre of vital interests);
   b. if the State in which he has his centre of vital interests cannot be determined, or if he has not a permanent home available to him in either State, he shall be deemed to be a resident only of the State in which he has an habitual abode;
   c. if he has a habitual abode in both States or in neither of them, he shall be deemed to be a resident of the State of which he is a national;
   d. if he is a national of both States or of neither of them the competent authorities of the Contracting States shall settle the question by mutual agreement.

3. Whereby reason of the provisions of paragraph 1, a person other than an individual is a resident of both Contracting States, then it shall be deemed to be a resident only of the State in which its place of effective management is situated.

Article 5: Permanent Establishment

1. For the purposes of this Agreement, the term "permanent establishment" means a fixed place of business through which the business of the enterprise is wholly or partly carried on.
2. The term "permanent establishment" includes especially:

   a. a place of management;
   b. a branch;
   c. an office;
   d. a factory;
   e. a workshop;
   f. a mine, an oil or gas well, a quarry or any other place of extraction of natural resources.

3. A building site or construction or installation project constitutes a permanent establishment only if it lasts more than six months.

4. Notwithstanding the preceding provisions of this Article, the term "permanent establishment" shall be deemed not to include:

   a. the use of facilities solely for the purpose of storage, display or delivery of goods or merchandise belonging to the enterprise;
   b. the maintenance of a stock of goods or merchandise belonging to the enterprise solely for the purpose of storage, display or delivery;
   c. the maintenance of a stock of goods or merchandise belonging to the enterprise solely for the purpose of processing by another enterprise;
   d. the maintenance of a fixed place of business solely for the purpose of purchasing goods or merchandise or of collecting information, for the enterprise;
   e. the maintenance of a fixed place of business solely for the purpose of carrying on, for the enterprise, any other activity of a preparatory or auxiliary character;
   f. the maintenance of a fixed place of business solely for any combination of activities mentioned in subparagraphs (a) to (e), provided that the overall activity of the fixed place of business resulting from this combination is of a preparatory or auxiliary character.

5. Notwithstanding the provisions of paragraphs 1 and 2, where a person—other than an agent of independent status to whom paragraph 6 applies—is acting on behalf of an enterprise and has, and habitually exercises, in a Contracting State an authority to conclude contracts in the name of the enterprise, that enterprise shall be deemed to have a permanent establishment in that State in respect of any activities which that person undertakes for the enterprise, unless the activities of such person are limited to those mentioned in paragraph 4 which, if exercised through a fixed place of business, would not make this fixed place of business a permanent establishment under the provisions of that paragraph.
6. An enterprise shall not be deemed to have a permanent establishment in a Contracting State merely because it carries on business in that State through a broker, general commission agent or any other agent of an independent status provided that such persons are acting in the ordinary course of their business.
7. The fact that a company which is a resident of a Contracting State controls or is controlled by a company which is a resident of the other Contracting State, or which carries on business in that other State (whether through a permanent establishment or otherwise), shall not of itself constitute either company a permanent establishment of the other.

Article 6: Income from Immovable Property

1. Income derived by a resident of a Contracting State from immovable property (including income from agriculture or forestry) situated in the other Contracting State may be taxed in that other State.
2. The term "immovable property" shall have the meaning which it has under the law of the Contracting State in which the property in question is situated.

The term shall in any case include property accessory to immovable property, livestock and equipment used in agriculture and forestry, rights to which the provisions of general law respecting landed property apply, usufruct of immovable property and rights to variable or fixed payments as consideration for the working of, or the right to work, mineral deposits, sources and other natural resources; ships, aircraft shall not be regarded as immovable property.

3. The provisions of paragraph 1 shall also apply to income derived from the direct use, letting, or use in any other form of immovable property.
4. The provisions of paragraphs 1 and 3 shall also apply to the income from immovable property of an enterprise and to income from immovable property used for the performance of independent professional services.

Article 7: Business Profits

1. The profits of an enterprise of a Contracting State shall be taxable only in that State unless the enterprise carries on business in the other Contracting State through a permanent establishment situated therein. If the enterprise carries on business as aforesaid, the profits of the enterprise may be taxed in the other State but only so much of them as is attributable to that permanent establishment.
2. Subject to the provisions of paragraph 3, where an enterprise of a Contracting State carries on business in the other Contracting State through a permanent establishment situated therein, there shall in each Contracting State be attributed to that permanent establishment the profits which it might be expected to make if it were a distinct and separate enterprise engaged in the same or similar activities under the same or similar conditions and dealing wholly independently with the enterprise of which it is a permanent establishment.
3. In determining the profits of a permanent establishment, there shall be allowed as deductions expenses which are incurred for the purposes of the business of the permanent establishment, including executive and general administrative expenses so incurred, whether in the State in which the permanent establishment is situated or elsewhere. However, no such deduction shall be allowed in respect of amounts, if any, paid (otherwise than towards reimbursement of actual expenses) by the permanent establishment to the head office of the enterprise or any of its other offices, by way of royalties, fees or other similar payments in return for the use of patents or other rights, or by way of commission, for specific services performed or for management, or, except in the case of a banking enterprise, by way interest on moneys lent to the permanent establishment. Likewise, no account shall be taken, in the determination of the profits of a permanent establishment, for amounts charged (otherwise than towards reimbursement of actual expenses), by the permanent establishment to the head office of the enterprise or any of its other offices, by way of royalties, fees or other similar payments in return for the use of patents or other rights, or by way of commission for specific services performed or for management, or, except in the case of a banking enterprise, by way of interest on moneys lent to the head office of the enterprise or any of its other offices.

4. Insofar as it has been customary in a Contracting State to determine the profits to be attributed to a permanent establishment on the basis of an apportionment of the total profits of the enterprise to its various parts, nothing in paragraph 2 shall preclude that Contracting State from determining the profits to be taxed by such an apportionment as may be customary; the method of apportionment adopted shall, however, be such that the result shall be in accordance with the principles contained in this Article.
5. No profits shall be attributed to a permanent establishment by reason of the mere purchase by that permanent establishment of goods or merchandise for the enterprise.
6. For the purposes of the preceding paragraphs, the profits to be attributed to the permanent establishment shall be determined by the same method year by year unless there is good and sufficient reason to the contrary.
7. Where profits include items of income which are dealt with separately in other Articles of this Agreement, then the provisions of those Articles shall not be affected by the provisions of this Article.

Article 8: Shipping and Air Transport.

1. Profits from the operation of ships or aircraft in international traffic shall be taxable only in the Contracting State in which the place of effective management of the enterprise is situated.
2. If the place of effective management of a shipping enterprise is aboard a ship, then it shall be deemed to be situated in the Contracting State in which the home harbour of the ship is situated, or, if there is no such home harbour, in the Contracting State of which the operator of the ship is a resident.
3. The provisions of paragraph 1 shall also apply to profits from the participation in a pool, a joint business or an international operating agency.

Article 9: Associated Enterprises.

1. Where:

   a. an enterprise of a Contracting State participates directly or indirectly in the management, control or capital of an enterprise of the other Contracting State, or
   b. the same persons participate directly or indirectly in the management, control or capital of an enterprise of a Contracting State and an enterprise of the other Contracting State, and in either case conditions are made or imposed between the two enterprises in their commercial or financial relations which differ from those which would be made between independent enterprises, then any profits which would, but for those conditions, have accrued to one of the enterprises, but, by reason of those conditions, have not so accrued, may be included in the profits of that enterprise and taxed accordingly.

2. Where a Contracting State includes in the profits of an enterprise of that State—and taxes accordingly—profits on which an enterprise of the other Contracting State has been charged to tax in that other State and the profits so included are profits which would have accrued to the enterprise of the first-mentioned State if the conditions made between the two enterprises had been those which would have been made between independent enterprises, then that other State shall make an appropriate adjustment to the amount of the tax charged therein on those profits. In determining such adjustment, due regard shall be had to the other provisions of this Agreement and the competent authorities of the Contracting States shall if necessary, consult each other.

Article 10: Dividends

1. Dividends paid by a company which is resident of a Contracting State to a resident of the other Contracting State may be taxed in that other State.
2. However, such dividends may also be taxed in the Contracting State of which the company paying the dividends is a resident and according to the laws of that State, but if the beneficial owner of the dividends is a resident of the other Contracting State, the tax so charged shall not exceed:

    a. 5 per cent of the gross amount of the dividends if the beneficial owner is a company (other than a partnership) which holds directly at least 25 per cent of the capital paying the dividends;
    b. 10 per cent of the gross amount of the dividends in all other cases.
    This paragraph shall not affect the taxation of the company in respect of the profits out of which the dividends are paid.

3. The term “dividends” as used in this Article means, income from shares, not being debt-claims, participation in profits, as well as income from other corporate rights which is subjected to the same taxation treatment as income from shares by the laws of the State of which the company making the distribution is a resident.
4. The provisions of paragraphs 1 and 2 shall not apply if the beneficial owner of the dividends, being a resident of a Contracting State, carries on business in the other Contracting State of which the company paying the dividends is a resident, through a permanent establishment situated therein or performs in that other State independent personal services from a fixed base situated therein, and the holding in respect of which the dividends are paid is effectively connected with such permanent establishment or fixed base. In such case, the provisions of Article 7 or Article 14, as the case may be, shall apply.
5. Where a company which is a resident of a Contracting State derives profits or income from the other Contracting State, that other State may not impose any tax on the dividends paid by the company except in so far as such dividends are paid to a resident of that other State or in so far as the holding in respect of which the dividends are paid is effectively connected with a permanent establishment or a fixed base situated in that other State, nor subject the company’s undistributed

profits to a tax on the company's undistributed profits, even if the dividends paid or the undistributed profits consist wholly or partly of profits or income arising in such other State.

Article 11: Interest

1. Interest arising in a Contracting State and paid to a resident of the other Contracting State may be taxed in that other State.
2. However, such interest may also be taxed in the Contracting State in which it arises and according to the laws of that State, but if the beneficial owner of the interest is a resident of the other Contracting State, the tax so charged shall not exceed 7 per cent of the gross amount of the interest.
3. Notwithstanding the provisions of paragraph 2, interest arising in a Contracting State and derived by the Government of the other Contracting State, a local authority and the Central Bank thereof or any financial institutions wholly owned by the Government of that other State, or by any other resident of that other State with respect to debt-claims financed by the Government of that other State, a local authority and the Central Bank thereof or any financial institutions wholly owned by the Government of that other State, shall be exempt from tax in the first-mentioned State.
4. The term "interest" as used in this Article means income from debt-claims of every kind, whether or not secured by mortgage and whether or not carrying a right to participate in the debtor's profits, and in particular, income from government securities and income from bonds or debentures, including premiums and prizes attaching to such securities, bonds or debentures. Penalty charges for late payment shall not be regarded as interest for the purpose of this Article.
5. The provisions of paragraphs 1 and 2 shall not apply if the beneficial owner of the interest, being a resident of a Contracting State, carries on business in the other Contracting State in which the interest arises, through a permanent establishment situated therein, or performs in that other State independent personal services from a fixed base situated therein, and the debt-claim in respect of which the interest is paid is effectively connected with such permanent establishment or fixed base. In such case, the provisions of Article 7 or Article 14, as the case may be, shall apply.
6. Interest shall be deemed to arise in a Contracting State when the payer is the Government of that State, a local authority thereof or a resident of that State. Where, however, the person paying the interest, whether he is a resident of a Contracting State or not, has in a Contracting State a permanent establishment or a fixed base in connection with which the indebtedness on which the interest is paid was incurred, and such interest is borne by such permanent establishment or fixed base, then such interest shall be deemed to arise in the State in which the permanent establishment or fixed base is situated.
7. Where, by reason of a special relationship between the payer and the beneficial owner or between both of them and some other person, the amount of the interest, having regard to the debt-claim for which it is paid, exceeds the amount which

would have been agreed upon by the payer and the beneficial owner in the absence of such relationship, the provisions of this Article shall apply only to the last mentioned amount. In such case, the excess part of the payments shall remain taxable according to the laws of each Contracting State, due regard being had to the other provisions of this Agreement.

Article 12: Royalties

1. Royalties arising in a Contracting State and paid to a resident of the other Contracting State may be taxed in that other State.
2. However, such royalties may also be taxed in the Contracting State in which they arise and according to the laws of that State, but if the beneficial owner of the royalties is a resident of the other Contracting State, the tax so charged shall not exceed 10 per cent of the gross amount of the royalties.
3. The term "royalties" as used in this Article means payments of any kind received as a consideration for the use of, or the right to use, any copyright of literary, artistic or scientific work, including cinematograph films, or films or tapes used for radio or television broadcasting, any patent, trade mark, design or models, plan, secret formula or process, or for information concerning industrial, commercial or scientific experience.
4. The provisions of paragraphs 1 and 2 shall not apply if the beneficial owner of the royalties being a resident of a Contracting State, carries on business in the other Contracting State in which the royalties arise, through a permanent establishment situated therein, or performs in that other State independent personal services from a fixed base situated therein, and the right or property in respect of which the royalties are paid is effectively connected with such permanent establishment or fixed base. In such case the provisions of Article 7 or Article 14, as the case may be, shall apply.
5. Royalties shall be deemed to arise in a Contracting State when the payer is that State, a local authority thereof or a resident of that State. Where, however, the person paying the royalties, whether he is a resident of a Contracting State or not, has in a Contracting State a permanent establishment or a fixed base in connection with which the liability to pay the royalties was incurred, and such royalties are borne by such permanent establishment or fixed base, then such royalties shall be deemed to arise in the State in which the permanent establishment or fixed base is situated.
6. Where, by reason of a special relationship between the payer and the beneficial owner or between both of them and some other person, the amount of the royalties, having regard to the use, right or information for which they are paid, exceeds the amount which would have been agreed upon by the payer and the beneficial owner in the absence of such relationship, the provisions of this Article shall apply only to the last-mentioned amount. In such case, the excess part of the payments shall remain taxable according to the laws of each Contracting State, due regard being had to the other provisions of this Agreement.

Article 13: Capital Gains

1. Gains derived by a resident of a Contracting State from the alienation of immovable property referred to in Article 6 and situated in the other Contracting State may be taxed in that other State.
2. Gains from the alienation of movable property forming part of the business property of a permanent establishment which an enterprise of a Contracting State has in the other Contracting State or of movable property pertaining to a fixed base available to a resident of a Contracting State in the other Contracting State for the purpose of performing independent personal services, including such gains from the alienation of such a permanent establishment (alone or with the whole enterprise) or of such fixed base, may be taxed in that other State.
3. Gains from the alienation of ships, aircraft or containers operated in international traffic or movable property pertaining to the operation of such ships, aircraft or containers, shall be taxable only in the Contracting State in which the place of effective management of the enterprise is situated.
4. Gains derived by a resident of a Contracting State from the alienation of shares deriving more than 50 per cent of their value directly or indirectly from immovable property situated in the other Contracting State may be taxed in that other State.
5. Gains from the alienation of any property other than that referred to in paragraphs 1, 2, 3 and 4 shall be taxable only in the Contracting State of which the alienator is a resident.

Article 14: Independent Personal Services

1. Income derived by a resident of a Contracting State in respect of professional services or other activities of an independent character shall be taxable only in that State except in the following circumstances:
   a. if he has a fixed base regularly available to him in the other Contracting State for the purpose of performing his activities; in that case, only so much of the income as is attributable to that fixed base may be taxed in that other Contracting State; or
   b. if his stay in the other State is for a period or periods aggregating 183 days or more in any twelve-month period commencing or ending in the fiscal year concerned; in that case, only so much of the income as is derived from his activities performed in that other State may be taxed in that other State.

2. The term "professional services" includes especially independent scientific, literary, artistic, educational or teaching activities as well as the independent activities of physicians, lawyers, engineers, architects, surgeons, dentists and accountants.

Article 15: Dependent Personal Services

1. Subject to the provisions of Articles 16, 18 and 19, salaries, wages and other similar remuneration derived by a resident of a Contracting State in respect

of an employment shall be taxable only in that State unless the employment is exercised in the other Contracting State. If the employment is so exercised, such remuneration as is derived therefrom may be taxed in that other State.

2. Notwithstanding the provisions of paragraph 1, remuneration derived by a resident of a Contracting State in respect of an employment exercised in the other Contracting State shall be taxable only in the first-mentioned State if:

   a. the recipient is present in the other State for a period or periods not exceeding in the aggregate 183 days in any twelve-month period commencing or ending in the fiscal year concerned; and
   b. the remuneration is paid by, or on behalf of, an employer who is not a resident of the other State; and
   c. the remuneration is not borne by a permanent establishment or a fixed base which the employer has in the other State.

3. Notwithstanding the preceding provisions of this Article, remuneration derived in respect of an employment exercised aboard a ship or aircraft operated in international traffic may be taxed in the Contracting State in which the place of effective management of the enterprise is situated.

Article 16: Directors' Fees

Directors' fees and other similar payments derived by a resident of a Contracting State in his capacity as a member of the board of directors of a company which is a resident of the other Contracting State may be taxed in that other State.

Article 17: Artistes and Sportsperson

1. Notwithstanding the provisions of Articles 14 and 15, income derived by a resident of a Contracting State as an entertainer, such as a theatre, motion picture, radio or television artiste, or a musician, or as a sportsperson, from his personal activities as such exercised in the other Contracting State, may be taxed in that other State.
2. Where income in respect of personal activities exercised by an entertainer or a sportsperson in his capacity as such accrues not to the entertainer or sportsperson himself but to another person, that income may, notwithstanding the provisions of Articles 7, 14 and 15, be taxed in the Contracting State in which the activities of the entertainer or sportsperson are exercised.
3. The provisions of paragraphs 1 and 2 shall not apply to the income from activities performed in a Contracting State by entertainers or sportspersons if the visit to that State is substantially supported by public funds of one or both of the Contracting States or local authorities thereof or the activity is exercised within the framework of cultural or 14 sports cooperation agreement between the Contracting States. In such a case, the income shall be taxable only in the Contracting State in which the entertainer or the sportsperson is a resident.

Article 18: Pensions

Subject to the provisions of paragraph 2 of Article 19, pensions and other similar remuneration paid to a resident of a Contracting State in consideration of past employment shall be taxable only in that State.

Article 19: Government Service

a. Remuneration, other than a pension, paid by a Contracting State or a local authority thereof to an individual in respect of services rendered to that State or authority shall be taxable only in that State.
b. However, such remuneration shall be taxable only in the other Contracting State if the services are rendered in that State and the individual is a resident of that State who:

    i. is a national of that State; or
    ii. did not become a resident of that State solely for the purpose of rendering the services.

c. Any pension paid by, or out of funds created by, a Contracting State or a local authority thereof to an individual in respect of services rendered to that State or authority shall be taxable only in that State.
d. However, such pension shall be taxable only in the other Contracting State if the individual is a resident of, and a national of, that State.

e. The provisions of Articles 15, 16, 17 and 18 shall apply to remuneration and pensions in respect of services rendered in connection with a business carried on by a Contracting State or a local authority thereof.

Article 20: Students and Apprentices

1. A student, apprentice or business trainee who is present in a Contracting State solely for the purpose of his education or training and who is, or immediately before being so present was, a resident of the other Contracting State, shall be exempt from tax in the first-mentioned State on payments received from outside that first-mentioned State for the purposes of his maintenance, education or training.
2. In respect of grants, scholarships and remuneration from employment not covered by paragraph 1, a student, apprentice or business trainee envisaged in paragraph 1 shall, in addition, be entitled during such education or training to the same exemptions, relief or reduction in respect of taxes available to residents of the State which he is visiting.

Article 21: Other Income

1. Items of income of a resident of a Contracting State, wherever arising, not dealt with in the foregoing Articles of this Agreement shall be taxable only in that State.

2. The provisions of paragraph 1 shall not apply to income, other than income from immovable property as defined in paragraph 2 of Article 6, if the beneficial owner of such income, being a resident of a Contracting State, carries on business in the other Contracting State through a permanent establishment situated therein, or performs in that other State independent personal services from a fixed base situated therein, and the right or property in respect of which the income is paid is effectively connected with such permanent establishment or fixed base. In such case the provisions of Article 7 or Article 14, as the case may be, shall apply.

Article 22: Capital

1. Capital represented by immovable property referred to in Article 6, owned by a resident of a Contracting State and situated in the other Contracting State, may be taxed in that other State.
2. Capital represented by movable property forming part of the business property of a permanent establishment which an enterprise of a Contracting State has in the other Contracting State or by movable property pertaining to a fixed base available to a resident of a Contracting State in the other Contracting State for the purpose of performing independent personal services, may also be taxed in that other State.
3. Capital represented by ships, aircraft and containers operated in international traffic and by movable property pertaining to the operation of such ships, aircraft and containers, shall be taxable only in the Contracting State of which the enterprise owning such property is a resident.
4. All other elements of capital of a resident of a Contracting State shall be taxable only in that State.

Article 23: Methods for Elimination of Double Taxation

1. In Algeria, double taxation shall be eliminated as follows:
   where a resident of Algeria derives income or owns capital which, in accordance with the provisions of this Agreement, may be taxed in China, Algeria shall deduct:

   a. from the tax on the income of the resident, an amount equal to the income tax paid in China;
   b. from the tax on the capital of the resident, an amount equal to the capital tax paid in China.
      Such deduction shall not, however, exceed that part of the tax on income or on capital, as computed before the deduction is given, which is attributable to the income or capital, as the case may be, which may be taxed in Algeria

2. In China, double taxation shall be eliminated as follows:

   a. where a resident of China derives income from or owns capital in Algeria, the amount of tax on that income or capital payable in Algeria in accordance with the provisions of this Agreement, may be credited against the Chinese tax imposed on that resident. The amount of the credit, however, shall not exceed the amount of the Chinese tax on that income or capital computed in accordance with the taxation laws and regulations of China;

b. where the income derived from Algeria is a dividend paid by a company which is a resident of Algeria to a company which is a resident of China and which owns not less than 10 per cent of the shares of the company paying the dividend, the credit shall take into account the tax paid to Algeria by the company paying the dividend in respect of its income.

Article 24: Non-Discrimination

1. Nationals of a Contracting State shall not be subjected in the other Contracting State to any taxation or any requirement connected therewith, which is other or more burdensome than the taxation and connected requirements to which nationals of that other State in the same circumstances, in particular with respect to residence, are or may be subjected. This provision shall, notwithstanding the provisions of Article 1, also apply to persons who are not residents of one or both of the Contracting States.
2. The taxation on a permanent establishment which an enterprise of a Contracting State has in the other Contracting State shall not be less favourably levied in that other State than the taxation levied on enterprises of that other State carrying on the same activities. This provision shall not be construed as obliging a Contracting State to grant to residents of the other Contracting State any personnel allowances, reliefs and reduction for taxation purposes on account of civil status or family responsibilities which it grants to its own residents.
3. Except where the provisions of paragraph 1 of Article 9, paragraph 7 of Article 11, or paragraph 6 of Article 12, apply, interest, royalties and other disbursements paid by an enterprise of a Contracting State to a resident of the other Contracting State shall, for the purpose of determining the taxable profits of such enterprise, be deductible under the same conditions as if they had been paid to a resident of the first-mentioned State. Similarly, any debts of an enterprise of a Contracting State to a resident of the other Contracting State shall, for the purpose of determining the taxable capital of such enterprise, be deductible under the same conditions as if they had been contracted to a resident of the first-mentioned State.
4. Enterprises of a Contracting State, the capital of which is wholly or partly owned or controlled, directly or indirectly, by one or more residents of the other Contracting State, shall not be subjected in the first-mentioned State to any taxation or any requirement connected therewith which is other or more burdensome than the taxation and connected requirements to which other similar enterprises of the first-mentioned State are or may be subjected.
5. The provisions of this Article shall, notwithstanding the provisions of Article 2, apply to taxes of every kind and description.

Article 25: Mutual Agreement Procedure

1. Where a person considers that the actions of one or both of the Contracting States result or will result for him in taxation not in accordance with the provisions of this Agreement, he may, irrespective of the remedies provided by the domestic law of those States, present his case to the competent authority of the Contracting State of which he is a resident or, if his case comes under paragraph 1 of Article 24, to that of the Contracting State of which he is a national. The case must be presented within three years from the first notification of the action resulting in taxation not in accordance with the provisions of the Agreement.
2. The competent authority shall endeavour, if the objection appears to it to be justified and if it is not itself able to arrive at a satisfactory solution, to resolve the case by mutual agreement with the competent authority of the other Contracting State, with a view to the avoidance of taxation which is not in accordance with the Agreement. Any agreement reached shall be implemented notwithstanding any time limits in the domestic law of the Contracting States.
3. The competent authorities of the Contracting States shall endeavour to resolve by mutual agreement any difficulties or doubts arising as to the interpretation or application of the Agreement. They may also consult together for the elimination of double taxation in cases not provided for in the Agreement.
4. The competent authorities of the Contracting States may communicate with each other directly for the purpose of reaching an agreement in the sense of the preceding paragraphs.

Article 26: Exchange of Information

1. The competent authorities of the Contracting States shall exchange such information as is necessary for carrying out the provisions of this Agreement or of the domestic laws concerning taxes of every kind and description imposed on behalf of the Contracting States, insofar as the taxation thereunder is not contrary to the Agreement. The exchange of information is not restricted by Articles 1 and 2. Any information received by a Contracting State shall be treated as secret in the same manner as information obtained under the domestic laws of that State and shall be disclosed only to persons or authorities (including courts and administrative bodies) concerned with the assessment or collection of, the enforcement or prosecution in respect of, or the determination of appeals in relation to, the taxes referred to in the first sentence. Such persons or authorities shall use the information only for such purposes. They may disclose the information in public court proceedings or in judicial decisions.
2. In no case shall the provisions of paragraph 1 be construed so as to impose on a Contracting State the obligation:

    a. to carry out administrative measures at variance with the laws and administrative practice of that or of the other Contracting State;
    b. to supply information which is not obtainable under the laws or in the normal course of the administration of that or of the other Contracting State;

c. to supply information which would disclose any trade, business, industrial, commercial or professional secret or trade process, or information, the disclosure of which would be contrary to public policy (order public).

Article 27: Members of Diplomatic Missions and Consular Posts.

Nothing in this Agreement shall affect the fiscal privileges of members of diplomatic missions or consular posts under the general rules of international law or under the provisions of special agreements.

Article 28: Entry into Force.

1. Each of the Contracting States shall notify the other completion of the procedure required by its law for the bringing into force of this Agreement. The Agreement shall enter into force on the date of the latter of these notifications.
2. The provisions of the Agreement shall apply:

   a. with regard to taxes withheld at source, in respect of amounts paid or credited on or after the first day of January next following the date upon which the Agreement enters into force; and
   b. with regard to other taxes, in respect of the taxable years beginning on or after the first day of January next following the date upon which the Agreement enters into forces.

Article 29: Termination

1. This Agreement shall remain in force indefinitely but either of the Contracting States may terminate the Agreement through diplomatic channels by giving to the other Contracting State a written notice of termination no later than 30 June of any calendar year starting five years after the year in which the Agreement enters into force.
2. In such event the Agreement shall cease to apply:

   a. with regard to taxes withheld at source, in respect of amounts paid or credited after the end of the calendar year in which such notice is given; and
   b. with regard to other taxes, in respect of the taxable years beginning after the end of the calendar year in which such notice is given.

IN WITNESS WHEREOF the undersigned, duly authorized thereto, have signed this Agreement.

DONE in duplicate at Beijing this sixth day of November 2006, in the Chinese, Arabic and English languages, all three texts being equally authentic. In case of divergence in interpretation, the English text shall prevail.

Chapter 2
Egypt

2.1 Country Profile

2.1.1 Introduction

Official name	Arab Republic of Egypt
Capital	Cairo
Government	Unitary semi-presidential republic
Population	104,124,440
Area	1,001,450 sq. km
Official language(s)	Arabic
Main religion(s)	Islam

(continued)

L. Riccardi and G. Riccardi, *China in Africa*,
https://doi.org/10.1007/978-981-16-1148-3_2

(continued)

Official name	Arab Republic of Egypt
Currency	Egyptian pound (EGP)
GDP	$1.204 trillion
GDP per capita	$12,700
Life expectancy	73.7

Source CIA Factbook, 2020

2.1.2 History

The Greek historian Herodotus called Egypt, "The Gift of the Nile," and along that life-giving river, the ancient Egyptians built their impressive civilization, where they ruled for three millennia. The regularity and richness of the annual Nile flood, coupled with the semi-isolation provided by deserts to both the east and the west, permitted the development of one of the greatest civilizations in history. After the rise of a unified kingdom around 3200 B.C., Egypt has been ruled by a series of dynasties. The last native dynasty fell to the Persians in 341 B.C., who were replaced by the Greeks, Romans, and Byzantines. The Arabs introduced Islam and the Arabic language in the 7th century and ruled for the next six centuries. This rich ancient history is still apparent in many aspects of modern Egyptian culture, specifically in rural areas.

In 1250, a local military caste, the Mamluks, took control and reigned until the invasion of the Ottoman Turks in 1517. During the Mamluk period, Egypt became the unrivalled political, economic and cultural centre of the eastern Arabic-speaking zone of the Muslim world. However, during the Ottoman regime, Egypt damaged civil society and economic institutions. The weakening of the economic system left Egypt vulnerable to foreign invasion.

Completion of the Suez Canal in 1869, built in partnership with the French, elevated Egypt as an important world transportation hub. In order to protect its investments, Britain seized control of Egypt's government in 1882, but nominal allegiance to the Ottoman Empire continued until 1914. Partially independent from the UK in 1922, Egypt acquired full sovereignty in 1952.

Inspired by the 2010 Tunisian revolution, Egyptian opposition groups sparked demonstrations and labour strikes across the country, culminating in President Hosni Mubarak's resignation in 2011. Egypt's military assumed national leadership until a new parliament was in place early 2012. Later that year, Mohammed Morsi won the presidential election. As a consequence of violent protests throughout the spring of 2013, against Morsi's government and the Muslim Brotherhood, the Egyptian Armed Forces intervened and removed Morsi from power. In July 2013, they substituted Morsi with interim President Adly Mansour. After the people's approval of the new constitution in January 2014, voters elected Abdel Fattah el-Sisi as president, who has been re-elected to a second four-year term in March 2018.

World view	1990	2000	2010	2020
Population, total (millions)	51,360	63,771	78,728	101,493
GDP (current US$) (billions)	96,087	104,752	230,024	353,003
GDP (% change)	2.3	5.3	5.1	5.8
GDP per capita (current $)	1,870	1,642	2,921	3,478
Inflation (%)	21.2	2.8	11.6	9.9

Source IMF World Economic Outlook database 2020/RsA Asia

2.1.3 Geography

Cairo is the capital and largest city of Egypt, as well as the 15th largest city in the world. The metropolitan area is the largest in the Middle East and the Arab world.

With a surface area of 1,001,450 sq./km, Egypt is the world's 30th largest country. Its land is separated from its neighbours by either the ocean or sparsely populated deserts. Egypt is separated from Libya and North Africa by the western desert, from Israel and Palestine (Gaza Strip) by the Sinai Desert and from Sudan by the Sahara Desert. Egypt's crucial role in geopolitics originates from its strategic position: a transcontinental nation that possesses a land bridge (the Isthmus of Suez) between Africa and Asia, traversed by the canal that connects the Mediterranean Sea with the Indian Ocean through the Red Sea.

About 96% of the Egyptian population lives in the Nile Valley, which makes up only 4% of the country. Most of the economic and social activity occurs in that area. The rest of the country is desert. While the rainfall in the desert is rare or non-existent, the Mediterranean coast has rain that is reliable enough to support marginal human activity, with some agriculture and farming. Natural resources include petroleum, natural gas, iron ore, phosphates, manganese, limestone, gypsum, talc, asbestos, lead, and zinc.

Most populated cities	
City	Population
Cairo	12,230,00
Alexandria	5,046,230
Giza	4,028,062
Shubra el Kheima	3,072,951
Port Said	1,357,352

Source Office National des Statistiques (ONS)

2.1.4 Government

Egypt has been governed through several constitutions. The first of these was the 1923 constitution, which was adopted just after Britain declared Egypt's independence. The political and cultural groundwork for modern Egypt was laid by that document, declaring it as an independent sovereign Islamic state. This constitution included a bicameral parliament, an independent judiciary, and a strong executive in the form of the King. The 1923 constitution was permanently abolished after the revolution in 1952, and the Republic of Egypt was declared in 1953.

Gamal Abdel Nasser led the new ruling junta to abolish all political parties. From this period, Egypt has had a "dominant party" system in which one party regularly controls an enormous majority in Parliament. The dominant party in Egypt is the National Democratic Party (NDP), which represents the political establishment. However, even though fourteen political parties exist in Egypt, only a few of them have been represented in Parliament.

The government is headed by a president who is elected for four years, with a possibility of two terms. The President chooses a Prime Minister and a Council of Ministers. The Parliament is elected for five years from 222 constituencies, each of which elects one person to represent workers, peasants, and one other. Moreover, the President can nominate leaders of parties that did not win any seats. In the late 1970s, some seats were put aside for women, but after an increase of save constituencies was allowed, this provision was ruled unconstitutional. Usually, there are few women ministers. However, one of the key roles for women in the current Egyptian political system is the role of the wife of a President. For example, the current "first lady" has taken on the role of organizing an awareness campaign for literacy and health to support the government's policies.

Voters approved a new constitution by referendum in 2014 and proceeded to elect former defence minister Abdelfattah Elsisi as President in May. Elsisi was re-elected to serve his second four-year term in March 2018. Elsisi's term in office was extended through 2024 and possibly through 2030 if re-elected for a third term due to a set of constitutional amendments approved by Egypt through a national referendum. The Amendments would also grant future Presidents as much as two consecutive six-year terms in office, allowing them to re-establish an upper legislative house, appoint one or more Vice Presidents, establish a 25% quota for female legislators, reinstate the military's role as guardian of Egypt, and extend presidential authority to appoint the heads of judicial councils.

Key political figures	
Title	Name
President	Abdel Fattah el-Sisi
Prime Minister	Mostafa Madbouly
Speaker of the House of Representatives	Ali Abdel Aal

Source The World Factbook—CIA, 2020

2.1.5 *Culture*

Egypt is recognised as a cultural trend-setter of the Arabic-speaking world. While contemporary Arabic and Middle Eastern culture are heavily influenced by Egyptian literature, film, music, and television, whereas foreign influences have affected the country's cuisine, this influence has mostly come from other areas of the Mediterranean, including Turkey, Greece, and the Levant. Due to a vast number of cultural influencers and intruders, Egypt has built a diversified cuisine with many different flavours. Egyptian cuisine has notable vegetarian dishes that rely heavily on legumes and vegetables. Even if mutton and chicken are ubiquitous, the pigeon is extremely popular as a delicacy. The Islam religion prohibits the consumption of alcohol, but locally brewed and fermented drinks are found.

Because of Egypt's history of occupation, Egyptian identity has evolved to accommodate Islam, Christianity, and Judaism. Throughout Egypt, the family remains the most important bond in the social ladder. This link is even more transparent among the Saʿīdī of Upper Egypt and the Bedouin of the deserts, where tribal identity is strong, and great importance is put into blood relationships. Even in the day-to-day conduct of state bureaucracy, business relationships are commonly facilitated by extensive patronage methods linking the local family with groups of relatives and friends. Having children is considered the greatest blessing in all social classes. Education is regarded as an important avenue for social mobility. Indeed, even low-income families invest in educating their children.

Football is by far the most popular sport in Egypt, and the Egyptian national football team called the "Pharaohs" had taken home the African Cup of Nations for a total of seven times, which includes a three-peat performance in 2006, 2008 and 2010.

For what concerns broadcast media, this is composed of a mix of state-run and private ones. State-run TV operates two national and six regional terrestrial networks, as well as a few satellite channels; dozens of private satellite channels and a large number of Arabic satellite channels are available for free; some limited satellite services are also available via subscription; state-run radio operates about thirty stations belonging to eight networks.

2.1.6 *Economy*

Global links	1990	2000	2010	2018
Merchandise trade (% of GDP)	27	20	36	40
Net barter of trade index (2000 = 100)	101	100	140	152
External debt stocks, total (DOD, current US$) (millions)	28,440	24,952	32,244	79,144

(continued)

(continued)

Global links	1990	2000	2010	2018
Net migration (thousands)	−460	−74	−275	–
Personal remittance, received (current US$) (million)	4,284	2,852	12,453	25,516
Foreign direct investment, net inflows (BoP, current US$ (million)	734	1,235	6,386	8,141
Net official development assistance received (current US$) (million)	6,065.2	1,370.8	599.16	2,063.74

Source World Development Indicators database/RsA Asia 2020

Economy	1990	2000	2010	2018
GDP (current US$) (billions)	42.98	99.84	218.89	250.89
GDP growth (annual %)	5.7	6.4	5.1	5.3
Inflation, GDP deflator (annual %)	17.7	3.9	10.1	21.4
Agriculture, value added (% of GDP)	19	15	13	11
Industry, value added (% of GDP)	27	31	36	35
Services, etc., value added (% of GDP)	50	46	47	51
Exports of goods and services (% of GDP)	20	16	21	19
Import of goods and services (% of GDP)	33	23	27	29
Gross capital formation (% of GDP)	29	20	20	17
Revenue, excluding grants (% of GDP)	23	24.3	24.8	21
Net lending (+)/ net borrowing (–) (% of GDP)	−2	−6.7	−7.7	–

Source World Development Indicators database/RsA Asia 2020

The Nile Valley is where most of Egypt's economic activity occurs. Before the opening of the markets, Egypt's economy was highly centralized. Although the constitution in 1971 described Egypt's economy based on socialism, meaning people control all the production, the public sector dominated the economy until the 1990s. However, before the 1971 constitution, Egypt's economy was best described as a free market.

Main Customers	
Export (% of export)	
United Arab Emirates	13%
Saudi Arabia	7.8%
Italy	6.6%
Turkey	6.4%
United Kingdom	4.7%
USA	4.5%
Lebanon	3.6%

Source ComTrade, 2020

Main suppliers	
Import (% of import)	
China	13%
Germany	8.8%
USA	5.4%
Italy	4.6%
Turkey	4.3%
Saudi Arabia	4.2%
Russia	3.8%
Ukraine	3.7%
South Korea	3.7%
Spain	3.4%

During the 1960s and early 1970s, the country experienced a major nationalization. Sectors impacted include industry, communications, banking and finance, and foreign trade. Private enterprise came gradually to find its scope restricted, but some space to manoeuvre was still left in real estate and agriculture. At the same time, the Egyptian government regulated all crucial aspects of production and distribution by imposing controls on agricultural prices, restricting foreign travel and the use of the foreign exchange, controlling rent, and appointing and supervising the board of directors of corporations.

Some restrictions were suppressed or relaxed in the last quarter of the 20th century, which allowed greater private-sector participation in many areas. Since the early 1970s, the government campaigned for increased foreign investment—initially receiving aids from oil-rich Arab countries. The normalization of Egyptian relations facilitated the return of several Japanese and Western corporations. In the early 1980s, increased allocations were made available for developing bridges, roads, telephone lines, oil pipelines, and other infrastructure. During the following decade, a series of IMF arrangements, coupled with massive external debt relief resulting from Egypt's participation in the Gulf War coalition, helped the country to improve its macroeconomic performance, and Egypt's economy became more resilient. This resilience occurred for two reasons: primarily because of new oil and natural gas discoveries, and secondly because the Western aid economy faced many hurdles.

Since 2000, the acceleration in the input of structural reforms, including fiscal, monetary policies, taxation, privatization, and new business legislation, helped Egypt to become a market-oriented economy and increased foreign investments. However, the general standard of living in Egypt remains low, as the government failed to equitably share the benefits of the GDP growth and improve the economic conditions for the broader population. Issues of unemployment and underemployment are widely developed across the country. These poor living conditions and limited job opportunities have contributed to public discontent and were a major factor leading to the January 2011 revolution that toppled Mubarak. The uprising had a negative effect on most sectors. The worst impact was felt in manufacturing, construction, and tourism. Since then, the uncertain security and political environment have restricted economic growth and failed to reduce unemployment, especially among the younger generation. In late 2016, to secure a deal with the IMF, Cairo floated its currency by introducing new taxes and cutting energy subsidies. Since the currency float, Egypt's high yield treasury bills have risen exponentially, enhancing both the dollar availability and central bank reserves.

Agriculture is one of the main sectors of the Egyptian economy. It contributes nearly as one-seventh of the GDP, employing one-fourth of the labour force, and it is an essential part of the foreign exchange. The government invests substantial capital in the form of canals, dams, drains, bridges, and water pumps as well as providing skilled labour.

State and markets	1990	2000	2010	2018
Time required to start a business (days)	–	40	13	12
Domestic credit provided by financial (% of GDP)	100.1	89	69.4	91.8
Tax revenue (% of GDP)	13.2	13.4	14.1	12.5
Military expenditure (%of GDP)	3.5	2.6	3.0	1.2
Individual using the Internet (% of population)	0	0.6	21.6	46.9
High-technology exports (% of manufactured exports)	–	0	1	0.9

Source World Development Indicators database/ RsA Asia 2020

The Biggest Egyptian Companies

Name	Industry	Sector	Headquarters	State-Owned
Air Arabia Egypt	Consumer Services	Airlines	Alexandria	No
Al-Mansour Automotive	Consumer Goods	Automobiles	Alexandria	No
Arab American Vehicles	Consumer Goods	Automobiles	Cairo	No
Arab Contractors	Industrials	Heavy Construction	Cairo	No
Bank of Alexandria	Financials	Banks	Alexandria	No
Banque du Caire	Financials	Banks	Cairo	No
BiscoMisr	Consumer Goods	Food Products	Cairo	No
Cairo Aviation	Consumer Services	Airlines	Cairo	No
Central Bank of Egypt	Financials	Banks	Cairo	Yes
Commercial International Bank	Financials	Banks	Cairo	No

(continued)

(continued)

The Biggest Egyptian Companies				
Name	Industry	Sector	Headquarters	State-Owned
Daily News Egypt	Consumer Services	Publishing	Giza	No
Egyptian Natural Gas Holding Company	Oil & Gas	Exploration & Production	Cairo	Yes
Egypt Post	Industrials	Delivery Services	Cairo	Yes
EgyptAir	Consumer Services	Airlines	Cairo	Yes
Egyptalum	Basic Materials	Aluminum	Nag Hammadi	No
Egyptian Engineering Agencies	Industrials	Automobiles	Cairo	No
Egyptian International Beverage Company	Consumer Goods	Brewers	Cairo	No
Egyptian National Railways	Industrials	Railroads	Cairo	No
Egyptian Natural Gas Company	Oil & Gas	Exploration & Production	New Cairo	No
Egy-Tech Engineering	Consumer Goods	Automobiles	Cairo	No
aSpace	Technology	Software	Alexandri‘	No
Etisalat Egypt	Telecommunications	Mobile Telecommunications	Cairo	No
EUC Construction – El Hazek	Industrials	Heavy Construction	Cairo	No
Ezz Steel	Basic Materials	Iron & Steel	Cairo	No
Gabbour Group	Consumer Goods	Automobiles	Cairo	No
Hassan Allam Sons	Industrials	Heavy Construction	Cairo	No
Herrawi Group	Consumer Goods	Food Products	Alexandria	No
Juhayna	Consumer Goods	Food Products	Giza	No
Manufacturing Commercial Vehicles	Industrials	Commercial Vehicles and Trucks	Cairo	No
Midwest Airlines	Consumer Services	Airlines	Cairo	No

(continued)

(continued)

The Biggest Egyptian Companies				
Name	Industry	Sector	Headquarters	State-Owned
Nasr	Consumer Goods	Automobiles	Cairo	Yes
National Bank of Egypt	Financials	Banks	Cairo	No
Nile Air	Consumer Services	Airlines	Cairo	No
Nilesat	Telecommunications	Mobile Telecommunications	Cairo	No
Orascom Construction Industries	Industrials	Heavy Construction	Cairo	No
Petroleum Air Services	Oil & Gas	Oil Equipment & Services	Cairo	No
Shotmed Paper Industries	Basic Materials	Paper	Giza	No
SICO Technology	Consumer Goods	Consumer Electronics	Cairo	No
Suez Canal Container Terminal	Industrials	Transportation Services	Port Said	No
Suez Steel	Basic Materials	Iron & Steel	Adabia	No
Telecom Egypt	Telecommunications	Fixed Line Telecommunications	Cairo	No
The Egyptian Gazette	Consumer Services	Publishing	Cairo	No
VertiKa	Technology	Software	Cairo	No

Source RsA Asia report 2020

2.1.7 Regulations

Indicator	Egypt, Arab Rep.	Middle East & North Africa	OECD members	Overall best performer
Starting a business				
Procedure—Man (number)	8	7.7	4.9	1.00 (New Zealand)
Time—Man (days)	14	18.6	8.5	0.5 (New Zealand)
Cost—Man (% of income per capita)	7.4	18.7	3.1	0 (UK)

(continued)

(continued)

Indicator	Egypt, Arab Rep.	Middle East & North Africa	OECD members	Overall best performer
Paid-in min. capital (% of income per capita)	0	9.9	8.7	0 (113 economies)
Dealing with construction permit				
Procedure—Men (number)	19	16.2	12.5	7 (Denmark)
Time–Men (days)	172	132.1	154.6	27.5 (The Republic of Korea)
Cost—Man (% of warehouse value)	1.9	4.3	1.6	0.1 (5 economies)
Building quality control index (0–15)	14.0	11.8	11.4	15 (3 economies)
Registering property				
Procedures (number)	8	5.7	4.6	1 (4 economies)
Time (days)	75	30.2	22.3	1 (3 economies)
Cost (% of property value)	1.1	6.0	4.2	0 (5 economies)
Quality of the land administration address (0–30)	7.0	13.4	22.7	29.00 (economies)
Getting credit				
Strength of legal rights index (0–12)	2	1.7	6.0	12 (4 economies)
Depth of credit information index (0–8)	8	4.8	6.6	8 (34 economies)
Credit registry coverage (% of adults)	7.8	14.0	18.3	100 (3 economies)
Credit bureau coverage (% of adults)	25.3	14.2	63.7	100 (23 economies)

Source World Development Indicators database/RsA Asia 2020

Tax or mandatory contribution	Payments (number)	Time (hour)	Statutory tax rate	Tax base	Total tax and contribution rate (% of profit)	Notes on TTR
Corporate Income Tax	1.0	165.0	26% on basic salary, 24% on variable salary	Gross salary	27.35	
Stamp duty on advertisements	1.0	69.0	22.5%	Taxable profit	13.58	
Property tax	1.0	Monthly rental value			0.82	
Tax on insurance contracts	1.0		1% and 10%	Insurance premium	0.05	
Value Added Tax (VAT)	12.0	158.0	10%	Value added	0.00	Not included
Payroll tax on employee	0.0		20%	Gross salaries	0.00	Withheld
Fuel tax	1.0			Consumption	0.00	Small amount

Source World Development Indicators database/RsA Asia 2020

2.2 Double Tax Agreement

Agreement Between the Government of the People's Republic of China and the Government of the Arab Republic of Egypt for the Avoidance of Double Taxation and the Prevention of Fiscal Evasion with Respect to Taxes on Income

The Government of the People's Republic of China and the Government of the Arab Republic of Egypt,

Desiring to conclude an Agreement for the avoidance of double taxation and the prevention of fiscal evasion with respect to taxes on income,

Have agreed as follows:

Article 1: Personal Scope

This Agreement shall apply to persons who are residents of one or both of the Contracting States.

Article 2: Taxes Covered

1. This Agreement shall apply to taxes on income imposed on behalf of a Contracting State or of its local authorities, irrespective of the manner in which they are levied.
2. There shall be regarded as taxes on income all taxes imposed on total income, or on elements of income, including taxes on gains from the alienation of movable or immovable property, as well as taxes on capital appreciation.
3. The existing taxes to which the Agreement shall apply are in particular:

    a. in China:
        i. the individual income tax;
        ii. the income tax for enterprises with foreign investment and foreign enterprises; and (hereinafter referred to as "Chinese tax")
    b. in Egypt:
        i. the tax on income derived from immovable property (including the agriculture land tax and the building tax);
        ii. the unified tax on income of individuals;
        iii. the tax on corporation profits;
        iv. the duty for the development of the financial resources of the State;
        v. supplementary taxes imposed as percentage of taxes mentioned above (hereinafter referred to as "Egyptian tax").

4. The Agreement shall also apply to any identical or substantially similar taxes which are imposed after the date of signature of this Agreement in addition to, or in place of, the existing taxes. The competent authorities of the Contracting States shall notify each other of any substantial changes which have been made in their respective taxation laws within a reasonable period of time after such changes.

Article 3: General Definitions

1. For the purposes of this Agreement, unless the context otherwise requires:

    a. the term "China" means the People's Republic of China; when used in geographical sense, means all the territory of the People's Republic of China, including its territorial sea, in which the Chinese laws relating to taxation apply, and any area beyond its territorial sea, within which the People's Republic of China has sovereign rights of exploration for and exploitation of resources of the sea-bed and its sub-soil and superjacent water resources in accordance with international law;
    b. the term "Egypt" means the Arab Republic of Egypt; when used in a geographical sense, the term "Egypt" includes:
        i. the territory of Egypt;
        ii. the territorial seas thereof; and

iii. the seabed and subsoil of the submarine areas adjacent to the coast thereof, but beyond the territorial sea, over which Egypt exercises sovereign rights, in accordance with international law for the purpose of exploration for the exploitation of the natural resources of such area, but only to the extent that the person, property or activity to which the Agreement is being applied is connected with such exploration or exploitation.

c. the terms "a Contracting State" and "the other Contracting State" mean China or Egypt, as the context requires;
d. the term "tax" means Chinese tax or Egyptian tax, as the context requires;
e. the term "person" includes an individual, a company and any other body of persons;
f. the term "company" means anybody corporate or any entity which is treated as a body corporate for tax purposes;
g. the terms "enterprise of a Contracting State" and "enterprise of the other Contracting State" mean, respectively, an enterprise carried on by a resident of a Contracting State and an enterprise carried on by a resident of the other Contracting State;
h. the term "national" means:
   i. any individual possessing the nationality of a Contracting State;
   ii. any legal person, partnership or association deriving its status as such from the laws in force in a Contracting State;
i. the term "international traffic" means any transport by a ship or aircraft operated by an enterprise which is a resident of a Contracting State, except when the ship or aircraft is operated solely between places in the other Contracting State;
j. the term "competent authority" means, in the case of China, the State Administration of Taxation or its authorized representative, and in the case of Egypt, the Minister of Finance or his authorized representative.

2. As regards the application of the Agreement by a Contracting State any term not defined therein shall, unless the context otherwise requires, have the meaning which it has under the law of that Contracting State concerning the taxes to which this Agreement applies.

Article 4: Resident

1. For the purposes of this Agreement, the term "resident of a Contracting State" means any person who, under the laws of that State, is liable to tax therein by reason of his domicile, residence, head office, place of effective management or any other criterion of a similar nature.
2. Whereby reason of the provisions of paragraph 1 an individual is a resident of both Contracting States, then his status shall be determined as follows:

   a. he shall be deemed to be a resident of the State in which he has a permanent home available to him; if he has a permanent home available to him in both

States, he shall be deemed to be a resident of the State with which his personal and economic relations are closer (centre of vital interests);

b. if the State in which he has his centre of vital interests cannot be determined, or if he has not a permanent home available to him in either State, he shall be deemed to be a resident of the State in which he has an habitual abode;

c. if he has an habitual abode in both States or in neither of them, he shall be deemed to be a resident of the State of which he is a national;

d. if he is a national of both States or of neither of them, the competent authorities of the Contracting States shall settle the question by mutual Agreement.

3. Where by reason of the provisions of paragraph 1 a person other than an individual is a resident of both Contracting States, then it shall be deemed to be a resident of the State in which the place of effective management of its business is situated. However, where such a person has the place of effective management of its business in one of the Contracting States and the place of head office of its business in the other Contracting state, then the competent authorities of the Contracting States shall determine by mutual Agreement the State of which the company shall be deemed to be a resident for the purposes of this Agreement.

Article 5: Permanent Establishment

1. For the purposes of this Agreement, the term "permanent establishment" means a fixed place of business through which the business of an enterprise is wholly or partly carried on.
2. The term "permanent establishment" includes especially:

   a. a place of management;
   b. a branch;
   c. an office;
   d. a factory;
   c. a workshop; and
   f. a mine, an oil or gas well, a quarry or any other place of extraction of natural resources; (g) a farm or a plantation.

3. The term "permanent establishment" likewise encompasses:

   a. a building site, a construction, assembly or installation project or supervisory activities in connection therewith, but only where such site, project or activities continue for a period of more than 12 months within and 24-month period;
   b. the furnishing of services, including consultancy services, by an enterprise through employees or other personnel, but only where activities of that nature continue (for the same or connected project) within the country for a period or periods aggregating more than 12 months within any 24 month period;

4. Notwithstanding the preceding provisions of this Article, the term "permanent establishment" shall be deemed not to include:

   a. the use of facilities solely for the purpose of storage, display or delivery of goods or merchandise belonging to the enterprise;
   b. the maintenance of a stock of goods or merchandise belonging to the enterprise solely for the purpose of storage, display or delivery;
   c. the maintenance of a stock of goods or merchandise belonging to the enterprise solely for the purpose of processing by another enterprise;
   d. the maintenance of a fixed place of business solely for the purpose of purchasing goods or merchandise or of collecting information, for the enterprise;
   e. the maintenance of a fixed place of business solely for the purpose of carrying on, for the enterprise, any other activity of a preparatory or auxiliary character;
   f. the maintenance of a fixed place of business solely for any combination of activities mentioned in sub-paragraphs (a) to (e), provided that the overall activity of the fixed place of business resulting from this combination is of a preparatory or auxiliary character.

5. Notwithstanding the provisions of paragraphs 1 and 2, where a person - other than an agent of an independent status to whom paragraph 6 applies - is acting in a Contracting State on behalf of an enterprise of the other Contracting State, has and habitually exercises, an authority to conclude contracts in the name of the enterprise, that enterprise shall be deemed to have a permanent establishment in the first-mentioned Contracting State in respect of any activities which that person undertakes for the enterprise, unless the activities of such person are limited to those mentioned in paragraph 4 which, if exercised through a fixed place of business, would not make this fixed place of business a permanent establishment under the provisions of that paragraph.
6. Notwithstanding the preceding provisions of this Article, an insurance enterprise of a Contracting State shall-except in regard to reinsurance-be deemed to have a permanent establishment in the other Contracting State if it collects premiums in the territory of that other State or insures risks situated therein through a person other than an agent of an independent status to whom paragraph 7 applies.
7. An enterprise of a Contracting State shall not be deemed to have a permanent establishment in the other Contracting State merely because it carries on business in that other State through a broker, general commission agent or any other agent of an independent status, provided that such persons are acting in the ordinary course of their business. However, when the activities of such an agent are devoted wholly or almost wholly on behalf of that enterprise, he will not be considered an agent of an independent status within the meaning of this paragraph.
8. The fact that a company which is a resident of a Contracting State controls or is controlled by a company which is a resident of the other Contracting State,

or which carries on business in that other State (whether through a permanent establishment or otherwise), shall not of itself constitute either company a permanent establishment of the other.

Article 6: Income from Immovable Property

1. Income derived by a resident of a Contracting State from immovable property (including income from agriculture or forestry) situated in the other Contracting State may be taxed in that other State.
2. The term "immovable property" shall have the meaning which it has under the law of the Contracting State in which the property in question is situated. The term shall in any case include property accessory to immovable property, livestock and equipment used in agriculture and forestry, rights to which the provisions of general law respecting landed property apply, usufruct of immovable property and rights to variable or fixed payments as consideration for the working of, or the right to work, mineral deposits, sources and other natural resources. Ships and aircraft shall not be regarded as immovable property.
3. The provisions of paragraph 1 shall apply to income derived from the direct use, letting, or use in any other form of immovable property.
4. The provisions of paragraphs 1 and 3 shall also apply to the income from immovable property of an enterprise and to income from immovable property used for the performance of independent personal services.

Article 7: Business Profits

1. The profits of an enterprise of a Contracting State shall be taxable only in that State unless the enterprise carries on business in the other Contracting State through a permanent establishment situated therein. If the enterprise carries on business as aforesaid, the profits of the enterprise may be taxed in the other State, but only so much of them as is attributable to that permanent establishment.
2. Subject to the provisions of paragraph 3, where an enterprise of a Contracting State carries on business in the other Contracting State through a permanent establishment situated therein, there shall in each Contracting State be attributed to 8 that permanent establishment the profits which it might be expected to make if it were a distinct and separate enterprise engaged in the same or similar activities under the same or similar conditions and dealing wholly independently with the enterprise of which it is a permanent establishment.
3. In determining the profits of a permanent establishment, there shall be allowed as deductions expenses which are incurred for the purposes of the business of the permanent establishment, including executive and general administrative expenses so incurred, whether in the State in which the permanent establishment is situated or elsewhere.
4. Insofar as it has been customary in a Contracting State to determine the profits to be attributed to a permanent establishment on the basis of an apportionment of the total profits of the enterprise to its various parts, nothing in paragraph 2 shall preclude that Contracting State from determining the profits to be taxed

by such an apportionment as may be customary. The method of apportionment adopted shall, however, be such that the result shall be in accordance with the principles contained in this Article.

5. No profits shall be attributed to a permanent establishment by reason of the mere purchase by that permanent establishment of goods or merchandise for the enterprise.
6. For the purposes of the preceding paragraphs, the profits to be attributed to the permanent establishment shall be determined by the same method year by year unless there is good and sufficient reason to the contrary.
7. Where profits include items of income which are dealt with separately in other Articles of this Agreement, then the provisions of those Articles shall not be affected by the provisions of this Article.

Article 8: Shipping and Air Transport

1. Profits of an enterprise which is a resident of a Contracting State from the operation of ships or aircraft in international traffic shall be taxable only in that Contracting State.
2. The provisions of paragraph 1 shall also apply to profits from the participation in a pool, a joint business or an international operating agency.

Article 9: Associated Enterprises

1. Where

   a. an enterprise of a Contracting State participates directly or indirectly in the management, control or capital of an enterprise of the other Contracting State, or
   b. the same persons participate directly or indirectly in the management, control or capital of an enterprise of a Contracting State and an enterprise of the other Contracting State, and in either case conditions are made or imposed between the two enterprises in their commercial or financial relations which differ from those which would be made between independent enterprises, then any profits which would, but for those conditions, have accrued to one of the enterprises, but, by reason of those conditions, have not so accrued, may be included in the profits of that enterprise and taxed accordingly.

2. Where a Contracting State includes in the profits of an enterprise of that State - and taxes accordingly - profits on which an enterprise of the other Contracting State has been charged to tax in that other State, and the profits so included are profits which would have accrued to the enterprise of the first-mentioned State if the conditions made between the two enterprises had been those which would have been made between independent enterprises, then that other State shall make an appropriate adjustment to the amount of the tax charged therein on those profits. In determining such adjustment, due regard shall be had to

the other provisions of this Agreement and the competent authorities of the Contracting States shall, if necessary, consult each other.

Article 10: Dividends

1. Dividends paid by a company which is a resident of a Contracting State to a resident of the other Contracting State may be taxed in that other State.
2. However, such dividends may also be taxed in the Contracting State of which the company paying the dividends is a resident and according to the laws of that State, but if the recipient is the beneficial owner of the dividends the tax so charged shall not exceed 8 per cent of the gross amount of the dividends. The competent authorities of the Contracting States shall by mutual agreement settle the mode of application of this limitation. This paragraph shall not affect the taxation of the company in respect of the profits out of which the dividends are paid.
3. The term "dividends" as used in this Article means income from shares, or other rights, not being debt-claims, participating in profits, as well as income from other corporate rights which is subjected to the same taxation treatment as income from shares by the laws of the State of which the company making the distribution is a resident.
4. The provisions of paragraphs 1 and 2 shall not apply if the beneficial owner of the dividends, being a resident of a Contracting State, carries on business in the other Contracting State of which the company paying the dividends is a resident, through a permanent establishment situated therein, or performs in that other State independent personal services from a fixed base situated therein, and the holding in respect of which the dividends are paid is effectively connected with such permanent establishment or fixed base. In such case the provisions of Article 7 or Article 14, as the case may be, shall apply.
5. Where a company which is a resident of a Contracting State derives profits or income from the other Contracting State, that other State may not impose any tax on the dividends paid by the company, except in so far as such dividends are paid to a resident of that other State or in so far as the holding in respect of which the dividends are paid is effectively connected with a permanent establishment or a fixed base situated in that other State, nor subject the company's undistributed profits to a tax on the company's undistributed profits, even if the dividends paid or the undistributed profits consist wholly or partly of profits or income arising in such other State.

Article 11: Interest

1. Interest arising in a Contracting State and paid to a resident of the other Contracting State may be taxed in that other State.
2. However, such interest may also be taxed in the Contracting State in which it arises and according to the laws of that State, but if the recipient is the beneficial owner of the interest the tax so charged shall not exceed 10 per cent of the gross

amount of the interest. The competent authorities of the Contracting States shall by mutual agreement settle the mode of application of this limitation.

3. Notwithstanding the provisions of paragraph 2, interest arising in a Contracting State and derived by the Government of the other Contracting State, a local authority and the Central Bank thereof or any financial institution wholly owned by the Government of that other State, or by any other resident of that other State with respect to debt-claims indirectly financed by the Government of that other State, a local authority, and the Central Bank thereof or any financial institution wholly owned by the Government of that other State, shall be exempt from tax in the first-mentioned State.
4. The term "interest" as used in this Article means income from debt-claims of every kind, whether or not secured by mortgage and whether or not carrying a right to participate in the debtor's profits, and in particular, income from government securities and income from bonds or debentures, including premiums and prizes attaching to such securities, bonds or debentures. Penalty charges for late payment shall not be regarded as interest for the purpose of this Article.
5. The provisions of paragraphs 1, 2 and 3 shall not apply if the beneficial owner of the interest, being a resident of a Contracting State, carries on business in the other Contracting State in which the interest arises, through a permanent establishment situated therein, or performs in that other State independent personal services from a fixed base situated therein, and the debt-claim in respect of which the interest is paid is effectively connected with such permanent establishment or fixed base. In such case the provisions of Article 7 or Article 14, as the case may be, shall apply.
6. Interest shall be deemed to arise in a Contracting State when the payer is the Government of that State, a local authority thereof or a resident of that State. Where, however, the person paying the interest, whether he is a resident of a Contracting State or not, has in a Contracting State a permanent establishment or a fixed base in connection with which the indebtedness on which the interest is paid was incurred, and such interest is borne by such permanent establishment or fixed base, then such interest shall be deemed to arise in the State in which the permanent establishment or fixed base is situated.
7. Where, by reason of a special relationship between the payer and the beneficial owner or between both of them and some other person, the amount of the interest, having regard to the debt-claim for which it is paid, exceeds the amount which would have been agreed upon by the payer and the beneficial owner in the absence of such relationship, the provisions of this Article shall apply only to the last-mentioned amount. In such case, the excess part of the payments shall remain taxable according to the laws of each Contracting State, due regard being had to the other provisions of this Agreement.

Article 12: Royalties

1. Royalties arising in a Contracting State and paid to a resident of the other Contracting State may be taxed in that other State.

2. However, such royalties may also be taxed in the Contracting State in which they arise, and according to the laws of that State, but if the recipient is the beneficial owner of the royalties, the tax so charged shall not exceed 8 per cent of the gross amount of the royalties. The competent authorities of the Contracting States shall by mutual agreement settle the mode of application of this limitation.
3. The term "royalties" as used in this Article means payments of any kind received as a consideration for the use of, or the right to use, any copyright of literary, artistic or scientific work, including cinematography films, or films or tapes for radio or television broadcasting, any patent, trade mark, design or model, plan, secret formula or process, or for the use of, or the right to use, industrial, commercial or scientific equipment, or for information concerning industrial, commercial or scientific experience.
4. The provisions of paragraphs 1 and 2 shall not apply if the beneficial owner of the royalties, being a resident of a Contracting State, carries on business in the other Contracting State in which the royalties arise, through a permanent establishment situated therein, or performs in that other State independent personal services from a fixed base situated therein, and the right or property in respect of which the royalties are paid is effectively connected with such permanent establishment or fixed base. In such case the provisions of Article 7 or Article 14, as the case may be, shall apply.
5. Royalties shall be deemed to arise in a Contracting State when the payer is the Government of that Contracting State, a local authority thereof or a resident of that Contracting State. Where, however, the person paying the royalties, whether he is a resident of a Contracting State or not, has in a Contracting State a permanent establishment or a fixed base in connection with which the liability to pay the royalties was incurred, and such royalties are borne by such permanent establishment or fixed base, then such royalties shall be deemed to arise in the State in which the permanent establishment or fixed base is situated.
6. Where, by reason of a special relationship between the payer and the beneficial owner or between both of them and some other person, the amount of the royalties, having regard to the use, right or information for which they are paid, exceeds the amount which would have been agreed upon by the payer and the beneficial owner in the absence of such relationship, the provisions of this Article shall apply only to the last-mentioned amount. In such case, the excess part of the payments shall remain taxable according to the laws of each Contracting State, due regard being had to the other provisions of this Agreement.

Article 13: Capital Gains

1. Gains derived by a resident of a Contracting State from the alienation of immovable property referred to in Article 6 and situated in the other Contracting State may be taxed in that other State.
2. Gains from the alienation of movable property forming part of the business property of a permanent establishment which an enterprise of a Contracting State has in the other Contracting State or of movable property pertaining to a

fixed base available to a resident of a Contracting State in the other Contracting State for the purpose of performing independent personal services, including such gains from the alienation of such a permanent establishment (alone or with the whole enterprise) or of such a fixed base, may be taxed in that other State.

3. Gains derived by an enterprise which is a resident of a Contracting State from the alienation of ships or aircraft operated in international traffic or movable property pertaining to the operation of such ships or aircraft, shall be taxable only in that Contracting State.
4. Gains from the alienation of shares of the capital stock of a company the property of which consists directly or indirectly principally of immovable property situated in a Contracting State may be taxed in that Contracting State.
5. Gains from the alienation of shares other than those mentioned in paragraph 4 representing a participation of at least 25 per cent in a company which is a resident of a Contracting State may be taxed in that State.
6. Gains from the alienation of any property other than that referred to in paragraphs 1 to 5, shall be taxable only in the Contracting State of which the alienator is a resident.

Article 14: Independent Personal Services

1. Income derived by a resident of a Contracting State in respect of professional services or other activities of an independent character shall be taxable only in that State except in one of the following circumstances, when such income may also be taxed in the other Contracting State:

   a. if he has a fixed base regularly available to him in the other Contracting State for the purpose of performing his activities; in that case, only so much of the income as is attributable to that fixed base may be taxed in that other State;
   b. if his stay in the other Contracting State is for a period or periods amounting to or exceeding in aggregate 183 days in the fiscal year concerned; in that case, only so much of the income as is derived from his activities performed in that other State may be taxed in that other State.

2. The term "professional services" includes especially independent scientific, literary, artistic, educational or teaching activities as well as the independent activities of physicians, lawyers, engineers, architects, dentists and accountants.

Article 15: Dependent Personal Services

1. Subject to the provisions of Articles 16, 18, 19,20 and 21, salaries, wages and other similar remuneration derived by a resident of a Contracting State in respect of an employment shall be taxable only in that State unless the employment is exercised in the other Contracting State. If the employment is so exercised, such remuneration as is derived therefrom may be taxed in that other State.

2. Notwithstanding the provisions of paragraph 1, remuneration derived by a resident of a Contracting State in respect of an employment exercised in the other Contracting State shall be taxable only in the first-mentioned State if:

   a. the recipient is present in the other State for a period or periods not exceeding in the aggregate 183 days in the fiscal year concerned; and
   b. the remuneration is paid by, or on behalf of, an employer who is not a resident of the other State; and
   c. the remuneration is not borne by a permanent establishment or a fixed base which the employer has in the other State.

3. Notwithstanding the provisions of paragraphs 1 and 2 of this Article, remuneration derived in respect of an employment exercised aboard a ship or aircraft operated by an enterprise which is a resident of a Contracting State in international traffic, shall be taxable only in that Contracting State.

Article 16: Directors' Fees

Directors' fees and other similar payments derived by a resident of a Contracting State in his capacity as a member of the board of directors of a company which is a resident of the other Contracting State may be taxed in that other State.

Article 17: Artistes and Sportsperson

1. Notwithstanding the provisions of Articles 14 and 15, income derived by a resident of a Contracting State as an entertainer, such as a theatre, motion picture, radio or television artiste, or a musician, or as a sportsman, from his personal activities as such exercised in the other Contracting State, may be taxed in that other State.
2. Where income in respect of personal activities exercised by an entertainer or a sportsman in his capacity as such accrues not to the entertainer or sportsman himself but to another person, that income may, notwithstanding the provisions of Articles 7, 14 and 15, be taxed in the Contracting State in which the activities of the entertainer or sportsman are exercised.
3. Notwithstanding the preceding provisions of this Article, income derived by entertainers or sportsmen who are residents of a Contracting State from the activities exercised in the other Contracting State under a plan of cultural exchange between the Governments of both Contracting States shall be exempt from tax in that other State.

Article 18: Pensions

1. Subject to the provisions of paragraph 2 of Article 19, pensions and other similar remuneration paid to a resident of a Contracting State in consideration of past employment shall be taxable only in that State.
2. Notwithstanding the provisions of paragraph 1, pensions paid and other similar payments made by the Government of a Contracting State or a local authority

thereof under a public welfare scheme of the social security system of that State shall be taxable only in that State.

Article 19: Government Service

a. Remuneration, other than a pension, paid by the Government of a Contracting State or a local authority thereof to an individual in respect of services rendered to the Government of that State or a local authority thereof, in the discharge of functions of a governmental nature, shall be taxable only in that State.

b. However, such remuneration shall be taxable only in the other Contracting State if the services are rendered in that other State and the individual is a resident of that other State who:

   i. is a national of that State; or
   ii. did not become a resident of that State solely for the purpose of rendering the services.

c. Any pension paid by, or out of funds to which contributions are made by the Government of a Contracting State or a local authority thereof to an individual in respect of services rendered to the Government of that State or a local authority thereof shall be taxable only in that State.

d. However, such pension shall be taxable only in the other Contracting State if the individual is a resident of, and a national of, that other State.

e. The provisions of Articles 15, 16, 17 and 18 shall apply to remuneration and pensions in respect of services rendered in connection with a business carried on by the Government of a Contracting State or a local authority thereof.

Article 20: Teachers and Researchers

1. Remuneration which an individual who is or was immediately before visiting a Contracting State, a resident of the other Contracting State and who is present in the first-mentioned State for the primary purpose of teaching, giving lectures or conducting research at an university, college, school or educational institution or scientific research institution recognized by the Government of the first-mentioned State derives for the purpose of such teaching, lectures or research shall not be taxed in the first-mentioned State, for a period of three years from the date of his first arrival in the first-mentioned State.
2. The provisions of paragraph 1 of this Article shall not apply to income from research if such research is undertaken not in the public interest but primarily for the private benefit of a specific person or persons.

Article 21: Students and Trainees

1. Payments which a student, business apprentice or trainee who is or was immediately before visiting a Contracting State a resident of the other Contracting State and who is present in the first-mentioned State solely for the purpose of

his education or training receives for the purpose of his maintenance, education or training shall not be taxed in that State, provided that such payments arise from sources outside that State.

2. In respect of grants, scholarships and remuneration from employment not covered by paragraph 1, a student, business apprentice or trainee described in paragraph 1 shall, in addition, be entitled during such education or training to the same exemptions, reliefs or reductions in respect of taxes available to residents of the State which he is visiting.

Article 22: Other Income

1. Items of income of a resident of a Contracting State, wherever arising, not dealt with in the foregoing Articles of this Agreement shall be taxable only in that State.
2. The provisions of paragraph 1 shall not apply to income, other than income from immovable property as defined in paragraph 2 of Article 6, if the recipient of such income, being a resident of a Contracting State, carries on business in the other Contracting State through a permanent establishment situated therein, or performs in that other State independent personal services from a fixed base situated therein, and the right or property in respect of which the income is paid is effectively connected with such permanent establishment or fixed base. In such case the provisions of Article 7 or Article 14, as the case may be, shall apply.

Article 23: Methods For Elimination Of Double Taxation

1. In China, double taxation shall be eliminated as follows:
   where a resident of China derives income from Egypt the amount of tax on that income payable in Egypt in accordance with the provisions of this Agreement, may be credited against the Chinese tax imposed on that resident. The amount of the credit, however, shall not exceed the amount of the Chinese tax on that income computed in accordance with the taxation laws and regulations of China.

2. In Egypt, double taxation shall be eliminated as follows:

   a. where a resident of Egypt derives income from China the amount of tax on that income payable in China in accordance with the provisions of this Agreement, may be credited against the Egyptian tax imposed on that resident. The amount of the credit, however, shall not exceed the amount of the Egyptian tax as computed before the deduction is given in accordance with the taxation laws and regulations of Egypt which is attributable to the income.
   b. Where, in accordance with any provision of this Agreement, income derived by a resident of Egypt, is exempt from tax in Egypt, Egypt may nevertheless, in calculating the amount of tax on the remaining income of such resident, take into account the exempted income.

Article 24: Non-Discrimination

1. Nationals of a Contracting State shall not be subjected in the other Contracting State to any taxation or any requirement connected therewith, which is other or more burdensome than the taxation and connected requirements to which nationals of that other State in the same circumstances are or may be subjected. This provision shall, notwithstanding the provisions of Article 1, also apply to persons who are not residents of one or both of the Contracting States.
2. The taxation on a permanent establishment which an enterprise of a Contracting State has in the other Contracting State shall not be less favourably levied in that other State than the taxation levied on enterprises of that other State carrying on the same activities. This provision shall not be construed as obliging a Contracting State to grant to residents of the other Contracting State any personal allowances, reliefs, and reductions for taxation purposes on account of civil status or family responsibilities which it grants to its own residents.
3. Except where the provisions of paragraph 1 of Article 9, paragraph 7 of Article 11, or paragraph 6 of Article 12, apply, interest, royalties and other disbursements paid by an enterprise of a Contracting State to a resident of the other Contracting State shall, for the purpose of determining the taxable profits of such enterprise, be deductible under the same conditions as if they had been paid to a resident of the first-mentioned State. Similarly, any debts of an enterprise of a Contracting State to a resident of the other Contracting State shall, for the purpose of determining the taxable capital of such enterprise, be deductible under the same conditions as if they had been contracted to a resident of the first-mentioned State.
4. Enterprises of a Contracting State, the capital of which is wholly or partly owned or controlled, directly or indirectly, by one or more residents of the other Contracting State, shall not be subjected in the first-mentioned State to any taxation or any requirement connected therewith which is other or more burdensome than the taxation and connected requirements to which other similar enterprises of the first-mentioned State are or may be subjected.

Article 25: Mutual Agreement Procedure

1. Where a person considers that the actions of one or both of the Contracting States result or will result for him in taxation not in accordance with the provisions of this Agreement, he may, irrespective of the remedies provided by the domestic law of those States, present his case to the competent authority of the Contracting State of which he is a resident or, if his case comes under paragraph 1 of Article 24, to that of the Contracting State of which he is a national. The case must be presented within 19 three years from the first notification of the action resulting in taxation not in accordance with the provisions of the Agreement.
2. The competent authority shall endeavour, if the objection appears to it to be justified and if it is not itself able to arrive at a satisfactory solution, to resolve the case by mutual Agreement with the competent authority of the other Contracting

State, with a view to the avoidance of taxation which is not in accordance with the Agreement. Any agreement reached shall be implemented notwithstanding any time limits in the domestic law of the Contracting States.

3. The competent authorities of the Contracting States shall endeavour to resolve by mutual Agreement any difficulties or doubts arising as to the interpretation or application of the Agreement. They may also consult together for the elimination of double taxation in cases not provided for in the Agreement.
4. The competent authorities of the Contracting States may communicate with each other directly for the purpose of reaching an agreement in the sense of paragraphs 2 and 3. When it seems advisable for reaching agreement, representatives of the competent authorities of the Contracting States may meet together for an oral exchange of opinions.

Article 26: Exchange of Information

1. The competent authorities of the Contracting States shall exchange such information as is necessary for carrying out the provisions of this Agreement or of the domestic laws of the Contracting States concerning taxes covered by the Agreement in so far as the taxation thereunder is not contrary to the Agreement, in particular for the prevention of evasion of such taxes. The exchange of information is not restricted by Article 1. Any information received by a Contracting State shall be treated as secret in the same manner as information obtained under the domestic laws of that State and shall be disclosed only to persons or authorities (including courts and administrative bodies) involved in the assessment or collection of, the enforcement or prosecution in respect of, or the determination of appeals in relation to, the taxes covered by the Agreement. Such persons or authorities shall use the information only for such purposes. They may disclose the information in public court proceedings or in judicial decisions.
2. In no case shall the provisions of paragraph 1 be construed so as to impose on a Contracting State the obligation:

   a. to carry out administrative measures at variance with the laws and administrative practice of that or of the other Contracting State;
   b. to supply information which is not obtainable under the laws or in the normal course of the administration of that or of the other Contracting State;
   c. to supply information which would disclose any trade, business, industrial, commercial or professional secret or trade process, or information, the disclosure of which would be contrary to public policy (order public).

Article 27: Diplomatic Agents and Consular Officers

Nothing in this Agreement shall affect the fiscal privileges of diplomatic agents or consular officers under the general rules of international law or under the provisions of special Agreements.

Article 28: Entry into Force

Each of the Contracting States shall notify to the other the completion of the procedures required by its law for the bringing into force of this Agreement. The Agreement shall enter into force on the thirtieth day following the date of the later of these notifications and shall thereupon have effect in both Contracting States:

a. in respect of taxes withheld at source, on income derived on or after 1 January in the calendar year next following the year in which the Agreement enters into force;
b. in respect of other taxes on income, for taxes chargeable for any tax year beginning on or after 1 January in the calendar year next following the year in which the Agreement enters into force.

Article 29: Termination

This Agreement shall continue in effect indefinitely but either of the Contracting State may, on or before the thirtieth day of June in any calendar year beginning after the expiration of a period of five years from the date of its entry into force, give to the other Contracting State, through the diplomatic channel, written notice of termination. In such event, the Agreement shall cease to have effect in both Contracting States:

a. in respect of taxes withheld at source, on income derived on or after 1 January in the calendar year next following the year in which the notice is given;
b. in respect of other taxes on income, for taxes chargeable for any tax year beginning on or after 1 January in the calendar year next following the year in which the notice is given.

IN WITNESS whereof the undersigned, duly authorized thereto, have signed this Agreement.

Done at Cairo on the 13th day of August 1997, in duplicate in the Chinese, Arabic and English languages, all texts being equally authentic. In case of divergence of interpretation, the English text shall prevail.

Chapter 3
Ethiopia

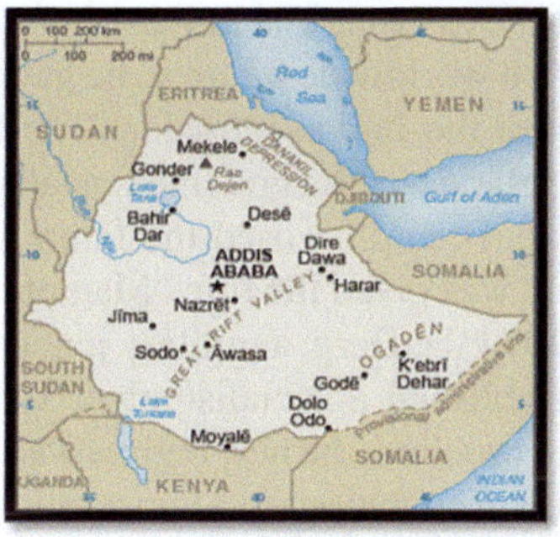

3.1 Country Profile

3.1.1 Introduction

Official Name	Federal Democratic Republic of Ethiopia
Capital	Addis Ababa
Government	Federal Parliamentary Republic
Population	108,113,150
Area	1,126,829 sq. km
Official language(s)	Amharic
Main religion(s)	Christianity, Islam
Currency	Birr (ETB)

(continued)

L. Riccardi and G. Riccardi, *China in Africa*,
https://doi.org/10.1007/978-981-16-1148-3_3

(continued)

Official Name	Federal Democratic Republic of Ethiopia
GDP	$200.6 billions
GDP per capita	$2,200
Life expectancy	67.5

Source CIA Factbook, 2020

3.1.2 History

The history of Ethiopia is unique among African countries, the ancient Ethiopian monarchy kept its freedom from colonial rule, except for the Italian fascist occupation from 1936 to 1941. The Italian invasion in 1935 made Emperor Haile Selassie I ("Ras Tafari") a worldwide figure as he gave an outstanding speech at the League of Nation to protest the Italian intrusion. The famous reggae singer Bob Marley considered Haile Selassie to be a god (the Rastafarian name coming from the Selassie's nickname Ras Tafari), and he used the famous LDN speech to write his song "War." Haile Selassie was given the title "Man of the Year" by the magazine Time in 1935.

In 1974 the Derg, a military junta, deposed Haile Selassie (who ruled since 1930) and established a socialist state. Torn by bloody uprisings, coups, and a massive refugee problem, the new regime was ultimately overthrown in 1991 by the Ethiopian People's Revolutionary Democratic Front (EPRDF). In 1994, a constitution was adopted, and Ethiopia's first multiparty elections were held in 1995. In May 1998, a border dispute with Eritrea led to the Eritrean-Ethiopian War, which ended with a peace treaty in 2000. The war cost both countries an estimated $1 million a day. The Eritrean-Ethiopian war had a negative impact on Ethiopia's economy but strengthened the ruling coalition. The final demarcation of the boundary is currently on hold due to Ethiopian objections to the Eritrea-Ethiopia Border Commission (EEBC). Ethiopia alleges that the EEBC acted beyond its mandate in issuing the coordinates and has not withdrawn troops from previously contested areas pronounced by the EEBC as belonging to Eritrea.

In August 2012, long-time leader Prime Minister Zenawi Meles died in the office. He was replaced by the Deputy Prime Minister Desalegn Hailermariam, marking the first peaceful transition of power in decades. But in August 2016, protests broke out across the country, and dozens of protesters were shot and killed by the police. The demonstrators demanded the end of human rights abuses, the release of political prisoners, and other regional requests. More recently, the government of Ethiopia declared one more time a nationwide state of emergency following the resignation of Prime Minister Hailemariam Desalegn. He is the first ruler in modern Ethiopian history to step down as previous leaders have died in office or being overthrown.

World view	1990	2000	2010	2020
Population, total (millions)	46.807	63.500	82.912	97.175
GDP (current US$) (billions)	12.595	8.235	29.917	103.607
GDP (% change)	2.602	9.838	10.6	7.198
GDP per capita (current $)	269.08	129.678	360.829	1,066.20
Inflation (%)	5.206	0.662	8.134	12.675

Source IMF World Economic Outlook database/RsA Asia 2020

3.1.3 Geography

With an area of 1,126,829 square kilometres, Ethiopia is the world's 27th largest country and the 10th largest in Africa. Bordering Kenya, Somalia, Eritrea, Djibouti, South Sudan, and Sudan, Ethiopia lies in the Horn of Africa, which is the easternmost part of the African continent. The country is dominated by a vast compound of mountains, plateaus, and lakes, divided by the Great Rift Valley, which runs southwest to northeast and is surrounded by lowlands, semi-desert, and steppes. This landscape diversity triggers wide variations in climate, soils, natural vegetation, and settlement patterns across the country.

Ethiopia's topography is comprised of deserts along its eastern border, the Choke and Mandebo mountains in the centre, and tropical forests in the south. Lake Tana, in the north, is the source of the Blue Nile. The lowest point of Ethiopia is the Afar Depression at 125 m, while the highest point of the country is Ras Dejen at 4,550 m.

Most populated cities	
City	Population
Addis Ababa	3,352,000
Adama	342,940
Gondar	341,991
Mek'ele	340,858
Hawassa	318,618

Source Office National des Statistiques (ONS)

3.1.4 Government

For almost sixteen hundred years, Ethiopia was ruled by a monarchy linked to the Orthodox Church. Haile Selassie, the last monarch of Ethiopia, was overthrown by the Derg communist military regime. In 1991, the EPRDF deposed the Derg and established a "democratic" government. In order to minimize ethnic strife in Ethiopia, the country is now an ethnic federation composed of eleven states.

Ethiopia is a federal parliamentary republic where the Prime Minister is the head of government, and the President is a figurehead with no real power. Whereas the executive power is exercised by the Government only, federal legislative power is vested in both the Government and the two Chambers of Parliament. The legislative branch consists of a bicameral legislation in which all people and ethnicities can be represented. However, Ethiopia has not achieved political equality. The ERPRD is an extension of the military organization that deposed the former military dictatorship, and the government is controlled by the Tigrean People's Liberation.

Concerning the political process, there is a universal suffrage for Ethiopian citizens age 18 and older. All peoples and nationalities are guaranteed by the constitution to participate in government, and each group is represented by at least one member in the House of Federation. Moreover, in the House of Peoples' Representatives, seats have been designated for underrepresented minorities. Women can participate in the political process, but the representation tends to be disproportionate. Around one-fifth of the seats in both legislative houses were held by women in the 2000s. In addition, several women have been justices of the Supreme court or cabinet ministers. The EPRDF coalition, comprising primarily Amhara, Oromo and Tigray groups, has been the ruling party since 1995 and the formation of the new republic. Other main political parties are the Coalition of Ethiopian Democratic Forces, the United Ethiopian Democratic Forces, and the Somali People's Democratic Party.

Ethiopia's first ethnic Oromo prime minister Abiy Ahmed Ali came into office in April 2018. ABIY announced that Ethiopia would reopen the border in September 2018 and accept the border ruling of 2000 in June 2018, prompting the reconciliation of Ethiopia and Eritrea, which was marked with a peace agreement in July 2018. Ethiopia's nearly 30-year ethnic-based ruling coalition, the EPRDF, merged into a single unity party called the Prosperity Part in November 2019, although one of the four constituent parties refused to join. Sahle-work Zewde, elected in October 2018, is the first female elected hear state in Ethiopia and currently the only female president in the whole of Africa.

Key political figures	
Title	Name
President	Sahle-Work Zewde
Prime Minister	Abyi Ahmed Ali
Speaker of the House of Federation	Keria Ibrahim
Speaker of the House of People's Representative	Tagesse Chafo
Deputy Prime Minister	Demeke Mekonnen

Source The World Factbook—CIA, 2020

3.1.5 Culture

Ethiopian arts are highly correlated to religion since thousands of years. Illuminated Bibles and manuscripts have been dated to the twelfth century, and the eight-hundred-year-old churches in Lalibela contain Christian paintings, manuscripts, and stone reliefs. Moreover, wood carvings and sculptures are quite common in the south, especially among the Konso. Several fine arts schools have been established in Addis Ababa that teach painting, etching, lettering, and sculpture. Many of Ethiopia's cultural institutions are in Addis Ababa, including the National Museum of Ethiopia, the National Library and Archive of Ethiopia, and the Museum of the Institute of Ethiopian Studies. Ethiopia's rich cultural history is also demonstrated around the country by various sites, several of which are within UNESCO World Heritage sites.

Traditional Ethiopian music is also diverse. Many of the songs in the Amharic language can be interpreted as having both a spiritual theme and a personal meaning. Ethiopian traditional literature is written primarily either in classical Ge'ez or in Amharic. However, after the country became independent from Italy in 1941, authors were encouraged to write with an emphasis on moral and patriotic themes.

In addition, Ethiopia's main sports are football and long-distance running. Ethiopian athletes have won many Olympic gold medals in long-distance running; world-renowned Ethiopian runners like Haile Gebrselassie, Kenenisa Bekele, and Tirunesh Djbaba hold several world records. Football is a national sport, and the national Ethiopian football team has made history by qualifying for the 2012 African Cup of Nations (CAF).

3.1.6 Economy

Economy	1990	2000	2010	2018
GDP (current US$) (billions)	12.18	8.24	29.93	84.36
GDP growth (annual %)	2.7	6.1	12.6	6.8
Inflation, GDP deflator (annual %)	3.3	9.5	1.4	12.5
Agriculture, value added (% of GDP)	50	45	41	31
Industry, value added (% of GDP)	9	11	9	27
Services, etc., value added (% of GDP)	36	37	42	36
Exports of goods and services (% of GDP)	…	…	17	8
Import of goods and services (% of GDP)	…	…	32	23
Gross capital formation (% of GDP)	0	0	0	34.1
Revenue, excluding grants (% of GDP)	12.3	11.8	10.8	9.0
Net lending (+)/net borrowing (−) (% of GDP)	−6.6	−4.2	−2.7	−4.0

Source World Development Indicators database/RsA Asia 2020

Ethiopia, the second-most populous country in Africa, is a one-party state with a planned economy. However, that has not always been the case. Under the reign of Haile Selassie, between 1930 and 1974, Ethiopia's economy centred around the free enterprise. At that time, the production and export of crops as coffee were advanced, and import-substituting manufactures, such as textiles and footwear, were established. Especially after World War II, banking, tourism, insurance, and transport began to participate more in the national economy. In 1974, the communist Derg regime took power until 1991. During this period, all means of production were nationalized, including land, housing, farms, and industry. In response to these policies, the smallholding farmers who form the backbone of Ethiopian agriculture became obviously reluctant to risk producing surplus foods for the market. Although land has remained nationalized, conditions in Ethiopia's countryside have improved slightly, as the regime has given considerable attention to rural development. Still, the issue of land ownership has remained contentious and has delayed the development of commercial agriculture.

However, despite progress generating from the 1990s economic reform, Ethiopia remains one of the poorest countries, not only in Africa but in the world. In 2001 the country qualified for debt relief under the Highly Indebted Poor Countries (HIPC) initiative of the International Monetary Fund (IMF) and World Bank. In 2005 Ethiopia benefited from 100 percent debt relief of loans from the IMF, the World Bank, and the African Development Bank. Following these events, Ethiopia grew at a rate between 8% and 11% (10.4% on average) annually for more than a decade before 2016, making the country one of the fastest-growing states among the 188 IMF member countries. Furthermore, since registering over 10% economic growth from 2004 through 2009, Ethiopia became the fastest-growing non-oil-dependent African economy in the years 2007 and 2008. This growth was driven by government investment in infrastructures, as well as sustained progress in the agricultural and service sectors. In 2008 and 2011, Ethiopia's economic performance and considerable development gains were challenged by high inflation and a difficult balance of payments situation. Loose monetary policy, high food prices, and substantial civil service wage increase triggered a surged in inflation up to 40%.

Although over 80% of Ethiopia's population is employed in the agricultural sector, services have surpassed agriculture as the principal source of GDP. Many other economic activities depend on agriculture, including marketing, processing and of course export of agricultural products. Agricultural production is overwhelmingly processed by small-scale farmers and enterprises, and a large part of commodity exports are provided by the small agricultural cash-crop sector. Principal crops include legumes, cereals, coffee, potatoes, oilseeds, and sugarcane. Therefore, Ethiopia's most promising resource is its agricultural land. Most of the reserve land is in parts of the country that have favourable climatic conditions for intensive agriculture. Although soil erosion and deforestation have strongly damaged the plateaus, almost half of the potentially cultivable land is still available for use.

Even today, agriculture is still contributing to almost half of Ethiopia's GDP. There are three types of agricultural activity. The first, and by far the most important, is the subsistence smallholder sector that produces most of the staple grains such as wheat, oats, corn, and barley as well as pulses like peas, lentils, and beans. These farm plots are small, ranging from 3 to 6 acres (equivalent to 1.2 to 2.5 hectares). Ethiopia's second type of agriculture is cash cropping, including products such as oilseeds, sugarcane, and beeswax. Coffee is the single most important export. Livestock raising is the third agricultural activity, which is essential in the peripheral lowlands of Ethiopia. Fishing is primarily artisanal and occurs on the country's rivers and inland lakes. Most of the locally sold fish are produced by small operators whose scale of operation and technology are inadequate for export production. Even if the fishing industry is small, production more than doubled during the 1990s.

Main suppliers	
Import (% of import)	
China	33.0%
Kuwait	7.8%
India	7.2%
United States	5.3%
Japan	3.7%
Saudi Arabia	3.2%
Italy	3.1%
Turkey	2.9%
Indonesia	2.5%
United Arab Emirates	2.3%

Main Customers	
Export (% of export)	
Somalia	12%
Kuwait	12%
Switzerland	11%
Netherlands	11%
China	7.3%
Saudi Arabia	6.3%
United States	4.9%
Germany	4.4%
Djibouti	3.9%
United Arab Emirates	3.3%

Source ComTrade, 2020

However, except for gold and tantalum, the role of minerals in Ethiopia's economy is small. Tantalum is mined in the south-central part of the country, whereas gold is extracted at Kibre Mengist in the south. Hydroelectricity is the most important source of power for industries and major cities, due to the 14 major rivers that run through Ethiopia. The most important power plants are those on the Awash River, the Blue Nile River, the Shebele River, the Omo River, and the Gilgel Gibe River. As of 2012, hydroelectric plants represented around 88.2% of the country's total installed electricity capacity, the remaining electrical power being generated from fossil fuels (8.3%), and other renewable sources (3.6%). However, some hydroelectric projects have generated considerable controversies, such as the Gilgel Gibe III dam and power station along the Omo River, which was opened in 2016. Ethiopia delivers roughly 81% of water volume to the Nile through the river basins of the Blue Nile, Sobat River, and Atbara. In 1959, Egypt and Sudan signed a bilateral treaty, the 1959 Nile Waters Agreement, which gave both countries exclusive maritime rights over the Nile waters. Since then, Egypt vetoed almost all projects in front of international institutions that aimed to utilize the local Nile tributaries. Consequently, this has made it difficult to finance hydropower and irrigation projects in western Ethiopia externally.

Also, in 2013, the electrification rate for the total population was 24%, with 85% coverage in urban areas and 10% coverage in rural areas. Most energy for domestic use in rural areas is derived primarily from firewood and charcoal, which has caused a strain in the remaining wood resources in the country. Ethiopia's long dependence on these sources has contributed to the depletion of its trees and the erosion of its soil. Thus, with the purpose of increasing access to electricity in rural areas, the government has begun to expand hydroelectric power generation.

State and markets	1990	2000	2010	2018
Time required to start a business (days)	...	47	20	32
Domestic credit provided by financial (% of GDP)	39.2	48.6	36.9	...
Tax revenue (% of GDP)	8.6	8.1	8.2	7.5
Military expenditure (% of GDP)	6.4	7.6	1.1	0.6
Mobile cellular subscriptions (per 100 people)	0	0	7.8	50.5
Individual using the Internet (% of population)	0	0	0.75	15.4
High-technology exports (% of manufactured exports)	...	0	4.45	17

Source World Development Indicators database/RsA Asia 2020

Manufacturing contributes about one-tenth (14%) of Ethiopia's GDP, and products are primarily for domestic consumption. The most important are tobacco, textiles, chemical products, leather and footwear, processed foods, and beverages. However, after the nationalization of the private sector before the 1974 revolution, the growth rate of the manufacturing sector declined. This was mainly triggered by an exodus of the foreign-owned and foreign-operated industry due to the revolution. The state is heavily engaged in the economy, as over 90 percent of large-scale industries are state-run, as opposed to less than 10 percent of the agriculture industry being state-run. Under the Ethiopian People's Revolutionary Democratic Front administration, there is both the public and private industry. Public industries include garment, steel, and textile industries, while much of the pharmaceutical industries are owned by shareholders.

The Biggest Ethiopian Companies				
Name	Industry	Sector	Headquarters	State-Owned
Anbessa City Bus Service Enterprise	Consumer Services	Travel & Tourism	Addis Ababa	No
Awash International Bank	Financials	Banks	Addis Ababa	No
Commercial Bank of Ethiopia	Financials	Banks	Addis Ababa	No
Cooperative Bank of Oromia	Financials	Banks	Addis Ababa	No
Debit Credit and Saving Institution SC	Financials	Banks	Mek'ele	No
Ethio Telecom	Telecommunications	Fixed Line Telecommunications	Addis Ababa	Yes
Ethiopia Commodity Exchange	Financials	Investment Services	Addis Ababa	No
Ethiopian Airlines	Consumer Services	Airlines	Addis Ababa	Yes
Harar Brewery	Consumer Goods	Brewers	Harar	No
Marathon Motors Engineering	Consumer Goods	Automobiles	Addis Ababa	No
National Bank of Ethiopia	Financials	Banks	Addis Ababa	Yes
Oromia International Bank	Financials	Banks	Addis Ababa	No
Salam Bus Line Share Company	Consumer Services	Travel & Tourism	Addis Ababa	No
Sky Bus Transport System	Consumer Service	Airlines	Addis Ababa	No

Source RsA Asia report 2018

3.1.7 Regulations

Indicator	Ethiopia.	Sub-Saharan Africa	OECD members	Overall Best Performer
Starting a business				
Procedure—Man (number)	12	7.6	4.9	1.00 (New Zealand)
Time—Man (days)	33	24.0	8.5	0.5 (New Zealand)
Cost—Man (% of income per capita)	57.8	49.9	3.1	0 (UK)

(continued)

(continued)

Indicator	Ethiopia.	Sub-Saharan Africa	OECD members	Overall Best Performer
Paid-in min. capital (% of income per capita)	0	25.6	8.7	0 (113 economies)
Dealing with construction permit				
Procedure–Men (number)	13	14.8	12.5	7 (Denmark)
Time–Men (days)	130	147.5	154.6	27.5 (The republic of Korea)
Cost—Man (% of warehouse value)	16.5	9.9	1.6	0.1 (5 economies)
Building quality control index (0–15)	7.0	8.0	11.4	15 (3 economies)
Registering property				
Procedures (number)	7	6.2	4.6	1 (4 economies)
Time (days)	52	59.3	22.3	1 (3 economies)
Cost (% of property value)	6.0	7.8	4.2	0 (5 economies)
Quality of the land administration address (0–30)	6.0	8.6	22.7	29.00 (economies)
Getting credit				
Strength of legal rights index (0–12)	3	5.1	6.0	12 (4 economies)
Depth of credit information index (0–8)	0	3.0	6.6	8 (34 economies)
Credit registry coverage (% of adults)	0.3	6.3	18.3	100 (3 economies)
Credit bureau coverage (% of adults)	0	8.2	63.7	100 (23 economies)

Source World Development Indicators database/RsA Asia 2020

Tax or mandatory contribution	Payments (number)	Time (hour)	Statutory tax rate	Tax base	Total tax and contribution rate (% of profit)	Notes on TTR
Corporate Income Tax	1.0	120.0	30%	Taxable profit	24.60	

(continued)

(continued)

Tax or mandatory contribution	Payments (number)	Time (hour)	Statutory tax rate	Tax base	Total tax and contribution rate (% of profit)	Notes on TTR
Capital gains tax	1.0	–	15%	Capital Gains	0.76	
Property tax	1.0	–	2 Birr	Square meter	0.38	
Tax on interest	0.0	–	5%	Interest Income	0.31	
License renewal fees	1.0	–	492 Birr	Fixed fee	0.10	
Value Added Tax (VAT)	12.0	72.0	15%	Value Added	0.00	Not included
Stamp duty on contracts	1.0	–	5 Birr	Fixed fee	0.00	Small amount
Fuel tax	1.0			Included into the fuel price	0.00	Small amount

Source World Development Indicators database/RsA Asia 2020

3.2 Double Tax Agreement

Agreement Between the Government of the People's Republic of China and the Government of the Federal Democratic Republic of Ethiopia for the Avoidance of Double Taxation and the Prevention of Fiscal Evasion with Respect to Taxes on Income

The Government of the People's Republic of China and the Government of the Federal Democratic Republic of Ethiopia,

Desiring to conclude an Agreement for the Avoidance of Double Taxation and the Prevention of Fiscal Evasion with respect to Taxes on Income (hereinafter referred to as the "Agreement"),

Have agreed as follows:

Article 1: Personal Scope

This Agreement shall apply to persons who are residents of one or both of the Contracting States.

Article 2: Taxes Covered

1. This Agreement shall apply to taxes on income imposed on behalf of a Contracting State or of its local authorities, irrespective of the manner in which they are levied.

There shall be regarded as taxes on income all taxes imposed on total income, or on elements of income, including taxes on gains from the alienation of movable or immovable property.

2. The existing taxes to which the Agreement shall apply are in particular:
   a. in China:
      i. the individual income tax;
      ii. the enterprise income tax; (hereinafter referred to as "Chinese tax");
   b. in Ethiopia:
      i. the tax on income and profit imposed by the Income Tax Proclamation No. 286/2002; and
      ii. the tax on income from mining, petroleum and agricultural activities imposed by respective proclamations; (hereinafter referred to as "Ethiopian tax").

3. The Agreement shall also apply to any identical or substantially similar taxes which are imposed after the date of signature of the Agreement in addition to, or in place of, the existing taxes. The competent authorities of the Contracting States shall notify each other of any substantial changes which have been made in their respective taxation laws within a reasonable period of time after such changes.

Article 3: General Definitions

1. For the purposes of this Agreement, unless the context otherwise requires:
   a. the term "China" means the People's Republic of China; when used in geographical sense, means all the territory of the People's Republic of China, including its territorial sea, in which the Chinese laws relating to taxation apply, and any area beyond its territorial sea, within which the People's Republic of China has sovereign rights of exploration for and exploitation of resources of the sea-bed and its sub-soil and superjacent water resources in accordance with international law and its domestic law;
   b. the term "Ethiopia" means the Federal Democratic Republic of Ethiopia; when used in a geographical sense, it means the national territory and any other area which in accordance with international law or the laws of Ethiopia is or may be designated as an area in which Ethiopia exercises sovereign rights or its jurisdiction;
   c. the terms "a Contracting State" and "the other Contracting State" mean China or Ethiopia as the context requires;
   d. the term "person" includes an individual, a company and any other body of persons;
   e. the term "company" means anybody corporate or any entity which is treated as a body corporate for tax purposes;
   f. the terms "enterprise of a Contracting State" and "enterprise of the other Contracting State" mean, respectively, an enterprise carried on by a resident

of a Contracting State and an enterprise carried on by a resident of the other Contracting State;

g. the term "national" means:
   i. any individual possessing the nationality of a Contracting State;
   ii. any legal person, partnership or association deriving its status as such from the laws in force in a Contracting State;
h. the term "international traffic" means any transport by a ship or aircraft operated by an enterprise which has its place of effective management in a Contracting State, except when the ship or aircraft is operated solely between places in the other Contracting State;
i. the term "competent authority" means:
   i. in the case of China, the State Administration of Taxation or its authorized representative; and
   ii. in the case of Ethiopia, the Minister of Finance and Economic Development or his authorized representative.

2. As regards the application of the Agreement by a Contracting State, any term not defined therein shall, unless the context otherwise requires, have the meaning which it has at that time under the law of that State concerning the taxes to which the Agreement applies.

Article 4: Resident

1. For the purposes of this Agreement, the term "resident of a Contracting State" means any person who, under the laws of that State, is liable to tax therein by reason of his domicile, residence, place of incorporation or registration, place of effective management or any other criterion of a similar nature, and also includes that State and any local authority thereof. This term, however, does not include any person who is liable to tax in that State in respect only of income from sources in that State.
2. Whereby reason of the provisions of paragraph 1 an individual is a resident of both Contracting States, then his status shall be determined as follows:

   a. he shall be deemed to be a resident only of the State in which he has a permanent home available to him; if he has a permanent home available to him in both States, he shall be deemed to be a resident of the State with which his personal and economic relations are closer (centre of vital interests);
   b. if the State in which he has his centre of vital interests cannot be determined, or if he has not a permanent home available to him in either State, he shall be deemed to be a resident only of the State in which he has an habitual abode;
   c. if he has a habitual abode in both States or in neither of them, he shall be deemed to be a resident only of the State of which he is a national;

d. if he is a national of both States or of neither of them, the competent authorities of the Contracting States shall settle the question by mutual agreement.

3. Whereby reason of the provisions of paragraph 1 a person other than an individual is a resident of both Contracting States, then it shall be deemed to be a resident only of the State in which its place of effective management is situated.

Article 5: Permanent Establishment

1. For the purposes of this Agreement, the term "permanent establishment" means a fixed place of business through which the business of an enterprise is wholly or partly carried on.
2. The term "permanent establishment" includes especially:

   a. a place of management;
   b. a branch;
   c. an office;
   d. a factory;
   e. a sales outlet;
   f. a workshop;
   g. a commercial warehouse;
   h. a farm, plantation or other place where agricultural, forestry, plantation or related activities are carried on; and
   i. a mine, an oil or gas well, a quarry or any other place of extraction of natural resources.

3. A building site or construction or installation project constitutes a permanent establishment only if it lasts more than 6 months.
4. Notwithstanding the preceding provisions of this Article, the term "permanent establishment" shall be deemed not to include:

   a. the use of facilities solely for the purpose of storage, display or delivery of goods or merchandise belonging to the enterprise;
   b. the maintenance of a stock of goods or merchandise belonging to the enterprise solely for the purpose of storage, display or delivery;
   c. the maintenance of a stock of goods or merchandise belonging to the enterprise solely for the purpose of processing by another enterprise;
   d. the maintenance of a fixed place of business solely for the purpose of purchasing goods or merchandise or of collecting information, for the enterprise;
   e. the maintenance of a fixed place of business solely for the purpose of carrying on, for the enterprise, any other activity of a preparatory or auxiliary character;
   f. the maintenance of a fixed place of business solely for any combination of activities mentioned in sub-paragraphs a) to e), provided that the overall

activity of the fixed place of business resulting from this combination is of a preparatory or auxiliary character.

5. Notwithstanding the provisions of paragraphs 1 and 2, where a person – other than an agent of an independent status to whom paragraph 6 applies—is acting on behalf of an enterprise and has, and habitually exercises, in a Contracting State an authority to conclude contracts in the name of the enterprise, that enterprise shall be deemed to have a permanent establishment in that State in respect of any activities which that person undertakes for the enterprise, unless the activities of such person are limited to those mentioned in paragraph 4 which, if exercised through a fixed place of business, would not make this fixed place of business a permanent establishment under the provisions of that paragraph.
6. An enterprise of a Contracting State shall not be deemed to have a permanent establishment in the other Contracting State merely because it carries on business in that other State through a broker, general commission agent or any other agent of an independent status, provided that such persons are acting in the ordinary course of their business. However, when the activities of such an agent are devoted wholly or almost wholly on behalf of that enterprise, he will not be considered an agent of an independent status within the meaning of this paragraph.
7. The fact that a company which is a resident of a Contracting State controls or is controlled by a company which is a resident of the other Contracting State, or which carries on business in that other State (whether through a permanent establishment or otherwise), shall not of itself constitute either company a permanent establishment of the other.

Article 6: Income from Immovable Property

1. Income derived by a resident of a Contracting State from immovable property (including income from agriculture or forestry) situated in the other Contracting State may be taxed in that other State.
2. The term "immovable property" shall have the meaning which it has under the law of the Contracting State in which the property in question is situated. The term shall in any case include property accessory to immovable property, livestock and equipment used in agriculture and forestry, rights to which the provisions of general law respecting landed property apply, usufruct of immovable property and rights to variable or fixed payments as consideration for the working of, or the right to work, mineral deposits, sources and other natural resources. Ships and aircraft shall not be regarded as immovable property.
3. The provisions of paragraph 1 shall apply to income derived from the direct use, letting, or use in any other form of immovable property.
4. The provisions of paragraphs 1 and 3 shall also apply to the income from immovable property of an enterprise and to income from immovable property used for the performance of independent personal services.

Article 7: Business Profits

1. The profits of an enterprise of a Contracting State shall be taxable only in that State unless the enterprise carries on business in the other Contracting State through a permanent establishment situated therein. If the enterprise carries on business as aforesaid, the profits of the enterprise may be taxed in the other State, but only so much of them as is attributable to that permanent establishment.
2. Subject to the provisions of paragraph 3, where an enterprise of a Contracting State carries on business in the other Contracting State through a permanent establishment situated therein, there shall in each Contracting State be attributed to that permanent establishment the profits which it might be expected to make if it were a distinct and separate enterprise engaged in the same or similar activities under the same or similar conditions and dealing wholly independently with the enterprise of which it is a permanent establishment.
3. In determining the profits of a permanent establishment, there shall be allowed as deductions expenses which are incurred for the purposes of the business of the permanent establishment, including executive and general administrative expenses so incurred, whether in the State in which the permanent establishment is situated or elsewhere. This provision shall apply subject to limitations under the domestic law.
4. Insofar as it has been customary in a Contracting State to determine the profits to be attributed to a permanent establishment on the basis of an apportionment of the total profits of the enterprise to its various parts, nothing in paragraph 2 shall preclude that Contracting State from determining the profits to be taxed by such an apportionment as may be customary. The method of apportionment adopted shall, however, be such that the result shall be in accordance with the principles contained in this Article.
5. No profits shall be attributed to a permanent establishment by reason of the mere purchase by that permanent establishment of goods or merchandise for the enterprise.
6. For the purposes of the preceding paragraphs, the profits to be attributed to the permanent establishment shall be determined by the same method year by year unless 7 there is good and sufficient reason to the contrary.
7. Where profits include items of income which are dealt with separately in other Articles of this Agreement, then the provisions of those Articles shall not be affected by the provisions of this Article.

Article 8: Shipping and Air Transport

1. Profits from the operation of ships or aircraft in international traffic shall be taxable only in the Contracting State in which the place of effective management of the enterprise is situated.
2. If the place of effective management of a shipping enterprise is aboard a ship, then it shall be deemed to be situated in the Contracting State in which the home harbour of the ship is situated, or, if there is no such home harbour, in the Contracting State of which the operator of the ship is a resident.

3. For the purposes of this Article, profits from the operation of ships or aircraft in international traffic particularly include:

   a. profits from the rental on a bareboat basis of ships or aircraft; and
   b. profits from the use, maintenance or rental of containers (including trailers and related equipment for the transport of containers) used for the transport of goods or merchandise.
   Where such rental or such use, maintenance or rental, as the case may be, is incidental to the operation of ships or aircraft in international traffic.

4. The provisions of paragraphs 1, 2 and 3 of this Article shall also apply to profits from the participation in a pool, a joint business or an international operating agency.

Article 9: Associated Enterprises

1. Where

   a. an enterprise of a Contracting State participates directly or indirectly in the management, control or capital of an enterprise of the other Contracting State, or
   b. the same persons participate directly or indirectly in the management, control or capital of an enterprise of a Contracting State and an enterprise of the other Contracting State, 8 and in either case conditions are made or imposed between the two enterprises in their commercial or financial relations which differ from those which would be made between independent enterprises, then any profits which would, but for those conditions, have accrued to one of the enterprises, but, by reason of those conditions, have not so accrued, may be included in the profits of that enterprise and taxed accordingly.

2. Where a Contracting State includes in the profits of an enterprise of that State—and taxes accordingly—profits on which an enterprise of the other Contracting State has been charged to tax in that other State and the profits so included are profits which would have accrued to the enterprise of the first-mentioned State if the conditions made between the two enterprises had been those which would have been made between independent enterprises, then that other State shall make an appropriate adjustment to the amount of the tax charged therein on those profits. In determining such adjustment, due regard shall be had to the other provisions of this Agreement and the competent authorities of the Contracting States shall, if necessary, consult each other.

Article 10: Dividends

1. Dividends paid by a company which is a resident of a Contracting State to a resident of the other Contracting State may be taxed in that other State.
2. However, such dividends may also be taxed in the Contracting State of which the company paying the dividends is a resident and according to the laws of

that State, but if the beneficial owner of the dividends is a resident of the other Contracting State, the tax so charged shall not exceed 5 per cent of the gross amount of the dividends. The competent authorities of the Contracting States shall by mutual agreement settle the mode of application of this limitation. This paragraph shall not affect the taxation of the company in respect of the profits out of which the dividends are paid.

3. The term "dividends" as used in this Article means income from shares or other rights, not being debt-claims, participating in profits, as well as income from other corporate rights which is subjected to the same taxation treatment as income from shares by the laws of the State of which the company making the distribution is a resident.
4. The provisions of paragraphs 1 and 2 shall not apply if the beneficial owner of the dividends, being a resident of a Contracting State, carries on business in the other Contracting State of which the company paying the dividends is a resident, through a permanent establishment situated therein, or performs in that other State independent personal services from a fixed base situated therein, and the holding in respect of which the dividends are paid is effectively connected with such permanent establishment or fixed base. In such case the provisions of Article 7 or Article 14, as the case may be, shall apply.
5. Where a company which is a resident of a Contracting State derives profits or income from the other Contracting State, that other State may not impose any tax on the dividends paid by the company, except insofar as such dividends are paid to a resident of that other State or insofar as the holding in respect of which the dividends are paid is effectively connected with a permanent establishment or a fixed base situated in that other State, nor subject the company's undistributed profits to a tax on the company's undistributed profits, even if the dividends paid or the undistributed profits consist wholly or partly of profits or income arising in such other State.

Article 11: Interest

1. Interest arising in a Contracting State and paid to a resident of the other Contracting State may be taxed in that other State.
2. However, such interest may also be taxed in the Contracting State in which it arises and according to the laws of that State, but if the beneficial owner of the interest is a resident of the other Contracting State, the tax so charged shall not exceed 7 per cent of the gross amount of the interest. The competent authorities of the Contracting States shall by mutual agreement settle the mode of application of this limitation.
3. Notwithstanding the provisions of paragraph 2, interest arising in a Contracting State and paid to, or on loans guaranteed or insured by, the Government, a local authority or the Central Bank of the other Contracting State shall be exempt from tax in the first-mentioned State.
4. The term "interest" as used in this Article means income from debt-claims of every kind, whether or not secured by mortgage and whether or not carrying a

right to participate in the debtor's profits, and in particular, income from government securities and income from bonds or debentures, including premiums and prizes attaching to such securities, bonds or debentures. Penalty charges for late payment shall not be regarded as interest for the purpose of this Article.

5. The provisions of paragraphs 1 and 2 shall not apply if the beneficial owner of the interest, being a resident of a Contracting State, carries on business in the other Contracting State in which the interest arises, through a permanent establishment situated therein, or performs in that other State independent personal services from a 10 fixed base situated therein, and the debt-claim in respect of which the interest is paid is effectively connected with such permanent establishment or fixed base. In such case the provisions of Article 7 or Article 14, as the case may be, shall apply.
6. Interest shall be deemed to arise in a Contracting State when the payer is a resident of that State. Where, however, the person paying the interest, whether he is a resident of a Contracting State or not, has in a Contracting State a permanent establishment or a fixed base in connection with which the indebtedness on which the interest is paid was incurred, and such interest is borne by such permanent establishment or fixed base, then such interest shall be deemed to arise in the State in which the permanent establishment or fixed base is situated.
7. Where, by reason of a special relationship between the payer and the beneficial owner or between both of them and some other person, the amount of the interest, having regard to the debt-claim for which it is paid, exceeds the amount which would have been agreed upon by the payer and the beneficial owner in the absence of such relationship, the provisions of this Article shall apply only to the last-mentioned amount. In such case, the excess part of the payments shall remain taxable according to the laws of each Contracting State, due regard being had to the other provisions of this Agreement.

Article 12: Royalties

1. Royalties arising in a Contracting State and paid to a resident of the other Contracting State may be taxed in that other State.
2. However, such royalties may also be taxed in the Contracting State in which they arise and according to the laws of that State, but if the beneficial owner of the royalties is a resident of the other Contracting State, the tax so charged shall not exceed 5 per cent of the gross amount of the royalties. The competent authorities of the Contracting States shall by mutual agreement settle the mode of application of this limitation.
3. The term "royalties" as used in this Article means payments of any kind received as a consideration for the use of, or the right to use, any copyright of literary, artistic or scientific work including cinematography films, or films or tapes for radio or television broadcasting, any patent, trade mark, design or model, plan, secret formula or process, or for the use of, or the right to use, industrial, commercial, or scientific equipment, or for information concerning industrial, commercial or scientific experience.

4. The provisions of paragraphs 1 and 2 shall not apply if the beneficial owner of the royalties, being a resident of a Contracting State, carries on business in the other Contracting State in which the royalties arise, through a permanent establishment situated therein, or performs in that other State independent personal services from a fixed base situated therein, and the right or property in respect of which the royalties are paid is effectively connected with such permanent establishment or fixed base. In such case the provisions of Article 7 or Article 14, as the case may be, shall apply.
5. Royalties shall be deemed to arise in a Contracting State when the payer is the Government of that Contracting State, a local authority thereof or a resident of that Contracting State. Where, however, the person paying the royalties, whether he is a resident of a Contracting State or not, has in a Contracting State a permanent establishment or a fixed base in connection with which the liability to pay the royalties was incurred, and such royalties are borne by such permanent establishment or fixed base, then such royalties shall be deemed to arise in the State in which the permanent establishment or fixed base is situated.
6. Where, by reason of a special relationship between the payer and the beneficial owner or between both of them and some other person, the amount of the royalties, having regard to the use, right or information for which they are paid, exceeds the amount which would have been agreed upon by the payer and the beneficial owner in the absence of such relationship, the provisions of this Article shall apply only to the last-mentioned amount. In such case, the excess part of the payments shall remain taxable according to the laws of each Contracting State, due regard being had to the other provisions of this Agreement.

Article 13: Capital Gains

1. Gains derived by a resident of a Contracting State from the alienation of immovable property referred to in Article 6 and situated in the other Contracting State may be taxed in that other State.
2. Gains from the alienation of movable property (including shares and other comparable interests in a company) forming part of the business property of a permanent establishment which an enterprise of a Contracting State has in the other Contracting State or of movable property pertaining to a fixed base available to a resident of a Contracting State in the other Contracting State for the purpose of performing independent personal services, including such gains from the alienation of such a permanent establishment (alone or with the whole enterprise) or of such a fixed base, may be taxed in that other State.
3. Gains from the alienation of ships or aircraft operated in international traffic or movable property pertaining to the operation of such ships or aircraft shall be taxable only in the Contracting State in which the place of effective management of the enterprise is situated.

4. Gains derived by a resident of a Contracting State from the alienation of shares deriving more than 50 per cent of their value directly or indirectly from immovable property situated in the other Contracting State may be taxed in that other State.
5. Gains from the alienation of any property other than that referred to in paragraphs 1 to 4, shall be taxable only in the Contracting State of which the alienator is a resident.

Article 14: Independent Personal Services

1. Income derived by a resident of a Contracting State in respect of professional services or other activities of an independent character shall be taxable only in that State except in one of the following circumstances, when such income may also be taxed in the other Contracting State:
   a. if he has a fixed base regularly available to him in the other Contracting State for the purpose of performing his activities; in that case, only so much of the income as is attributable to that fixed base may be taxed in that other State;
   b. if his stay in the other Contracting State is for a period or periods amounting to or exceeding in the aggregate 183 days in any twelve month period commencing or ending in the calendar year concerned; in that case, only so much of the income as is derived from his activities performed in that other State may be taxed in that other State.
2. The term "professional services" includes especially independent scientific, literary, artistic, educational or teaching activities as well as the independent activities of physicians, lawyers, engineers, architects, dentists and accountants.

Article 15: Dependent Personal Services

1. Subject to the provisions of Articles 16, 18, 19, 20 and 21, salaries, wages and other similar remuneration derived by a resident of a Contracting State in respect of an employment shall be taxable only in that State unless the employment is exercised in the other Contracting State. If the employment is so exercised, such remuneration as is derived therefrom may be taxed in that other State.
2. Notwithstanding the provisions of paragraph 1, remuneration derived by a resident of a Contracting State in respect of an employment exercised in the other Contracting State shall be taxable only in the first-mentioned State if:
   a. the recipient is present in the other State for a period or periods not exceeding in the aggregate 183 days in any twelve-month period commencing or ending in the calendar year concerned; and
   b. the remuneration is paid by, or on behalf of, an employer who is not a resident of the other State; and
   c. the remuneration is not borne by a permanent establishment or a fixed base which the employer has in the other State.

3. Notwithstanding the preceding provisions of this Article, remuneration derived in respect of an employment exercised aboard a ship or aircraft operated in international traffic, shall be taxable only in the Contracting State in which the place of the effective management of the enterprise is situated.

Article 16: Directors Fees

Directors' fees and other similar payments derived by a resident of a Contracting State in his capacity as a member of the board of directors of a company which is a resident of the other Contracting State may be taxed in that other State.

Article 17: Artistes and Sportsmen

1. Notwithstanding the provisions of Articles 14 and 15, income derived by a resident of a Contracting State as an entertainer, such as a theatre, motion picture, radio or television artiste, or a musician, or as a sportsman, from his personal activities as such exercised in the other Contracting State, may be taxed in that other State.
2. Where income in respect of personal activities exercised by an entertainer or a sportsman in his capacity as such accrues not to the entertainer or sportsman himself but to another person, that income may, notwithstanding the provisions of Articles 7, 14 and 15, be taxed in the Contracting State in which the activities of the entertainer or sportsman are exercised.
3. Notwithstanding the provisions of paragraphs 1 and 2, income derived from the activities referred to in paragraph 1 within the framework of cultural or sports exchanges agreed to by the Governments of the Contracting States and carried out other than for the purpose of profit shall be exempt from tax in the Contracting State in which these activities are exercised.

Article 18: Pensions

1. Subject to the provisions of paragraph 2 of Article 19, pensions and other similar remuneration paid to a resident of a Contracting State in consideration of past employment shall be taxable only in that State.
2. Notwithstanding the provisions of paragraph 1, pensions paid, and other similar payments made by the Government of a Contracting State or a local authority thereof under a public welfare scheme of the social security system of that State shall be taxable only in that State.

Article 19: Government Service

a. Salaries, wages and other similar remuneration, other than a pension, paid by the Government of a Contracting State or a local authority thereof to an individual in respect of services rendered to that State or a local authority thereof, shall be taxable only in that State.

b. However, such salaries, wages and other similar remuneration shall be taxable only in the other Contracting State if the services are rendered in that other State and the individual is a resident of that other State who:

   i. is a national of that State; or
   ii. did not become a resident of that State solely for the purpose of rendering the services.

c. Any pension paid by, or out of funds created by a Contracting State or a local authority thereof to an individual in respect of services rendered to the Government of that State or a local authority thereof shall be taxable only in that State.
d. However, such pension shall be taxable only in the other Contracting State if the individual is a resident of, and a national of, that other State.
e. The provisions of Articles 15, 16, 17 and 18 shall apply to salaries, wages, pensions and other similar remuneration in respect of services rendered in connection with a business carried on by a Contracting State or a local authority thereof.

Article 20: Teachers and Researchers

1. Remuneration which an individual who is or was immediately before visiting a Contracting State a resident of the other Contracting State and who is present in the first-mentioned State for the primary purpose of teaching, giving lectures or conducting research at the invitation of any university, college, school or other similar non-profitable educational institution or scientific research institution recognized by the Government of the first-mentioned State derives for the purpose of such teaching, lectures or research shall not be taxed in the first-mentioned State, for a period of three years from the date of his first arrival in the first-mentioned State.
2. The provisions of paragraph 1 of this Article shall not apply to income from research if such research is undertaken not in the public interest but primarily for the private benefit of a specific person or persons.

Article 21: Students and Trainees

1. Payments which a student, business apprentice or trainee who is or was immediately before visiting a Contracting State a resident of the other Contracting State and who is present in the first-mentioned State solely for the purpose of his education or training receives for the purpose of his maintenance, education or training shall not be taxed in that State, provided that such payments arise from sources outside that State.
2. A student or business apprentice who is or was immediately before visiting a Contracting State a resident of the other Contracting State and who is present in the first-mentioned State for a continuous period not exceeding four year shall not be taxed in the first-mentioned State in respect of remuneration for

services rendered in that state, provided that the services are in connection with his studies or training and the remuneration constitutes earnings necessary for his maintenance.

Article 22: Other Income

1. Items of income of a resident of a Contracting State, wherever arising, not dealt with in the foregoing Articles of this Agreement shall be taxable only in that State.
2. The provisions of paragraph 1 shall not apply to income, other than income from immovable property as defined in paragraph 2 of Article 6, if the recipient of such income, being a resident of a Contracting State, carries on business in the other Contracting State through a permanent establishment situated therein, or performs in that other State independent personal services from a fixed base situated therein, and the right or property in respect of which the income is paid is effectively connected with such permanent establishment or fixed base. In such case the provisions of Article 7 or Article 14, as the case may be, shall apply.

Article 23: Methods for Elimination of Double Taxation

1. In China, double taxation shall be eliminated as follows:

   a. Where a resident of China derives income from Ethiopia, the amount of tax on that income payable in Ethiopia in accordance with the provisions of this Agreement, may be credited against the Chinese tax imposed on that resident. The amount of the credit, however, shall not exceed the amount of the Chinese tax on that income computed in accordance with the taxation laws and regulations of China.
   b. Where the income derived from Ethiopia is dividend paid by a company which is a resident of Ethiopia to a company which is a resident of China and which owns not less than 20 per cent of the shares of the company paying the dividend, the credit shall take into account the tax paid to Ethiopia by the company paying the dividend in respect of its income.

2. In Ethiopia, double taxation shall be eliminated as follows:
   Where a resident of Ethiopia derives income, which in accordance with the provisions of this Agreement may be taxed in China, Ethiopia shall allow as a deduction from the tax on the income of that resident, an amount equal to the income tax paid in China. Such deduction shall not, however, exceed that part of the income tax, as computed before the deduction is given, which is attributable, as the case may be, to the income which may be taxed in China.
3. For the purposes of this Article, where business profits arising in a Contracting State are exempt or taxed at a reduced rate in that State for a limited period of time in accordance with the laws and regulations of that State, then the tax on such business profits which have been exempt or taxed at a reduced rate in

that State shall be credited against the tax on business profits owing in the State where the beneficial owner of the business profits is a resident.

Article 24: Non-Discrimination

1. Nationals of a Contracting State shall not be subjected in the other Contracting State to any taxation or any requirement connected therewith, which is other or more burdensome than the taxation and connected requirements to which nationals of that other State in the same circumstances are or may be subjected. This provision shall, notwithstanding the provisions of Article 1, also apply to persons who are not residents of one or both of the Contracting States.
2. The taxation on a permanent establishment which an enterprise of a Contracting State has in the other Contracting State shall not be less favourably levied in that other State than the taxation levied on enterprises of that other State carrying on the same activities. This provision shall not be construed as obliging a Contracting State to grant to residents of the other Contracting State any personal allowances, reliefs and reductions for taxation purposes on account of civil status or family responsibilities which it grants to its own residents.
3. Except where the provisions of paragraph 1 of Article 9, paragraph 7 of Article 11, or paragraph 6 of Article 12, apply, interest, royalties and other disbursements paid by an enterprise of a Contracting State to a resident of the other Contracting State shall, for the purpose of determining the taxable profits of such enterprise, be deductible under the same conditions as if they had been paid to a resident of the first-mentioned State.
4. Enterprises of a Contracting State, the capital of which is wholly or partly owned or controlled, directly or indirectly, by one or more residents of the other Contracting State, shall not be subjected in the first-mentioned State to any taxation or any requirement connected therewith which is other or more burdensome than the taxation and connected requirements to which other similar enterprises of the first-mentioned State are or may be subjected.
5. The provisions of this Article shall, notwithstanding the provisions of Article 2, apply to taxes of every kind and description.

Article 25: Mutual Agreement Procedure

1. Where a person considers that the actions of one or both of the Contracting States result or will result for him in taxation not in accordance with the provisions of this Agreement, he may, irrespective of the remedies provided by the domestic law of those States, present his case to the competent authority of the Contracting State of which he is a resident or, if his case comes under paragraph 1 of Article 24, to that of the Contracting State of which he is a national. The case must be presented within three years from the first notification of the action resulting in taxation not in accordance with the provisions of the Agreement.
2. The competent authority shall endeavour, if the objection appears to it to be justified and if it is not itself able to arrive at a satisfactory solution, to resolve the case by mutual agreement with the competent authority of the other Contracting

State, with a view to the avoidance of taxation which is not in accordance with the Agreement. Any agreement reached shall be implemented notwithstanding any time limits in the domestic law of the Contracting States.

3. The competent authorities of the Contracting States shall endeavour to resolve by mutual agreement any difficulties or doubts arising as to the interpretation or application of the Agreement. They may also consult together for the elimination of double taxation in cases not provided for in the Agreement.
4. The competent authorities of the Contracting States may communicate with each other directly for the purpose of reaching an agreement in the sense of paragraphs 2 and 3. When it seems advisable for reaching agreement, representatives of the competent authorities of the Contracting States may meet together for an oral exchange of opinions.

Article 26: Exchange of Information

1. The competent authorities of the Contracting States shall exchange such information as is necessary for carrying out the provisions of this Agreement or of the domestic laws of the Contracting States concerning taxes covered by the Agreement, insofar as the taxation thereunder is not contrary to the Agreement, in particular for the prevention of evasion of such taxes. The exchange of information is not restricted by Articles 1 and 2.
2. Any information received by a Contracting State shall be treated as secret and shall be disclosed only to persons or authorities (including courts and administrative bodies) involved in the assessment or collection of, the enforcement or prosecution in respect of, or the determination of appeals in relation to, the taxes covered by the Agreement. Such persons or authorities shall use the information only for such purposes. They may disclose the information in public court proceedings or in judicial decisions.
3. In no case shall the provisions of paragraphs 1 and 2 be construed so as to impose on a Contracting State the obligation:

   a. to carry out administrative measures at variance with the laws and administrative practice of that or of the other Contracting State;
   b. to supply information which is not obtainable under the laws or in the normal course of the administration of that or of the other Contracting State;
   c. to supply information which would disclose any trade, business, industrial, commercial or professional secret or trade process, or information, the disclosure of which would be contrary to public policy (order public).

Article 27: Diplomatic Agents and Consular Officers

Nothing in this Agreement shall affect the fiscal privileges of diplomatic agents or consular officers under the general rules of international law or under the 19
provisions of special agreements.

Article 28: Entry into Force

This Agreement shall enter into force on the thirtieth day of the latter of the notification through which the Contracting States shall notify each other that the internal legal procedures for the entry into force of this Agreement have been complied with and its provisions shall have effect with respect to income derived during the taxable years beginning on or after the first day of January next following that in which this Agreement enters into force.

Article 29: Termination

This Agreement shall continue in effect indefinitely but either of the Contracting States may, on or before the thirtieth day of June in any calendar year beginning after the expiration of a period of five years from the date of its entry into force, give written notice of termination to the other Contracting State through the diplomatic channels. In such event this Agreement shall cease to have effect with respect to income derived during the taxable years beginning on or after the first day of January in the calendar year next following that in which the notice of termination is given.

IN WITNESS whereof the undersigned, duly authorized thereto, have signed this Agreement.

Done at____ on this day of ____, ____, in duplicate in the Chinese and English languages, both texts being equally authentic.

Chapter 4
Morocco

4.1 Country Profile

4.1.1 Introduction

Official name	Kingdom of Morocco
Capital	Rabat
Government	Parliamentary Constitutional Monarchy
Population	35,561,654
Area	446,550 sq. km
Official language(s)	Arabic, Berber, French

(continued)

L. Riccardi and G. Riccardi, *China in Africa*,
https://doi.org/10.1007/978-981-16-1148-3_4

(continued)

Official name	Kingdom of Morocco
Main religion(s)	Islam
Currency	Dirham (MAD)
GDP	$298.6 billion
GDP per capita	$8,600
Life expectancy	73.3

Source CIA Factbook, 2020

4.1.2 History

Morocco was conquered by the Moroccan Muslim dynasty for the first time in 788. Then in the 16th century, the Sa'adi monarchy inaugurated a golden age, raising laws and a policy against foreign invaders. In the 17th century, the Alouite Dynasty took leadership of Morocco. The current royal family belongs to this Dynasty. In addition, since 1860, when Spain occupied the north of the country, European powers eroded the sovereignty of Morocco, and in 1912 the French imposed a protectorate over Morocco. Only 44 years later, Morocco obtained independence from France after a long struggle for freedom. In 1956, the city of Tangier and most of the Spanish possession were turned over to the new country. In the next year, the new country of Morocco was established, Sultan Mohammed V changed the country into a constitutional monarchy, and he was declared King. In 1976 the Spanish army was pulled back from Western Sahara, so Morocco extended its administrative control to 80% of this territory. However, the UN does not recognize Morocco as administrator of Western Sahara.

During the Arab Spring in early 2011, Morocco was involved in riots and pro-democracy protests, which spread all over the country, forcing King Mohammed VI to implement a reform program. By a popular referendum in July 2011, the constitution was reformed, redistributing some powers to Parliament and Prime Minister, even though ultimate authority remains in the hands of the monarch. During the election in November 2011, the Justice and Development Party (PJD), a moderate Islamic Party, became the first Islamist party in the Morocco Government's history, winning most of the seats in the Parliament. The other election was held in October 2016 when the PJD reinforced their power in Parliament.

World view	1990	2000	2010	2020
Population, total (millions)	24.167	28.283	32.182	35.952
GDP (current US$) (billions)	30.18	38.859	93.217	124.539
GDP (% change)	4.035	1.913	3.816	3.688

(continued)

(continued)

World view	1990	2000	2010	2020
GDP per capita (current $)	1,248.81	1,373.92	2,896.56	3,464.02
Inflation (%)	6.026	1.923	0.994	1.1

Source IMF World Economic Outlook database 2020/RsA Asia

4.1.3 Geography

Morocco is in the northwest of Africa; its geographical position is along the Strait of Gibraltar. It is the only African country to have both Atlantic and Mediterranean coastlines. Morocco is the 59th largest country in the world. The total land area measures 446,300 square km, and there is only 250 square km of water surface. Much of the surface of Morocco is mountainous: The Atlas Mountains are located further inland, and the Rif Mountains are located along the northern coast; at the same time, the mountains are surrounded by large plateaus, valleys of grasslands and fertile coasts. The south-eastern region of Morocco is covered by the Sahara Desert. The highest peak of Morocco is Jebel Toubkal, which measures 4,165 m high, and Sebkha Tah is the lowest point at-59 m high. The most important river is the Moulouya River. The source is in the Atlas Mountains, and it flows into The Mediterranean Sea.

Morocco has both a Mediterranean and desert climate. The mild weather along the coast becomes more extreme as one moves further inland. During the summer, it is warm and dry with peak temperatures above 35 °C, but the night is cold, especially in the desert, where the minimum temperature can be as low as 5 °C. During the winter, the climate is mild along the coastline with temperatures averaging between 12 to 25 °C, while it is cold in the inland area, with temperatures ranging from 5 °C to −7 °C. The wettest seasons are spring and autumn.

However, there are serious issues regarding land degradation and soil erosion. 47.1% of the land is exploited for permanent pasture. This overgrazing of livestock intensifies desertification and the destruction of vegetation. Another issue is the containment of raw sewage and the oil pollution of coastal waters. Minimal environmental regulations enforced by the government have had repercussions on the water supply, especially during the cyclical period of droughts that characterize deserts.

Most populated cities	
City	Population
Casablanca	3,144,909
Rabat	1,655,753
Fes	964,891

(continued)

(continued)

Most populated cities	
City	Population
Sale	903,485
Marrakesh	839,296

Source Office National des Statistiques (ONS)

4.1.4 Government

The Kingdom of Morocco is a constitutional monarchy with an elected parliament. The government is based on Islamic law as well as the French and Spanish civil law systems. There are three main branches of government: executive, legislative, juridical. The first one includes the King, who has a hereditary position which is held for life; in addition, the King appoints the council of ministers and the prime minister. The legislative power is held and split by two chambers (bicameral parliament): The Chamber of Counsellors (270 members), which is selected by local councils, professional organizations and labour syndicates for nine years term; and the Chamber of Representatives (325 members), which are elected by a popular vote for six years term. The judicial power is held by the Supreme Court of Judges, presided over by the King.

The administration in Morocco is divided into 37 provinces. Every province is led by a governor appointed directly by the King. The first King of independent Morocco was Mohammed V of the Alaouite dynasty. In 1961, the throne was taken by his son Hassan II, who accepted the Royal Charter proclaimed by his father. In this way, Hassan II began to transform Morocco into a constitutional monarchy. Hassan II presided over Morocco for 38 years, becoming the longest-serving King in the Arab world. In 1999, Hassan II died, leaving the throne to his son, Mohammed VI.

In the present day, the politics of Morocco are characterized by multiple political parties, most of which belong to two major groups: The National Entete and The Democratic Bloc. The former is a coalition, created in 1993, of rightist political parties. The latter is an opposition coalition, formed in 1992, of leftist political parties. In addition, there are many Islamic fundamentalist parties, and while these groups are not legal, they are unofficially tolerated. The first constitution was drafted in 1962. It was not accepted by the public because most of the power was in the hands of the King. After a period of a state of emergency, as well as two unsuccessful military coups in 1971 and 1972, another constitution was created, which increased the number of directly appointed parliamentary members.

Key political figures	
Title	Name
King	Mohamed VI
Prime Minister	Saadeddine Othmani

Source The World Factbook—CIA, 2020

4.1.5 Culture

The Moroccan culture is a union between the indigenous Berber and colonial styles. This merger is reflected in every type of cultural expression: architecture, literature, cuisine, and art. Morocco's architectural style is shaped by indigenous Berber, the foreign invaders from the Arab world, Spain, Portugal, and France, who all brought religious and cultural influences. Big cities, such as Rabat and Casablanca, are full of modern and elegant buildings that sharply contrast with the older, more traditional architecture.

The interactions between different groups of people in Morocco have created a diversified cuisine, one that is a mix between Barber, European, and Mediterranean styles. Chicken and lamb are the most common meats in Morocco, and pork is forbidden in accordance with the Islamic faith. The most famous dishes are Couscous and Harira soup. Couscous is a dish made with granulated seminola grains, mutton or beef, and a variety of vegetables. It is eaten by all Moroccans and is referred to as the national dish. The most common drink is Atai, a type of green tea with mint. Like all Arab countries, tea is the fundamental base of the Moroccan culture, and is served during the meals, and also throughout the day. A Moroccan social event is not complete without tea. It is the first thing that is offered to a guest, and a rejection is almost intolerable. However, like every country that follows the Law of Sharia, Moroccans cannot eat during the thirty days of Ramadan, when every Islamic person in the country must fast from dawn until dusk.

Another key component of Moroccan culture is sport. Football is the most common sport in the country. In 1986, Morocco was the first country belonging to the African and Arab areas to overcome the first round of the FIFA World Cup.

The first newspapers to appear in Morocco were El Eco de Tetuàn (founded in 1860), published in Spanish, and Maghreb Al Aksa, a weekly newspaper (founded in 1877) published in English. Today, the government owns many media outlets, such as radio and television.

4.1.6 Economy

Global links	1990	2000	2010	2018
Merchandise trade (% of GDP)	37.1	48.8	57.0	67.5
Net barter of trade index (2000 = 100)	84.9	100.0	104.9	128.3
External debt stocks, total (DOD, current US$) (billion)	25.0	20.8	27.3	49.1
Net migration (thousands)	–	–	–	–
Personal remittance, received (current US$) (million)	2,006.4	2,161.0	6422.5	6,919.4
Foreign direct investment, net inflows (BoP, current US$ (million)	165.1	426.6	1,240.6	3,544.4
Net official development assistance received (current US$) (million)	1,241.1	447.4	985.5	811.7

Source World Development Indicators database/RsA Asia 2020

Economy	1990	2000	2010	2018
GDP (current US$) (billions)	30.2	38.9	93.2	117.9
GDP growth (annual %)	3.4	1.9	3.8	3.0
Inflation, GDP deflator (annual %)	7.7	−0.7	1.0	1.1
Agriculture, value added (% of GDP)	15.1	11.9	12.9	12.3
Industry, value added (% of GDP)	27.6	27.0	25.7	25.9
Services, etc., value added (% of GDP)	45.0	50.6	51.0	50.0
Exports of goods and services (% of GDP)	24.6	26.8	32.2	38.7
Import of goods and services (% of GDP)	30.1	32.4	43.0	49.3
Gross capital formation (% of GDP)	31.1	26.4	34.1	33.5
Revenue, excluding grants (% of GDP)	21.1	–	26.6	25.8
Net lending (+)/net borrowing (–) (% of GDP)	−2.1	–	−4.0	−3.7

Source World Development Indicators database/RsA Asia 2020

Morocco's proximity to the Mediterranean Sea and Europe has been key to its economic growth. Its low-cost labour and economic policy opened Morocco to an international market, and over recent years the strength of the government to improve the port, transportation infrastructures, and industrial facilities places Morocco at the centre for business throughout Africa. However, this has not always been the case; during the 80 s and 90 s, Morocco was drowning in debts. This continued until the government welcomed austerity measures and reforms in order to open the market. Therefore, Morocco could boost exports and, at the same time, cut subsidies for gasoline, which allowed the government to embrace renewable energy and placed a target to get 50% of the country's energy from greener sources.

Morocco's GDP growth in 2017 was at 4.1%. One of the most important growth elements was agriculture. Although, in 2016, the country was hit by a dramatic change of weather. The agriculture sector, which made up almost 15% of Morocco's total GDP, was dragged downward. Nevertheless, 2017 was still a very favourable year for the agricultural sector, and this balanced the performance of the primary sectors bringing with it a sector of livestock, fruit, and fisheries. In 2017 a new investment project was implemented over the whole country called the Industrial Acceleration Plan. This replaced a similar plan that had been called National Pact for Industrial Emergence. This plan of development exploits influxes of foreign investments and joint venture in order to boost the automotive sector and use synergies with the local industries to create sectors which are new for Morocco, including renewable energy.

Exports boosted when Morocco signed the bilateral Free Trade Agreement with the US in 2006 and Advanced Status agreement with the UE in 2008. Due to these agreements in 2016, the country becomes the 51st largest export economy in the world, with a value of export of US$ 22.9 billion. Morocco is a big importer with a value of imported products over US$ 41 billion, and it is evident that the trade balance is negative of US$ 18.8 billion, this gap has increased over the last years, for example in 1995 the negative trade balance was USD 2.03 billion in net imports. The current deficit was reduced from 4.4% of GDP in 2016 to around 4% in 2017; this improvement is due to legislative reforms and an increase in foreign direct investment. The change was reflected even when the total public debt decreased from 64.7% of GDP in 2016 to 63% in 2017, and the inflation was below 1%.

Over the past twenty years, the Moroccan government has embarked reforms ranging from taxation to welfare. On one side, the country has carried out a careful fiscal decentralization of the civil services, reinforced the control of the state-owned enterprise, and controlled social spending in order to protect vulnerable segments of the population.

Main Customers	
Export (% of export)	%
Spain	33.13
France	30.00
Italy	6.88
USA	5.00
India	5.00
Turkey	5.00
United Kingdom	3.8
Germany	3.75
Brazil	3.75
Netherland	3.13

Source ComTrade, 2020

Main suppliers	
Import (% of import)	%
Spain	23.40
France	19.50
China	13.48
USA	9.57
Germany	8.87
Italy	8.16
Turkey	6.38
Portugal	4.26
Russian Federation	3.55
Saudi Arabia	2.84

State and markets	1990	2000	2010	2018
Time required to start a business (days)	–	–	12	9
Domestic credit provided by financial (% of GDP)	36.7	77.3	101.5	110.8
Tax revenue (% of GDP)	18.7	–	22.8	21.9
Military expenditure (%of GDP)	3.5	2.2	3.4	3.1
Mobile cellular subscriptions (per 100 people)	0.0	8.1	98.9	124.2
Individual using the Internet (% of population)	0.0	0.7	52.0	64.8
High-technology exports (% of manufactured exports)	–	11.3	7.7	4.0

Source World Development Indicators database/RsA Asia 2020

4.1.7 Regulations

Morocco is 40th in the ranking of 190 economies on the ease of starting a business. Starting a business in Morocco requires four procedures and takes 9.5 days. The first step is to obtain a Certificat Négatif to register the company name; the second step is to pay stamp duty; the third step is to register for patent tax, the tribunal of Commerce, social security, and taxation and the last step is to make a company stamp.

However, for registering properties, Morocco's rating is not as high. Morocco stands at 87th in a ranking of 190 economies. This procedure requires six steps and 22 days. The first step is conducted due diligence at the Commercial Court Registry; the second one is complete due diligence at the Land Registry; the third step is for both parties to sign the sales contract and have it be authenticated by the notary; the fourth step is obtaining an "Attestation Fiscale" from Regional General Tax Authority; the next step is to complete the Registration of the deed with the Tax

Authority; the last one is that the buyer must apply for the inscription of the registered deed on the land registers. In addition, another reliable score to evaluate property is to use the quality of land administration index, which is the sum of scorers on the reliability of infrastructure, transparency of information, geographic coverage, land dispute resolutions, and equal access to property rights indices. This index ranges from 0 to 30 points, where a higher score means better quality, and Morocco gets 14.0 points.

To further understand the economic country profile, the ease of getting credit is also analysed. Morocco stands at 101 in the ranking of 190 economies; furthermore, the economy has a score of 7.0 points out of 8 about the depth of credit information index and 2 points out of 12 about the strength of legal rights index. In addition, Morocco also stands at 41 in the ranking of 190 economies on the ease of paying taxes, in order to improve the system of tax payment Morocco in 2016 created an electronic platform for filing and payment corporate income tax, VAT and labour taxes.

The last aspect to be considered is the labour market regulation, which relates to hiring workers, working hours, redundancy, measuring several aspects of job quality such as the availability of maternity leave, paid sick leave, and equal treatment of man and woman at the workplace. The law of hiring and working in Morocco guarantees a minimum wage of 282.9 USD per month, the maximum number of working days per week is 6, an overtime work premium of 25% of hourly pay and the number of paid annual leave for a worker with five years of tenure is 19.5 days.

Over the last decades, globalization has also significantly increased the ease of doing business in the world and, of course, in Morocco. Doing business records the time and cost associated with the logical process of exporting and importing goods, measuring the time and cost associated with: documentary compliance, border compliance, and domestic transport within the overall process of exporting or importing a shipment of goods. Globally, Morocco stands at 63 in the ranking of 190 economies on the ease of trading across borders, getting 81.12 points, and the Regional Average of the Middle East & North Africa is 55.98. In 2015, the government approved a reform to ease the trading across the border by reducing the number of export documents, and in 2017 a new reform was deliberated opening one single window system in order to reduce the time of importing goods.

Indicator	Zimbabwe	Sub-Saharan Africa	OECD members	Overall best performer
Starting a business				
Procedure—Man (number)	4	7.6	4.9	1.00 (New Zealand)
Time—Man (days)	9.5	24.0	8.5	0.5 (New Zealand)
Cost–Man (% of income per capita)	7.9	49.9	3.1	0 (UK)

(continued)

(continued)

Indicator	Zimbabwe	Sub-Saharan Africa	OECD members	Overall best performer
Paid-in min. capital (% of income per capita)	0.0	25.6	8.7	0 (113 economies)
Dealing with construction permit				
Procedure—Men (number)	13	14.8	12.5	7 (Denmark)
Time—Men (days)	88.5	147.5	154.6	27.5 (Korea Rep.)
Cost—Man (% of warehouse value)	3.5	9.9	1.6	0.1 (5 economies)
Building quality control index (0–15)	13	8.0	11.4	15 (3 economies)
Registering property				
Procedures (number)	6	6.2	4.6	1 (4 economies)
Time (days)	22	59.3	22.3	1 (3 economies)
Cost (% of property value)	5.9	7.8	4.2	0 (5 economies)
Quality of the land administration address (0–30)				
Getting credit				
Strength of legal rights index (0–12)	2.0	5.1	6.0	12 (4 economies)
Depth of credit information index (0–8)	7	3.0	6.6	8 (34 economies)
Credit registry coverage (% of adults)	24.6	6.3	18.3	100 (3 economies)

Source World Development Indicators database/RsA Asia 2020

4.2 Double Tax Agreement

Agreement Between the Government of the People's Republic of China and the Government of the Kingdom of Morocco for the Avoidance of Double Taxation and the prevention of Fiscal Evasion with Respect to Taxes on Income.

The government of the People's Republic of China and the government of the Kingdom of Morocco, desiring to conclude an Agreement for the avoidance of double taxation and the prevention of fiscal evasion with respect to taxes on income,

Have Agreed as follows:

Article 1: Persons Covered

This Agreement shall apply to persons who are residents of one or both of the Contracting States.

Article 2: Taxes Covered

1. This Agreement shall apply to taxes on income imposed on behalf of a Contracting State or of its political subdivisions or local authorities, irrespective of the manner in which they are levied.
2. There shall be regarded as taxes on income all taxes imposed on total income, or on elements of income, including taxes on gains from the alienation of movable or immovable property, taxes on the total amounts of wages or salaries paid by enterprises as well as taxes on capital appreciation.
3. The existing taxes to which the Agreement shall apply are in particular:
   a. in the case of China:
      i. the individual income tax;
      ii. the income tax for enterprises with foreign investment and foreign enterprises;
      (hereinafter referred to as "Chinese tax"); and

   b. in the case of the Kingdom of Morocco:
      i. the general income tax;
      ii. the corporation tax;
      (hereinafter referred to as "Moroccan tax").

4. The Agreement shall also apply to any identical or substantially similar taxes which are imposed after the date of signature of the Agreement in addition to, or in place of, the existing taxes. The competent authorities of the Contracting States shall notify each other of any substantial changes which have been made in their respective taxation laws within a reasonable period of time after such changes.

Article 3: General Definitions

1. For the purposes of this Agreement, unless the context otherwise requires:
   a. the terms "a Contracting State" and " the other Contracting State" mean China or Morocco as the context requires;
   b. the term "China" means the People's Republic of China; when used in geographical sense, means all the territory of the People's Republic of China, including its territorial sea, in which the Chinese laws relating to taxation apply, and any area beyond its territorial sea, within which the People's Republic of China has sovereign rights of exploration for and exploitation of resources of the sea-bed and its sub-soil and superjacent water resources in accordance with international law;

c. the term "Morocco" means the Kingdom of Morocco and, when used in geographical sense the term "Morocco" includes:
   i. the territory of the Kingdom of Morocco, the territorial sea thereof, and
   ii. the maritime areas beyond the territorial sea, including the seabed and subsoil thereof (continental shelf) and the exclusive economic zone over which Morocco exercises sovereign rights, in accordance with its domestic laws and international law, for the purpose of exploration and exploitation of the natural resources of such areas;
d. the term "tax" means Chinese tax or Moroccan tax, as the context requires;
e. the term "person" includes an individual, a company and any other body of persons;
f. the term "company" means anybody corporate or any entity which is treated as a body corporate for tax purposes;
g. the terms "enterprise of a Contracting State" and "enterprise of the other Contracting State" mean respectively an enterprise carried on by a resident of a Contracting State and an enterprise carried on by a resident of the other Contracting State;
h. the term "international traffic" means any transport by a ship or aircraft operated by an enterprise that has its place of effective management (e.g. head office) in a Contracting State, except when the ship or aircraft is operated solely between places in the other Contracting State;
i. the term "competent authority" means:
   i. in the case of China, the State Administration of Taxation or its authorised representative;
   ii. in the case of Morocco, the Minister of Economy and Finance or his authorised representative;
j. the term "national" means:
   i. any individual possessing the nationality of a Contracting State;
   ii. any legal person, partnership or association deriving its status as such from the laws in force in a Contracting State.

2. As regards the application of the Agreement at any time by a Contracting State, any term not defined therein shall, unless the context otherwise requires, have the meaning that it has at that time under the law of that State for the purposes of the taxes to which the Agreement applies, any meaning under the applicable tax laws of that State prevailing over a meaning given to the term under other laws of that State.

Article 4: Resident

1. For the purposes of this Agreement, the term "resident of a Contracting State" means any person who, under the laws of that State, is liable to tax therein by reason of his domicile, residence, place of head office, place of management or any other criterion of a similar nature, and also includes that State and any

political subdivision or local authority thereof. This term, however, does not include any person who is liable to tax in that State in respect only of income from sources in that State.

2. Whereby reason of the provisions of paragraph 1 an individual is a resident of both Contracting States, then his status shall be determined as follows:

   a. he shall be deemed to be a resident only of the State in which he has a permanent home available to him; if he has a permanent home available to him in both States, he shall be deemed to be a resident only of the State with which his personal and economic relations are closer (centre of vital interests);
   b. if the State in which he has his centre of vital interests cannot be determined, or if he has not a permanent home available to him in either State, he shall be deemed to be a resident only of the State in which he has an habitual abode;
   c. if he has an habitual abode in both States or in neither of them, he shall be deemed to be a resident only of the State of which he is a national;
   d. if he is a national of both States or of neither of them, the competent authorities of the Contracting States shall settle the question by mutual agreement.

3. Where by reason of the provisions of paragraph 1 a person other than an individual is a resident of both Contracting States, then it shall be deemed to be a resident only of the Contracting State in which the place of effective management (e.g. head office) is situated.

Article 5: Permanent Establishment

1. For the purposes of this Agreement, the term "permanent establishment" means a fixed place of business through which the business of an enterprise is wholly or partly carried on.
2. The term "permanent establishment" includes especially:

   a. a place of management;
   b. a branch;
   c. an office;
   d. a factory;
   e. a workshop;
   f. a mine, an oil or gas well, a quarry or any other place of extraction of natural resources;
   g. a sales outlet;
   h. a farm or plantation.

3. The term "permanent establishment" also encompasses:

a. a building site, a construction, assembly or installation project or supervisory activities in connection therewith, but only if such site, project or activities lasts more than six months;
b. the furnishing of services, including consultancy services, by an enterprise through employees or other personnel engaged by the enterprise for such purpose, but only if activities of that nature continue (for, the same or a connected project) within a Contracting State for a period or periods aggregating more than 6 months within any twelve-month period.

4. Notwithstanding the preceding provisions of this Article, the term "permanent establishment" shall be deemed not to include:

a. the use of facilities solely for the purpose of storage, display or delivery of goods or merchandise belonging to the enterprise;
b. the maintenance of a stock of goods or merchandise belonging to the enterprise solely for the purpose of storage, display or delivery;
c. the maintenance of a stock of goods or merchandise belonging to the enterprise solely for the purpose of processing by another enterprise;
d. the maintenance of a fixed place of business solely for the purpose of purchasing goods or merchandise or of collecting information for the enterprise;
e. the maintenance of a fixed place of business solely for the purpose of carrying on, for the enterprise, any other activity of a preparatory or auxiliary character;
f. the maintenance of a fixed place of business solely for any combination of activities mentioned in sub-paragraphs a) to e), provided that the overall activity of the fixed place of business resulting from this combination is of a preparatory or auxiliary character.

5. Notwithstanding the provisions of paragraphs 1 and 2, where a person—other than an agent of an independent status to whom paragraph 7 applies—is acting in a Contracting State on behalf of an enterprise of the other Contracting State, that enterprise shall be deemed to have a permanent establishment in the first-mentioned Contracting State in respect of any activities which that person undertakes for the enterprise, if such a person:

a. has and habitually exercises in that State an authority to conclude contracts in the name of the enterprise, unless the activities of such person are limited to those mentioned in paragraph 4 which, if exercised through a fixed place of business, would not make this fixed place of business a permanent establishment under the provisions of that paragraph; or
b. has no such authority, but habitually maintains in the first-mentioned State a stock of goods or merchandise from which he regularly delivers goods or merchandise on behalf of the enterprise.

6. Notwithstanding the preceding provisions of this Article, an insurance enterprise of a Contracting State shall, except in regard to re-insurance, be deemed to have a

permanent establishment in the other Contracting State if it collects premiums in the territory of that other State or insures risks situated therein through a person other than an agent of an independent status to whom paragraph 7 applies.

7. An enterprise of a Contracting State shall not be deemed to have a permanent establishment in the other Contracting State merely because it carries on business in that other State through a broker, general commission agent or any other agent of an independent status, provided that such persons are acting in the ordinary course of their business. However, when the activities of such an agent are devoted wholly or almost wholly on behalf of that enterprise, and conditions are made or imposed between that enterprise and the agent in their commercial and financial relations which differ from those which would have been made between independent enterprises, he will not be considered an agent of an independent status within the meaning of this paragraph.
8. The fact that a company which is a resident of a Contracting State controls or is controlled a company which is a resident of the other Contracting State, or which carries on business in that other State (whether through a permanent establishment or otherwise), shall not of itself constitute either company a permanent establishment of the other.

Article 6: Income from Immovable Property

1. Income derived by a resident of a Contracting State from immovable property (including income from agriculture or forestry) situated in the other Contracting State may be taxed in that other State.
2. The term "immovable property" shall have the meaning which it has under the law of the Contracting State in which the property in question is situated. The term shall in any case include property accessory to immovable property, livestock and equipment used in agriculture and forestry, rights to which the provisions of general law respecting landed property apply, usufruct of immovable property and rights to variable or fixed payments as consideration for the working of, or the right to work, mineral deposits, sources and other natural resources; ships and aircraft shall not be regarded as immovable property.
3. The provisions of paragraph 1 shall apply to income derived from the direct use, letting or use in any other form of immovable property.
4. The provisions of paragraphs 1 and 3 shall also apply to the income from immovable property of an enterprise and to income from immovable property used for the performance of independent personal services.
5. Where the ownership of shares or other corporate rights in a company or another legal entity entitles the owner of such shares or corporate rights to the enjoyment of immovable property held by the company or the other legal entity, income derived by the owner from the use, letting or use in any other form of his right of enjoyment may be taxed in the Contracting State in which the immovable property is situated.

Article 7: Business Profits

1. The profits of an enterprise of a Contracting State shall be taxable only in that State unless the enterprise carries on business in the other Contracting State through a permanent establishment situated therein. If the enterprise carries on business as aforesaid, the profits of the enterprise may be taxed in the other State, but only so much of them as is attributable to that permanent establishment.
2. Subject to the provisions of paragraph 3, where an enterprise of a Contracting State carries on business in the other Contracting State through a permanent establishment situated therein, there shall in each Contracting State be attributed to that permanent establishment the profits which it might be expected to make if it were a distinct and separate enterprise engaged in the same of similar activities under the same or similar conditions and dealing wholly independently with the enterprise of which it is a permanent establishment.
3. In determining the profits of a permanent establishment, there shall be allowed as deductions expenses which are incurred for the purposes of the business of the permanent establishment, including executive and general administrative expenses so incurred, whether in the State in which the permanent establishment is situated or elsewhere. However, no such deduction shall be allowed in respect of amounts, if any, paid (otherwise than towards reimbursement of actual expenses)by the permanent establishment to the head office of the enterprise or any of its other office, by way of royalties, fees or other similar payments in return for the use of patents or other rights, or by way of commission for specific services performed or for management, or, except in the case of a banking enterprise, by way of interest on moneys lent to the permanent establishment. Likewise, no account shall be taken, in the determination of the profits of a permanent establishment, for such payments, charged by the permanent establishment of the head office of the enterprise or any of its other offices.
4. Insofar as it has been customary in a Contracting State to determine the profits to be attributed to a permanent establishment on the basis of an apportionment of the total profits of the enterprise to its various parts, nothing in paragraph 2 shall preclude that Contracting State from determining the profits to be taxed by such an apportionment as may be customary; the method of apportionment adopted shall, however, be such that the result shall be in accordance with the principles contained in this article.
5. No profits shall be attributed to a permanent establishment by reason of the mere purchase by that permanent establishment of goods or merchandise for the enterprise.
6. For the purposes of the preceding paragraphs, the profits to be attributed to the permanent establishment shall be determined by the same method year by year unless there is good and sufficient reason to the contrary.
7. Where profits include items of income which are dealt with separately in other Articles of this Agreement, then the provisions of those Articles shall not be affected by the provisions of this Article.

Article 8: Shipping and Air Transport

1. Profits from the operation of ships or aircraft in international traffic shall be taxable only in the Contracting State in which the place of effective management (e.g. head office) of the enterprise is situated.
2. If the place of effective management (e.g. head office) of a shipping enterprise is aboard a ship, then it shall be deemed to be situated in the Contracting State in which the home harbour of the ship is situated, or, if there is no such home harbour, in the Contracting State of which the operator of the ship is a resident.
3. The provisions of paragraph 1 shall also apply to profits from the participation in a pool, a joint business or an international operating agency.
4. For the purposes of this article, profits derived by an enterprise of a Contracting State from the operation of ships or aircraft in international traffic shall include, inter alia, profits incidental to the profits, such as use or rental of containers, to which the provisions of paragraph I apply.

Article 9: Associated Enterprises

1. Where:

    a. an enterprise of a Contracting State participates directly or indirectly in the management, control or capital of an enterprise of the other Contracting State, or
    b. the same persons participate directly or indirectly in the management, control or capital of an enterprise of a Contracting State and an enterprise of the other Contracting State, and in either case conditions are made or imposed between the two enterprises in their commercial or financial relations which differ from those which would be made between independent enterprises, then any profits which would, but for those conditions, have accrued to one of the enterprises, but, by reason of those conditions, have not so accrued, may be included in the profits of that enterprise and taxed accordingly.

2. Where a Contracting State includes in the profits of an enterprise of that State—and taxes accordingly—profits on which an enterprise of the other Contracting State has been charged to tax in that other State and the profits so included are profits which would have accrued to the enterprise of the first-mentioned State if the conditions made between the two enterprises had been those which would have been made between independent enterprises, then that other State shall make an appropriate adjustment to the amount of the tax charged therein on those profits. In determining such adjustment, due regard shall be had to the other provisions of this Agreement and the competent authorities of the Contracting States shall, if necessary, consult each other.

Article 10: Dividends

1. Dividends paid by a company which is a resident of a Contracting State to a resident of the other Contracting State may be taxed in that other State.
2. However, such dividends may also be taxed in the Contracting State of which the company paying the dividends is a resident and according to the laws of that State, but if the beneficial owner of the dividends is a resident of the other Contracting State, the tax so charged shall not exceed 10 per cent of the gross amount of the dividends.
3. The term "dividends" as used in this Article means income from shares, "jouissance" shares or "jouissance" rights, mining shares, founders' shares or other rights, not being debt-claims, participating in profits, as well as income from other corporate rights which is subjected to the same taxation treatment as income from shares by the laws of the State of which the company making the distribution is a resident.
4. The provisions of paragraphs 1 and 2 shall not apply if the beneficial owner of the dividends, being a resident of a Contracting State, carries on business in the other Contracting State of which the company paying the dividends is a resident, through a permanent establishment situated therein, or performs in that other State independent personal services from a fixed base situated therein, and the holding in respect of which the dividends are paid is effectively connected with such permanent establishment or fixed base. In such case the provisions of Article 7 or Article 14, as the case may be, shall apply.
5. Where a company which is a resident of a Contracting State derives profits or income from the other Contracting State, that other State may not impose any tax on the dividends paid by the company, except insofar as such dividends are paid to a resident of that other State or insofar as the holding in respect of which the dividends are paid is effectively connected with a permanent establishment or a fixed base situated in that other State, nor subject the company's undistributed profits to a tax on the company's undistributed profits, even if the dividends paid or the undistributed profits consist wholly or partly of profits or income arising in such other State.
6. Notwithstanding any other provision of this Agreement, where a company which is a resident of a Contracting State has a permanent establishment in the other Contracting State, the profits taxable under paragraph 1 of Article 7 may be subject to a withholding tax in that other State, in accordance with its tax laws, but the tax so charged shall not exceed I 0 per cent of the amount of those profits after deducting therefrom the corporate income tax imposed thereon in that other State.

Article 11: Interest

1. Interest arising in a Contracting State and paid to a resident of the other Contracting State may be taxed in that other State.
2. However, such interest may also be taxed in the Contracting State in which it arises and according to the laws of that State, but if the beneficial owner

of the interest is a resident of the other Contracting State, the tax so charged shall not exceed 10 per cent of the gross amount of the interest. The competent authorities of the Contracting States shall by mutual agreement settle the mode of application of this limitation.

3. Notwithstanding the provisions of paragraph 2, interest arising in a Contracting State and paid to the Government of the other Contracting State shall be exempt from tax in the first- mentioned Contracting State. The term "Government" means:

   a. in the case of China, the Government of China and shall include:
      i. the People's Bank of China;
      ii. the State Development Bank of China;
      iii. the Export-Import Bank of China;
      iv. the Agriculture Development Bank of China;
      v. any institution wholly or mainly owned by the Government of China, as may be agreed from time to time between the competent authorities of the Contracting States, as far as the loans in consideration of which the interest is paid are guaranteed by the Government of China.
   b. in the case of Morocco, the Government of Morocco and shall include:
      i. the central bank of Morocco;
      ii. any institution wholly or mainly owned by the Government of Morocco, as may be agreed from time to time between the competent authorities of the Contracting States as far as the loans in consideration of which the interest is paid are guaranteed by the Government of Morocco.

4. The term "interest" as used in this Article means income from debt-claims of every kind, whether or not secured by mortgage and whether or not carrying a right to participate in the debtor's profits, and in particular, income from government securities and income from bonds or debentures, including premiums and prizes attaching to such securities, bonds or debentures. Penalty charges for late payment shall not be regarded as interest for the purpose of this Article.
5. The provisions of paragraphs 1, 2 and 3 shall not apply if the beneficial owner of the interest, being a resident of a Contracting State, carries on business in the other Contracting State in which the interest arises, through a permanent establishment situated therein, or performs in that other State independent personal services from a fixed base situated therein, and the debt- claim in respect of which the interest is paid is effectively connected with such permanent establishment or fixed base. In such case the provisions of article 7 or article 14, as the case may be, shall apply.
6. Interest shall be deemed to arise in a Contracting State when the payer is that State itself, a political subdivision, a local authority or a resident of that State. Where, however, the person paying the interest, whether he is a resident of a Contracting State or not, has in a Contracting State a permanent establishment or a fixed base in connection with which the indebtedness on which the interest is paid was incurred, and such interest is borne by such permanent establishment

or fixed base, then such interest shall be deemed to arise in the State in which the permanent establishment or fixed base is situated.

7. Where, by reason of a special relationship between the payer and the beneficial owner or between both of them and some other person, the amount of the interest, having regard to the debt-claim for which it is paid, exceeds the amount which would have been agreed upon by the payer and the beneficial owner in the absence of such relationship, the provisions of this Article shall apply only to the last-mentioned amount. In such case, the excess part of the payments shall remain taxable according to the laws of each Contracting State, due regard being had to the other provisions of this Agreement.

Article 12: Royalties

1. Royalties arising in a Contracting State and paid to a resident of the other Contracting State may be taxed in that other State.
2. However, such royalties may also be taxed in the Contracting State in which they arise, and according to the law of that State, but if the beneficial owner of the royalties is a resident of the other Contracting State, the tax so charged shall not exceed 10 per cent of the gross amount of the royalties. The competent authorities of the Contracting States shall by mutual agreement settle the mode of application of this limitation.
3. The term "royalties" as used in this article means payments of any kind received as a consideration for the use of, or the right to use, any copyright of literary, artistic or scientific work including cinematograph films, or films or tapes used for radio or television broadcasting, any patent, trade mark, design or model, plan, secret formula or process, or for the use of, or the right to use, agricultural, industrial, commercial or scientific equipment, or for information concerning agricultural, industrial, commercial or scientific experience.
4. The provisions of paragraphs 1 and 2 shall not apply if the beneficial owner of the royalties, being a resident of a Contracting State, carries on business in the other Contracting State in which the royalties arise, through a permanent establishment situated therein, or performs in that other Contracting State independent personal services from a fixed base situated therein, and the right or property in respect of which the royalties are paid is effectively connected with such permanent establishment or fixed base. In such case the provisions of article 7 or article 14, as the case may be, shall apply.
5. Royalties shall be deemed to arise in a Contracting State when the payer is that State itself, a political subdivision, a local authority or a resident of that State. Where, however, the person paying the royalties, whether he is a resident of a Contracting State or not, has in a Contracting State a permanent establishment or a fixed base in connection with which the liability to pay the royalties was incurred, and such royalties are borne by such permanent establishment or fixed base, then such royalties shall be deemed to arise in the State in which the permanent establishment or fixed base is situated.

6. Where, by reason of a special relationship between the payer and the beneficial owner or between both of them and some other person, the amount of the royalties, having regard to the use, right or information for which they are paid, exceeds the amount which would have been agreed upon by the payer and the beneficial owner in the absence of such relationship, the provisions of this Article shall apply only to the last-mentioned amount. In such case, the excess part of the payments shall remain taxable according to the laws of each Contracting State, due regard being had to the other provisions of this Agreement.

Article 13: Capital Gains

1. Gains derived by a resident of a Contracting State from the alienation of immovable property referred to in Article 6 and situated in the other Contracting State may be taxed in that other State.
2. Gains from the alienation of movable property forming part of the business property of a permanent establishment which an enterprise of a Contracting State has in the other Contracting State or of movable property pertaining to a fixed base available to a resident of a Contracting State in the other Contracting State for the purpose of performing independent personal services, including such gains from the alienation of such a permanent establishment (alone or with the whole enterprise) or of such fixed base, may be taxed in that other State.
3. Gains from the alienation of ships or aircraft operated in international traffic or movable property pertaining to the operation of such ships or aircraft, shall be taxable only in the Contracting State in which the place of effective management (e.g. head office) of the enterprise is situated.
4. Gains from the alienation of shares of the capital stock of a company, the property of which consists directly or indirectly principally of immovable property situated in a Contracting State may be taxed in that Contracting State.
5. Gains from the alienation of any property other than that referred to in paragraphs 1 to 4, shall be taxable only in the Contracting State of which the alienator is a resident.

Article 14: Independent Personal Services

1. Income derived by a resident of a Contracting State in respect of professional services or other activities of an independent character shall be taxable only in that State except in the following circumstances, when such income may also be taxed in the other Contracting State:

   a. If he has a fixed base regularly available to him in the other Contracting State for the purpose of performing his activities; in that case, only so much of the income as is attributable to that fixed base may be taxed in the other Contracting State; or
   b. If his stay in the other Contracting State is for a period or periods amounting to or exceeding in the aggregate 183 days in any twelve-month period commencing or ending in the fiscal year concerned; in that case, only so

much of the income as is derived from his activities performed in that other State may be taxed in that other State.

2. The term "professional services" includes especially independent scientific, literary, artistic, educational or teaching activities as well as the independent activities of physicians, lawyers, engineers, architects, dentists and accountants.

Article 15: Dependent Personal Services

1. Subject to the provisions of Articles 16,18,19,20 and 21, salaries, wages and other similar remuneration derived by a resident of a Contracting State in respect of an employment shall be taxable only in that State unless the employment is exercised in the other Contracting State. If the employment is so exercised, such remuneration as is derived therefrom may be taxed in that other State.
2. Notwithstanding the provisions of paragraph 1, remuneration derived by a resident of a Contracting State in respect of an employment exercised in the other Contracting State shall be taxable only in the first-mentioned State if:

   a. The recipient is present in the other State for a period or periods not exceeding in the aggregate 183 days in any twelve-month period commencing or ending in the fiscal year concerned; and
   b. the remuneration is paid by, or on behalf of, an employer who is not a resident of the other State; and
   c. the remuneration is not borne by a permanent establishment or a fixed base which the employer has in the other State.

3. Notwithstanding the preceding provisions of this Article, remuneration derived in respect of an employment exercised aboard a ship or aircraft operated in international traffic, shall be taxed in the Contracting State in which the place of effective management (e.g. head office) of the enterprise is situated.

Article 16: Directors' Fees and Remuneration of Top-Level Managerial Officials

1. Directors' fees and other similar payments derived by a resident of a Contracting State in his capacity as a member of the board of directors of a company which is a resident of the other Contracting State may be taxed in that other State.
2. Salaries, wages and other similar remuneration derived by a resident of a Contracting State in his capacity as an official in a top-level managerial position of a company which is a resident of the other Contracting State may be taxed in that other State.

Article 17: Artistes and Sportsmen

1. Notwithstanding the provisions of Articles 14 and 15, income derived by a resident of a Contracting State as an entertainer, such as a theatre, motion picture, radio or television artiste, or a musician, or as a sportsman, from his personal activities as such exercised in the other Contracting State, may be taxed in that other State.

2. Where income in respect of personal activities exercised by an entertainer or a sportsman in his capacity as such accrues not to the entertainer or sportsman himself but to another person, that income may, notwithstanding the provisions of Articles 7, 14 and 15, be taxed in the Contracting State in which the activities of the entertainer or sportsman are exercised.
3. Notwithstanding the provisions of paragraphs 1 and 2 of this Article, income derived by entertainers or sportsmen who are residents of a Contracting State from the activities exercised in the other Contracting State shall be exempt from tax in that other Contracting State if such activities are supported wholly or mainly from public funds of the Government of either Contracting State or take place under a plan of cultural exchange between the Governments of the Contracting States.

Article 18: Pensions

1. Subject to the provisions of paragraph 2 of Article 19, pensions, life annuities and other similar remuneration paid to a resident of a Contracting State in consideration of past employment shall be taxable only in that State.
2. Notwithstanding the provisions of paragraph 1, pensions paid, and other payments made under a public scheme which is part of the social security system of a Contracting State shall be taxable only in that State.

Article 19: Government Service

a. Salaries, wages and other similar remuneration, other than a pension, paid by a Contracting State or a political subdivision or a local authority thereof to an individual in respect of services rendered to that State or subdivision or authority shall be taxable only in that State.

b. However, such salaries, wages and other similar remuneration shall be taxable only in the other Contracting State if the services are rendered in that other State and the individual is a resident of that State who:

   i. is a national-of that State; or
   ii. did not become a resident of that State solely for the purpose of rendering the services.

c. Any pension paid by, or out of funds created by, a Contracting State or a political subdivision or a local authority thereof to an individual, in respect of services rendered to that State or subdivision or authority shall be taxable only in that State.

d. However, such pension shall be taxable only in the other Contracting State if the individual is a resident of, and a national of, that other State.

e. The provisions of Articles 15, 16, 17 and 18, shall apply to salaries, wages and other similar remuneration and to pensions in respect of services rendered in connection with a business carried on by a Contracting State or a political subdivision or a local authority thereof.

Article 20: Students

1. Payments which a student, business apprentice or trainee who is or was immediately before visiting a Contracting State a resident of the other Contracting State and who is present in the first-mentioned State solely for the purpose of his education or training receives for the purpose of his maintenance, education or training shall not be taxed in that State, provided that such payments arise from sources outside that State.
2. In respect of grants, scholarships and remuneration from employment not covered by paragraph 1, a student or business apprentice described in paragraph 1 shall, in addition, be entitled during such education or training to the same exemptions, reliefs or reductions in respect of taxes available to residents of the State which he is visiting.

Article 21: Teachers and Researchers

1. Remuneration which an individual, who is or was immediately before visiting a Contracting State, a resident of the other Contracting State and who is present in the first-mentioned State for the primary purpose of teaching, giving lectures or conducting research at a university, college, school or educational institution or scientific research institution recognized by the Government of the first-mentioned State, derives for the purpose of such teaching, lectures or research shall not be taxed in the first-mentioned State, for a period of two years from the date of his first arrival in the first-mentioned State.
2. The provisions of paragraph 1 of this Article shall not apply to income from research if such research is undertaken not in the public interest but primarily for the private benefit of a specific person or persons.

Article 22: Other Income

1. Items of income of a resident of a Contracting State, wherever arising, not dealt with in the foregoing Articles of this Agreement shall be taxable only in that State.
2. The provisions of paragraph 1 shall not apply to income, other than income from immovable property as defined in paragraph 2 of Article 6, if the recipient of such income, being a resident of a Contracting State, carries on business in the other Contracting State through a permanent establishment situated therein, or performs in that other State independent personal services from a fixed base situated therein, and the right or property in respect of which the income is paid is effectively connected with such permanent establishment or fixed base. In such case the provisions of Article 7 or Article 14, as the case may be, shall apply.

Article 23: Methods for the Elimination of Double Taxation

1. Where a resident of a Contracting State derives income in the other Contracting State the amount of tax on that income payable in that other State in accordance with the provision of this Agreement, may be credited against the tax imposed on that resident in the first-mentioned State. The amount of the credit, however, shall not exceed the amount of the tax of the first-mentioned State on that income computed in accordance with the taxation laws and regulations of the first-mentioned State.
2. Where in accordance with any provision of this Agreement income derived by a resident of a Contracting State is exempt from tax in that State, such State may nevertheless, in calculating the amount of tax on the remaining income of such resident, take into account the exempted income.
3. For the purpose of paragraph 1, the tax paid in a Contracting State shall be deemed to include the tax which would have been payable but for the legal provisions concerning tax reduction, exemption or other tax incentives for a limited period of time in accordance with the laws of that State for the promotion of economic development

Article 24: Non-Discrimination

1. Nationals of a Contracting State shall not be subjected in the other Contracting State to any taxation or any requirement connected therewith, which is other or more burdensome than the taxation and connected requirements to which nationals of that other State in the same circumstances, in particular with respect to residence, are or may be subjected. This provision shall, notwithstanding the provisions of Article 1, also apply to persons who are not residents of one or both of the Contracting States.
2. The taxation on a permanent establishment which an enterprise of a Contracting State has in the other Contracting State shall not be less favourably levied in that other State than the taxation levied on enterprises of that other State carrying on the same activities. This provision shall not be construed as obliging a Contracting State to grant to residents of the other Contracting State any personal allowances, reliefs and reductions for taxation purposes on account of civil status or family responsibilities which it grants to its own residents.
3. Except where the provisions of paragraph 1 of Article 9, paragraph 7 of Article 11, or paragraph 6 of Article 12 apply, interest, royalties and other disbursements paid by an enterprise of a Contracting State to a resident of the other Contracting State shall, for the purpose of determining the taxable profits of such enterprise, be deductible under the same conditions as if they had been paid to a resident of the first– mentioned State.
4. Enterprises of a Contracting State, the capital of which is wholly or partly owned or controlled, directly or indirectly, by one or more residents of the other Contracting State, shall not be subjected in the first- mentioned State to any taxation or any requirement connected therewith which is other or more

burdensome than the taxation and connected requirements to which other similar enterprises of the first mentioned State are or may be subjected.

5. In no case shall the provisions of this Article be construed as preventing either Contracting State from:
imposing a tax as described in paragraph 6 of Article 10;
applying the provisions of its domestic law as regards thin capitalisation and the burden of proof in respect of the allowance of expenses.
6. The provisions of this Article shall, notwithstanding the provisions of Article 2, apply to taxes of every kind and description.

Article 25: Mutual Agreement Procedure

1. Where a person considers that the actions of one or both of the Contracting States result or will result for him in taxation not in accordance with the provisions of this Agreement, he may, irrespective of the remedies provided by the domestic law of those States, present his case to the competent authority of the Contracting State of which he is a resident or, if his case comes under paragraph 1 of Article 24, to that of the Contracting State of which he is a national. The case must be presented within three years from the first notification of the actions resulting in taxation not in accordance with the provisions of the Agreement.
2. The competent authority shall endeavour, if the objection appears to it to be justified and if it is not itself able to arrive at a satisfactory solution, to resolve the case by mutual agreement with the competent authority of the other Contracting State, with a view to the avoidance of taxation which is not in accordance with this Agreement. Any agreement reached shall be implemented notwithstanding any time limits in the domestic law of the Contracting States.
3. The competent authorities of the Contracting States shall endeavour to resolve by mutual agreement any difficulties or doubts arising as to the interpretation or application of the Agreement. They may also consult together for the elimination of double taxation in cases not provided for in the Agreement.
4. The competent authorities of the Contracting States may communicate with each other directly, including through a joint commission consisting of themselves or their representatives, for the purpose of reaching an agreement in the sense of the preceding paragraphs.

Article 26: Exchange of Information

1. The competent authorities of the Contracting States shall exchange such information as is necessary for carrying out the provisions of tiffs Agreement or of the domestic laws of the Contracting States concerning taxes covered by the Agreement, insofar as the taxation thereunder is not contrary to the Agreement. The exchange of information is not restricted by Article 1. Any information received by a Contracting State shall be treated as secret in the same manner as information obtained under the domestic law of that State and shall be disclosed only to persons or authorities (including courts and administrative bodies) involved in the assessment or collection of, the enforcement or prosecution in respect of, or

the determination of appeals in relation to, the taxes covered by the Agreement. Such persons or authorities shall use the information only for such purposes. They may disclose the information in public court proceedings or in judicial decisions.

2. In no case shall the provisions of paragraph 1 be construed so as to impose on Contracting State the obligation:
   a. to carry out administrative measures at variance with the laws and administrative practice of that or of the other Contracting State;
   b. to supply information which is not obtainable under the laws or in the normal course of the administration of that or of the other Contracting State;
   c. to supply information which would disclose any trade, business, industrial, commercial or professional secret or trade process, or information, the disclosure of which would be contrary to public policy (order public).

Article 27: Members of Diplomatic Missions and Consular Posts

Nothing in this Agreement shall affect the fiscal privileges of members of diplomatic missions or consular posts under the general rules of international law or under the provisions of special agreements.

Article 28: Entry into Force

Each of the Contracting States shall notify to the other the completion of the procedures required by its law for the bringing into force of this Agreement. The Agreement shall enter into force on the thirtieth day following the date of these notifications and shall thereupon have effect in both Contracting States:

a. in respect of taxes withheld at source, on income derived on or after 1 January in the calendar year next following the year in which the Agreement enters into force;
b. in respect of other taxes on income, for taxes chargeable for any tax year beginning on or after 1 January in the calendar year next following the year in which the Agreement enters into force.

Article 29: Termination

This Agreement shall continue in effect indefinitely but either of the Contracting States may, at least six months before the end of any calendar year beginning after the expiration of a period of five years from the date of its entry into force, give to the other Contracting State, through the diplomatic channels, written notice of termination. In such event, the Agreement shall cease to have effect in both Contracting States:

a. in respect of taxes withheld at source, on income derived on or after 1 January in the calendar year next following the year in which the notice is given;

b. in respect of other taxes on income, for taxes chargeable for any tax year beginning on or after 1 January in the calendar year next following the year in which the notice is given.

IN WITNESS WHEREOF the undersigned, duly authorised thereto, have signed this Agreement.

Done in duplicate at Rabat, this 27th day of August 2002, in the Chinese, Arabic and English languages, all texts being equally authentic. In case of divergence of interpretation, the English text shall prevail.

Chapter 5
South Africa

5.1 Country Profile

5.1.1 Introduction

Official Name	Republic of South Africa
Capital	Pretoria
Government	Constitutional Republic
Population	56,463,617
Area	1,221,037 square km
Official language(s)	Afrikaans, English, Zulu

(continued)

L. Riccardi and G. Riccardi, *China in Africa*,
https://doi.org/10.1007/978-981-16-1148-3_5

(continued)

Official Name	Republic of South Africa
Main religion(s)	Protestant
Currency	South African Rand
GDP	$767.2 billion
GDP per capita	$13,600
Life expectancy	64.8

Source CIA Factbook, 2020

5.1.2 *History*

Between 200,000 to 100,000 years ago, the evolution of modern humans began from Africa, and these people were called the San. Later, they gathered with the Khoi shepherds from the north who were moving south. Together, they became the KhoiSan. The KhoiSan descended to the Western Cape at the same time. Their descendants, about 1,000 years later, formed the Mapungubwe African Kingdom and began trading with India, Arabia, and China.

In 1652, Jan van Riebeeck and his 90 strongmen arrived from the Netherlands and set up a marine refuelling station in Cape Town. This was a geographically and politically significant stop on the only commercial route from Europe and the Americas to India, the "Spice Islands" of the West Indies, and to the East. Over the next 200 years, different waves of other European and Indian settlers arrived. Subsequently, the Dutch, British, and to some extent, the French clashed for control of the Cape. The British eventually triumphed in 1806. The Dutch Boers thus began their journey back to the country to escape British domination. This period also signed the beginning of the Mfecane (dispersion, crushing) of Africans, which began in Zululand, crossed the Drakensberg, and swept the South African province of Free State. Encouraged by the growing militarism of the Zulu warrior king Shaka, the region of South Africa became a confusing whirlwind of movements and massacres. The eventual arrival of land-hungry Voortrekkers and British settlers in 1820 further reinforced the conflicts. In the late 1800 s, South Africa's immense riches in gold and diamonds were discovered. Later, its platinum resources were also found.

The 20th century saw the end of the South African War (also known as the Second Boer War) which took place from 1899 to 1902, as well as the creation of the South African Union in 1910, South Africa's involvement in the First World War and the Second World War alongside the Allies, the short victory of the predominantly Afrikaner National Party in 1948 and, in the years that followed, the formulation of apartheid. Apartheid was a period of nearly 50 years of institutional racism and the elimination of people of colour, during which the African National Congress (ANC) was banned, and its leaders, including Nelson Mandela, imprisoned on Robben

Island. The opening of the ANC, the release of Mandela and his fellow prisoners, and the democratic elections of 1994 were the signifiers of the birth of a new South Africa.

Since that time, South Africa has struggled to address apartheid-era imbalances in decent housing, education, and health care. In recent years, Jacob Zuma became president in 2009 and was re-elected in 2014, but was forced to resign in February 2018 after numerous corruption scandals and gains by opposition parties in municipal elections in 2016. His successor, Cyril Ramaphosa, has pledged to crackdown on corruption and shore up state-owned enterprises and is the ANC's likely candidate for May 2019 national elections.

World view	1990	2000	2010	2020
Population, total (millions)	36.79	44.9	51.329	59.72
GDP (current US$) (billions)	115.533	136.453	375.304	369.854
GDP (% change)	−0.318	4.155	3.04	1.079
GDP per capita (current $)	3,140.34	3,039.04	7,311.74	6,193.17
Inflation (%)	14.213	5.389	4.264	5.169

Source IMF World Economic Outlook database 2020/RsA Asia

5.1.3 Geography

South Africa is a big country located on the southern tip of the African continent. It has more than 50 million people from a multitude of different cultures. The territory covers an area of 1,221,037 km^2 and is bigger than Germany, France, and Italy combined. The country has about 3,000 km of coastline. The southeast coast is warmed by the Agulhas Current, which comes from the equator region, while the Atlantic coast is touched by the cold Benguela Current. The differences in temperature between these two currents are the origin of the contrasts that exist in terms of vegetation and climate between the east and the west sides of the country. Bordered to the north by Namibia, Botswana, Zimbabwe, and Mozambique, South Africa also surrounds two small independent countries, Lesotho and Swaziland.

Administratively, South Africa is divided into nine provinces, Eastern Cape, Northern Cape, Western Cape, Free State, Gauteng, Kwazulu-Natal, Limpopo, Mpumalanga, North West, North West Province. The province of Northern Cape is the largest of the South African provinces by size, but it is the least populated. As for Gauteng, the smallest of the provinces, it generates one-third of the national GDP.

South Africa can also be divided into two main regions, an inner plateau, and the coastal plain. The two regions are separated by hills and mountains, including the famous Drakensberg, which rises to 3482 meters. The ocean that surrounds South

Africa enjoys a rather temperate climate even if there are significant climatic differences from one region to another. The province of Kwazulu-Natal has a subtropical climate with a high hygrometry rate in summer. The southern part of Gauteng experiences hot summers with some torrential storms, while the northern part of the region has mild winters. Western Cape has a Mediterranean climate with hot, dry summers and cold, wet winters. The South African climate is mild throughout the year, with an annual rainfall of about 500 mm compared to a global average of 857 mm. The seasons are reversed compared to Europe. The South African summer starts in October and ends in March, and the temperatures are between 15° and 35°, while the winter is from April to September and has temperatures ranging from 0° or less, to 20° at midday.

The immense wealth of South African wildlife is one of their main tourist attractions. South Africa hosts the three largest land mammals: elephants, rhinoceroses, and hippopotamuses. As for the five big wild animals (lions, elephants, leopards, buffalos, rhinoceroses), they are the pride of natural parks. But there are also giraffes, antelopes, marine fauna, and many birds, including the ostrich and the penguin of the Cape. The flora is in the image of the diversity of the country. South Africa alone accounts for one-tenth of the world's botanical heritage, some 25,000 species. In the Cape region, there are 8,500 species of plants, of which 2,500 grow on the peninsula alone, and 5,000 exist nowhere else.

Most populated cities

City	Population
Cape Town	3,443,441
Durban	3,120,282
Johannesburg	2,026,469
Soweto	1,695,047
Pretoria	1,619,438

Source Office National des Statistiques (ONS)

5.1.4 Government

The Republic of South Africa is a parliamentary republic.

Since 1984, the President was head of the state and head of the Government. Ministers were appointed by the President, and the President was elected by those in Parliament. However, this political system was segregated between 1991–1994.

In 1994, the first multiracial elections were held. Since then, the country's political system has been dominated by the ANC, who received 65.9% of the votes in the last general elections. The national party, which established apartheid and dominated the country's politics between 1948 and 1994, left after they merged with ANC in 2005.

The official opposition is the Democratic Alliance, which received 16.7% of the votes. The extreme right-wing identity (1%), the far-left Pan-African (1%), and some ethnic parties (7%) or Christian Democrats also are included in the political landscape.

Key political figures	
Title	Name
President	Matamela Cyril Ramaphosa
Deputy President	David Mabuza
Chair of the National Council	Amos Masondo
Speaker of the National Assembly	Thandi Modise
Chief Justice	Mogoeng Mogoeng

Source The World Factbook—CIA, 2020

5.1.5 Culture

Football is the most popular sport in South Africa, due to the low resources required to play it. In 2010, South Africa hosted the FIFA World Cup for the first time. South Africa also has more than 600,000 rugby players. In 1995, the national South African team (the Springboks) won the Rugby World Cup at home, and Nelson Mandela, the South African president, wore a shirt of François Pienaar (who is a white South African). This sport symbolises South Africa's reconciliation. Other main sports also practiced in South Africa are cycling, cricket, and golf.

Another popular interest in South Africa is theatre, which has always been of great importance, as it allows South Africans to convey political messages to their illiterate comrades. The Market Theatre in Johannesburg is the most famous in the country.

Another popular art form in South Africa is literature, which has also gained worldwide recognition. South Africa has published books which were written by English-speaking authors such as Nadine Gordimer (Nobel Prize for literature) and by Afrikaners, such as André Brink or Breytenbach, whose books were translated into English. Despite the popularity of literature, black writers often remain unrecognised internationally, though this is beginning to change.

South Africans also have the richest palette of music in the whole African continent. The popular music styles include rock, jazz, classical, gospel, rap, reggae, maskanda, mbaqanga, kwaito, and many others.

5.1.6 Economy

Global links	1990	2000	2010	2018
Merchandise trade (% of GDP)	36	44	50	57
Net barter of trade index (2000 = 100)	104	100	141	146
External debt stocks, total (DOD, current US$) (billion)	0	25.44	108.39	179.31
Net migration (thousands)	–	–	–	–
Personal remittance received (current US$) (million)	135.5	324.7	1069.5	929.1
Foreign direct investment, net inflows (BoP, current US$ (million)	−75.72	−968.83	−3963.27	−5569.46
Net official development assistance received (current US$) (million)	–	490.0	1,036.2	914.8

Source World Development Indicators database/RsA Asia 2020

Economy	1990	2000	2010	2018
GDP (current US$) (billions)	115.55	136.36	375.35	368.29
GDP growth (annual %)	−0.3	4.2	3	0.8
Inflation, GDP deflator (annual %)	15.5	8.8	6.4	3.9
Agriculture, value added (% of GDP)	4	3	2	2
Industry, value added (% of GDP)	36	29	27	26
Services, etc., value added (% of GDP)	50	59	61	61
Exports of goods and services (% of GDP)	24	27	29	30
Import of goods and services (% of GDP)	18	24	27	30
Gross capital formation (% of GDP)	19	16	19	18
Revenue, excluding grants (% of GDP)	25.5	25.7	28.1	31.6
Net lending (+)/net borrowing (−) (% of GDP)	−3.4	−1.9	−4.0	−5.1

Source World Development Indicators database/RsA Asia 2020

South Africa, which is Africa's largest economy, accounts for more than 30% of the continent's GNP and is among the most promising emerging markets in the world. Classified as a "middle-income country" by the World Bank, it has uniquely combined an economy comparable to that of developed countries. It is the only African member in the G20, and it collaborates with OECD in the framework of the Enhanced Engagement Program. Ranked as the 26th largest industrialized nation, South Africa is also a member of major international financial institutions and plays a major role in promoting the goals of developing countries. In December 2010, South Africa also joined Brazil, Russia, India, and China in the BRIC, which has since been known as the BRICS.

When the world suffered from the economic crisis, South Africa managed to preserve itself due to its prudent monetary and fiscal policy management. South Africa, which has reformed its economy, has excellent growth rates: it experienced 62 quarters of uninterrupted economic growth between 1993 and 2007, and GDP growth reached 5.1%. However, the Eurozone did affect South Africa. Although The World Bank data showed GDP growth was 3.1% in 2017, it was just 1.3% in 2008. A strict control policy has also permitted the South African Central Bank to contain its inflation. In July 2012, inflation consecutively fell for three quarters and eventually reached 4.9%. This helped to protect the standard of living of South Africans, especially those in the poorest households.

South Africa also has a large and diversified industrial base (30% of GDP). A mineral-rich subsoil means South Africa remains the world's leading producer for minerals such as gold, platinum, rhodium, chromium, manganese, and vanadium. The country owns 80% of the world's manganese reserves, 72% of the world's chromium, 88% of the world's platinum group, 40% of the world's gold reserves, 27% of the world's vanadium reserves and 60% of the world's coal reserves. The automotive industry also occupies a prominent place in South Africa's economy as it accounts for 6.5% of its GDP. In addition, South Africa's aerospace industry has recognized expertise in the design and manufacture of high value-added products, and consequently, energy contributes to 15% of South Africa's gross domestic product. Thus, South Africa's sophisticated financial structure awards them with a stock market whose capitalization ranks among the top 20 in the world.

Main Customers	
Export (% of export)	%
China	9.20
USA	7.40
Germany	5.00
Botswana	4.80
Namibia	4.70
Japan	4.30
UK	4.30
India	2.90
Belgium	3.10
Mozambique	3.10

Source ComTrade, 2020

Main Suppliers	
Import (% of import)	%
Germany	18.10
USA	11.80

(continued)

(continued)

Main Suppliers	
Import (% of import)	%
India	6.70
USA	4.20
Saudi Arabia	3.80
Japan	3.40
France	3.00
UK	2.90
Thailand	2.90
Nigeria	2.80

State and markets	1990	2000	2010	2018
Time required to start a business (days)	–	–	45	40
Domestic credit provided by financial (% of GDP)	53.9	70.5	81.4	79.0
Tax revenue (% of GDP)	23.1	23.3	25	27.5
Military expenditure (%of GDP)	3.9	1.4	1.1	1.0
Mobile cellular subscriptions (per 100 people)	0	18.5	98.4	159.9
Individual using the Internet (% of population)	0	5.3	24	54
High-technology exports (% of manufactured exports)	–	7	5.97	5.31

Source World Development Indicators database/RsA Asia 2020

The Biggest Algerian Companies				
Name	Industry	Sector	Headquarters	State-Owned
Standard Bank	Financials	Bank	Johannesburg	Yes
First Rand	Financials	Bank	Johannesburg	No
Sasol	Oil & Gas	Oil	Johannesburg	Yes
Sanlam	Financials	Insurance	Cape Town	Yes
Telkom	Telecommunication	Mobile Telecommunication	Pretoria	Yes
MTN	Telecommunication	Mobile Telecommunication	Johannesburg	No
Remgro	–	Conglomerate	Stellenbosch	No
Bidvest Group	–	Conglomerate	Johannesburg	No
Impala Platinum	–	Mining	Johannesburg	No
Imperial Holdings	–	Transport	Ekurhuleni	No

(continued)

(continued)

The Biggest Algerian Companies

Name	Industry	Sector	Headquarters	State-Owned
Barloworld	–	Conglomerate	Johannesburg	No
Naspers	–	Media	Cape Town	No
Metropolitan Holdings	Financials	Financial Services	Cape Town	Yes
Gold Fields	–	Mining	Johannesburg	No
Sappi	–	Paper	Johannesburg	Yes
Steinhoff	Financials	Financial Services	Johannesburg	Yes
Alexander Forbes	Financials	Financial Services	Johannesburg	Yes
Tiger Brands	Consumer Goods	Food	Johannesburg	Yes

Source RsA Asia report 2020

5.1.7 Regulations

South Africa has embraced international trade, and this now accounts for 60% of the country's GDP. It shipped US$89.5 billion goods in 2017, which was an increase of 20.8% since 2016 (the value of exports is nevertheless down 5.9% compared to 2013). South Africa's main trading partners are China (9.6%), the United States (7.5%), Germany (7.1%), Japan (4.7%), India (4.7%), Botswana (4.3%) and Namibia (4%). The country mainly exports precious stones and precious metals (which accounts for 16.7% of the total).

5.2 Double Tax Agreement

Agreement Between the Government of the People's Republic of China and the Government of the Republic of South Africa for the Avoidance of Double Taxation and the Prevention of Fiscal Evasion with Respect to Taxes on Income

The Government of the People's Republic of China and the Government of The Republic of South Africa,

Desiring to conclude an Agreement for the avoidance of double taxation and the prevention of fiscal evasion with respect to taxes on income,

Have agreed as follows:

Article 1: Personal Scope

This Agreement shall apply to persons who are residents of one or both of the Contracting States.

Article 2: Taxes Covered

1. This Agreement shall apply to taxes on income imposed on behalf of a Contracting State or a political subdivision or a local authority thereof, irrespective of the manner in which they are levied.
2. The existing taxes to which the Agreement shall apply are in particular:

   a. in China:
      i. the individual income tax;
      ii. the income tax for enterprises with foreign investment and foreign enterprises;
      (hereinafter referred to as "Chinese tax")

   b. in South Africa:
      i. the income tax;
      ii. the secondary tax on companies;
      (hereinafter referred to as "South African tax")

3. The Agreement shall also apply to any identical or substantially similar taxes which are imposed by either contracting State after the date of signature of the Agreement in addition to, or in place of, the existing taxes. The competent authorities of the Contracting States shall notify each other of any substantial changes which have been made in their respective taxation laws within a reasonable period of time after such changes.

Article 3: General Definitions

1. For the purposes of this Agreement, unless the context otherwise requires:

   a. the term "China" means the People's Republic of China; when used in a geographical sense, means all the territory of the People's Republic of China, including its territorial sea, in which the Chinese laws relating to taxation apply, and any area beyond its territorial sea, within which the People's Republic of China has sovereign rights of exploration for and exploitation of resources of the sea-bed and its sub-soil and superjacent water resources in accordance with international law;
   b. the term "South Africa" means the Republic of South Africa and, when used in a geographical sense, includes the territorial sea thereof as well as any area outside the territorial sea, including the continental shelf, which has been or may hereafter be designated, under the laws of South Africa and in accordance with international law, as an area within which South Africa may exercise sovereign rights or jurisdiction;
   c. the terms "a Contracting State" and "the other Contracting State" mean China or South Africa, as the context requires;
   d. the term "tax" means Chinese tax or South African tax, as the context requires;

e. the term "person" includes an individual, a company, and any other body of persons;
f. the term "company" means anybody corporate or any entity which is treated as a body corporate for tax purposes;
g. the terms "enterprise of a Contracting State" and "enterprise of the other Contracting State" mean, respectively, an enterprise carried on by a resident of a Contracting State and an enterprise carried on by a resident of the other Contracting State;
h. the term "national" means:
   i. any individual possessing the nationality of a Contracting State;
   ii. any legal person, partnership or association deriving its status as such from the laws in force in a Contracting State;
i. the term "international traffic" means any transport by a ship or aircraft operated by an enterprise of a Contracting State except when the ship or aircraft is operated solely between places in the other Contracting State;
j. the term "competent authority" means, in the case of China, the State Administration of Taxation or its authorized representative, and in the case of South Africa, the Commissioners for the South African Revenue Service of his authorized representative.

2. As regards the application of the Agreement at any time by a Contracting State, any term not defined therein shall, unless the context otherwise requires, have the meaning that it has at that time under the law of that Contracting State for the purposes of the taxes to which the Agreement applies, any meaning under the applicable tax laws of that Contracting State prevailing over a meaning given to the term under other laws of that Contracting State.

Article 4: Resident

1. For the purposes of this Agreement, the term "resident of a Contracting State" means:

   a. in China, any person who, under the laws of China, is liable to tax therein by reason of his domicile, residence, place of head office or any other criterion of a similar nature;
   b. in South Africa, any individual who is ordinarily resident in South Africa and any other person which has its place of effective management in South Africa;
   c. that State and any political subdivision or local authority thereof.

2. Whereby reason of the provisions of paragraph 1 an individual is a resident of both Contracting States, then his status shall be determined as follows:

   a. he shall be deemed to be a resident only of the State in which he has a permanent home available to him; if he has a permanent home available to him in both States, he shall be deemed to be a resident only of the State with which his personal and economic relations are closer (centre of vital interests);

b. if the State in which he has his centre of vital interests cannot be determined, or if he has not a permanent home available to him in either State, he shall be deemed to be a resident only of the State in which he has an habitual abode;

c. if he has a habitual abode in both States or in neither of them, he shall be deemed to be a resident only of the State of which he is a national;

d. if he is a national of both States or of neither of them, the competent authorities of the Contracting States shall settle the question by mutual agreement.

3. Where, by reason of the provisions of paragraph 1, a person other than an individual is a resident of both Contracting States, then it shall be deemed to be a resident of the State in which its place of effective management or its head office is situated. However, if such person has a place of effective management in a Contracting State and has a head office in the other Contracting State, the competent authorities of the Contracting States shall by mutual agreement determine the State of which the person in question is a resident.

Article 5: Permanent Establishment

1. For the purposes of this Agreement, the term "permanent establishment" means a fixed place of business through which the business of an enterprise is wholly or partly carried on.
2. The term "permanent establishment" includes especially:

   a. a place of management;
   b. a branch;
   c. an office;
   d. a factory;
   e. a workshop; and
   f. a mine, an oil or gas well, a quarry or any other place of extraction of natural resources.

3. The term "permanent establishment" likewise encompasses:

   a. a building site, a construction, assembly or installation project or supervisory activities in connection therewith, but only where such site, project or activities continue for a period of more than 12 months;
   b. the furnishing of services, including consultancy services, by and enterprise through employees or other personnel engaged by the enterprise for such purpose, but only where activities of that nature continue (for the same or a connected project) within a Contracting State for a period or periods aggregating more than 12 months within any twenty four month period.

4. Notwithstanding the preceding provisions of this Article, the term "permanent establishment" shall be deemed not to include:

a. the use of facilities solely for the purpose of storage, display or delivery of goods or merchandise belonging to the enterprise;
b. the maintenance of a stock of goods or merchandise belonging to the enterprise solely for the purpose of storage, display or delivery;
c. the maintenance of a stock of goods or merchandise belonging to the enterprise solely for the purpose of processing by another enterprise;
d. the maintenance of a fixed place of business solely for the purpose of purchasing goods or merchandise or of collecting information, for the enterprise;
e. the maintenance of a fixed place of business solely for the purpose of carrying on, for the enterprise, any other activity of a preparatory or auxiliary character;
f. the maintenance of a fixed place of business solely for any combination of activities mentioned in subparagraphs (a) to (e), provided that the overall activity of the fixed place of business resulting from this combination is of a preparatory or auxiliary character.

5. Notwithstanding the provisions of paragraphs 1 and 2, where a person - other than an agent of an independent status to whom paragraph 6 applies - is acting in a Contracting State on behalf of an enterprise of the other Contracting State, and has, and habitually exercises, an authority to conclude contracts in the name of the enterprise, that enterprise shall be deemed to have a permanent establishment in the first-mentioned Contracting State in respect of any activities which that person undertakes for the enterprise, unless the activities of such person are limited to those mentioned in paragraph 4 which, if exercised through a fixed place of business, would not make this fixed place of business a permanent establishment under the provisions of that paragraph.
6. An enterprise of a Contracting State shall not be deemed to have a permanent establishment in the other Contracting State merely because it carries on business in that other State through a broker, general commission agent or any other agent of an independent status, provided that such persons are acting in the ordinary course of their business.
7. The fact that a company which is a resident of a Contracting State controls or is controlled by a company which is a resident of the other Contracting State, or which carries on business in that other State (whether through a permanent establishment or otherwise), shall not of itself constitute either company a permanent establishment of the other.

Article 6: Income from Immovable Property

1. Income derived by a resident of a Contracting State from immovable property (including income from agriculture or forestry) situated in the other Contracting State may be taxed in that other State.
2. The term “immovable property” shall have the meaning which it has under the law of the Contracting State in which the property in question is situated.

The term shall in any case include property accessory to immovable property, livestock and equipment used in agriculture and forestry, rights to which the provisions of general 7 law respecting landed property apply, usufruct of immovable property and rights to variable or fixed payments as consideration for the working of, or the right to work, mineral deposits, sources and other natural resources. Ships and aircraft shall not be regarded as immovable property.

3. The provisions of paragraph 1 shall apply to income derived from the direct use, letting, or use in any other form of immovable property.
4. The provisions of paragraphs 1 and 3 shall also apply to the income from immovable property of an enterprise and to income from immovable property used for the performance of independent personal services.

Article 7: Business Profits

1. The profits of an enterprise of a Contracting State shall be taxable only in that State unless the enterprise carries on business in the other Contracting State through a permanent establishment situated therein. If the enterprise carries on business as aforesaid, the profits of the enterprise may be taxed in the other State, but only so much of them as is attributable to that permanent establishment.
2. Subject to the provisions of paragraph 3, where an enterprise of a Contracting State carries on business in the other Contracting State through a permanent establishment situated therein, there shall in each Contracting State be attributed to that permanent establishment the profits which it might be expected to make if it were a distinct and separate enterprise engaged in the same or similar activities under the same or similar conditions and dealing wholly independently with the enterprise of which it is a permanent establishment.
3. In determining the profits of a permanent establishment, there shall be allowed as deductions expenses which are incurred for the purposes of the business of the permanent establishment, including executive and general administrative expenses so incurred, whether in the State in which the permanent establishment is situated or elsewhere.
4. Insofar as it has been customary in a Contracting State to determine the profits to be attributed to a permanent establishment on the basis of an apportionment of the total profits of the enterprise to its various parts, nothing in paragraph 2 shall preclude that Contracting State from determining the profits to be taxed by such an apportionment as may be customary. The method of apportionment adopted shall, however, be such that the result shall be in accordance with the principles contained in this Article.
5. No profits shall be attributed to a permanent establishment by reason of the mere purchase by that permanent establishment of goods or merchandise for the enterprise.
6. For the purposes of the preceding paragraphs, the profits to be attributed to the permanent establishment shall be determined by the same method year by year unless there is good and sufficient reason to the contrary.

7. Where profits include items of income which are dealt with separately in other Articles of this Agreement, then the provisions of those Articles shall not be affected by the provisions of this Article.

Article 8: Shipping and Air Transport

1. Profits of an enterprise of a Contracting State from the operation of ships or aircraft in international traffic shall be taxable only in that State.
2. The provisions of paragraph 1 shall also apply to profits from the participation in a pool, a joint business or an international operating agency.

Article 9: Associated Enterprises

1. Where
   a. an enterprise of a Contracting State participates directly or indirectly in the management, control or capital of an enterprise of the other Contracting State, or
   b. the same persons participate directly or indirectly in the management, control or capital of an enterprise of a Contracting State and an enterprise of the other Contracting State,
   c. and in either case conditions are made or imposed between the two enterprises in their commercial or financial relations which differ from those which would be made between independent enterprises, then any profits which would, but for those conditions, have accrued to one of the enterprises, but, by reason of those conditions, have not so accrued, may be included in the profits of that enterprise and taxed accordingly.
2. Where a Contracting State includes in the profits of an enterprise of that State—and taxes accordingly—profits on which an enterprise of the other Contracting State has been charged to tax in that other State and the profits so included are profits which would have accrued to the enterprise of the first-mentioned State if the conditions made between the two enterprises had been those which would have been made between independent enterprises, then that other State shall make an appropriate adjustment to the amount of the tax charged therein on those profits. In determining such adjustment, due regard shall be had to the other provisions of this Agreement and the competent authorities of the Contracting States shall, if necessary, consult each other.

Article 10: Dividends

1. Dividends paid by a company which is a resident of a Contracting State to a resident of the other Contracting State may be taxed in that other State.
2. However, such dividends may also be taxed in the Contracting State of which the company paying the dividends is a resident and according to the laws of that State, but if the beneficial owner of the dividends is a resident of the other Contracting State, the tax so charged shall not exceed 5 per cent of the gross

amount of the dividends. The competent authorities of the Contracting States shall by mutual agreement settle the mode of application of this limitation.

This paragraph shall not affect the taxation of the company in respect of the profits out of which the dividends are paid.

3. The term "dividends" as used in this Article means income from shares, or other rights, not being debt-claims, participating in profits, as well as income from other corporate rights which is subjected to the same taxation treatment as income from shares by the laws of the State of which the company making the distribution is a resident.
4. The provisions of paragraphs 1 and 2 shall not apply if the beneficial owner of the dividends, being a resident of a Contracting State, carries on business in the other Contracting State of which the company paying the dividends is a resident, through a permanent establishment situated therein, or performs in that other State independent personal services from a fixed base situated therein, and the holding in respect of which the dividends are paid is effectively connected with such permanent establishment or fixed base. In such case the provisions of Article 7 or Article 14, as the case may be, shall apply.
5. Where a company which is a resident of a Contracting State derives profits or income from the other Contracting State, that other State may not impose any tax on the dividends paid by the company, except insofar as such dividends are paid to a resident of that other State or insofar as the holding in respect of which the dividends are paid is effectively connected with a permanent establishment or a fixed base situated in that other State, nor subject the company's undistributed profits to a tax on the company's undistributed profits, even if the dividends paid or the undistributed profits consist wholly or partly of profits or income arising in such other State.

Article 11: Interest

1. Interest arising in a Contracting State and paid to a resident of the other Contracting State may be taxed in that other State.
2. However, such interest may also be taxed in the Contracting State in which it arises and according to the laws of that State, but if the beneficial owner of the interest is a resident of the other Contracting State, the tax so charged shall not exceed 10 per cent of the gross amount of the interest. The competent authorities of the Contracting States shall by mutual agreement settle the mode of application of this limitation.
3. Notwithstanding the provisions of paragraph 2, interest arising in a Contracting State and derived by the Government of the other Contracting State, a political subdivision, a local authority and the Central Bank thereof or any financial institution wholly owned by the Government of that other State, or by any other resident of that other State with respect to debt-claims indirectly financed by the Government of that other State, a political subdivision, a local authority and the Central Bank thereof or any financial institution wholly owned by the

Government of that other State, shall be exempt from tax in the first-mentioned State.

4. The term "interest" as used in this Article means income from debt-claims of every kind, whether or not secured by mortgage and whether or not carrying a right to participate in the debtor's profits, and in particular, income from government securities and income from bonds or debentures, including premiums and prizes attaching to such securities, bonds or debentures. Penalty charges for late payment shall not be regarded as interest for the purpose of this Article.
5. The provisions of paragraphs 1, 2 and 3 shall not apply if the beneficial owner of the interest, being a resident of a Contracting State, carries on business in the other Contracting State in which the interest arises, through a permanent establishment situated therein, or performs in that other State independent personal services from a fixed base situated therein, and the debt-claim in respect of which the interest is paid is effectively connected with such permanent establishment or fixed base. In such case the provisions of Article 7 or Article 14, as the case may be, shall apply.
6. Interest shall be deemed to arise in a Contracting State when the payer is a resident of that State, Where, however, the person paying the interest, whether he is a resident of a Contracting State or not, has in a Contracting State a permanent establishment or a fixed base in connection with which the indebtedness on which the interest is paid was incurred, and such interest is borne by such permanent establishment or fixed base, then such interest shall be deemed to arise in the State in which the permanent establishment or fixed base is situated.
7. Where, by reason of a special relationship between the payer and the beneficial owner or between both of them and some other person, the amount of the interest, having regard to the debt-claim for which it is paid, exceeds the amount which would have been agreed upon by the payer and the beneficial owner in the absence of such relationship, the provisions of this Article shall apply only to the last-mentioned amount. In such case, the excess part of the payments shall remain taxable according to the laws of each Contracting State, due regard being had to the other provisions of this Agreement.

Article 12: Royalties

1. Royalties arising in a Contracting State and paid to a resident of the other Contracting State may be taxed in that other State.
2. However, such royalties may also be taxed in the Contracting State in which they arise, and according to the laws of that State, but if the beneficial owner of the royalties is a resident of the other Contracting State, the tax so charged shall not exceed:

    a. in the case of royalties referred to in subparagraph
    b. of paragraph 3 of this Article, 10 per cent of the gross amount of the royalties; (b) in the case of royalties referred to in subparagraph (b) of paragraph 3 of this Article, 10 per cent of the adjusted amount of the royalties. For

the purpose of this subparagraph "the adjusted amount" means 70 per cent of the gross amount of the royalties.

3. The term "royalties" as used in this Article comprises:
   a. payments of any kind received as a consideration for the use of, or the right to use, any copyright of literary, artistic or scientific work, including cinematograph films, and films, tapes or discs for radio or television broadcasting, or any patent, know-how, trade mark, design or model, plan, secret formula or process; and
   b. payments of any kind received as a consideration for the use of, or the right to use, any industrial, commercial or scientific equipment.
4. The provisions of paragraphs 1 and 2 shall not apply if the beneficial owner of the royalties, being a resident of a Contracting State, carries on business in the other Contracting State in which the royalties arise, through a permanent establishment situated therein, or performs in that other State independent personal services from a fixed base situated therein, and the right or property in respect of which the royalties are paid is effectively connected with such permanent establishment or fixed base. In such case the provisions of Article 7 or Article 14, as the case may be, shall apply.
5. Royalties shall be deemed to arise in a Contracting State when the payer is a resident of that State, Where, however, the person paying the royalties, whether he is a resident of a Contracting State or not, has in a Contracting State a permanent establishment or a fixed base in connection with which the liability to pay the royalties was incurred, and such royalties are borne by such permanent establishment or fixed base, then such royalties shall be deemed to arise in the State in which the permanent establishment or fixed base is situated.
6. Where, by reason of a special relationship between the payer and the beneficial owner or between both of them and some other person, the amount of the royalties, having regard to the use, right or information for which they are paid, exceeds the amount which would have been agreed upon by the payer and the beneficial owner in the absence of such relationship, the provisions of this Article shall apply only to the last-mentioned amount. In such case, the excess part of the payments shall remain taxable according to the laws of each Contracting State, due regard being had to the other provisions of this Agreement.

Article 13: Capital Gains

1. Gains derived by a resident of a Contracting State from the alienation of immovable property referred to in Article 6 and situated in the other Contracting State may be taxed in that other State.
2. Gains from the alienation of movable property forming part of the business property of a permanent establishment which an enterprise of a Contracting State has in the other Contracting State or of movable property pertaining to a fixed base available to a resident of a Contracting State in the other Contracting State for the purpose of performing independent personal services, including

such gains from the alienation of such a permanent establishment (alone or with the whole enterprise) or of such a fixed base, may be taxed in that other State.

3. Gains of an enterprise of a Contracting State from the alienation of ships or aircraft operated in international traffic or movable property pertaining to the operation of such ships or aircraft shall be taxable only in that State.
4. Gains from the alienation of shares of the capital stock of a company the property of which consists directly or indirectly principally of immovable property situated in a Contracting State may be taxed in that Contracting State.
5. Gains from the alienation of shares other than those mentioned in paragraph 4 representing a participation of at least 25 per cent in a company which is a resident of a Contracting State may be taxed in that State.
6. Gains from the alienation of any property other than that referred to in the preceding paragraphs, shall be taxable only in the Contracting State of which the alienator is a resident.

Article 14: Independent Personal Services

1. Income derived by a resident of a Contracting State in respect of professional services or other activities of an independent character shall be taxable only in that State except in one of the following circumstances, when such income may also be taxed in the other Contracting State:

   a. if he has a fixed base regularly available to him in the other Contracting State for the purpose of performing his activities; in that case, only so much of the income as is attributable to that fixed base may be taxed in that other State;
   b. if his stay in the other Contracting State is for a period or periods amounting to or exceeding in the aggregate 183 days in any twelve month period commencing or ending in the fiscal year concerned; in that case, only so much of the income as is derived from his activities performed in that other State may be taxed in that other State.

2. The term “professional services” includes especially independent scientific, literary, artistic, educational or teaching activities as well as the independent activities of physicians, lawyers, engineers, architects, dentists and accountants.

Article 15: Dependent Personal Services

1. Subject to the provisions of Articles 16, 18, 19, 20 and 21, salaries, wages and other similar remuneration derived by a resident of a Contracting State in respect of an employment shall be taxable only in that State unless the employment is exercised in the other Contracting State. If the employment is so exercised, such remuneration as is derived therefrom may be taxed in that other State.
2. Notwithstanding the provisions of paragraph 1, remuneration derived by a resident of a Contracting State in respect of an employment exercised in the other Contracting State shall be taxable only in the first-mentioned State if:

a. the recipient is present in the other State for a period or periods not exceeding in the aggregate 183 days in any twelve-month period Commencing or ending in the fiscal year concerned; and
b. the remuneration is paid by, or on behalf of, an employer who is not a resident of the other State; and
c. the remuneration is not borne by a permanent establishment or a fixed base which the employer has in the other State.

3. Notwithstanding the preceding provisions of this Article, remuneration derived in respect of an employment exercised aboard a ship or aircraft operated in international traffic by an enterprise of a Contracting State may be taxable in that State.

Article 16: Directors' Fees

Directors' fees and other similar payments derived by a resident of a Contracting State in his capacity as a member of the board of directors of a company which is a resident of the other Contracting State may be taxed in that other State.

Article 17: Entertainers and Sportspersons

1. Notwithstanding the provisions of Articles 14 and 15, income derived by a resident of a Contracting State as an entertainer, such as a theatre, motion picture, radio or television artiste, or a musician, or as a sportsman, from his personal activities as such exercised in the other Contracting State, may be taxed in that other State.
2. Where income in respect of personal activities exercised by an entertainer or a sportsman in his capacity as such accrues not to the entertainer or sportsman himself 15 but to another person, that income may, notwithstanding the provisions of Articles 7, 14 and 15, be taxed in the Contracting State in which the activities of the entertainer or sportsman are exercised.
3. Notwithstanding the preceding provisions of this Article, income derived by entertainers or sportspersons who are residents of a Contracting State from the activities exercised in the other Contracting State shall be exempt from tax in that other Contracting State if such activities are supported wholly or mainly from public funds of the Government of either Contracting State, a political subdivision or a local authority thereof, or take place under a plan of cultural exchange between the Governments of the Contracting States.

Article 18: Pensions

1. Subject to the provisions of paragraph 2 of Article 19, pensions and other similar remuneration paid to a resident of a Contracting State in consideration of past employment shall be taxable only in that State.
2. Notwithstanding the provisions of paragraph 1, pensions paid and other similar payments made by the Government of a Contracting State, a political subdivision or a local authority thereof under a public welfare scheme of the social security system of that State shall be taxable only in that State.

Article 19: Government Service

a. Salaries, wages and other similar remuneration, other than a pension, paid by a Contracting State or a political subdivision or a local authority thereof to an individual in respect of services rendered to that State or a political subdivision or a local authority thereof, shall be taxable only in that State.
b. However, such salaries, wages and other similar remuneration shall be taxable only in the other Contracting State if the services are rendered in that State and the individual is a resident of that State who:
c. is a national of that State; or
d. did not become a resident of that State solely for the purpose of rendering the services.
e. Any pension paid by, or out of funds created by, a Contracting State or a political subdivision or a local authority thereof to an individual in respect of services rendered to that State or a political subdivision or a local authority thereof shall be taxable only in that State.
f. However, such pension shall be taxable only in the other Contracting State if the individual is a resident of, and a national of, that other State.
g. The provisions of Articles 15, 16, 17 and 18 shall apply to salaries, wages and other similar remuneration, and to pensions in respect of services rendered in connection with a business carried on by the Government of a Contracting State or a political subdivision or a local authority thereof.

Article 20: Teachers and Researchers

1. Remuneration which an individual who is or was immediately before visiting a Contracting State, a resident of the other Contracting State and who is present in the first-mentioned State for the primary purpose of teaching, giving lectures or conducting research at a university, college, school or educational institution or scientific research institution recognized by the Government of the first-mentioned State, derives for the purpose of such teaching, lectures or research shall not be taxed in the first-mentioned State, for a period of two years from the date of his first arrival in the first-mentioned State.
2. The provisions of paragraph 1 of this Article shall not apply to income from research if such research is undertaken not in the public interest but primarily for the private benefit of a specific person or persons.

Article 21: Students and Trainees

1. Payments which a student, business apprentice or trainee who is or was immediately before visiting a Contracting State a resident of the other Contracting State and who is present in the first-mentioned State solely for the purpose of his education training receives for the purpose of his maintenance, education or training shall not be taxed in that State, provided that such payments arise from sources outside that State.

2. In respect of grants, scholarships and remuneration from employment not covered by paragraph 1, a student, business apprentice or trainee described in paragraph 1 shall, in addition, be entitled during such education or training to the same exemptions, reliefs or reductions in respect of taxes available to residents of the State which he is visiting.

Article 22: Other Income

1. Items of income of a resident of a Contracting State, wherever arising, not dealt with in the foregoing Articles of this Agreement shall be taxable only in that State.
2. The provisions of paragraph 1 shall not apply to income, other than income from immovable property as defined in paragraph 2 of Article 6, if the recipient of such income, being a resident of a Contracting State, carries on business in the other Contracting State through a permanent establishment situated therein, or performs in that other State independent personal services from a fixed base situated therein, and the right or property in respect of which the income is paid is effectively connected with such permanent establishment or fixed base. In such case, the provisions of Article 7 or Article 14, as the case may be, shall apply.
3. Notwithstanding the provisions of paragraphs 1 and 2, items of income of a resident of a Contracting State not dealt with in the foregoing Articles of the Agreement and arising in the other Contracting State may also be taxed in that other State.

Article 23: Methods for Elimination of Double Taxation

Double taxation shall be eliminated as follows:

1. In China, where a resident of China derives income from South Africa the amount of the South African tax paid on that income in accordance with the provisions of this Agreement, may be credited against the Chinese tax imposed on that resident. The amount of the credit, however, shall not exceed the amount of the Chinese tax on that income computed in accordance with the taxation laws and regulations of China.
2. In South Africa, Chinese tax paid by residents of South Africa in respect of income taxable in China, in accordance with the provisions of the Agreement, shall be deducted from the taxes due according to South African fiscal law. Such deduction shall not, however, exceed an amount which bears to the total South African tax payable the same ratio as the income concerned bears to the total income.

Article 24: Non-Discrimination

1. Nationals of a Contracting State shall not be subjected in the other Contracting State to any taxation or any requirement connected therewith, which is other

or more burdensome than the taxation and connected requirements to which nationals of that other State in the same circumstances are or may be subjected. This provision shall, notwithstanding the provisions of Article 1, also apply to persons who are not residents of one or both of the Contracting States.

2. The taxation on a permanent establishment which an enterprise of a Contracting State has in the other Contracting State shall not be less favourably levied in that other State than the taxation levied on enterprises of that other State carrying on the same activities. This provision shall not be construed as obliging a Contracting State to grant to residents of the other Contracting State any personal allowances, reliefs and reductions for taxation purposes on account of civil status or family responsibilities which it grants to its own residents.
3. Except where the provisions of paragraph 1 of Article 9, paragraph 7 of Article 11, or paragraph 6 of Article 12, apply, interest, royalties and other disbursements paid by an enterprise of a Contracting State to a resident of the other Contracting State shall, for the purpose of determining the taxable profits of such enterprise, be deductible under the same conditions as if they had been paid to a resident of the first-mentioned State.
4. Enterprises of a Contracting State, the capital of which is wholly or partly owned or controlled, directly or indirectly, by one or more residents of the other Contracting State, shall not be subjected in the first-mentioned State to any taxation or any requirement connected therewith which is other or more burdensome than the taxation and connected requirements to which other similar enterprises of the first-mentioned State are or may be subjected.
5. The provisions of this Article shall, notwithstanding the provisions of Article 2, apply to taxes of every kind and description.

Article 25: Mutual Agreement Procedure

1. Where a person considers that the actions of one or both of the Contracting States result or will result for him in taxation not in accordance with the provisions of this Agreement, he may, irrespective of the remedies provided by the domestic law of those States, present his case to the competent authority of the Contracting State of which he is a resident or, if his case comes under paragraph 1 of Article 24, to that of 19 the Contracting State of which he is a national. The case must be presented within three years from the first notification of the action resulting in taxation not in accordance with the provisions of the Agreement.
2. The competent authority shall endeavour, if the objection appears to it to be justified and if it is not itself able to arrive at a satisfactory solution, to resolve the case by mutual agreement with the competent authority of the other Contracting State, with a view to the avoidance of taxation which is not in accordance with the Agreement. Any agreement reached shall be implemented notwithstanding any time limits in the domestic law of the Contracting States.
3. The competent authorities of the Contracting States shall endeavour to resolve by mutual agreement any difficulties or doubts arising as to the interpretation or

application of the Agreement. They may also consult together for the elimination of double taxation in cases not provided for in the Agreement.

4. The competent authorities of the Contracting States may communicate with each other directly for the purpose of reaching an agreement in the sense of paragraphs 2 and 3. When it seems advisable for reaching agreement, representatives of the competent authorities of the Contracting States may meet together for an oral exchange of opinions.

Article 26 Exchange of Information

1. The competent authorities of the Contracting States shall exchange such information as is necessary for carrying out the provisions of this Agreement or of the domestic laws of the Contracting States concerning taxes covered by the Agreement insofar as the taxation thereunder is not contrary to the Agreement. The exchange of information is not restricted by Article 1. Any information received by a Contracting State shall be treated as secret in the same manner as information obtained under the domestic laws of that State and shall be disclosed only to persons or authorities (including courts and administrative bodies) concerned with the assessment or collection of, the enforcement or prosecution in respect of, or the determination of appeals in relation to, the taxes covered by the Agreement. Such persons or authorities shall use the information only for such purposes. They may disclose the information in public court proceedings or in judicial decisions.
2. In no case shall the provisions of paragraph 1 be construed so as to impose on a Contracting State the obligation:

   a. to carry out administrative measures at variance with the laws and administrative practice of that or of the other Contracting State;
   b. to supply information which is not obtainable under the laws or in the normal course of the administration of that or of the other Contracting State;
   c. to supply information which would disclose any trade, business, industrial, commercial or professional secret or trade process, or information, the disclosure of which would be contrary to public policy (order public).

Article 27: Members of Diplomatic Missions and Consular Posts

Nothing in this Agreement shall affect the fiscal privileges of members of diplomatic missions or consular posts under the general rules of international law or under the provisions of special agreements.

Article 28: Entry into Force

Each of the Contracting States shall notify to the other the completion of the procedures required by its law for the bringing into force of this Agreement. The Agreement shall enter into force on the thirtieth day following the date of the later of these notifications and shall have effect as respects income derived during the taxable years beginning on or after the first day of January next following that in which the Agreement enters into force.

Article 29: Termination

This Agreement shall continue in effect indefinitely but either of the Contracting States may, on or before the thirtieth day of June in any calendar year beginning after the expiration of a period of five years from the date of its entry into force, give written notice of termination to the other Contracting State through the diplomatic channel. In such event the Agreement shall cease to have effect as respects income derived during the taxable years beginning on or after the first day of January in the calendar year next following that in which the notice of termination is given.

IN WITNESS whereof the undersigned, duly authorized thereto, have signed this Agreement.

Done at Pretoria on the 25th day of April 2000, in duplicate in the Chinese and English languages, both texts being equally authentic.

For the Government of the People's Republic of China

For the Government of the Republic of South Africa

Chapter 6
Tunisia

6.1 Country Profile

6.1.1 Introduction

Official Name	Republic of Tunisia
Capital	Tunis
Government	Parliamentary Republic
Population	11,721,177
Area	163,610.00 sq. km

(continued)

L. Riccardi and G. Riccardi, *China in Africa*,
https://doi.org/10.1007/978-981-16-1148-3_6

(continued)

Official Name	Republic of Tunisia
Official language(s)	Arabic, French, Berber
Main religion(s)	Muslim
Currency	Dinar (TND)
GDP	$137,7 billion
GDP per capita	$11,900
Life expectancy	76.3

Source CIA, 2020

6.1.2 History

Tunisia's history has very ancient origins. The Sahara Desert, the Atlas Mountains, and the opening of the Mediterranean Sea all contribute a fundamental role within the famous city of Carthage. The Vandals occupied the region in the 5th century and documented a series of occupations. In the 6th century, Byzantines conquered this area, and during the 8th century, Arabs took possession of the country. It was during this era that one of the most prestigious sanctuaries was built, the Great Mosque of Kairouan, built in 670 A.D., and is now the oldest standing minaret worldwide. This region declined around the 12th century when Tunisia succumbed under the command of Barbarossa. In 1574, the Ottoman Empire then took a permanent acquisition of Tunisia and ruled the country until 1881. From this point, control was then given to a French dominion, which lasted for 75 years. After World War I, independence spread in Tunisia, and they finally became an independent state in 1956. Tunisia's first president Habib Bourguiba dominated the country for 31 years and is known for repressing Islamic fundamentalism and for providing women with rights, which is a unique event in the Muslim nation. But in 1987, Bourguiba was declared medically incapable of continuing his government and was replaced by Zine el Abidine Ben Ali.

While under Zine el Abidine Ben Ali's control, the Tunisian Parliament approved laws that made the country more democratic, however according to the Amnesty International reforms, the approved laws were a cover to create a positive image. This positive image was not maintained as the government also enhanced censorship on freedom of the press and political pluralism. This policy intensified the frustration and anger of the people and resulted in a revolution. On 17 December 2010, a 26-year old street vendor set himself on fire in protest of the humiliation inflicted on him by a municipal official. This triggered a mass protest and riots spread all over the country. This wind of change soon widened to other countries in the north of Africa and the Middle East, which consequently gave rise to the revolution known as the Arab Spring. On 14 January 2011, Ben Ali left both the government and Tunisia.

In the same year, elections for the new Constituent Assembly were held. During these elections, human rights activist Moncef Marzouki was voted as the interim president. In February 2012, the Assembly drafted the new constitution, and after several iterations, the document was ratified in January 2014. During the 2014 elections, which took place under the country's new constitution, Beji Caid Essebsi was elected to the presidency, but the government is looking for a balance between their economic and social problems.

World view	1990	2000	2010	2020
Population, total (millions)	8.233	9.699	10.64	11.903
GDP (current US$) (billions)	13.474	21.474	44.054	39.61
GDP (% change)	7.075	4.299	3.511	2.428
GDP per capita (current $)	1,636.64	2,213.95	4,140.47	3,327.72
Inflation (%)	6.502	2.77	4.361	5.436

Source IMF World Economic Outlook database 2020/RsA Asia

6.1.3 Geography

Tunisia is the smallest country in North Africa. The main geographical points of interest are the Atlas Mountains, which are situated in the north of Tunisia, and the Sahara Desert, which is in the south. To the north and east of the mountains are low hills and flat coasts. A part of Tunisia is covered by a portion of the Sahara, and the centre of the country is covered by the Grand Erg Oriental, which is also known as the "field of sand dunes." Tunisia owns Kerkennah Island, which is no more than 13 m above sea level, and Jerba Island, which is situated close to the mainland by an Antique Roman road. The total area of Tunisia measures 163,610 sq. km, and it is the 94th largest country in the world.

The climate in the north of Tunisia is mild: rainy during the winter and hot during the summer. The highest point in Tunisia is Jebel ech Chambi, which is 1,544 m high, and the lowest point is Shatt al Gharsah at 17 m. There are many sources of water in Tunisia; however, the main one is the Medjerda River, which has a length of 450 km. Besides the river, there is also a lagoon between Tunis and the Gulf of Tunis (37 sq km). The country is also characterized by a series of dry salt lakes on the northern edge of the Sahara.

However, in Tunisia, there are weighty issues about desertification, soil erosion, overgrazing, deforestation, containment of raw sewage, and the oil pollution in water. Consequently, this lack of control has had repercussions on the health of the population. In addition, Tunisia also has a problem with earthquakes, flooding, and droughts. However, since the opening of the sea, important natural resources now include fish and salt.

Most populated cities	
City	Population
Tunis	693,210
Sfax	277,278
Sousse	164,123
Midoun	120,000
Kairouan	119,794

Source Office National des Statistiques (ONS)

6.1.4 Government

The conventional name of Tunisia is The Republic of Tunisia. Tunisia is a Parliamentary Republic headed by a President. The Republic of Tunisia is a representative democracy where the power is in the hands of the President, who is head of the state, and the Prime Minister is head of the Government and the unicameral Parliament. Tunisia's legal system is a mix between the civil law, that comes from the French civil code, and the Islamic law. However, the Law of Personal Status is still based on Islamic law despite the abolishment of the Sharia courts in 1956.

But after the fall of Ben Ali in 2011, Tunisia was pushed towards becoming more democratic. In January 2014, a new constitution was ratified, and according to this, Tunisia was a free state. In October 2014, elections under the new constitution were held, following the Arab Spring, and Tunisia was also included in the European Neighbourhood Policy (ENP). Under the power of Ben Ali, there were only three independent opposition parties: PDP, FDTL, and Tajdid. However, since the revolution, the number of legalized parties has grown rapidly. Now there are more than 100 legal parties, including those under the Ben Ali government. A unique peculiarity in Tunisia for the Arab world government is the number of seats held by women. In 2011, women at the constituent assembly held between 24% and 31% of all seats. Another characteristic that belongs to the new government is its code of Personal Status; in fact, it is one of the most progressive civil codes in North Africa and amongst the Muslim world, and the Law of Personal Status is now also applied to all Tunisians regardless of their religion.

Key political figures	
Title	Name
President	Kais Saied
Prime Minister	Elyes Fakhfakh

Source The World Factbook—CIA, 2020

6.1.5 *Culture*

The history of Tunisia reveals an intense and rich past. Over the last three thousand years, there have been invasions conducted by different ethnicities, and Tunisian culture has had to become a merger of different civilizations. In addition to native Amazigh, there are Carthaginian, Roman Africans, Arab and French. Furthermore, much of the population have tried to obtain control of their territory, and consequently, this has left signs of their dominions in every aspect of the culture.

The stronger presences of the Carthaginian Republic, the Roman Empire, and other left monuments are one of the most beautiful archaeological sites in the world. In Tunisia, two architectural styles are dominant: Islamic and Roman styles fill buildings with spiritual inspiration and religious decorations.

Tunisia's ethnic diversity is reflected in its cuisine. Traditional Tunisian cuisine is Mediterranean and very spicy, and their national dish is Couscous, semolina (minuscule grains, prepared with a stew of meat) and vegetables. However, Tunisians located near the coast eat mainly seafood, eggs, and bread. The most common drink in Tunisia is tea. Like every Arab country, tea is served during meals and throughout the day. Social events require that tea must be served, and like every country following the Law of Sharia, Tunisians cannot eat during the thirty days of Ramadan, when every Islamic person in the country must fast from dawn until dusk.

Another vital aspect of Tunisian culture is their media. Tunisia's broadcast media is mainly under the control of the government. The Tunisian State runs the Tunisian Radio and television establishment. Just one TV show and three radio stations are under private-owned control and are focused on national news. The government, through the Office National de la Telediffusion, has control of the broadcast facilities and transmitters. Even if the freedom of the press is guaranteed, more than half of the newspapers are privately owned, and almost all the media support the government line.

Finally, regarding sports in Tunisia, football is the most spread. Their national team, The Eagles of Carthage, won the 2004 African Cup of Nations, which they hosted. They have also taken part in the FIFA World Cup four times.

Football is the most famous sport in Tunisia as already said, however at the same time, handball is undoubtedly quite common. Their national team has participated in many Handball World Championships, and they even hosted the 2005 Handball World Championship, where they took the fourth place. They have also won the African Cup a staggering 9 times.

6.1.6 *Economy*

Due to the structural reform, Tunisia's economy is finally beginning to grow. GDP growth in 2015 and 2016 was at 1%, but in 2017, the economic growth increased to be above 2%, and the forecasts for 2018 and 2019 are predicted to be higher than

3%. This acceleration is due to two elements: the first is the rise in external demand, which is improving the industrial sector (in particular industries of phosphate and gas) and the non-manufacturing sector. Secondly, since 2011, Tunisia has pursued economic revitalization through public spending. This policy helps both public and private consumption.

Furthermore, Tunisia has several other positive factors which are supporting their economic growth. The first one is tourism. After years of terrorism tormenting Tunisia, the improvement in security has revived the tourist industry. This brought a 32% increase in tourism in 2017, and this is also likely to improve the balance of payments. In addition, following an experiment with socialist economic policies in the 1960s, Tunisia embarked on a successful strategy that focused on bolstering exports, foreign investment, and tourism, all of which are now become central to the country's economy. Key exports now include textiles and apparel, food products, petroleum products, chemicals, and phosphates. France, Germany, and Spain are expected to drive up exports, and at the same time, Tunisia may benefit from the dividends of the strategic reforms adopted since 2015. These include the law on public-private partnerships established on 27 November 2015, and the law established on 30 September 2016, which was to boost the investment rate in accordance with the Strategic Development Plan 2016–2020. This anticipates there will be a 5% increase in GDP by 2020.

Global links	1990	2000	2010	2018
Merchandise trade (% of GDP)	73.5	67.1	87.7	95.5
Net barter of trade index (2000 = 100)	109.2	100.0	112.9	119.2
External debt stocks, total (DOD, current US$) (billion)	7.7	11.4	22.5	34.6
Net migration (thousands)	–	–	–	–
Personal remittance received (current US$) (million)	551.0	795.9	2,063.3	1,902.2
Foreign direct investment, net inflows (BoP, current US$ (million)	76.3	750.7	1,334.5	988.9
Net official development assistance received (current US$) (million)	392.5	222.8	550.1	805.2

Source World Development Indicators database/RsA Asia 2020

Economy	1990	2000	2010	2018
GDP (current US$) (billions)	12.3	21.5	44.0	39.9
GDP growth (annual %)	7.9	4.7	3.5	2.5
Inflation, GDP deflator (annual %)	4.5	3.3	3.8	6.9
Agriculture, value added (% of GDP)	17.7	11.3	8.2	10.4
Industry, value added (% of GDP)	33.6	30.2	31.5	22.7
Services, etc., value added (% of GDP)	48.7	58.5	60.3	59.1
Exports of goods and services (% of GDP)	43.6	39.5	49.5	48.9

(continued)

(continued)

Economy	1990	2000	2010	2018
Import of goods and services (% of GDP)	50.6	42.9	54.7	62.0
Gross capital formation (% of GDP)	27.1	26.1	26.6	19.7
Revenue, excluding grants (% of GDP)	30.7	26.5	29.0	–
Net lending (+)/net borrowing (–) (% of GDP)	−3.2	−2.4	−1.4	–

Source World Development Indicators database/RsA Asia 2020

Main Customer	
Export (% of export)	
France	4.3%
Italy	2.4%
Germany	1.4%
Algeria	0.7%
Spain	0.5%
Libya	0.4%
Belgium	0.2%
USA	0.2%

Source ComTrade

Main Supplier	
Import (% of import)	
France	3.0%
Italy	2.8%
China	1.8%
Turkey	0.9%
Spain	0.8%
Algeria	0.7%
USA	0.7%
Russian Federation	0.6%

State and markets	1990	2000	2010	2018
Time required to start a business (days)	–	–	13.0	9.0
Domestic credit provided by financial (% of GDP)	62.5	59.7	62.2	93.9
Tax revenue (% of GDP)	20.0	19.3	20.1	–
Military expenditure (%of GDP)	2.0	1.5	1.3	2.1
Mobile cellular subscriptions (per 100 people)	0.0	1.2	104.5	127.7

(continued)

(continued)

Individual using the Internet (% of population)	0.0	2.8	36.8	64.2
High-technology exports (% of manufactured exports)	2.1	3.4	4.9	6.1

6.1.7 Regulations

According to data collected by *Doing Business*, starting a business in Tunisia requires 9 procedures and takes 11 days. Globally, Tunisia stands at 103 in the ranking of 190 economies on the ease of starting a business (regional average Middle East and North Africa is 80.35).

In relation to registering a property, Tunisia globally stands at 92 in the ranking of 190 economies on the ease of registering property (regional average Middle East and North Africa are 60.64). The procedure which takes most of the time is the last one, as 30 days are needed to complete the title deed at the Land Property Administration. Registering a property will require 4 procedures and takes 39 days.

For getting credit, the economy of Tunisia has a score of 6.0 on the depth of credit information index and a score of 3.0 on the strength of legal rights index. Globally, Tunisia stands at 101 in the ranking of 190 economies on the ease of getting credit (45.0 points, firmly above the regional African and Middle East score: 28.75).

Regarding the ease of paying taxes, the Tunisian government has an issue with facilitating the processes of paying taxes. Tunisia stands at 106 in the ranking of 190 economies on the ease of paying taxes; however, this is the only index below the regional average.

Trading across the border is a fundamental element to understanding the economy of a country. Globally, Tunisia stands at 92 in the ranking of 190 economies on the ease of trading across borders, far above the average of the African region. The most significant reforms to ease the trading are the following: in 2011, Tunisia upgraded its electronic data interchange system for imports and exports, which speed up the assembly of import documents, and in 2016, Tunisia reduced its border compliance time for both exporting and importing. This was achieved by improving the efficiency of its state-owned port handling company and investing in the port infrastructure.

The final aspect to be considered is the labour market regulation. This relates to hiring workers, working hours, redundancy, maternity leave, paid sick leave, and equal treatment of men and women at the workplace. The law for hiring and working in Tunisia guarantees a minimum wage of US$ 256.8 per month, the maximum number of working days per week is 6, an overtime work premium of 25% of hourly pay and the number of paid annual leave for a worker with 5 years of tenure is 19.

Indicator	Tunisia	Sub-Saharan Africa	OECD members	Overall Best Performer
Starting a business				
Procedure–Man (number)	9	7.6	4.9	1.00 (New Zealand)
Time–Man (days)	11	24.0	8.5	0.5 (New Zealand)
Cost–Man (% of income per capita)	4.7	49.9	3.1	0 (UK)
Paid-in min. capital (% of income per capita)	0	25.6	8.7	0 (113 economies)
Dealing with construction permit				
Procedure – Men (number)	17	14.8	12.5	7 (Denmark)
Time–Men (days)	93	147.5	154.6	27.5 (Korea Rep.)
Cost–Man (% of warehouse value)	2.5	9.9	1.6	0.1 (5 economies)
Building quality control index (0–15)	11	8.0	11.4	15 (3 economies)
Registering property				
Procedures (number)	4	6.2	4.6	1 (4 economies)
Time (days)	39	59.3	22.3	1 (3 economies)
Cost (% of property value)	6.1	7.8	4.2	0 (5 economies)
Quality of the land administration address (0–30)				
Getting credit				
Strength of legal rights index (0–12)	3	5.1	6.0	12 (4 economies)
Depth of credit information index (0–8)	6	3.0	6.6	8 (34 economies)
Credit registry coverage (% of adults)	27.5	6.3	18.3	100 (3 economies)

Source World Development Indicators database/RsA Asia 2020

6.2 Double Tax Agreement

Agreement Between the Government of the People's Republic of China and the Government of the Republic of Tunisia for the Avoidance of Double Taxation and the Prevention of Fiscal Evasion with Respect to Taxes on Income

The Government of the People's Republic of China and the Government of the Republic of Tunisia,

Desiring to conclude an Agreement for the avoidance of double taxation and the prevention of fiscal evasion with respect to taxes on income,

Have agreed as follows:

Article 1: Personal Scope

This Agreement shall apply to persons who are residents of one or both of the Contracting States.

Article 2: Taxes Covered

1. This Agreement shall apply to taxes on income imposed on behalf of a Contracting State or of its political subdivisions or local authorities, irrespective of the manner in which they are levied.
2. There shall be regarded as taxes on income all taxes imposed on total income, or on elements of income, including taxes on gains from the alienation of movable or immovable property, as well as taxes on capital appreciation.
3. The existing taxes to which the Agreement shall apply are in particular:

    a. in China:
        i. the individual income tax;
        ii. the income tax for enterprises with foreign investment and foreign enterprises.
        (hereinafter referred to as "Chinese tax")

    b. in Tunisia:
        i. the income tax;
        ii. the corporation tax.

4. The Agreement shall also apply to any identical or substantially similar taxes which are imposed after the date of signature of the Agreement in addition to, or in place of, the existing taxes. The competent authorities of the Contracting States shall notify each other of any substantial changes which have been made in their respective taxation laws.

Article 3: General Definitions

1. For the purposes of this Agreement, unless the context otherwise requires:

    a. The term "China" means the People's Republic of China; when used in geographical sense, means all the territory of the People's Republic of

China, including its territorial sea, in which the Chinese laws relating to taxation apply, and any area beyond its territorial sea, within which the People′s Republic of China has sovereign rights of exploration for and exploitation of resources of the sea bed and its sub soil and superjacent water resources in accordance with international law;

b. the term "Tunisia" means the territory of the Republic of Tunisia including any area adjacent to the territorial waters of Tunisia and its space area on which, in accordance with international law, Tunisia can exercise the rights pertaining to the sea bed, marine sub soil and to their natural resources;
c. the terms "a Contracting State" and "the other Contracting State" mean China or Tunisia as the context requires;
d. the term "tax" means Chinese tax or Tunisian tax as the context requires;
e. the term "person" includes an individual, a company and any other body of persons;
f. the term "company" means anybody corporate or any entity which is treated as a body corporate for tax purposes;
g. the terms "enterprise of a Contracting State" and "enterprise of the other Contracting State" mean, respectively, an enterprise carried on by a resident of a Contracting State and an enterprise carried on by a resident of the other Contracting State;
h. the term "national" means:
    i. any individual possessing the nationality of a Contracting State;
    ii. any legal person, partnership or association deriving its status as such from the laws in force in a Contracting State;
i. the term "international traffic" means any transport by a ship or aircraft operated by an enterprise which has its head office(place of effective management)in a Contracting State, except when the ship or aircraft is operated solely between places in the other Contracting State;
j. the term "competent authority" means, in the case of China, the State Administration of Taxation or its authorized representative, and in the case of Tunisia the Minister of finance or his authorized representative.

2. As regards the application of the Agreement by a Contracting State, any term not defined therein shall, unless the context otherwise requires, have the meaning which it has under the law of that Contracting State concerning the taxes to which the Agreement applies.

Article 4: Resident

1. For the purposes of this Agreement, the term "resident of a Contracting State" means any person who, under the laws of that State, is liable to tax therein by reason of his domicile, residence, place of head office (place of effective management) or any other criterion of a similar nature.
2. Whereby reason of the provisions of paragraph 1 an individual is a resident of both Contracting States, then his status shall be determined as follows:

a. he shall be deemed to be a resident of the State in which he has a permanent home available to him; if he has a permanent home available to him in both States, he shall be deemed to be a resident of the State with which his personal and economic relations are closer (centre of vital interests);
b. if the State in which he has his centre of vital interests cannot be determined, or if he has not a permanent home available to him in either State, he shall be deemed to be a resident of the State in which he has an habitual abode;
c. if he has a habitual abode in both States or in neither of them, he shall be deemed to be a resident of the State of which he is a national;
d. if he is a national of both States or of neither of them, the competent authorities of the Contracting States shall settle the question by mutual agreement.

3. Where by reason of the provisions of paragraph 1 a person other than an individual is a resident of both Contracting States, then it shall be deemed to be a resident of the State in which its head office(place of effective management)is situated.

Article 5: Permanent Establishment

1. For the purposes of this Agreement, the term "permanent establishment" means a fixed place of business through which the business of an enterprise is wholly or partly carried on.
2. The term "permanent establishment" includes especially:

a. a place of management;
b. a branch;
c. an office;
d. a factory;
e. a workshop; and
f. a mine, an oil or gas well, a quarry or any other place of extraction of natural resources.

3. The term "permanent establishment" likewise encompasses:
a building site, a construction, assembly or installation project or supervisory activities in connection therewith, but only where such site, project or activities continue for a period of more than six months.

4. Notwithstanding the preceding provisions of this Article, the term "permanent establishment" shall be deemed not to include:

a. the use of facilities solely for the purpose of storage, display or delivery of goods or merchandise belonging to the enterprise;
b. the maintenance of a stock of goods or merchandise belonging to the enterprise solely for the purpose of storage, display or delivery;
c. the maintenance of a stock of goods or merchandise belonging to the enterprise solely for the purpose of processing by another enterprise;

d. the maintenance of a fixed place of business solely for the purpose of purchasing goods or merchandise or of collecting information, for the enterprise;
e. the maintenance of a fixed place of business solely for the purpose of carrying on, for the enterprise, any other activity of a preparatory or auxiliary character;
f. the maintenance of a fixed place of business solely for any combination of activities mentioned in sub paragraphs a) to e), provided that the overall activity of the fixed place of business resulting from this combination is of a preparatory or auxiliary character.

5. Notwithstanding the provisions of paragraphs 1 and 2,where a person—other than an agent of an independent status to whom paragraph 7 applies—is acting in a Contracting State on behalf of an enterprise of the other Contracting State, has and habitually exercises an authority to conclude contracts in the name of the enterprise, that enterprise shall be deemed to have a permanent establishment in the first mentioned Contracting State in respect of any activities which that person undertakes for the enterprise, unless the activities of such person are limited to those mentioned in paragraph 4 which, if exercised through a fixed place of business, would not make this fixed place of business a permanent establishment under the provisions of that paragraph.
6. Notwithstanding the preceding provisions of this Article, an insurance enterprise of a Contracting State shall, except in regard to reinsurance, be deemed to have a permanent establishment in the other Contracting State if it collects premiums in the territory of that other State or insures risks situated therein through a person other than an agent of an independent status to whom paragraph 7 applies.
7. An enterprise of a Contracting State shall not be deemed to have a permanent establishment in the other Contracting State merely because it carries on business in that other State through a broker, general commission agent or any other agent of an independent status, provided that such persons are acting in the ordinary course of their business. However, when the activities of such an agent are devoted wholly or almost wholly on behalf of that enterprise, he will not be considered an agent of an independent status within the meaning of this paragraph.
8. The fact that a company which is a resident of a Contracting State controls or is controlled by a company which is a resident of the other Contracting State, or which carries on business in that other State (whether through a permanent establishment or otherwise),shall not of itself constitute either company a permanent establishment of the other.

Article 6: Income from Immovable Property

1. Income derived by a resident of a Contracting State from immovable property (including income from agriculture or forestry) situated in the other Contracting State may be taxed in that other State.
2. The term "immovable property" shall have the meaning which it has under the law of the Contracting State in which the property in question is situated. The term shall in any case include property accessory to immovable property, livestock and equipment used in agriculture and forestry, rights to which the provisions of general law respecting landed property apply, usufruct of immovable property and rights to variable or fixed payments as consideration for the working of, or the right to work, mineral deposits, sources and other natural resources. Ships and aircraft shall not be regarded as immovable property.
3. The provisions of paragraph 1 shall apply to income derived from the direct use, letting or use in any other form of immovable property.
4. The provisions of paragraphs 1 and 3 shall also apply to the income from immovable property of an enterprise and to income from immovable property used for the performance of independent personal services.

Article 7: Business Profits

1. The profits of an enterprise of a Contracting State shall be taxable only in that State unless the enterprise carries on business in the other Contracting State through a permanent establishment situated therein. If the enterprise carries on business as aforesaid, the profits of the enterprise may be taxed in the other State, but only so much of them as is attributable to that permanent establishment.
2. Subject to the provisions of paragraph 3,where an enterprise of a Contracting State carries on business in the other Contracting State through a permanent establishment situated therein, there shall in each Contracting State be attributed to that permanent establishment the profits which it might be expected to make if it were a distinct and separate enterprise engaged in the same or similar activities under the same or similar conditions and dealing wholly independently with the enterprise of which it is a permanent establishment.
3. In determining the profits of a permanent establishment, there shall be allowed as deductions expenses which are incurred for the purposes of the business of the permanent establishment, including executive and general administrative expenses so incurred, whether in the State in which the permanent establishment is situated or elsewhere. However, no such deduction shall be allowed in respect of amounts, if any, paid (otherwise than towards reimbursement of actual expenses)by the permanent establishment to the head office of the enterprise or any of its other offices, by way of royalties, fees or other similar payments in return for the use of patents or other rights, or by way of commission, for specific services performed or for management, or, except in the case of a banking enterprise, by way of interest on moneys lent to the permanent establishment. Likewise, no account shall be taken, in the determination of

the profits of a permanent establishment, for amounts charged(otherwise than towards reimbursement of actual expenses),by the permanent establishment to the head office of the enterprise or any of its other offices, by way of royalties, fees or other similar payments in return for the use of patents or other rights, or by way of commission for specific services performed or for management, or, except in the case of a banking enterprise by way of interest on moneys lent to the head office of the enterprise or any of its other offices.

4. Insofar as it has been customary in a Contracting State to determine the profits to be attributed to a permanent establishment on the basis of an apportionment of the total profits of the enterprise to its various parts, nothing in paragraph 2 shall preclude that Contracting State from determining the profits to be taxed by such an apportionment as may be customary. The method of apportionment adopted shall, however, be such that the result shall be in accordance with the principles contained in this Article.
5. No profits shall be attributed to a permanent establishment by reason of the mere purchase by that permanent establishment of goods or merchandise for the enterprise.
6. For the purposes of the preceding paragraphs, the profits to be attributed to the permanent establishment shall be determined by the same method year by year unless there is good and sufficient reason to the contrary.
7. Where profits include items of income which are dealt with separately in other Articles of this Agreement, then the provisions of those Articles shall not be affected by the provisions of this Article.

Article 8: Shipping and Air Transport

1. Profits from the operation of ships or aircraft in international traffic shall be taxable only in the Contracting State in which the place of head office (place of effective management) of the enterprise is situated.
2. If the place of head office (place of effective management) of a shipping enterprise is aboard a ship, then it shall be deemed to be situated in the Contracting State in which the home harbour of the ship is situated, or, if there is no such home harbour, in the Contracting State of which the operator of the ship is a resident.
3. The provisions of paragraph 1 shall also apply to profits from the participation in a pool, a joint business or an international operating agency.

Article 9: Associated Enterprises

1. Where

    a. an enterprise of a Contracting State participates directly or indirectly in the management, control or capital of an enterprise of the other Contracting State, or

b. the same persons participate directly or indirectly in the management, control or capital of an enterprise of a Contracting State and an enterprise of the other Contracting State,

and in either case conditions are made or imposed between the two enterprises in their commercial or financial relations which differ from those which would be made between independent enterprises, then any profits which would, but for those conditions, have accrued to one of the enterprises, but, by reason of those conditions, have not so accrued, may be included in the profits of that enterprise and taxed accordingly.

2. Where a Contracting State includes in the profits of an enterprise of that State—and taxes accordingly—profits on which an enterprise of the other Contracting State has been charged to tax in that other State and the profits so included are profits which would have accrued to the enterprise of the first mentioned State if the conditions made between the two enterprises had been those which would have been made between independent enterprises, then that other State shall make an appropriate adjustment to the amount of the tax charged therein on those profits. In determining such adjustment, due regard shall be had to the other provisions of this Agreement and the competent authorities of the Contracting States shall, if necessary, consult each other.

Article 10: Dividends

1. Dividends paid by a company which is a resident of a Contracting State to a resident of the other Contracting State may be taxed in that other State.
2. However, such dividends may also be taxed in the Contracting State of which the company paying the dividends is a resident and according to the laws of that State, but if the recipient is the beneficial owner of the dividends the tax so charged shall not exceed eight per cent of the gross amount of the dividends. The competent authorities of the Contracting States shall by mutual agreement settle the mode of application of this limitation.
   This paragraph shall not affect the taxation of the company in respect of the profits out of which the dividends are paid.
3. The term "dividends" as used in this Article means income from shares, or other rights, not being debt claims, participating in profits, as well as income from other corporate rights which is subjected to the same taxation treatment as income from shares by the laws of the State of which the company making the distribution is a resident.
4. The provisions of paragraphs 1 and 2 shall not apply if the beneficial owner of the dividends, being a resident of a Contracting State, carries on business in the other Contracting State of which the company paying the dividends is a resident, through a permanent establishment situated therein, or performs in that other State independent personal services from a fixed base situated therein, and the holding in respect of which the dividends are paid is effectively connected

with such permanent establishment or fixed base. In such case the provisions of Article 7 or Article 14, as the case may be, shall apply.

5. Where a company which is a resident of a Contracting State derives profits or income from the other Contracting State, that other State may not impose any tax on the dividends paid by the company, except insofar as such dividends are paid to a resident of that other State or insofar as the holding in respect of which the dividends are paid is effectively connected with a permanent establishment or a fixed base situated in that other State, nor subject the company′s undistributed profits to a tax on the company′s undistributed profits, even if the dividends paid or the undistributed profits consist wholly or partly of profits or income arising in such other State.

Article 11: Interest

1. Interest arising in a Contracting State and paid to a resident of the other Contracting State may be taxed in that other State.
2. However, such interest may also be taxed in the Contracting State in which it arises and according to the laws of that State, but if the recipient is the beneficial owner of the interest the tax so charged shall not exceed ten per cent of the gross amount of the interest. The competent authorities of the Contracting States shall by mutual agreement settle the mode of application of this limitation.
3. Notwithstanding the provisions of paragraph 2,interest arising in a Contracting State and derived by the Government of the other Contracting State, a local authority and the Central Bank thereof or any financial institution wholly owned by the Government of that other State, or by any other resident of that other State with respect to debt claims indirectly financed by the Government of that other State, a local authority, and the Central Bank thereof or any financial institution wholly owned by the Government of that other State, shall be exempt from tax in the first mentioned State.
4. The term "interest" as used in this Article means income from debt claims of every kind, whether or not secured by mortgage and whether or not carrying a right to participate in the debtor′s profits, and in particular, income from government securities and income from bonds or debentures, including premiums and prizes attaching to such securities, bonds or debentures. Penalty charges for late payment shall not be regarded as interest for the purpose of this Article.
5. The provisions of paragraphs 1,2 and 3 shall not apply if the beneficial owner of the interest, being a resident of a Contracting State, carries on business in the other Contracting State in which the interest arises, through a permanent establishment situated therein, or performs in that other State independent personal services from a fixed base situated therein, and the debt claim in respect of which the interest is paid is effectively connected with such permanent establishment or fixed base. In such case the provisions of Article 7 or Article 14, as the case may be, shall apply.
6. Interest shall be deemed to arise in a Contracting State when the payer is the Government of that State, a local authority thereof or a resident of that State.

Where, however, the person paying the interest, whether he is a resident of a Contracting State or not, has in a Contracting State a permanent establishment or a fixed base in connection with which the indebtedness on which the interest is paid was incurred, and such interest is borne by such permanent establishment or fixed base, then such interest shall be deemed to arise in the State in which the permanent establishment or fixed base is situated.

7. Where, by reason of a special relationship between the payer and the beneficial owner or between both of them and some other person, the amount of the interest, having regard to the debt claim for which it is paid, exceeds the amount which would have been agreed upon by the payer and the beneficial owner in the absence of such relationship, the provisions of this Article shall apply only to the last mentioned amount. In such case, the excess part of the payments shall remain taxable according to the laws of each Contracting State, due regard being had to the other provisions of this Agreement.

Article 12: Royalties

1. Royalties arising in a Contracting State and paid to a resident of the other Contracting State may be taxed in that other State.
2. However, such royalties may also be taxed in the Contracting State in which they arise and according to the laws of that State, but if the recipient is the beneficial owner of the royalties, the tax so charged shall not exceed:
   10 per cent of the gross amount of the royalties paid for the use of, or the right to use, any copyright of literary, artistic or scientific work including cinematography films, or films or tapes for radio or television broadcasting, any patent, trade mark, design or model, plan, secret formula or process, or for the use of, or the right to use, industrial, commercial or scientific experience;
   5 per cent of the gross amount of the royalties paid for technical or economic studies or for technical assistance.
   The competent authorities of the Contracting States shall by mutual agreement settle the mode of application of this limitation.

2. The provisions of paragraphs 1 and 2 shall not apply if the beneficial owner of the royalties, being a resident of a Contracting State, carries on business in the other Contracting State in which the royalties arise, through a permanent establishment situated therein, or performs in that other State independent personal services from a fixed base situated therein, and the right or property in respect of which the royalties are paid is effectively connected with such permanent establishment or fixed base. In such case the provisions of Article 7 or Article 14, as the case may be, shall apply.
3. Royalties shall be deemed to arise in a Contracting State when the payer is the Government of that Contracting State, a local authority thereof or a resident of that Contracting State. Where, however, the person paying the royalties, whether he is a resident of a Contracting State or not, has in a Contracting State a permanent establishment or a fixed base in connection with which the

liability to pay the royalties was incurred, and such royalties are borne by such permanent establishment or fixed base, then such royalties shall be deemed to arise in the State in which the permanent establishment or fixed base is situated.

4. Where, by reason of a special relationship between the payer and the beneficial owner or between both of them and some other person, the amount of the royalties, having regard to the use, right or information for which they are paid, exceeds the amount which would have been agreed upon by the payer and the beneficial owner in the absence of such relationship, the provisions of this Article shall apply only to the last mentioned amount. In such case, the excess part of the payments shall remain taxable according to the laws of each Contracting State, due regard being had to the other provisions of this Agreement.

Article 13: Capital Gains

1. Gains derived by a resident of a Contracting State from the alienation of immovable property referred to in Article 6 and situated in the other Contracting State may be taxed in that other State.
2. Gains from the alienation of movable property forming part of the business property of a permanent establishment which an enterprise of a Contracting State has in the other Contracting State or of movable property pertaining to a fixed base available to a resident of a Contracting State in the other Contracting State for the purpose of performing independent personal services, including such gains from the alienation of such a permanent establishment (alone or with the whole enterprise) or of such a fixed base, may be taxed in that other State.
3. Gains from the alienation of ships or aircraft operated in international traffic or movable property pertaining to the operation of such ships or aircraft shall be taxable only in the Contracting State in which the place of head office (place of effective management) of the enterprise is situated. 4. Gains from the alienation of any property other than that referred to in paragraphs 1 to 3, shall be taxable only in the Contracting State of which the alienator is a resident.

Article 14: Independent Personal Services

1. Income derived by a resident of a Contracting State in respect of professional services or other activities of an independent character shall be taxable only in that State except in one of the following circumstances, when such income may also be taxed in the other Contracting State:

   a. if the has a fixed base regularly available to him in the other Contracting State for the purpose of performing his activities; in that case, only so much of the income as is attributable to that fixed base may be taxed in that other State;
   b. if his stay in the other Contracting State is for a period or periods amounting to or exceeding in the aggregate 183 days in any twelve month period commencing or ending in the fiscal year concerned in that case, only so

much of the income as is derived from his activities performed in that other State may be taxed in that other State.

2. The term "professional services" includes especially independent scientific, literary, artistic, educational or teaching activities as well as the independent activities of physicians, lawyers, engineers, architects, dentists and accountants.

Article 15: Dependent Personal Services

1. Subject to the provisions of Articles 16,18,19,20 and 21, salaries, wages and other similar remuneration derived by a resident of a Contracting State in respect of an employment shall be taxable only in that State unless the employment is exercised in the other Contracting State. If the employment is so exercised, such remuneration as is derived therefrom may be taxed in that other State.
2. Notwithstanding the provisions of paragraph 1, remuneration derived by a resident of a Contracting State in respect of an employment exercised in the other Contracting State shall be taxable only in the first mentioned State if:

   a. the recipient is present in the other State for a period or periods not exceeding in the aggregate 183 days in any twelve-month period commencing or ending in the fiscal year concerned; and
   b. the remuneration is paid by, or on behalf of, an employer who is not a resident of the other State; and
   c. the remuneration is not borne by a permanent establishment or a fixed base which the employer has in the other State.

3. Notwithstanding the preceding provisions of this Article, remuneration derived in respect of an employment exercised aboard a ship or aircraft operated in international traffic, shall be taxable only in the Contracting State in which the place of head office (place of effective management) of the enterprise is situated.

Article 16: Directors' Fees

Directors′ fees and other similar payments derived by a resident of a Contracting State in his capacity as a member of the board of directors of a company which is a resident of the other Contracting State may be taxed in that other State.

Article 17: Artistes and Sportsman

1. Notwithstanding the provisions of Articles 14 and 15, Income derived by a resident of a Contracting State as an entertainer, such as a theatre, motion picture, radio or television artiste, or a musician, or as a sportsman, from his personal activities as such exercised in the other Contracting State, may be taxed in that other State.
2. Where income in respect of personal activities exercised by an entertainer or a sportsman in his capacity as such accrues not to the entertainer or sportsman himself but to another person, that income may, notwithstanding the provisions

of Articles 7,14 and 15, be taxed in the Contracting State in which the activities of the entertainer or sportsman are exercised.

3. Notwithstanding the preceding provisions of this Article, income derived by entertainers or sportsmen who are residents of a Contracting State from the activities exercised in the other Contracting State under a plan of cultural exchange between the Governments of both Contracting States shall be exempt from tax in that other State.

Article 18: Pensions

1. Subject to the provisions of paragraph 2 of Article 19, pensions and other similar remuneration paid to a resident of a Contracting State in consideration of past employment shall be taxable only in that State.
2. Notwithstanding the provisions of paragraph 1, pensions paid and other similar payments made by the Government of a Contracting State or a political subdivision or a local authority thereof under a public welfare scheme of the social security system of that State shall be taxable only in that State.

Article 19: Government Service

a. Remuneration, other than a pension, paid by the Government of a Contracting State or a political subdivision or a local authority thereof to an individual in respect of services rendered to the Government of that State or a political subdivision or a local authority thereof, in the discharge of functions of a governmental nature, shall be taxable only in that State.
b. However, such remuneration shall be taxable only in the other Contracting State if the services are rendered in that other State and the individual is a resident of that other State who:

    i. is a national of that State; or
    ii. did not become a resident of that State solely for the purpose of rendering the services.

c. Any pension paid by, or out of funds to which contributions are made by the Government of a Contracting State or a local authority thereof to an individual in respect of services rendered to the Government of that State or a local authority thereof shall be taxable only in that State.
d. However, such pension shall be taxable only in the other Contracting State if the individual is a resident of, and a national of, that other State.

e. The provisions of Articles 15,16,17 and 18 shall apply to remuneration and pensions in respect of services rendered in connection with a business carried on by the Government of a Contracting State or a political subdivision or local authority thereof.

Article 20: Teachers and Researchers

1. Remuneration which an individual who is or was immediately before visiting a Contracting State, a resident of the other Contracting State and who is present in the first mentioned State for the primary purpose of teaching, giving lectures or conducting research at a university, college, school or educational institution or scientific research institution recognized by the Government of the first mentioned State derives for the purpose of such teaching, lectures or research shall not be taxed in the first mentioned State, for a period of two years from the date of his first arrival in the first mentioned State.
2. The provisions of paragraph 1 of this Article shall not apply to income from research if such research is undertaken not in the public interest but primarily for the private benefit of a specific person or persons.

Article 21: Students and Trainees

1. Payments which a student, business apprentice or trainee who is or was immediately before visiting a Contracting State a resident of the other Contracting State and who is present in the first mentioned State solely for the purpose of his education or training receives for the purpose of his maintenance, education or training shall not be taxed in that State, provided that such payments arise from sources outside that State.
2. In respect of grants, scholarships and remuneration from employment not covered by paragraph 1, a student, business apprentice or trainee described in paragraph 1 shall, in addition, be entitled during such education or training to the same exemptions, reliefs or reductions in respect of taxes available to residents of the State which he is visiting.

Article 22: Other Income

1. Items of income of a resident of a Contracting State, wherever arising, not dealt with in the foregoing Articles of this Agreement shall be taxable only in that State.
2. The provisions of paragraph 1 shall not apply to income, other than income from immovable property as defined in paragraph 2 of Article 6, if the recipient of such income, being a resident of a Contracting State, carries on business in the other Contracting State through a permanent establishment situated therein, or performs in that other State independent personal services from a fixed base situated therein, and the right or property in respect of which the income is paid is effectively connected with such permanent establishment or fixed base. In such case the provisions of Article 7 or Article 14, as the case may be, shall apply.

Article 23: Methods for Elimination of Double Taxation

1. Where a resident of one Contracting State derives income from the other Contracting State, the amount of tax on the income payable in the other

Contracting State in accordance with the provisions of this Agreement may be credited against the tax imposed by the first mentioned State on that resident. The amount of the credit, however, shall not exceed the amount of the tax imposed by the first mentioned State on that income computed in accordance with the taxation laws and regulations of the Contracting State.

2. Where the income derived from one Contracting State is a dividend paid by a company which is a resident of the Contracting State to a company which is a resident of the other Contracting State and which owns not less than ten per cent of the shares of the company paying the dividend, the credit shall take into account the tax paid in the first mentioned State by the company paying the dividend in respect of the profits out of which the dividend is paid.
3. The tax paid in a Contracting State mentioned in paragraphs 1 and 2 of this Article, shall be deemed to include the tax which would have been payable but for the legal provisions concerning tax reduction, exemption or other tax incentives of the Contracting States for the promotion of economic development.

Article 24: Non-Discrimination

1. Nationals of a Contracting State shall not be subjected in the other Contracting State to any taxation or any requirement connected therewith, which is other or more burdensome than the taxation and connected requirements to which nationals of that other State in the same circumstances, in particular with respect to residence, are or may be subjected. This provision shall, notwithstanding the provisions of Article 1, also apply to persons who are not residents of one or both of the Contracting States.
2. The taxation on a permanent establishment which an enterprise of a Contracting State has in the other Contracting State shall not be less favourably levied in that other State than the taxation levied on enterprises of that other State carrying on the same activities. This provision shall not be construed as obliging a Contracting State to grant to residents of the other Contracting State any personal allowances, reliefs and reductions for taxation purposes on account of civil status or family responsibilities which it grants to its own residents.
3. Except where the provisions of paragraph 1 of Article 9, paragraph 7 of Article 11, or paragraph 6 of Article 12, apply, interest, royalties and other disbursements paid by an enterprise of a Contracting State to a resident of the other Contracting State shall, for the purpose of determining the taxable profits of such enterprise, be deductible under the same conditions as if they had been paid to a resident of the first mentioned State.
4. Enterprises of a Contracting State, the capital of which is wholly or partly owned or controlled, directly or indirectly, by one or more residents of the other Contracting State, shall not be subjected in the first mentioned State to any taxation or any requirement connected therewith which is other or more burdensome than the taxation and connected requirements to which other similar enterprises of the first mentioned State are or may be subjected.

Article 25: Mutual agreement Procedure

1. Where a person considers that the actions of one or both of the Contracting States result or will result for him in taxation not in accordance with the provisions of this Agreement, he may, irrespective of the remedies provided by the domestic law of those States, present his case to the competent authority of the Contracting State of which he is a resident or, if his case comes under paragraph 1 of Article 24, to that of the Contracting State of which he is a national. The case must be presented within three years from the first notification of the action resulting in taxation not in accordance with the provisions of the Agreement.
2. The competent authority shall endeavour, if the objection appears to it to be justified and if it is not itself able to arrive at a satisfactory solution, to resolve the case by mutual agreement with the competent authority of the other Contracting State, with a view to the avoidance of taxation which is not in accordance with the Agreement. Any agreement reached shall be implemented notwithstanding any time limits in the domestic law of the Contracting States.
3. The competent authorities of the Contracting States shall endeavour to resolve by mutual agreement any difficulties or doubts arising as to the interpretation or application of the Agreement. They may also consult together for the elimination of double taxation in cases not provided for in the Agreement.
4. The competent authorities of the Contracting States may communicate with each other directly for the purpose of reaching an agreement in the sense of paragraphs 2 and 3. When it seems advisable for reaching agreement, representatives of the competent authorities of the Contracting States may meet together for an oral exchange of opinions.

Article 26: Exchange of Information

1. The competent authorities of the Contracting States shall exchange such information as is necessary for carrying out the provisions of this Agreement or of the domestic laws of the Contracting States concerning taxes covered by the Agreement, insofar as the taxation thereunder is not contrary to the Agreement, in particular for the prevention of evasion of such taxes. The exchange of information is not restricted by Article 1. Any information received by a Contracting State shall be treated as secret and shall be disclosed only to persons or authorities (including courts and administrative bodies) involved in the assessment or collection of, the enforcement or prosecution in respect of, or the determination of appeals in relation to, the taxes covered by the Agreement. Such persons or authorities shall use the information only for such purposes. They may disclose the information in public court proceedings or in judicial decisions.
2. In no case shall the provisions of paragraph 1 be construed so as to impose on a Contracting State the obligation:

    a. to carry out administrative measures at variance with the laws and administrative practice of that or of the other Contracting State;

b. to supply information which is not obtainable under the laws or in the normal course of the administration of that or of the other Contracting State;
c. to supply information which would disclose any trade, business, industrial, commercial or professional secret or trade process, or information, the disclosure of which would be contrary to public policy (order public).

Article 27: Diplomatic Agents and Consular Officers

Nothing in this Agreement shall affect the fiscal privileges of diplomatic agents or consular officers under the general rules of international law or under the provisions of special agreements.

Article 28: Entry into Force

This Agreement shall enter into force on the thirtieth day after the latter of the dates on which diplomatic notes indicating the completion of internal legal procedures necessary in each country for the entry into force of this Agreement have been exchanged. This Agreement shall have effect as respects income derived during the taxable years beginning on or after the first day of January of the year following that in which this Agreement enters into force.

Article 29: Termination

This Agreement shall continue in effect indefinitely but either of the Contracting States may, on or before the thirtieth day of June in any calendar year beginning after the expiration of a period of five years from the date of its entry into force, give written notice of termination to the other Contracting State through the diplomatic channels. In such event this Agreement shall cease to have effect as respects income derived during the taxable years beginning on or after the first day of January in the calendar year next following that in which the notice of termination is given.

IN WITNESS whereof the undersigned, duly authorized thereto, have signed this Agreement.

Done at Tunis on the 16 day of April 2002, in duplicate in the Chinese, Arabic, French and English languages, all texts being equally authentic.

In case of divergence in interpretation, the English text shall prevail.

For the Government of the People's Republic of China
Minister of Foreign Trade and Economic Cooperation
Shi Guangsheng
For the Government of the Republic of Tunisia.

Chapter 7
Zimbabwe

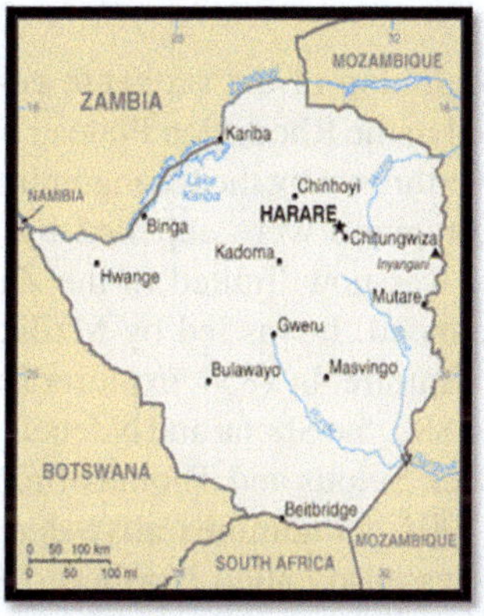

7.1 Country Profile

7.1.1 Introduction

Official Name	Republic of Zimbabwe
Capital	Harare
Government	Semi-presidential republic
Population	14,546,314
Area	390,757 sq. km

(continued)

L. Riccardi and G. Riccardi, *China in Africa*,
https://doi.org/10.1007/978-981-16-1148-3_7

(continued)

Official Name	Republic of Zimbabwe
Official language(s)	Shona, Ndebele, English
Main religion(s)	Protestant
Currency	United States Dollar
GDP	$34.27 billion
GDP per capita	$2,300
Life expectancy	62.3

Source CIA Factbook, 2020

7.1.2 History

The beginning of the sixteenth century brought the arrival of the Portuguese, who invested in the Rhodesian Plateau by the Zambezi Valley. In 1684, the Torwa dynasty was overthrown by the Changamire clan, which founded the Rozwi Empire. In 1690, the Portuguese were expelled by Monomatapa troops, but the domain of the old empire was now limited to the Zambezi Valley. In 1840, a Ndebele military state was founded. It was led by Mzilikazi of the Zulu Xumalo clan on the ruins of the Rozwi Empire. In 1854, explorer David Livingstone arrived at Victoria Falls. Then in 1870–1880, the Shona and Ndebele territories were explored by Europeans, including Frederick Selous and Thomas Baines.

In 1901, an administrative division was created between the northern Zambezi territories, also called Northern Rhodesia, and those to the south, called Southern Rhodesia. Settlers and mining companies supported this grouping in preparation for independence under white domination, following the South African model. In 1964, the federation was dissolved. Northern Rhodesia was renamed Zambia and Nyasaland was renamed Malawi, and both declare their independence. In 1978, internal agreements took place between the Rhodesian government and moderate black nationalist movements for the establishment of a new assembly and a multiracial government. In 1979, the ephemeral state of Zimbabwe-Rhodesia was created and then reinstated in the United Kingdom, before the Lancaster House agreements paved the way for Zimbabwe's independence and a redistribution of land after 10 years.

In 1980, fifteen years after Ian Smith's unilateral declaration of independence, the British granted independence to Southern Rhodesia, which took the name of Zimbabwe, and it became a member of the Commonwealth. Former guerrilla leader Robert Mugabe became the new prime minister. In 1987, after a constitutional amendment, Robert Mugabe became the president of Zimbabwe on December 31. In the 1990s, several events accentuate the regime's authoritarianism. On November 21, 2017, President Mugabe was forced to resign following a coup orchestrated on November 15, 2017 by General Sibusiso Moy.

Mnangagwa, Mugabe's vice president, was inaugurated president days later, promising to hold presidential elections in 2018.

World view	1990	2000	2010	2020
Population, total (millions)	9.786	11.693	12.34	15.189
GDP (current US$) (billions)	10.144	11.34	12.042	12.868
GDP (% change)	n/a	−4.231	19.683	2.721
GDP per capita (current $)	1,036.53	969.824	975.851	847.163
Inflation (%)	1.345	4.475	3.045	49.698

Source IMF World Economic Outlook database 2020/RsA Asia

7.1.3 Geography

Zimbabwe is a country in southern Africa with no access to the sea. It covers an area of 390,757 sq. kilometres (61st world country in terms of area). It shares its 3066 km border with Zambia, South Africa, Botswana, and Mozambique. Victoria Falls, near the town of Livingstone in Zambia, is part of the river and is among the largest and most impressive waterfalls in the world at 1,700 m wide and up to 108 m high. It has been listed as a UNESCO World Heritage since 1989.

The highest point of Zimbabwe is Inyangani at 2,592 m.; the lowest point is the junction of the Runde and Save Rivers at 162 m. The Save River, or Sabi River, is a 400 km river in south-eastern Africa, which flows through Zimbabwe and Mozambique. Natural resources in Zimbabwe include coal, chromium ore, asbestos, gold, nickel, copper, iron ore, vanadium, lithium, tin, and platinum group metals.

Zimbabwe's most important agricultural outputs, which are grown in the more fertile regions, are tobacco, corn, cotton, wheat, coffee, sugarcane, and peanuts. The country also relies on livestock, which includes sheep, goats, and pigs.

Zimbabwe has a temperate, tropical climate with a rainy season extending from late October to March. The landscapes are composed of savannas and tropical evergreen forests in the moist and mountainous regions of the east. The average annual temperature is 25°C. The fauna is made up of many mammals, including hippopotamus, rhinoceros, baboon, giraffe, zebra, warthog, and many others with a total of about 350 different mammal species throughout the country.

Most populated cities	
City	Population
Harare	1,542,813
Bulawayo	699,385
Chitungwiza	340,360

(continued)

(continued)

Most populated cities	
City	Population
Mutare	184,205
Gweru	146,073

Source Office National des Statistiques (ONS)

7.1.4 Government

The Republic of Zimbabwe is a semi-presidential republic that took its independence from the English on April 18, 1980. Therefore, April 18 is called "Independence Day." The new constitution was voted by referendum on March 16, 2013, approved by parliament on May 9 and effective May 22, 2013. Suffrage has been universal throughout the country for 18 years.

The new chief of state is President Emmerson Dambudzo Mnangagwa, who has been in office since November 24, 2017. He was preceded by Robert Gabriel Mugabe, who resigned on November 21, 2017, after ruling for 37 years.

Key political figures	
Title	Name
President	Emmerson Mnangagwa
1st Vice President	Constantino Chiwenga
2nd Vice President	Kembo Mohadi

Source The World Factbook—CIA, 2020

7.1.5 Culture

Sports are very present in Zimbabwe, especially football, rugby, cricket, tennis, hockey, polo, and golf. Some athletes are known around the world, such as swimmer Kirsty Coventry, golfer Nick Price or football players Matthew Rusike and Peter Ndlovu. Zimbabwe participated for the first time in the Olympic Games under its current name in 1980 and has sent athletes to compete in every Summer Olympic Games since then. The 2014 Winter Olympics in Sochi marked Zimbabwe's first participation at the Winter Olympic Games.

One method of enjoying sports in Zimbabwe is through the media. The only radio broadcast in the whole country is Radio Zimbabwe. It broadcasts to the country, including the most remote areas. It broadcasts in English, Shona, and Ndebele.

Southern Rhodesia, the former name of Zimbabwe, was one of the first African countries to have a television channel. The Rhodesian Broadcasting Corporation's first broadcasts began in 1960, and at the time, only the main agglomerations were covered. In 1984, black-and-white transmissions gave way to colour. Two years later, in 1986, the second TV channel of the ZBC was launched in Harare. This TV channel was replaced in 1997 by the independent television channel Joy TV, which stopped broadcasting in 2002 in favour of satellite channels.

Another important aspect of culture is food. In Zimbabwe, the main food is sadza, a kind of thick and firm polenta. It is often accompanied by tsunga (a thick or diluted stew), with vegetables or curdled milk and, sometimes, beef or chicken. Locals often make the sadza into a ball and dip it in the stew. The Zimbabwean cuisine is marked by vegetables such as corn on the cob, squash, beans, and peanuts. Rice is grown in some areas but is not commonly eaten in rural areas.

7.1.6 Economy

Global links	1990	2000	2010	2018
Merchandise trade (% of GDP)	40	56	58	27
Net barter of trade index (2000 = 100)	97	100	112	110
External debt stocks, total (DOD, current US$) (billion)	3.32	3.91	6.78	12.29
Net migration (thousands)	–	–	–	–
Personal remittance received (current US$) (million)	0.8	–	1413.2	1730
Foreign direct investment, net inflows (BoP, current US$ (million)	−12.2	23.2	122.6	744.6
Net official development assistance received (current US$) (million)	334.3	175.6	712.5	793.6

Source World Development Indicators database/RsA Asia 2020

Economy	1990	2000	2010	2018
GDP (current US$) (billions)	8.78	6.69	12.04	31.00
GDP growth (annual %)	7.0	−3.1	19.7	6.2
Inflation, GDP deflator (annual %)	−0.9	0.6	4.1	28
Agriculture, value added (% of GDP)	15	16	10	12
Industry, value added (% of GDP)	30	–	21	33
Services, etc., value added (% of GDP)	45	70	58	46
Exports of goods and services (% of GDP)	23	38	30	23
Import of goods and services (% of GDP)	22	35	63	38
Gross capital formation (% of GDP)	17	13	19	13

(continued)

(continued)

Economy	1990	2000	2010	2018
Revenue, excluding grants (% of GDP)	–	–	19.4	18.2
Net lending (+)/net borrowing (–) (% of GDP)	–	–	3.1	−8.1

Source World Development Indicators database/RsA Asia 2020

Despite possessing enormous natural resources and fertile land, Zimbabwe is facing an economic disaster unprecedented since its independence, due to the mismanagement of Robert Mugabe's administration. Since 2000, the country has been in a state of hyperinflation. At the end of 2006, a US $2 billion loan was obtained from the People's Republic of China. Zimbabwe's involvement in the war in the Democratic Republic of Congo has weighed heavily on the country's economy, costing hundreds of millions of dollars. Furthermore, by January 2008, the annual hyperinflation rate reached 100,580.2% while the unemployment rate is close to 80%. In July 2008, the yearly inflation record rate officially stood at 231 million.

Main Customer	
Export (% of export)	
South Africa	79.4%
Mozambique	9.5%
United Arab Emirates	4.1%
Zambia	2.5%
Belgium	1.6%
Botswana	1.0%
Kenya	0.4%
France	0.3%

Source ComTrade

Main Suplier	
Import (% of import)	
South Africa	79.4%
Singapore	21.5%
China	7.0%
Zambia	3.5%
India	3.2%
Mozambique	3.1%
Japan	1.9%
United Kingdom	1.8%

The unemployment rate exceeds 70% of the active population in the early 2010s. Since 2001, more than three million people have left Zimbabwe because of the economic crisis. About 1.2 million Zimbabweans work in South Africa, mainly in the sectors of mining and agriculture. The agriculture sector in Zimbabwe suffered from the poor land allocation in 1999 and 2000.

In terms of natural resources, Zimbabwe has the second-largest platinum reserve in the world, after South Africa and other major diamond mines. Zimbabwe's trade consists of exporting 65% of its electricity, and then importing energy from South Africa, Mozambique, and Zambia.

State and markets	1990	2000	2010	2018
Time required to start a business (days)	–	–	87	32
Domestic credit provided by financial (% of GDP)	22.6	40.4	21.1	48
Tax revenue (% of GDP)	–	–	17.4	16.2
Military expenditure (%of GDP)	4.7	3.4	1.0	2.2
Mobile cellular subscriptions (per 100 people)	0	2.2	60.6	89.4
Individual using the Internet (% of population)	0	0.4	6.4	23.1
High-technology exports (% of manufactured exports)	1.4	1.6	0.9	2.1

Source World Development Indicators database/RsA Asia 2020

Since 2002, when the United States and the European Union attacked the country with sanctions, China has increased its influence by providing loans and donations. In 2015, President Xi Jinping made an official visit, initiating a $5.6 billion cooperation plan, which included mining, public works, and land. At the diplomatic level, China blocked all sanctions against the country at the UN Security Council. Historically, China had supported ZANU against Ian Smith's pro-Western white power, and current President Emmerson Mnangagwa was based in China in the 1960s, weaving networks that grew over the years.

The Biggest Zimbabwe Companies

Name	Industry	Sector	Headquarters
African Distillers	Consumer goods	Distillers and vintners	Stapleford
Agricultural Development Bank of Zimbabwe	Financials	Banks	Harare
Air Zimbabwe	Consumer services	Airlines	Harare
ART Holdings	Basic materials	Paper	Harare
Beitbridge Bulawayo Railway	Industrials	Railroads	Beitbridge
Bindura Nickel Corporation	Basic materials	General mining	Bindura
Border Timbers	Basic materials	Forestry	Mutare
Cairns Holdings	Consumer goods	Food & beverage	Harare
CBZ Bank Limited	Financials	Banks	Harare
CBZ Holdings	Financials	Financial services	Harare

(continued)

(continued)

The Biggest Zimbabwe Companies			
Name	Industry	Sector	Headquarters
CFX Bank	Financials	Banks	Harare
Colcom Foods	Consumer goods	Food products	Harare
Cotton Company of Zimbabwe	Basic materials	Forestry	Harare
Dairibord	Consumer goods	Food products	Harare
Delta Corporation	Consumer goods	Beverages	Harare
Ecobank Zimbabwe	Financials	Banks	Harare
Econet Wireless Zimbabwe	Telecommunications	Mobile telecommunications	Harare
Fastjet Zimbabwe	Consumer services	Airlines	Harare
FBC Bank	Financials	Banks	Harare
Hippo Valley Estate	Consumer goods	Food products	Chiredzi'
Interfin Bank	Financials	Banks	Harare
Kingdom Bank limited	Financials	Banks	Harare
MBCA Bank	Financials	Banks	Harare
Meikles	Consumer services	Hotels	Harare
National Railways of Zimbabwe	Industrials	Railroads	Bulawayo
New Limpopo Bridge Ltd	Industrials	Heavy construction	Beitbridge
Royal Bank of Zimbabwe	Financials	Banks	Harare
Sable Chemicals	Basic materials	Specialty chemicals	Kwekwe
Standard Chartered Zimbabwe	Financials	Banks	Harare
Tanganda Tea	Consumer goods	Beverages	Mutare
Time Bank Zimbabwe	Financials	Banks	Harare
TM Supermarket	Consumer services	Food retailers & wholesalers	Harare
Trust Banking Corporation	Financials	Banks	Harare
TSL Limited	Consumer goods	Tobacco	Harare
Zimbabwe Broadcasting Corporation	Consumer services	Broadcasting & entertainment	Harare
Zimbabwe Iron and Steel Company	Basic Materials	Iron & steel	Kwekwe
Zimbabwe flyafrica.com	Consumer services	Airlines	Harare
Zimbabwe Stock Exchange	Financials	Investment services	Harare
Zimbabwe United Passenger Company	Consumer services	Travel & tourism	Harare

(continued)

(continued)

The Biggest Zimbabwe Companies			
Name	Industry	Sector	Headquarters
Zimplow Limited	Industrials	Industrial goods & services	Bulawayo
ZimPost	Industrials	Industrial transportation	Harare
Zimswitch	Industrials	Financial administration	Harare

Source RsA Asia 2020

7.1.7 Regulations

The value-added tax in Zimbabwe is 15%, and the corporate tax is 25%. A 3% levy is usually made for the fight against AIDS. However, the most commonly reported problem by foreign companies operating in Zimbabwe is Zimbabwe's trade barriers customs clearance, as delays can take several weeks or months.

7.2 Double Tax Agreement

Agreement Between the Government of the People's Republic of China and the Government of the Republic of Zimbabwe for the Avoidance of Double Taxation and the Prevention of Fiscal Evasion with Respect to Taxes on Income.

The Government of the People's Republic of China and the Government of the Republic of Zimbabwe.

Desiring to conclude an Agreement for the avoidance of double taxation and the prevention of fiscal evasion with respect to taxes on income (hereinafter referred to as "the Agreement"),

Have agreed as follows:

Article 1: Personal Scope

This Agreement shall apply to persons who are residents of one or both of the Contracting States.

Article 2: Taxes Covered

1. This Agreement shall apply to taxes on income imposed on behalf of a Contracting State or of its local authorities, irrespective of the manner in which they are levied.

2. There shall be regarded as taxes on income all taxes imposed on total income, or on elements of income, including taxes on gains from the alienation of movable or immovable property, as well as taxes on capital appreciation.
3. The existing taxes to which the Agreement shall apply are in particular:

   a. in China,
      i. the individual income tax;
      ii. the enterprise income tax;
      (hereinafter referred to as "Chinese tax");

   b. in Zimbabwe:
      i. the income tax;
      ii. the non-resident shareholders' tax;
      iii. the non-residents' tax on fees;
      iv. the non-residents' tax on royalties;
      v. the capital gains tax, and
      vi. the residents' tax on interest;
      (hereinafter referred to as "Zimbabwean tax").

4. The Agreement shall also apply to any identical or substantially similar taxes which are imposed after the date of signature of the Agreement in addition to, or in place of, the existing taxes. The competent authorities of the Contracting States shall notify each other of any significant changes which have been made in their respective taxation laws within a reasonable period of time after such changes.

Article 3: General Definitions

1. For the purposes of this Agreement, unless the context otherwise requires:

   a. the term "China" means the People's Republic of China; when used in geographical sense, means all the territory of the People's Republic of China, including its land territory, internal waters, territorial sea and the air space above them, in which the Chinese laws relating to taxation apply, and any area beyond its territorial sea, within which the People's Republic of China has sovereign rights or jurisdiction in accordance with international law and its internal law;
   b. the term "Zimbabwe" means the Republic of Zimbabwe;
   c. the terms "a Contracting State" and "the other Contracting State" mean China or Zimbabwe as the context requires;
   d. the term "tax" means Chinese tax or Zimbabwean tax as the context requires;
   e. the term "person" includes an individual, an estate, a trust, a company and any other body of persons;
   f. the term "company" means anybody corporate or any entity which is treated as a body corporate for tax purposes;

g. the term "enterprise" applies to the carrying on of any business;
h. the terms "enterprise of a Contracting State" and "enterprise of the other Contracting State" mean, respectively, an enterprise carried on by a resident of a Contracting State and an enterprise carried on by a resident of the other Contracting State;
i. the term "national" means:
   i. any individual possessing the nationality of a Contracting State;
   ii. any legal person, partnership or association deriving its status as such from the laws in force in a Contracting State;
j. the term "business" includes the performance of professional services and of other activities of an independent character;
k. the term "international traffic" means any transport by a ship, a boat, an aircraft, or a road or rail transport vehicle operated by an enterprise of a Contracting State except when the ship, boat, aircraft or road or rail transport vehicle is operated solely between places in the other Contracting State;
l. the term "competent authority" means:
   i. in the case of China, the State Administration of Taxation or its authorized representative, and
   ii. in the case of Zimbabwe, Commissioner General of the Zimbabwe Revenue Authority or his authorized representative.

2. As regards the application of the Agreement by a Contracting State, any term not defined therein shall, unless the context otherwise requires, have the meaning which it has under the law of that Contracting State concerning the taxes to which the Agreement applies.

Article 4: Resident

1. For the purposes of this Agreement, the term "resident of a Contracting State" means any person who, under the laws of that State, is liable to tax therein by reason of his domicile, residence, place of incorporation, place of effective management or any other criterion of a similar nature. This term, however, does not include any person who is liable to tax in that State in respect only of income from sources in that State.
2. Whereby reason of the provisions of paragraph 1 an individual is a resident of both Contracting States, then his status shall be determined as follows:

   a. he shall be deemed to be a resident of the State in which he has a permanent home available to him; if he has a permanent home available to him in both States, he shall be deemed to be a resident of the State with which his personal and economic relations are closer (centre of vital interests);
   b. if the State in which he has his centre of vital interests cannot be determined, or if he has not a permanent home available to him in either State, he shall be deemed to be a resident of the State in which he has a habitual abode;

c. if he has a habitual abode in both States or in neither of them, he shall be deemed to be a resident of the State of which he is a national;
d. if he is a national of both States or of neither of them, the competent authorities of the Contracting States shall settle the question by mutual agreement.

3. Whereby reason of the provisions of paragraph 1, a person other than an individual is a resident of both Contracting States, then it shall be deemed to be a resident only of the State in which its place of effective management is situated.

Article 5: Permanent Establishment

1. For the purposes of this Agreement, the term "permanent establishment" means a fixed place of business through which the business of an enterprise is wholly or partly carried on.
2. The term "permanent establishment" includes especially:

   a. a place of management;
   b. a branch;
   c. an office;
   d. a factory;
   e. a workshop, and
   f. a mine, an oil or gas well, a quarry or any other place of extraction of natural resources.

3. The term "permanent establishment" also encompasses:

   a. a building site, a construction, assembly or installation project or supervisory activities in connection therewith, but only if such site, project or activities last more than twelve months;
   b. the furnishing of services, including consultancy services, by an enterprise through employees or other personnel engaged by the enterprise for such purpose, but only if activities of that nature continue within a Contracting State for a period or periods aggregating more than six months within any twelve-month period.

4. Notwithstanding the preceding provisions of this Article, the term "permanent establishment" shall be deemed not to include:

   a. the use of facilities solely for the purpose of storage, display or delivery of goods or merchandise belonging to the enterprise;
   b. the maintenance of a stock of goods or merchandise belonging to the enterprise solely for the purpose of storage, display or delivery;
   c. the maintenance of a stock of goods or merchandise belonging to the enterprise solely for the purpose of processing by another enterprise;
   d. the maintenance of a fixed place of business solely for the purpose of purchasing goods or merchandise or of collecting information, for the enterprise;

e. the maintenance of a fixed place of business solely for the purpose of carrying on, for the enterprise, any other activity of a preparatory or auxiliary character;
f. the maintenance of a fixed place of business solely for any combination of activities mentioned in sub-paragraphs a) to e), provided that the overall activity of the fixed place of business resulting from this combination is of a preparatory or auxiliary character.

5. Notwithstanding the provisions of paragraphs 1 and 2, where a person—other than an agent of an independent status to whom paragraph 6 applies—is acting on behalf of an enterprise and has, and habitually exercises, in a Contracting State an authority to conclude contracts in the name of the enterprise, that enterprise shall be deemed to have a permanent establishment in that State in respect of any activities which that person undertakes for the enterprise, unless the activities of such person are limited to those mentioned in paragraph 4, which, if exercised through a fixed place of business, would not make this fixed place of business a permanent establishment under the provisions of that paragraph.
6. An enterprise of a Contracting State shall not be deemed to have a permanent establishment in the other Contracting State merely because it carries on business in that other State through a broker, general commission agent or any other agent of an independent status, provided that such persons are acting in the ordinary course of their business. However, when the activities of such an agent are devoted wholly or almost wholly on behalf of that enterprise, he will not be considered an agent of an independent status within the meaning of this paragraph.
7. The fact that a company which is a resident of a Contracting State controls or is controlled by a company which is a resident of the other Contracting State, or which carries on business in that other State (whether through a permanent establishment or otherwise), shall not of itself constitute either company a permanent establishment of the other.

Article 6: Income from Immovable Property

1. Income derived by a resident of a Contracting State from immovable property (including income from agriculture or forestry) situated in the other Contracting State may be taxed in that other State.
2. The term “immovable property” shall have the meaning which it has under the law of the Contracting State in which the property in question is situated. The term shall in any case include property accessory to immovable property, livestock and equipment used in agriculture and forestry, rights to which the provisions of general law respecting landed property apply, usufruct of immovable property and rights to variable or fixed payments as consideration for the working of, or the right to work, mineral deposits, sources and other natural resources. Ships and aircrafts shall not be regarded as immovable property.
3. The provisions of paragraph 1 shall apply to income derived from the direct use, letting, or use in any other form of immovable property.

4. The provisions of paragraphs 1 and 3 shall also apply to the income from immovable property of an enterprise.

Article 7: Business Profits

1. The profits of an enterprise of a Contracting State shall be taxable only in that State unless the enterprise carries on business in the other Contracting State through a permanent establishment situated therein. If the enterprise carries on business as aforesaid, the profits of the enterprise may be taxed in the other State, but only so much of them as is attributable to that permanent establishment.
2. Subject to the provisions of paragraph 3, where an enterprise of a Contracting State carries on business in the other Contracting State through a permanent establishment situated therein, there shall in each Contracting State be attributed to that permanent establishment the profits which it might be expected to make if it were a distinct and separate enterprise engaged in the same or similar activities under the same or similar conditions and dealing wholly independently with the enterprise of which it is a permanent establishment.
3. In determining the profits of a permanent establishment, there shall be allowed as deductions expenses which are incurred for the purposes of the business of the permanent establishment, including executive and general administrative expenses so incurred, whether in the State in which the permanent establishment is situated or elsewhere.
4. Insofar as it has been customary in a Contracting State to determine the profits to be attributed to a permanent establishment on the basis of an apportionment of the total profits of the enterprise to its various parts, nothing in paragraph 2 shall preclude that Contracting State from determining the profits to be taxed by such an apportionment as may be customary. The method of apportionment adopted shall, however, be such that the result shall be in accordance with the principles contained in this Article.
5. No profits shall be attributed to a permanent establishment by reason of the mere purchase by that permanent establishment of goods or merchandise for the enterprise.
6. For the purposes of the preceding paragraphs, the profits to be attributed to the permanent establishment shall be determined by the same method year by year unless there is good and sufficient reason to the contrary.
7. Where profits include items of income which are dealt with separately in other Articles of this Agreement, then the provisions of those Articles shall not be affected by the provisions of this Article.

Article 8: International Traffic

1. Profits of an enterprise of a Contracting State from the operation or rental of ships boats, aircrafts, or rail or road transport vehicles in international traffic and the rental of containers and related equipment which is incidental to the operation of ships, boats, aircraft, rail or road transport vehicles in international traffic

shall be taxable only in the Contracting State in which the place of effective management of the enterprise is situated.

2. If the place of effective management of a shipping enterprise is aboard a ship or boat, then it shall be deemed to be situated in the Contracting State in which the home harbour of the ship or boat is situated, or, if there is no such home harbour, in the Contracting State of which the operator of the ship or boat is a resident.
3. The provisions of paragraph 1 of this Article shall also apply to profits from the participation in a pool, a joint business or an international operating agency.

Article 9: Associated Enterprises

1. Where

    a. an enterprise of a Contracting State participates directly or indirectly in the management, control or capital of an enterprise of the other Contracting State, or
    b. the same persons participate directly or indirectly in the management, control or capital of an enterprise of a Contracting State and an enterprise of the other Contracting State, and in either case conditions are made or imposed between the two enterprises in their commercial or financial relations which differ from those which would be made between independent enterprises, then any profits which would, but for those conditions, have accrued to one of the enterprises, but, by reason of those conditions, have not so accrued, may be included in the profits of that enterprise and taxed accordingly.

2. Where a Contracting State includes in the profits of an enterprise of that State—and taxes accordingly—profits on which an enterprise of the other Contracting State has been charged to tax in that other State and the profits so included are profits which would have accrued to the enterprise of the first-mentioned State if the conditions made between the two enterprises had been those which would have been made between independent enterprises, then that other State shall make an appropriate adjustment to the amount of the tax charged therein on those profits. In determining such adjustment, due regard shall be had to the other provisions of this Agreement and the competent authorities of the Contracting States shall if necessary, consult each other.

Article 10: DividendsArticle 10: Dividends

1. Dividends paid by a company which is a resident of a Contracting State to a resident of the other Contracting State may be taxed in that other State.
2. However, such dividends may also be taxed in the Contracting State of which the company paying the dividends is a resident and according to the laws of that State, but if the beneficial owner of the dividends is a resident of the other Contracting State, the tax so charged shall not exceed:

a. two point five per cent (2.5%) of the gross amount of the dividends if the beneficial owner is a company which controls directly or indirectly at least 25 per cent of the company paying the dividends;

b. seven point five per cent (7.5%) of the gross amount of the dividends in all other cases.

The competent authorities of the Contracting States shall by mutual agreement settle the mode of application of these limitations.

This paragraph shall not affect the taxation of the company in respect of the profits out of which the dividends are paid.

3. The term "dividends" as used in this Article means income from shares or other rights, not being debt-claims, participating in profits, as well as income from other corporate rights which is subjected to the same taxation treatment as income from shares by the laws of the State of which the company making the distribution is a resident.
4. The provisions of paragraphs 1 and 2 shall not apply if the beneficial owner of the dividends, being a resident of a Contracting State, carries on business in the other Contracting State of which the company paying the dividends is a resident, through a permanent establishment situated therein, and the holding in respect of which the dividends are paid is effectively connected with such permanent establishment. In such case the provisions of Article 7 shall apply.
5. Where a company which is a resident of a Contracting State derives profits or income from the other Contracting State, that other State may not impose any tax on the dividends paid by the company, except insofar as such dividends are paid to a resident of that other State or insofar as the holding in respect of which the dividends are paid is effectively connected with a permanent establishment situated in that other State, nor subject the company's undistributed profits to a tax on the company's undistributed profits, even if the dividends paid or the undistributed profits consist wholly or partly of profits or income arising in such other State.
6. The provisions of this Article shall not apply if it was the main purpose or one of the purposes of any person concerned with the creation or assignment of the shares or other rights in respect of which the dividend is paid to take advantage of this Article by means of that creation or assignment.

Article 11: Interest

1. Interest arising in a Contracting State and paid to a resident of the other Contracting State may be taxed in that other State.
2. However, such interest may also be taxed in the Contracting State in which it arises and according to the laws of that State, but if the beneficial owner of the interest is a resident of the other Contracting State, the tax so charged shall not exceed seven point five per cent (7.5%) of the gross amount of the interest. The competent authorities of the Contracting States shall by mutual agreement settle the mode of application of this limitation.

3. Notwithstanding the provisions of paragraph 2, interest arising in a Contracting State and derived by the Government of the other Contracting State, a local authority and the Central Bank thereof or any financial institution wholly owned by the Government of that other State, or by any other resident of that other State with respect to debt-claims indirectly financed by the Government of that other State, a local authority, and the Central Bank thereof or any financial institution wholly owned by the Government of that other State, shall be exempt from tax in the first-mentioned State.
4. The term "interest" as used in this Article means income from debt-claims of every kind, whether or not secured by mortgage and whether or not carrying a right to participate in the debtor's profits, and in particular, income from government securities and income from bonds or debentures, including premiums and prizes attaching to such securities, bonds or debentures. Penalty charges for late payment shall not be regarded as interest for the purpose of this Article.
5. The provisions of paragraphs 1, 2 and 3 shall not apply if the beneficial owner of the interest, being a resident of a Contracting State, carries on business in the other Contracting State in which the interest arises, through a permanent establishment situated therein, and the debt-claim in respect of which the interest is paid is effectively connected with such permanent establishment. In such case the provisions of Article 7 shall apply.
6. Interest shall be deemed to arise in a Contracting State when the payer is the Government of that State, a local authority thereof or a resident of that State. Where, however, the person paying the interest, whether he is a resident of a Contracting State or not, has in a Contracting State a permanent establishment in connection with which the indebtedness on which the interest is paid was incurred, and such interest is borne by such permanent establishment, then such interest shall be deemed to arise in the State in which the permanent establishment is situated.
7. Where, by reason of a special relationship between the payer and the beneficial owner or between both of them and some other person, the amount of the interest, having regard to the debt-claim for which it is paid, exceeds the amount which would have been agreed upon by the payer and the beneficial owner in the absence of such relationship, the provisions of this Article shall apply only to the last-mentioned amount. In such case, the excess part of the payments shall remain taxable according to the laws of each Contracting State, due regard being had to the other provisions of this Agreement.
8. The provisions of this Article shall not apply if it was the main purpose or one of the purposes of any person concerned with the creation or assignment of the debt-claim in respect of which the interest is paid to take advantage of this Article by means of that creation or assignment.

Article 12: Royalties

1. Royalties arising in a Contracting State and paid to a resident of the other Contracting State may be taxed in that other State.

2. However, such royalties may also be taxed in the Contracting State in which they arise and according to the laws of that State, but if the beneficial owner of the royalties is a resident of the other Contracting State, the tax so charged shall not exceed seven point five per cent (7.5%) of the gross amount of the royalties. The competent authorities of the Contracting States shall by mutual agreement settle the mode of application of this limitation.
3. Notwithstanding the provisions of paragraph 2, royalties arising in a Contracting State and derived by the Government of the other Contracting State and a local authority thereof shall be exempt from tax in the first-mentioned State.
4. The term "royalties" as used in this Article means payments of any kind received as a consideration for the use of, or the right to use, any copyright of literary, artistic or scientific work including cinematography films, any patent, trade mark, design or model, plan, secret formula or process, or for information concerning industrial, commercial or scientific experience.
5. The provisions of paragraphs 1 and 2 shall not apply if the beneficial owner of the royalties, being a resident of a Contracting State, carries on business in the other Contracting State in which the royalties arise, through a permanent establishment situated therein, and the right or property in respect of which the royalties are paid is effectively connected with such permanent establishment. In such case the provisions of Article 7 shall apply.
6. Royalties shall be deemed to arise in a Contracting State when the payer is the Government of that Contracting State, a local authority thereof or a resident of that Contracting State. Where, however, the person paying the royalties, whether he is a resident of a Contracting State or not, has in a Contracting State a permanent establishment in connection with which the liability to pay the royalties was incurred, and such royalties are borne by such permanent establishment, then such royalties shall be deemed to arise in the State in which the permanent establishment is situated.
7. Where, by reason of a special relationship between the payer and the beneficial owner or between both of them and some other person, the amount of the royalties, having regard to the use, right or information for which they are paid, exceeds the amount which would have been agreed upon by the payer and the beneficial owner in the absence of such relationship, the provisions of this Article shall apply only to the last-mentioned amount. In such case, the excess part of the payments shall remain taxable according to the laws of each Contracting State, due regard being had to the other provisions of this Agreement.
8. The provisions of this Article shall not apply if it was the main purpose or one of the purposes of any person concerned with the creation or assignment of the rights in respect of which the royalties are paid to take advantage of this Article by means of that creation or assignment.

Article 13: Capital Gains

1. Gains derived by a resident of a Contracting State from the alienation of immovable property referred to in Article 6 and situated in the other Contracting State may be taxed in that other State.
2. Gains from the alienation of movable property forming part of the business property of a permanent establishment which an enterprise of a Contracting State has in the other Contracting State, including such gains from the alienation of such a permanent establishment (alone or with the whole enterprise), may be taxed in that other State.
3. Gains from the alienation of ships, aircraft, boats, road or rail transport vehicles operated in international traffic by an enterprise of a Contracting State or movable property pertaining to the operation of such ships, aircraft, boats, road or rail transport vehicles shall be taxable only in the Contracting State in which the place of effective of management of the enterprise is situated.
4. Gains derived by a resident of a Contracting State from the alienation of shares deriving more than 50 percent of their value directly or indirectly from immovable property situated in the other Contracting State may be taxed in that other State.
5. Gains from the alienation of shares other than those mentioned in paragraph 4 representing a participation of at least 50 per cent in a company which is a resident of a Contracting State may be taxed in that State.
6. Gains from the alienation of any property other than that referred to in the preceding paragraphs of this Article, shall be taxable only in the Contracting State of which the alienator is a resident.

Article 14: Income from Employment

1. Subject to the provisions of Articles 15, 17, 18 and 19, salaries, wages and other similar remuneration derived by a resident of a Contracting State in respect of an employment shall be taxable only in that State unless the employment is exercised in the other Contracting State. If the employment is so exercised, such remuneration as is derived therefrom may be taxed in that other State.
2. Notwithstanding the provisions of paragraph 1, remuneration derived by a resident of a Contracting State in respect of an employment exercised in the other Contracting State shall be taxable only in the first-mentioned State if:

   a. the recipient is present in the other State for a period or periods not exceeding in the aggregate 183 days in the calendar year concerned; and
   b. the remuneration is paid by, or on behalf of, an employer who is not a resident of the other State; and
   c. the remuneration is not borne by a permanent establishment which the employer has in the other State.

3. Notwithstanding the preceding provisions of this Article, remuneration derived in respect of an employment exercised aboard a ship, a boat, an aircraft or a

road or rail transport vehicle operated in international traffic by an enterprise of a Contracting State, shall be taxable only in that State.

Article 15: Directors' Fees

Directors' fees and other similar payments derived by a resident of a Contracting State in his capacity as a member of the board of directors of a company which is a resident of the other Contracting State may be taxed in that other State.

Article 16: Artistes and Sportspersons

1. Notwithstanding the provisions of Article 14, income derived by a resident of a Contracting State as an entertainer such as a theatre, motion picture, radio or television artiste, or a musician, or as a sportsperson, from his personal activities as such exercised in the other Contracting State, may be taxed in that other State.
2. Where income in respect of personal activities exercised by an entertainer or a sportsperson in his capacity as such accrues not to the entertainer or sportsperson himself but to another person, that income may, notwithstanding the provisions of Articles 7 and 14, be taxed in the Contracting State in which the activities of the entertainer or sportsperson are exercised.
3. Notwithstanding the preceding provisions of this Article, income derived by entertainers or sportsmen who are residents of a Contracting State from the activities exercised in the other Contracting State under a plan of cultural exchange between the Governments of both Contracting States shall be exempt from tax in that other State.

Article 17: Pensions

1. Subject to the provisions of paragraph 2 of Article 18, pensions and other similar remuneration paid to a resident of a Contracting State in consideration of past employment shall be taxable only in that State.
2. Notwithstanding the provisions of paragraph 1, pensions paid and other similar payments made by the Government of a Contracting State or a local authority thereof under a public welfare scheme of the social security system of that State, shall be taxable only in that State.

Article 18: Government Service

a. Salaries, wages and other similar remuneration, other than a pension, paid by a Contracting State or a local authority thereof to an individual in respect of services rendered to that State or authority shall be taxable only in that State.
b. However, such salaries, wages and other similar remuneration shall be taxable only in the other Contracting State if the services are rendered in that State and the individual is a resident of that State who:

   i. is a national of that State; or
   ii. did not become a resident of that State solely for the purpose of rendering the services.

c. Any pension paid by, or out of funds created by a Contracting State or a local authority thereof to an individual in respect of services rendered to that State or authority shall be taxable only in that State.
d. However, such pension shall be taxable only in the other Contracting State if the individual is a resident of, and a national of, that State.
e. The provisions of Articles 14, 15, 16 and 17 shall apply to salaries, wages and other similar remuneration in respect of services rendered in connection with a business carried on by a Contracting State or a local authority thereof.

Article 19: Teachers and Researchers

1. Remuneration which an individual who is or was immediately before visiting a Contracting State, a resident of the other Contracting State and who is present in the first-mentioned State for the primary purpose of teaching, giving lectures or conducting research at a university, college, school or educational institution or scientific research institution recognized by the Government of the first-mentioned State derives for the purpose of such teaching, lectures or research shall not be taxed in the first-mentioned State, for a period of three years from the date of his first arrival in the first-mentioned State.
2. The provisions of paragraph 1 of this Article shall not apply to income from research if such research is undertaken not in the public interest but primarily for the private benefit of a specific person or persons.

Article 20: Students

1. Payments which a student or business trainee or apprentice who is or was immediately before visiting a Contracting State a resident of the other Contracting State and who is present in the first-mentioned State solely for the purpose of his education or training receives for the purpose of his maintenance, education or training shall not be taxed in that State, provided that such payments arise from sources outside that State.
2. In respect of grants, scholarships and remuneration from employment not covered by paragraph 1, a student, business apprentice or trainee described in paragraph 1 shall, in addition, be entitled during such education or training to the same exemptions, reliefs or reductions in respect of taxes available to residents of the State which he is visiting.

Article 21: Other Income

1. Items of income of a resident of a Contracting State, wherever arising, not dealt with in the foregoing Articles of this Agreement shall be taxable only in that State.
2. The provisions of paragraph 1 shall not apply to income, other than income from immovable property as defined in paragraph 2 of Article 6, if the recipient of such income, being a resident of a Contracting State, carries on business in the other Contracting State through a permanent establishment situated therein,

and the right or property in respect of which the income is paid is effectively connected with such permanent establishment. In such case the provisions of Article 7 shall apply.

Article 22: Methods for the Elimination of Double Taxation

1. In China, double taxation shall be eliminated as follows:
   a. Where a resident of China derives income from Zimbabwe, the amount of tax on that income payable in Zimbabwe in accordance with the provisions of this Agreement may be credited against the Chinese tax imposed on that resident. The amount of the credit, however, shall not exceed the amount of the Chinese tax on that income computed in accordance with the taxation laws and regulations of China.
   b. Where the income derived from Zimbabwe is dividend paid by a company which is a resident of Zimbabwe to a company which is a resident of China and which owns not less than 10% of the shares of the company paying the dividend, the credit shall take into account the tax paid in Zimbabwe by the company paying the dividend in respect of the profits out of which the dividend is paid.
2. In Zimbabwe, double taxation shall be eliminated as follows:
   Subject to the provisions of the laws of Zimbabwe regarding the allowance as a credit against Zimbabwean tax of the tax payable in a territory outside Zimbabwe (which shall not affect the general principle hereof) Chinese tax payable, whether directly or by deduction, in respect of taxable income or chargeable gains from sources within China shall be allowed as a credit against any Zimbabwean tax computed by reference to the same taxable income or chargeable gains by reference to which the Chinese tax is computed. The amount of the credit, however, shall not exceed the amount of the Zimbabwean tax on that income computed in accordance with the taxation laws and regulations of Zimbabwe.

Article 23 Non-Discrimination

1. Nationals of a Contracting State shall not be subjected in the other Contracting State to any taxation or any requirement connected therewith, which is other or more burdensome than the taxation and connected requirements to which nationals of that other State in the same circumstances, in particular with respect to residence, are or may be subjected. This provision shall, notwithstanding the provisions of Article 1, also apply to persons who are not residents of one or both of the Contracting States.
2. The taxation on a permanent establishment which an enterprise of a Contracting State has in the other Contracting State shall not be less favourably levied in that other State than the taxation levied on enterprises of that other State carrying on the same activities. This provision shall not be construed as obliging a Contracting State to grant to residents of the other Contracting State any

personal allowances, reliefs and reductions for taxation purposes on account of civil status or family responsibilities which it grants to its own residents.

3. Except where the provisions of paragraph 1 of Article 9, paragraph 7 of Article 11, or paragraph 7 of Article 12 apply, interest, royalties and other disbursements paid by an enterprise of a Contracting State to a resident of the other Contracting State shall, for the purpose of determining the taxable profits of such enterprise, be deductible under the same conditions as if they had been paid to a resident of the first-mentioned State. Similarly, any debts of an enterprise of a Contracting State to a resident of the other Contracting State shall, for the purpose of determining the taxable capital of such enterprise, be deductible under the same conditions as if they had been contracted to a resident of the first-mentioned State.
4. Enterprises of a Contracting State, the capital of which is wholly or partly owned or controlled, directly or indirectly, by one or more residents of the other Contracting State, shall not be subjected in the first-mentioned State to any taxation or any requirement connected therewith which is other or more burdensome than the taxation and connected requirements to which other similar enterprises of the first-mentioned State are or may be subjected.
5. The provisions of this Article shall, notwithstanding the provisions of Article 2, apply to taxes of every kind and description.

Article 24: Mutual Agreement Procedure

1. Where a person considers that the actions of one or both of the Contracting States result or will result for him in taxation not in accordance with the provisions of this Agreement, he may, irrespective of the remedies provided by the domestic law of those States, present his case to the competent authority of the Contracting State of which he is a resident or, if his case comes under paragraph 1 of Article 23, to that of the Contracting State of which he is a national. The case must be presented within three years from the first notification of the action resulting in taxation not in accordance with the provisions of the Agreement.
2. The competent authority shall endeavour, if the objection appears to it to be justified and if it is not itself able to arrive at a satisfactory solution, to resolve the case by mutual agreement with the competent authority of the other Contracting State, with a view to the avoidance of taxation which is not in accordance with the Agreement. Any agreement reached shall be implemented notwithstanding any time limits in the domestic law of the Contracting States.
3. The competent authorities of the Contracting States shall endeavour to resolve by mutual agreement any difficulties or doubts arising as to the interpretation or application of the Agreement. They may also consult together for the elimination of double taxation in cases not provided for in the Agreement.
4. The competent authorities of the Contracting States may communicate with each other directly for the purpose of reaching an agreement in the sense of the preceding paragraphs. When it seems advisable for reaching agreement,

representatives of the competent authorities of the Contracting States may meet together for an oral exchange of opinions.

Article 25: Exchange of Information

1. The competent authorities of the Contracting States shall exchange such information as is foreseeably relevant for carrying out the provisions of this Agreement or to the administration or enforcement of the domestic laws concerning taxes of every kind and description imposed on behalf of the Contracting States, or local authorities, insofar as the taxation thereunder is not contrary to the Agreement. The exchange of information is not restricted by Articles 1 and 2.
2. Any information received under paragraph 1 by a Contracting State shall be treated as secret in the same manner as information obtained under the domestic laws of that State and shall be disclosed only to persons or authorities (including courts and administrative bodies) concerned with the assessment or collection of, the enforcement or prosecution in respect of, the determination of appeals in relation to the taxes referred to in paragraph 1, or the oversight of the above. Such persons or authorities shall use the information only for such purposes. They may disclose the information in public court proceedings or in judicial decisions.
3. In no case shall the provisions of paragraphs 1 and 2 be construed so as to impose on a Contracting State the obligation:

   a. to carry out administrative measures at variance with the laws and the administrative practice of that or of the other Contracting State;
   b. to supply information which is not obtainable under the laws or in the normal course of the administration of that or of the other Contracting State;
   c. to supply information which would disclose any trade, business, industrial, commercial or professional secret or trade process, or information, the disclosure of which would be contrary to public policy ("ordre public").

4. If information is requested by a Contracting State in accordance with this Article, the other Contracting State shall use its information gathering measures to obtain the requested information, even though that other State may not need such information for its own tax purposes. The obligation contained in the preceding sentence is subject to the limitations of paragraph 3 but in no case shall such limitations be construed to permit a Contracting State to decline to supply information solely because it has no domestic interest in such information.
5. In no case shall the provisions of paragraph 3 be construed to permit a Contracting State to decline to supply information solely because the information is held by a bank, other financial institution, nominee or person acting in an agency or a fiduciary capacity or because it relates to ownership interests in a person.

Article 26: Members of Diplomatic Missions and Consular Posts

Nothing in this Agreement shall affect the fiscal privileges of members of diplomatic missions or consular posts under the general rules of international law or under the provisions of special agreements.

Article 27: Entry into Force

Each of the Contracting States shall notify the other through diplomatic channels of the completion of the procedures required by law for the bringing into force of this Agreement. This Agreement shall enter into force on the date of the receipt of the latter notification. The provisions of this Agreement shall have effect as respects income derived during the taxable years beginning on or after the first day of January in the calendar year next following that in which this Agreement enters into force.

Article 28: Termination

This Agreement shall continue in effect indefinitely but either Contracting State may, on or before the thirtieth day of June in any calendar year beginning after the expiration of a period of five years from the date of its entry into force, give a written notice of termination to the other Contracting State through diplomatic channels. The provisions of this Agreement shall cease to have effect as respects income derived during the taxable years beginning on or after the first day of January in the calendar year next following that in which the notice of termination is given.

IN WITNESS whereof the undersigned, duly authorized thereto, have signed this Agreement.

DONE at Harare on the 1st day of December 2015, in duplicate in the Chinese and English languages, both texts being equally authentic.

For the Government of the People's Republic of China
Wang Jun
For the Government of the Republic of Zimbabwe
Chinamas

Chapter 8
China's Investments in Africa

The population of African Continent has surpassed one billion since 2010. It is expected to be more than four billion by the end of the century, almost as much as in Asia. This demographic growth will make a faster-growing domestic demand, which will also be supported by an increased purchasing power thanks to remittances from the Africans emigrated abroad. In the face of this challenge, the continent's leaders understand that the private sector must play a forward-looking role; for this reason, African governments are making efforts to create a suitable environment for private sector-led activities and hence, encourage foreign direct investments.

On the other hand, over the past two decades, China's robust economic growth and rapidly expanding presence in global markets have greatly intensified its trade ties with Africa. China, with its latest growth, has fuelled a steadily rising demand for oil, minerals, and other primary commodities, many of which are abundant in sub-Saharan Africa. China has now become a major development partner for countries throughout the continent, and its trade, investment, diplomatic, and political relationships with African countries continue to strengthen.

The African resources China imports are varied: oil, iron ore, timber, and copper. In exchange for broad access to resources, China exports cheap manufactured goods back to its trading partners, builds much-needed infrastructure, provides foreign direct investments, and loans out billions of dollars.

The table below contains data about China's investment projects in Africa started in 2014.

Funding agency	Recipient	Amount (thousands)	Currency	Sector
Unspecified Chinese Government Institution, Government Agency	Africa, regional	10.000.000	USD	Unallocated/Unspecified

(continued)

L. Riccardi and G. Riccardi, *China in Africa*,
https://doi.org/10.1007/978-981-16-1148-3_8

(continued)

Funding agency	Recipient	Amount (thousands)	Currency	Sector
Unspecified Chinese Government Institution, Government Agency	Africa, regional	28.540	USD	Emergency Response
Unspecified Chinese Government Institution, Government Agency	Africa, regional			Energy Generation and Supply
China Development Bank (CDB), Government Agency	Africa, regional			Energy Generation and Supply
Unspecified Chinese Government Institution, Government Agency	Africa, regional	500.000	CNY	Emergency Response
China Center for Disease Control and Prevention (China-CDC), Government Agency	Africa, regional			Emergency Response
China Center for Disease Control and Prevention (China-CDC), Government Agency	Africa, regional			Emergency Response
Export-Import Bank of China, Government Agency	Africa, regional	170.000	USD	Transport and Storage
Unspecified Chinese Government Institution, Government Agency	Angola	180.000	CNY	Unallocated/Unspecified
Unspecified Chinese Government Institution, Government Agency	Angola			Health
Unspecified Chinese Government Institution, Government Agency	Angola	350	CNY	Other Social infrastructure. and services
China Development Bank (CDB), Government Agency	Angola	2.000.000	USD	Energy Generation and Supply

(continued)

(continued)

Funding agency	Recipient	Amount (thousands)	Currency	Sector
Export-Import Bank of China, Government Agency	Angola	54.900	USD	Energy Generation and Supply
Unspecified Chinese Government Institution, Government Agency	Benin	840	USD	Emergency Response
Unspecified Chinese Government Institution, Government Agency	Botswana			Education
Unspecified Chinese Government Institution, Government Agency	Botswana			Government and Civil Society
Unspecified Chinese Government Institution, Government Agency	Botswana			Education
Unspecified Chinese Government Institution, Government Agency	Botswana			Education
Unspecified Chinese Government Institution, Government Agency	Botswana			Education
Chinese Embassy/Consulate, Government Agency	Botswana	175	BWP	Support to NGOs and GO
Unspecified Chinese Government Institution, Government Agency	Burundi	100	USD	Emergency Response
Unspecified Chinese Government Institution, Government Agency	Burundi			Health
Unspecified Chinese Government Institution, Government Agency	Burundi	100	USD	Government and Civil Society

(continued)

(continued)

Funding agency	Recipient	Amount (thousands)	Currency	Sector
Unspecified Chinese Government Institution, Government Agency	Burundi	5.000	CNY	Government and Civil Society
Export-Import Bank of China, Government Agency	Burundi	14.980	USD	Communications
Unspecified Chinese Government Institution, Government Agency	Burundi			Food Aid/Food Assistance
Unspecified Chinese Government Institution, Government Agency	Burundi			Emergency Response
Unspecified Chinese Government Institution, Government Agency	Burundi	31.600	USD	Other Multisector
Unspecified Chinese Government Institution, Government Agency	Burundi			Unallocated/Unspecified
Unspecified Chinese Government Institution, Government Agency	Cameroon			Health
Unspecified Chinese Government Institution, Government Agency	Cameroon			Agriculture, Forestry and Fishing
Unspecified Chinese Government Institution, Government Agency	Cameroon			Government and Civil Society
Export-Import Bank of China, Government Agency	Cameroon	81.400	USD	Communications
Export-Import Bank of China, Government Agency	Cameroon	385.808,808	USD	Transport and Storage
Unspecified Chinese Government Institution, Government Agency	Cape Verde			Health

(continued)

(continued)

Funding agency	Recipient	Amount (thousands)	Currency	Sector
Unspecified Chinese Government Institution, Government Agency	Cape Verde	150.000	USD	Unallocated/Unspecified
Unspecified Chinese Government Institution, Government Agency	Cape Verde	500	USD	Emergency Response
Unspecified Chinese Government Institution, Government Agency	Comoros			Health
Unspecified Chinese Government Institution, Government Agency	Congo, Dem. Rep.	5.000	USD	Health
Unspecified Chinese Government Institution, Government Agency	Congo, Dem. Rep.			Health
Unspecified Chinese Government Institution, Government Agency	Congo, Dem. Rep.			Education
Unspecified Chinese Government Institution, Government Agency	Congo, Dem. Rep.			Education
Unspecified Chinese Government Institution, Government Agency	Congo, Rep.	815	USD	Health
Unspecified Chinese Government Institution, Government Agency	Congo, Rep.	50.000	XAF	General Environmental Protection
Export-Import Bank of China, Government Agency	Cote D'Ivoire	210.000	USD	Transport and Storage
Export-Import Bank of China, Government Agency	Cote D'Ivoire	91.480	USD	Water Supply and Sanitation

(continued)

(continued)

Funding agency	Recipient	Amount (thousands)	Currency	Sector
Unspecified Chinese Government Institution, Government Agency	Djibouti			Health
Unspecified Chinese Government Institution, Government Agency	Djibouti	16.000	USD	Other Multisector
Unspecified Chinese Government Institution, Government Agency	Egypt	150.000	CNY	Other Multisector
Unspecified Chinese Government Institution, Government Agency	Equatorial Guinea			Health
Export-Import Bank of China, Government Agency	Ethiopia	177.000	USD	Transport and Storage
Export-Import Bank of China, Government Agency	Ethiopia	1.400.000	ETB	Transport and Storage
Export-Import Bank of China, Government Agency	Ethiopia	485.000	ETB	Transport and Storage
Unspecified Chinese Government Institution, Government Agency	Ethiopia			Health
Chinese Embassy/Consulate, Government Agency	Ethiopia	1.000	ETB	Education
Unspecified Chinese Government Institution, Government Agency	Gabon			Health
Unspecified Chinese Government Institution, Government Agency	Ghana	5.000	CNY	Health
Unspecified Chinese Government Institution, Government Agency	Ghana	833	USD	Emergency Response

(continued)

(continued)

Funding agency	Recipient	Amount (thousands)	Currency	Sector
Unspecified Chinese Government Institution, Government Agency	Guinea			Health
Unspecified Chinese Government Institution, Government Agency	Guinea			Health
Unspecified Chinese Government Institution, Government Agency	Guinea	1.000	CNY	Health
Unspecified Chinese Government Institution, Government Agency	Guinea	5.000	USD	Health
Unspecified Chinese Government Institution, Government Agency	Guinea	2.000	USD	Emergency Response
Unspecified Chinese Government Institution, Government Agency	Guinea	30.000	CNY	Emergency Response
Export-Import Bank of China, Government Agency	Kenya	1.600.000	USD	Transport and Storage
Unspecified Chinese Government Institution, Government Agency	Kenya			Agriculture, Forestry and Fishing
Unspecified Chinese Government Institution, Government Agency	Kenya			Health
Unspecified Chinese Government Institution, Government Agency	Kenya			Education
Unspecified Chinese Government Institution, Government Agency	Kenya			Education

(continued)

(continued)

Funding agency	Recipient	Amount (thousands)	Currency	Sector
Unspecified Chinese Government Institution, Government Agency	Kenya	9.200.000	KES	Energy Generation and Supply
Unspecified Chinese Government Institution, Government Agency	Kenya			Emergency Response
Unspecified Chinese Government Institution, Government Agency	Kenya	10.000	USD	General Environmental Protection
Unspecified Chinese Government Institution, Government Agency	Kenya	2.000.000	KES	Unallocated/Unspecified
Unspecified Chinese Government Institution, Government Agency	Kenya	2.000.000	KES	Unallocated/Unspecified
Unspecified Chinese Government Institution, Government Agency	Kenya			Education
Unspecified Chinese Government Institution, Government Agency	Kenya	20	USD	General Environmental Protection
Unspecified Chinese Government Institution, Government Agency	Kenya			Health
Export-Import Bank of China, Government Agency	Kenya	1.633.000	USD	Transport and Storage
Unspecified Chinese Government Institution, Government Agency	Kenya			General Environmental Protection
Unspecified Chinese Government Institution, Government Agency	Kenya	2.000	KES	Education

(continued)

(continued)

Funding agency	Recipient	Amount (thousands)	Currency	Sector
Unspecified Chinese Government Institution, Government Agency	Kenya			Education
Unspecified Chinese Government Institution, Government Agency	Lesotho			Education
Unspecified Chinese Government Institution, Government Agency	Liberia	4.000	USD	Transport and Storage
Unspecified Chinese Government Institution, Government Agency	Liberia			Industry, Mining, Construction
Unspecified Chinese Government Institution, Government Agency	Liberia	1.000	CNY	Health
Unspecified Chinese Government Institution, Government Agency	Liberia	6.500	CNY	Communications
Unspecified Chinese Government Institution, Government Agency	Liberia	20	USD	Health
Unspecified Chinese Government Institution, Government Agency	Liberia	1.000	USD	Emergency Response
Unspecified Chinese Government Institution, Government Agency	Liberia	2.000	USD	Food Aid/Food Assistance
Unspecified Chinese Government Institution, Government Agency	Liberia	211,781	USD	Emergency Response
Unspecified Chinese Government Institution, Government Agency	Liberia	80.000	CNY	Unallocated/Unspecified

(continued)

(continued)

Funding agency	Recipient	Amount (thousands)	Currency	Sector
China Development Bank (CDB), Government Agency	Liberia	150	USD	Emergency Response
People's Liberation Army of China, Government Agency	Liberia			Emergency Response
Unspecified Chinese Government Institution, Government Agency	Liberia			Health
People's Liberation Army of China, Government Agency	Liberia	40	USD	Emergency Response
Unspecified Chinese Government Institution, Government Agency	Liberia			Government and Civil Society
Unspecified Chinese Government Institution, Government Agency	Liberia	1.000	CNY	Emergency Response
Unspecified Chinese Government Institution, Government Agency	Libya			Health
Unspecified Chinese Government Institution, Government Agency	Madagascar			Health
Unspecified Chinese Government Institution, Government Agency	Malawi	5.000.000	MWK	Energy Generation and Supply
Unspecified Chinese Government Institution, Government Agency	Malawi	8.000	USD	Other Multisector
Unspecified Chinese Government Institution, Government Agency	Malawi	17.000	USD	Other Multisector
Unspecified Chinese Government Institution, Government Agency	Malawi			Energy Generation and Supply

(continued)

(continued)

Funding agency	Recipient	Amount (thousands)	Currency	Sector
Unspecified Chinese Government Institution, Government Agency	Mali			Health
Unspecified Chinese Government Institution, Government Agency	Mali	493.000	CNY	Communications
Unspecified Chinese Government Institution, Government Agency	Mali			Emergency Response
Unspecified Chinese Government Institution, Government Agency	Mali	18.000.000	XOF	Unallocated/Unspecified
Unspecified Chinese Government Institution, Government Agency	Mali	8.000.000	XOF	Unallocated/Unspecified
Unspecified Chinese Government Institution, Government Agency	Mali			Education
Unspecified Chinese Government Institution, Government Agency	Mali	8.000.000	USD	Transport and Storage
Unspecified Chinese Government Institution, Government Agency	Mali	80.000	XOF	Health
Unspecified Chinese Government Institution, Government Agency	Mali	420.000	XOF	Health
Unspecified Chinese Government Institution, Government Agency	Mauritania	15.000	EUR	Health
Unspecified Chinese Government Institution, Government Agency	Mauritania			Health

(continued)

(continued)

Funding agency	Recipient	Amount (thousands)	Currency	Sector
Unspecified Chinese Government Institution, Government Agency	Mauritania			Health
Unspecified Chinese Government Institution, Government Agency	Mauritania	3.300	USD	Water Supply and Sanitation
Export-Import Bank of China, Government Agency	Morocco	300.000	USD	Energy Generation and Supply
China Development Bank (CDB), Government Agency	Morocco	100.000	USD	Business and Other Services
Export-Import Bank of China, Government Agency	Mozambique	133.000	USD	Communications
Unspecified Chinese Government Institution, Government Agency	Mozambique			Emergency Response
Export-Import Bank of China, Government Agency	Mozambique	120.000	USD	Transport and Storage
Unspecified Chinese Government Institution, Government Agency	Namibia	2.110,174	NAD	Health
Unspecified Chinese Government Institution, Government Agency	Namibia	800.000	NAD	Transport and Storage
Unspecified Chinese Government Institution, Government Agency	Namibia	50.000	NAD	Other Social infrastructure. and services
Unspecified Chinese Government Institution, Government Agency	Nigeria	10.000	CNY	Health
Unspecified Chinese Government Institution, Government Agency	Nigeria			Education

(continued)

(continued)

Funding agency	Recipient	Amount (thousands)	Currency	Sector
Unspecified Chinese Government Institution, Government Agency	Nigeria			Government and Civil Society
Unspecified Chinese Government Institution, Government Agency	Rwanda			Education
Unspecified Chinese Government Institution, Government Agency	Rwanda	642,304	USD	Energy Generation and Supply
Unspecified Chinese Government Institution, Government Agency	Rwanda	50.000	CNY	Unallocated/Unspecified
Unspecified Chinese Government Institution, Government Agency	Rwanda			Education
Unspecified Chinese Government Institution, Government Agency	Rwanda	26.508,751	USD	Government and Civil Society
Unspecified Chinese Government Institution, Government Agency	Rwanda			Education
Unspecified Chinese Government Institution, Government Agency	Senegal	30	USD	Health
Unspecified Chinese Government Institution, Government Agency	Seychelles			Other Multisector
Unspecified Chinese Government Institution, Government Agency	Sierra Leone			Health
Unspecified Chinese Government Institution, Government Agency	Sierra Leone	10.000	CNY	Health

(continued)

(continued)

Funding agency	Recipient	Amount (thousands)	Currency	Sector
Unspecified Chinese Government Institution, Government Agency	Sierra Leone			Emergency Response
Unspecified Chinese Government Institution, Government Agency	Sierra Leone			Health
Unspecified Chinese Government Institution, Government Agency	Sierra Leone			Emergency Response
Unspecified Chinese Government Institution, Government Agency	Sierra Leone			Emergency Response
Unspecified Chinese Government Institution, Government Agency	Sierra Leone			Health
Unspecified Chinese Government Institution, Government Agency	Sierra Leone	1.000	CNY	Emergency Response
Unspecified Chinese Government Institution, Government Agency	Sierra Leone	1.000	USD	Emergency Response
China Center for Disease Control and Prevention (China-CDC), Government Agency	Sierra Leone	4.350	USD	Emergency Response
Unspecified Chinese Government Institution, Government Agency	Sierra Leone			Emergency Response
China Development Bank (CDB), Government Agency	Sierra Leone	150	USD	Emergency Response
Unspecified Chinese Government Institution, Government Agency	Sierra Leone	2.000	USD	Emergency Response

(continued)

(continued)

Funding agency	Recipient	Amount (thousands)	Currency	Sector
Unspecified Chinese Government Institution, Government Agency	Sierra Leone	48.000	USD	Emergency Response
Unspecified Chinese Government Institution, Government Agency	Sierra Leone			Emergency Response
Unspecified Chinese Government Institution, Government Agency	Sierra Leone	10.000	CNY	Emergency Response
Unspecified Chinese Government Institution, Government Agency	Somalia	20	USD	Emergency Response
Unspecified Chinese Government Institution, Government Agency	Somalia			Health
Unspecified Chinese Government Institution, Government Agency	Somalia	20	USD	Emergency Response
Unspecified Chinese Government Institution, Government Agency	South Sudan	400	CNY	Health
Unspecified Chinese Government Institution, Government Agency	South Sudan			Energy Generation and Supply
Unspecified Chinese Government Institution, Government Agency	South Sudan	1.600	USD	Emergency Response
Unspecified Chinese Government Institution, Government Agency	South Sudan	200	USD	Emergency Response
Unspecified Chinese Government Institution, Government Agency	South Sudan			Emergency Response

(continued)

(continued)

Funding agency	Recipient	Amount (thousands)	Currency	Sector
Unspecified Chinese Government Institution, Government Agency	South Sudan	24.000	USD	Unallocated/Unspecified
Unspecified Chinese Government Institution, Government Agency	South Sudan	3.000	USD	Emergency Response
Unspecified Chinese Government Institution, Government Agency	South Sudan	150.000	CNY	Unallocated/Unspecified
Unspecified Chinese Government Institution, Government Agency	South Sudan	30.000	CNY	Emergency Response
Unspecified Chinese Government Institution, Government Agency	South Sudan			Emergency Response
Export-Import Bank of China, Government Agency	Sudan	700.000	USD	Transport and Storage
Unspecified Chinese Government Institution, Government Agency	Sudan			Action Relating to Debt
Unspecified Chinese Government Institution, Government Agency	Sudan			Transport and Storage
Unspecified Chinese Government Institution, Government Agency	Sudan	36.000	USD	Other Multisector
Unspecified Chinese Government Institution, Government Agency	Sudan	14.000	USD	Agriculture, Forestry and Fishing
Unspecified Chinese Government Institution, Government Agency	Sudan	76.000	USD	Agriculture, Forestry and Fishing

(continued)

(continued)

Funding agency	Recipient	Amount (thousands)	Currency	Sector
Unspecified Chinese Government Institution, Government Agency	Suriname			Transport and Storage
Unspecified Chinese Government Institution, Government Agency	Suriname			Education
China Development Bank (CDB), Government Agency	Tanzania	2.000.000	USD	Trade and Tourism
Unspecified Chinese Government Institution, Government Agency	Tanzania			Health
Unspecified Chinese Government Institution, Government Agency	Tanzania	52.000.000	TZS	Unallocated/Unspecified
Unspecified Chinese Government Institution, Government Agency	Tanzania	26.000.000	TZS	Unallocated/Unspecified
Unspecified Chinese Government Institution, Government Agency	Tanzania	400.000	TZS	Government and Civil Society
Unspecified Chinese Government Institution, Government Agency	Tanzania			Government and Civil Society
Unspecified Chinese Government Institution, Government Agency	Tanzania	30.000	TZS	Emergency Response
Unspecified Chinese Government Institution, Government Agency	Tanzania	3	USD	Education
Unspecified Chinese Government Institution, Government Agency	Tanzania			Education

(continued)

(continued)

Funding agency	Recipient	Amount (thousands)	Currency	Sector
Unspecified Chinese Government Institution, Government Agency	Tanzania	200.000	USD	Water Supply and Sanitation
Export-Import Bank of China, Government Agency	Tanzania	136.000	USD	Energy Generation and Supply
Unspecified Chinese Government Institution, Government Agency	Tanzania			Education
Unspecified Chinese Government Institution, Government Agency	Tanzania			Other Multisector
China Ministry of Commerce, Government Agency	Togo	820	USD	Health
Unspecified Chinese Government Institution, Government Agency	Togo	420.000	XOF	Health
Unspecified Chinese Government Institution, Government Agency	Tunisia			Health
Unspecified Chinese Government Institution, Government Agency	Tunisia	80.000	CNY	Other Multisector
Unspecified Chinese Government Institution, Government Agency	Tunisia			Energy Generation and Supply
Unspecified Chinese Government Institution, Government Agency	Uganda	10.000	CNY	Health
Export-Import Bank of China, Government Agency	Uganda	482.500	USD	Energy Generation and Supply
Chinese Embassy/Consulate, Government Agency	Uganda			Education

(continued)

(continued)

Funding agency	Recipient	Amount (thousands)	Currency	Sector
Unspecified Chinese Government Institution, Government Agency	Uganda			Education
Unspecified Chinese Government Institution, Government Agency	Uganda			Agriculture, Forestry and Fishing
Unspecified Chinese Government Institution, Government Agency	Uganda			Health
Unspecified Chinese Government Institution, Government Agency	Uganda	800	USD	Energy Generation and Supply
Unspecified Chinese Government Institution, Government Agency	Uganda			Government and Civil Society
Unspecified Chinese Government Institution, Government Agency	Uganda	763	USD	Education
Unspecified Chinese Government Institution, Government Agency	Uganda			Agriculture, Forestry and Fishing
Unspecified Chinese Government Institution, Government Agency	Uganda			Government and Civil Society
Unspecified Chinese Government Institution, Government Agency	Uganda			Health
Unspecified Chinese Government Institution, Government Agency	Zambia			Health
Unspecified Chinese Government Institution, Government Agency	Zambia			Health

(continued)

(continued)

Funding agency	Recipient	Amount (thousands)	Currency	Sector
Unspecified Chinese Government Institution, Government Agency	Zambia	90.000.000	USD	Health
Export-Import Bank of China, Government Agency	Zambia	41.000	USD	Energy Generation and Supply
Unspecified Chinese Government Institution, Government Agency	Zambia	32.000	USD	Other Multisector
Unspecified Chinese Government Institution, Government Agency	Zambia	32.000	USD	Other Multisector
Export-Import Bank of China, Government Agency	Zambia	360.000	USD	Transport and Storage
Unspecified Chinese Government Institution, Government Agency	Zambia			Transport and Storage
Unspecified Chinese Government Institution, Government Agency	Zambia			Education
Unspecified Chinese Government Institution, Government Agency	Zambia			Support to NGOs and GO
Unspecified Chinese Government Institution, Government Agency	Zambia			Other Social infrastructure. and services
Unspecified Chinese Government Institution, Government Agency	Zambia	23,593	ZMW	Other Social infrastructure. and services
Unspecified Chinese Government Institution, Government Agency	Zambia			Other Social infrastructure. and services

(continued)

(continued)

Funding agency	Recipient	Amount (thousands)	Currency	Sector
Unspecified Chinese Government Institution, Government Agency	Zambia			Education
Export-Import Bank of China, Government Agency	Zimbabwe	218.000	USD	Communications
Unspecified Chinese Government Institution, Government Agency	Zimbabwe	23.000	USD	Industry, Mining, Construction
Export-Import Bank of China, Government Agency	Zimbabwe	89.000	USD	Health
Unspecified Chinese Government Institution, Government Agency	Zimbabwe			Education
Unspecified Chinese Government Institution, Government Agency	Zimbabwe			Education
Export-Import Bank of China, Government Agency	Zimbabwe	319.000	USD	Energy Generation and Supply
Unspecified Chinese Government Institution, Government Agency	Zimbabwe			Energy Generation and Supply
Unspecified Chinese Government Institution, Government Agency	Zimbabwe	500	USD	Emergency Response
Unspecified Chinese Government Institution, Government Agency	Zimbabwe	30	USD	Government and Civil Society
Unspecified Chinese Government Institution, Government Agency	Zimbabwe			Health

Source Aiddata, 2014

Chapter 9
Belt Road Initiative

The Belt Road Initiative is a development strategy adopted by the Chinese Government, which focuses on connectivity and cooperation between China, Europe, and Africa. It plans substantial investments in transportation infrastructure, mainly through Asia and Eastern Europe. China's ODI to countries along OBOR grew 23.8% year-on-year in 2015 and was up 60% year-on-year in the first half of 2016.

Much of China's outbound direct investment (ODI) in Africa is intricately linked to trade. Africa has benefited from China's rising ODI outflows, but no more so than other regions. Indeed, Chinese investments have increased worldwide and, mainly in Asia, China's most important ODI recipient. The ambitious Belt Road Initiative drives this global trend.

Throughout sub-Saharan Africa, China is investing most heavily in energy and the extractive industries, a pattern similar to its investment strategy in other parts of the world. In West Africa, however, Chinese ODI is unusually concentrated in the transportation sector. From 2005 to 2012, the West African transportation sector received 36% of China's total ODI flows to the region, substantially higher the 14% average worldwide. Transport equipment is overwhelmingly related to mineral extraction, a sector where Chinese firms are highly concentrated. Transportation was followed by the mining and metallurgy sector with 32% of total regional investment, also well above the 16% average worldwide. Energy attracted the third-largest share of Chinese ODI at 28%, lower than the 46% worldwide average.

The table below contains data about China's investment projects in Africa related to The Belt Road Initiative.

L. Riccardi and G. Riccardi, *China in Africa*,
https://doi.org/10.1007/978-981-16-1148-3_9

Region	Country	Projects (Name)	Sector	Segments	Investment, Mio USD	Stage	Commencement, year	Expected completion, year	EPC company/ Project consultant
Africa	Angola	Benguela Railway	Transport	Railways	1830	Completed			China Railway Construction Corporation (CRCC)
Africa	Ethiopia	Djibouti-Ethiopia Railway Line, Ethiopia & Djibouti	Transport	Railways	4000	Completed			China Railway Construction Corporation (CRCC)
Africa	Ethiopia	Addis Ababa Light Rail	Transport	Railways	475	Completed			Company A
Africa	Kenya	Mombasa-Nairobi Railway	Transport	Railways	3804	Completed		2017	China Communications Construction Company (CCCC)
Africa	Nigeria	Abuja-Kaduna Railway	Transport	Railways	850	Completed			China Railway Construction Corporation (CRCC)
Africa	Nigeria	Lagos-Calabar Railway	Transport	Railways	11100	Under construction	2014		China Railway Construction Corporation (CRCC)
Africa	Nigeria	Abuja Rail Mass Transit Phase II	Transport	Railways	1473	Under construction	2017		China Railway Construction Corporation (CRCC)

(continued)

(continued)

Region	Country	Projects (Name)	Sector	Segments	Investment, Mio USD	Stage	Commencement, year	Expected completion, year	EPC company/ Project consultant
Africa	Sudan	Khartoum-Port Sudan railway	Transport	Railways	1154	Completed			Company A

Source Centre for Strategic & International Studies (CSIS), Economist

Appendix 1
Sources: Africa Report, *RsA Asia, 2020*

Top 5 Economies in Africa

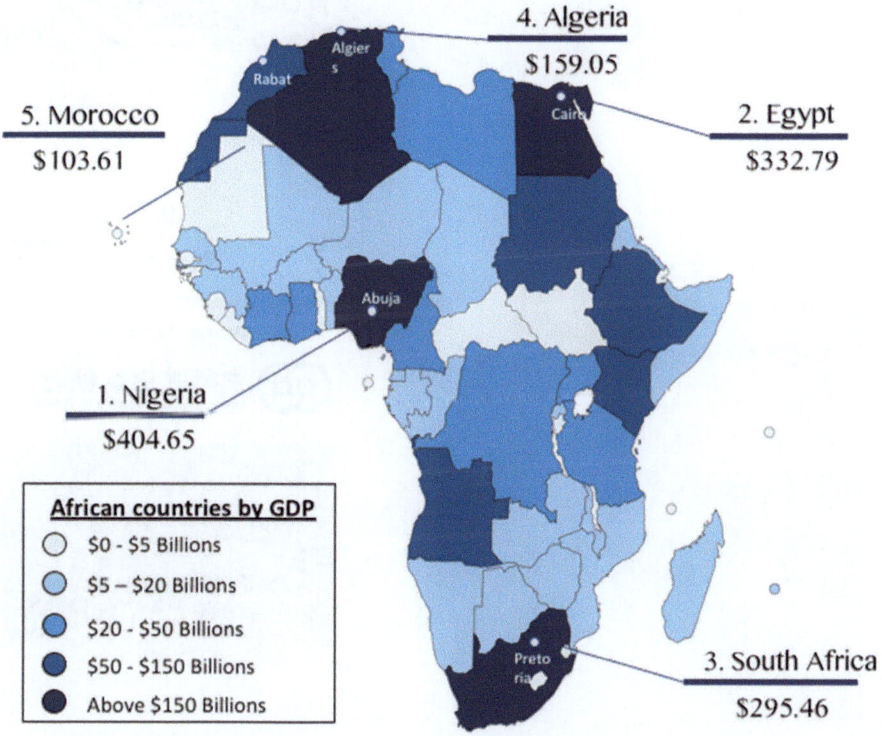

L. Riccardi and G. Riccardi, *China in Africa*,
https://doi.org/10.1007/978-981-16-1148-3

10 Biggest Chinese Funded Projects in Africa

10

Mozambique

Mepanda Nkua Dam and hydroelectric station

Amount: *$3.1 billion*

中国进出口银行
THE EXPORT-IMPORT BANK OF CHINA

9

Kenya

Nairobi – Mombasa standard gauge railway

Amount: *$3.4 billion*

中国进出口银行
THE EXPORT-IMPORT BANK OF CHINA

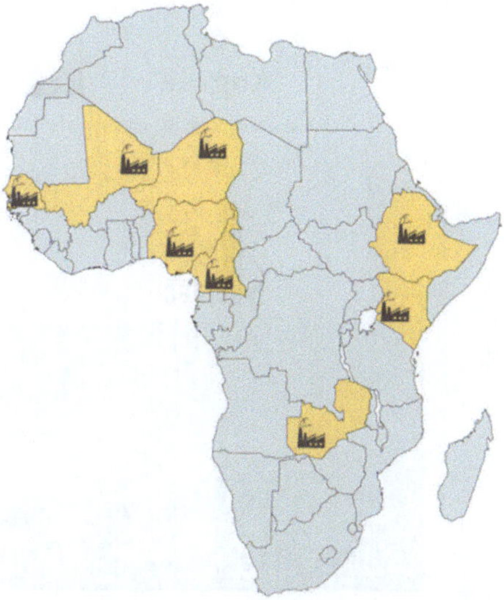

8

Regional

Cements plants in Cameroon, Ethiopia, Kenya, Mali, Niger, Nigeria, Senegal and Zambia

Amount: *$4.34 billion*

SINOMA 中国中材国际工程股份有限公司 SINOMA INTERNATIONAL ENGINEERING CO., LTD.

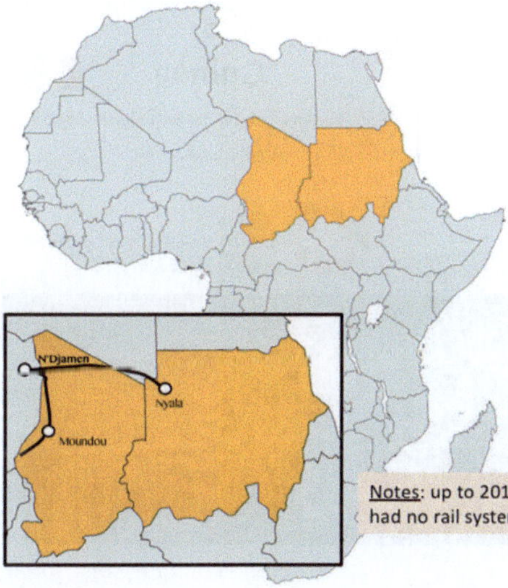

Notes: up to 2012, Chad had no rail system

7

Regional

Chad-Sudan 1,344-km railway network

Amount: *$5.6 billion*

中国土木工程集团有限公司 CHINA CIVIL ENGINEERING CONSTRUCTION CORPORATION

6

Angola

Construction of an oil refinery

Amount: *$4.34 billion*

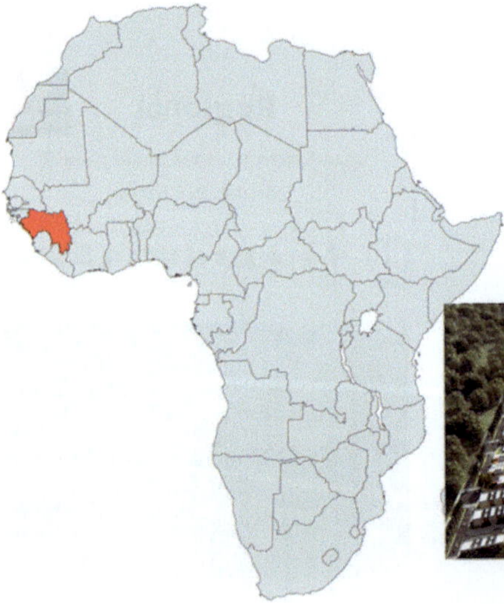

5

Guinea

Joint Venture to fund infrastructural projects

Amount: *$7 billion*

China International Fund Limited
中國國際基金有限公司

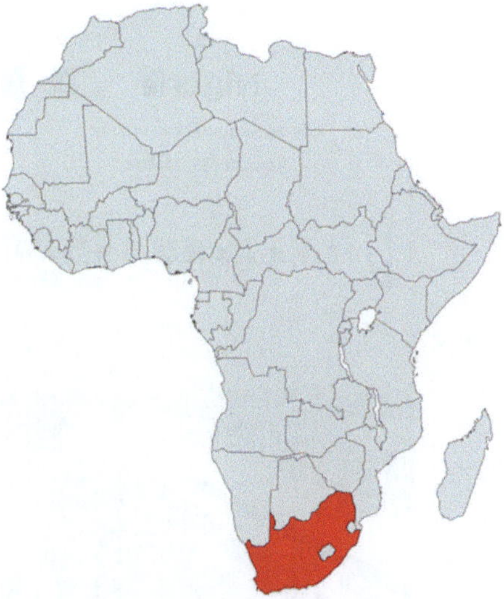

4

South Africa

Mini-City outside Johannesburg (100,000 ha)

Amount: *$7 billion*

ZENDAI

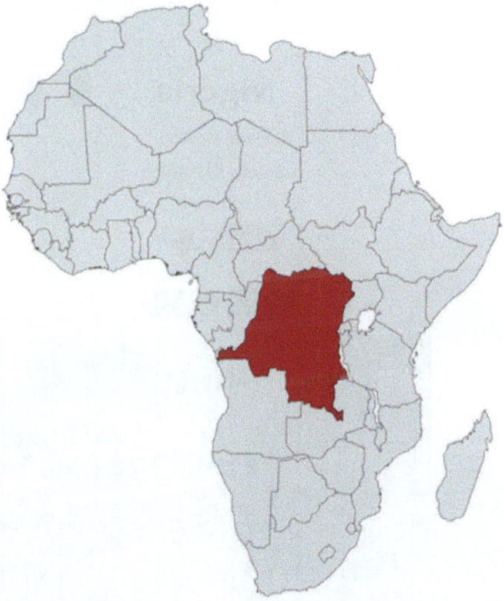

3

DR Congo

Infrastructures for mines barter deal (Sicomines)

Amount: *$7.16 billion*

中国进出口银行

THE EXPORT-IMPORT BANK OF CHINA

2

Nigeria

Lagos-Kano railway project

Amount: *$8.3 billion*

中国土木工程集团有限公司
CHINA CIVIL ENGINEERING CONSTRUCTION CORPORATION

1

Nigeria

Coastal Railway

Amount: *$12 billion*

CRCC
中国铁建

Amount Granted by China in Africa

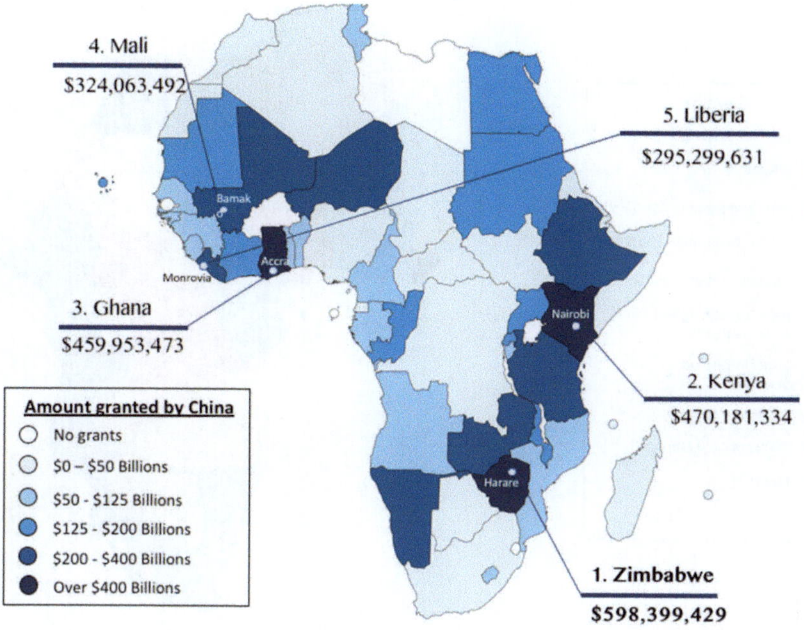

Amount Invested by China in Africa

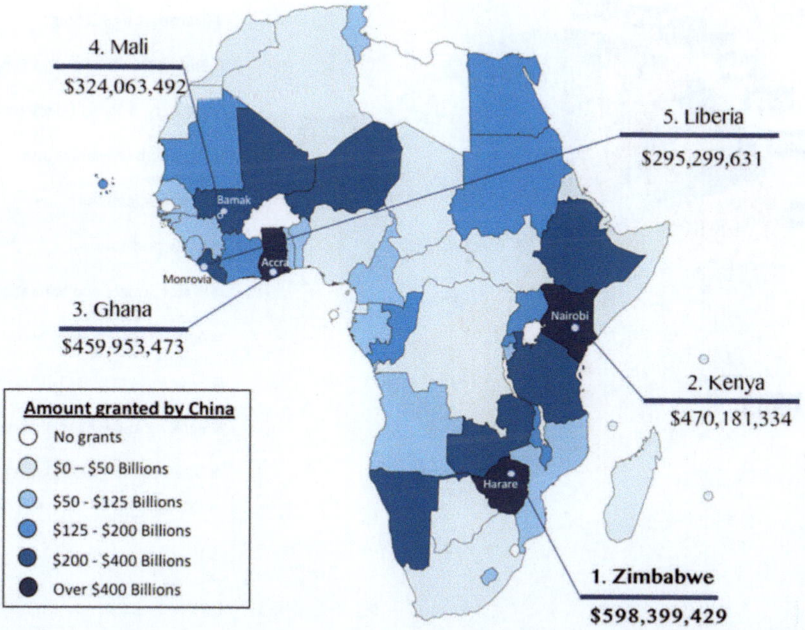

Chinese Investments Leading Sectors by Country

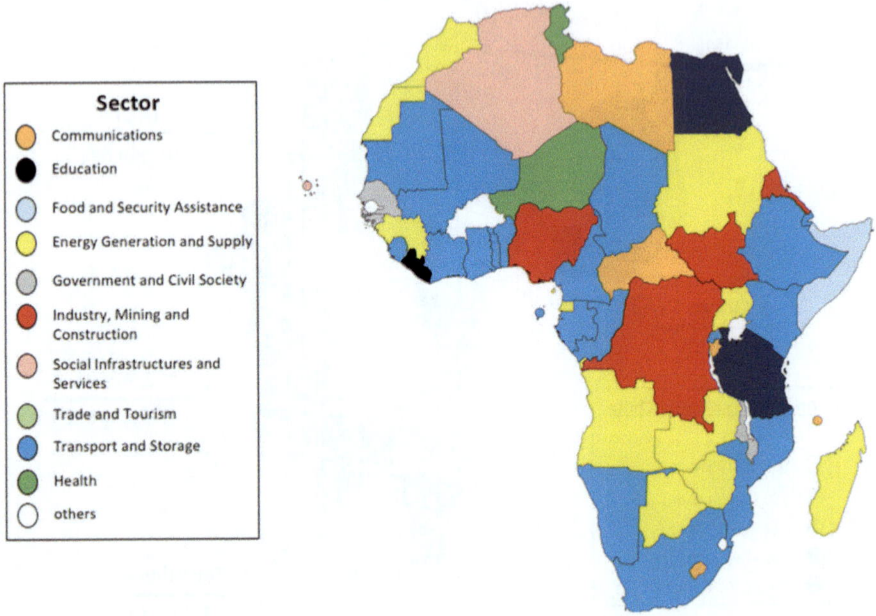

Chinese Investments Leading Sectors for Africa

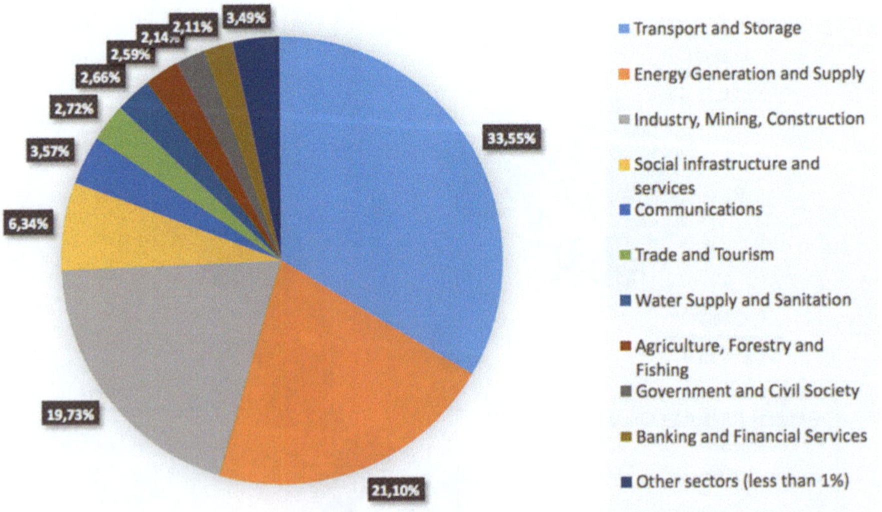

Scopes of Investments: Mining Example

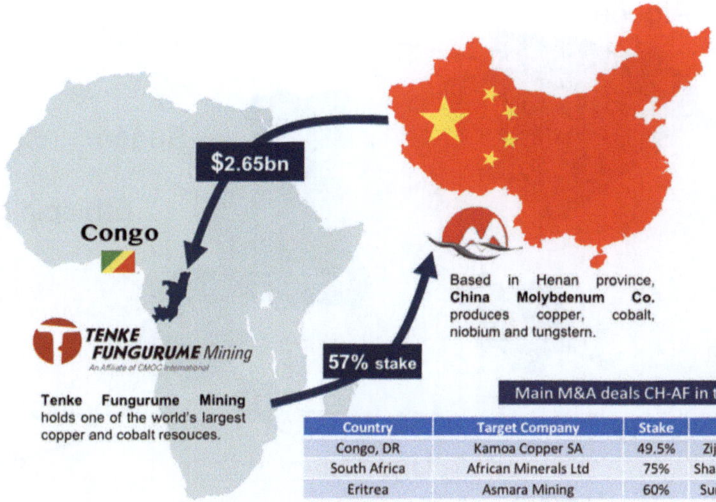

Main M&A deals CH-AF in the Mining Industry

Country	Target Company	Stake	Bidder	US$m
Congo, DR	Kamoa Copper SA	49.5%	Zijin Mining Group	412
South Africa	African Minerals Ltd	75%	Shandong Iron Group	170
Eritrea	Asmara Mining	60%	Sunridge Gold Corp	78

African BRI Countries by Tax Rate

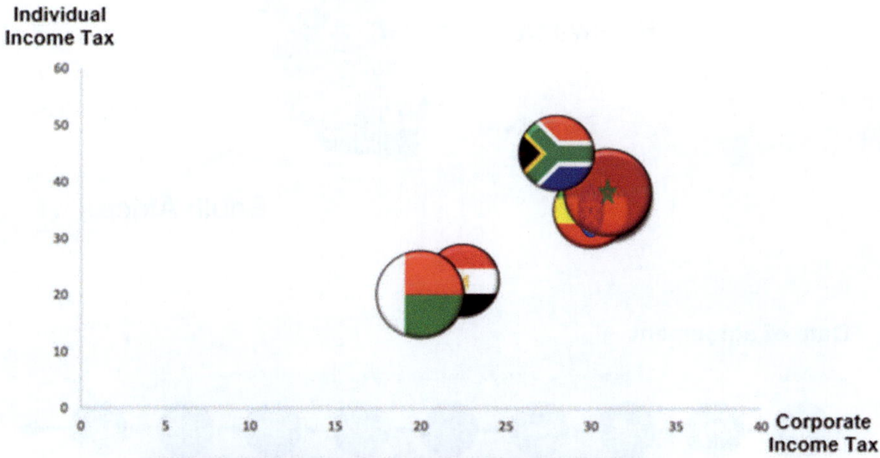

Country	CIT (%)	IIT (%)	VAT (%)
Egypt	22,5	22,5	14
Ethiopia	30	35	15
Madagascar	20	20	20
Morocco	31	38	20
South Africa	28	45	15

China—Africa Double Tax Treaties

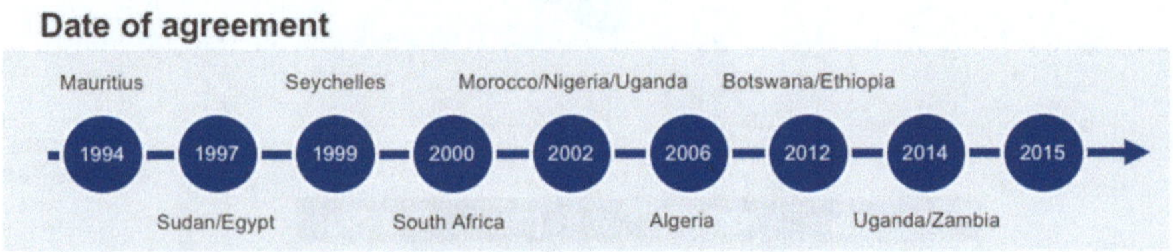

Appendix 2
African Country Data

*Data for Appendix 2 comes from *The World Bank, 2018*

	1990	2000	2010	2018
Algeria				
Population, total	25,758,869	31,042,235	35,977,455	42,228,429
Population growth (annual %)	2.57	1.36	1.81	2.01
GDP growth (annual %)	0.80	3.80	3.60	1.40
Inflation, GDP deflator (annual %)	30.26	22.67	16.12	7.56
Exports of goods and services (% of GDP)	23.44	42.07	38.45	25.62
Imports of goods and services (% of GDP)	24.94	20.79	31.42	32.34
GDP (current US$ billions)	62.05	54.79	161.21	173.76
Angola				
Population, total	11,848,386	16,395,473	23,356,246	30,809,762
Population growth (annual %)	3.38	3.28	3.67	3.28
GDP growth (annual %)	−3.45	3.05	4.86	−2.13
Inflation, GDP deflator (annual %)	14.01	418.02	31.69	34.84
Exports of goods and services (% of GDP)	33.33	89.69	61.54	30.03
Imports of goods and services (% of GDP)	33.33	62.86	42.58	29.43
GDP (current US$ billions)	11.23	9.13	83.80	105.75
Benin				
Population, total	4,978,496	6,865,951	9,199,259	11,485,048
Population growth (annual %)	3.24	2.98	2.81	2.73

(continued)

L. Riccardi and G. Riccardi, *China in Africa*,
https://doi.org/10.1007/978-981-16-1148-3

(continued)

	1990	2000	2010	2018
GDP growth (annual %)	8.98	5.86	2.11	6.70
Inflation, GDP deflator (annual %)	2.18	4.34	0.88	0.59
Exports of goods and services (% of GDP)	19.18	20.61	23.07	27.30
Imports of goods and services (% of GDP)	26.54	26.74	28.36	34.55
GDP (current US$ billions)	1.96	3.51	9.54	14.25
Botswana				
Population, total	1,286,756	1,643,334	1,987,105	2,254,126
Population growth (annual %)	3.34	2.03	1.71	2.20
GDP growth (annual %)	6.77	1.99	8.56	4.45
Inflation, GDP deflator (annual %)	6.30	14.17	8.92	0.93
Exports of goods and services (% of GDP)	55.06	51.83	43.64	39.36
Imports of goods and services (% of GDP)	49.79	40.09	51.26	37.77
GDP (current US$ billions)	3.79	5.79	12.79	18.62
Burkina Faso				
Population, total	8,811,034	11,607,942	15,605,217	19,751,535
Population growth (annual %)	2.66	2.84	3.02	2.87
GDP growth (annual %)	−0.60	1.82	5.37	6.83
Inflation, GDP deflator (annual %)	1.81	−0.82	6.81	2.37
Exports of goods and services (% of GDP)	10.97	9.53	19.23	30.79
Imports of goods and services (% of GDP)	24.46	24.98	29.64	37.24
GDP (current US$ billions)	3.10	2.63	8.98	14.12
Burundi				
Population, total	5,438,957	6,378,871	8,675,602	11,175,378
Population growth (annual %)	2.45	1.77	3.26	3.17
GDP growth (annual %)	3.50	−0.86	5.12	1.61
Inflation, GDP deflator (annual %)	5.99	38.94	8.56	−2.85
Exports of goods and services (% of GDP)	7.87	6.32	9.70	9.40
Imports of goods and services (% of GDP)	27.78	16.23	29.80	29.81
GDP (current US$ billions)	1.13	0.87	2.03	3.04

(continued)

(continued)

	1990	2000	2010	2018
Cabo Verde				
Population, total	337,950	428,188	492,654	543,767
Population growth (annual %)	2.02	1.82	1.22	1.16
GDP growth (annual %)	0.69	14.28	1.47	5.08
Inflation, GDP deflator (annual %)	2.35	−7.90	0.51	1.53
Exports of goods and services (% of GDP)	17.13	27.01	32.67	48.78
Imports of goods and services (% of GDP)	68.82	60.51	61.77	68.21
GDP (current US$ billions)	0.31	0.54	1.66	1.98
Cameroon				
Population, total	11,780,088	15,513,945	20,341,241	25,216,237
Population growth (annual %)	3.05	2.62	2.75	2.61
GDP growth (annual %)	−6.11	3.55	3.42	4.06
Inflation, GDP deflator (annual %)	1.64	5.21	1.91	1.60
Exports of goods and services (% of GDP)	20.18	25.91	22.17	19.31
Imports of goods and services (% of GDP)	17.31	24.94	26.95	23.70
GDP (current US$ billions)	11.15	10.08	26.14	38.68
Central African Republic				
Population, total	2,806,734	3,640,427	4,386,768	4,666,377
Population growth (annual %)	2.20	2.29	1.13	1.52
GDP growth (annual %)	−2.15	−2.49	4.63	3.79
Inflation, GDP deflator (annual %)	1.84	8.51	4.21	−1.22
Exports of goods and services (% of GDP)	17.07	20.37	11.63	18.88
Imports of goods and services (% of GDP)	25.88	25.29	22.80	46.98
GDP (current US$ billions)	1.44	0.91	2.14	2.22
Chad				
Population, total	5,963,252	8,355,654	11,952,136	15,477,751
Population growth (annual %)	3.23	3.68	3.33	3.02
GDP growth (annual %)	−4.18	−0.88	13.55	2.64
Inflation, GDP deflator (annual %)	8.01	5.29	6.39	5.11
Exports of goods and services (% of GDP)	13.48	16.89	36.85	36.00
Imports of goods and services (% of GDP)	27.91	34.68	43.55	37.88

(continued)

(continued)

	1990	2000	2010	2018
GDP (current US$ billions)	1.74	1.39	10.66	11.27
Comoros				
Population, total	411,594	542,357	689,692	832,322
Population growth (annual %)	2.95	2.52	2.41	2.24
GDP growth (annual %)	5.09	10.85	3.80	3.43
Inflation, GDP deflator (annual %)	2.18	−4.46	1.65	1.16
Exports of goods and services (% of GDP)	8.84	8.84	9.64	13.25
Imports of goods and services (% of GDP)	26.92	26.92	29.91	29.85
GDP (current US$ billions)	0.43	0.35	0.91	1.18
Democratic Republic of the Congo				
Population, total	34,612,023	47,105,826	64,563,854	84,068,091
Population growth (annual %)	3.37	2.55	3.33	3.23
GDP growth (annual %)	−6.57	−6.91	7.11	5.76
Inflation, GDP deflator (annual %)	108.96	2630.12	20.79	30.14
Exports of goods and services (% of GDP)	29.50	11.45	41.11	33.62
Imports of goods and services (% of GDP)	29.20	15.56	49.64	37.34
GDP (current US$ billions)	9.35	19.09	21.57	47.23
Republic of the Congo				
Population, total	2,356,737	3,127,411	4,273,731	5,244,363
Population growth (annual %)	2.73	2.89	3.05	2.58
GDP growth (annual %)	1.00	7.58	8.75	1.03
Inflation, GDP deflator (annual %)	−1.03	47.04	20.72	22.24
Exports of goods and services (% of GDP)	51.78	80.30	85.12	98.89
Imports of goods and services (% of GDP)	19.04	43.61	54.70	56.02
GDP (current US$ billions)	2.80	3.22	12.01	11.26
Ivory Coast				
Population, total	11,924,877	16,454,668	20,532,950	25,069,229
Population growth (annual %)	3.61	2.60	2.33	2.55
GDP growth (annual %)	−1.10	−2.07	2.02	7.43
Inflation, GDP deflator (annual %)	−4.52	2.25	5.39	0.43
Exports of goods and services (% of GDP)	31.69	40.78	50.63	29.80

(continued)

(continued)

	1990	2000	2010	2018
Imports of goods and services (% of GDP)	27.11	33.86	43.33	29.25
GDP (current US$ billions)	10.80	10.72	24.88	43.01
Djibouti				
Population, total	590,398	717,584	851,146	958,920
Population growth (annual %)	4.60	2.47	1.70	1.56
GDP growth (annual %)	–	0.42	3.49	5.46
Inflation, GDP deflator (annual %)	–	2.40	3.95	1.30
Exports of goods and services (% of GDP)	53.84	35.06	–	148.78
Imports of goods and services (% of GDP)	78.43	50.38	–	178.88
GDP (current US$ billions)	0.45	0.55	1.13	2.96
Egypt				
Population, total	56,134,475	68,831,561	82,761,235	98,423,595
Population growth (annual %)	2.43	1.93	1.98	2.03
GDP growth (annual %)	5.67	6.37	5.15	5.31
Inflation, GDP deflator (annual %)	17.74	3.94	10.11	21.43
Exports of goods and services (% of GDP)	20.35	16.20	21.35	18.91
Imports of goods and services (% of GDP)	32.57	22.82	26.59	29.37
GDP (current US$ billions)	42.98	99.84	218.89	250.89
Equatorial Guinea				
Population, total	419,188	606,181	943,639	1,308,974
Population growth (annual %)	3.04	4.11	4.56	3.65
GDP growth (annual %)	−1.76	18.21	−8.92	−6.36
Inflation, GDP deflator (annual %)	10.35	64.74	24.91	11.17
Exports of goods and services (% of GDP)	38.99	122.06	85.76	58.81
Imports of goods and services (% of GDP)	164.35	212.07	58.91	45.70
GDP (current US$ billions)	0.11	1.05	16.31	13.28
Eritrea				
Population, total	3,113,311	3,392,801	4,390,840	–
Population growth (annual %)	1.34	2.70	1.85	–
GDP growth (annual %)	–	−3.14	2.19	–
Inflation, GDP deflator (annual %)	–	24.98	11.57	–

(continued)

(continued)

	1990	2000	2010	2018
Exports of goods and services (% of GDP)	–	9.67	4.79	–
Imports of goods and services (% of GDP)	–	58.21	23.35	–
GDP (current US$ billions)	–	0.71	2.12	–
Ethiopia				
Population, total	47,887,865	66,224,804	87,639,964	109,224,559
Population growth (annual %)	3.43	2.88	2.78	2.62
GDP growth (annual %)	2.73	6.07	12.55	6.81
Inflation, GDP deflator (annual %)	3.27	9.46	1.44	12.52
Exports of goods and services (% of GDP)	..	..	..	8.37
Imports of goods and services (% of GDP)	..	..	..	22.80
GDP (current US$ billions)	12.18	8.24	29.93	84.36
Gabon				
Population, total	949,488	1,228,360	1,624,140	2,119,275
Population growth (annual %)	2.75	2.41	3.46	2.60
GDP growth (annual %)	5.19	−1.88	7.09	0.84
Inflation, GDP deflator (annual %)	15.36	28.09	16.56	7.15
Exports of goods and services (% of GDP)	46.04	69.03	57.66	50.54
Imports of goods and services (% of GDP)	30.86	32.67	31.49	21.51
GDP (current US$ billions)	5.95	5.07	14.36	16.85
Gambia				
Population, total	955,593	1,317,703	1,793,196	2,280,102
Population growth (annual %)	4.27	3.13	3.00	2.95
GDP growth (annual %)	3.56	5.50	5.91	6.55
Inflation, GDP deflator (annual %)	11.96	2.22	5.64	5.20
Exports of goods and services (% of GDP)	59.90	25.80	14.67	21.85
Imports of goods and services (% of GDP)	71.58	30.56	26.34	41.51
GDP (current US$ billions)	0.32	0.78	1.54	1.63
Ghana				
Population, total	14,773,277	19,278,856	24,779,619	29,767,108
Population growth (annual %)	2.88	2.45	2.49	2.19
GDP growth (annual %)	3.33	3.70	7.90	6.26

(continued)

(continued)

	1990	2000	2010	2018
Inflation, GDP deflator (annual %)	31.17	27.23	16.60	10.21
Exports of goods and services (% of GDP)	16.88	48.80	29.48	35.26
Imports of goods and services (% of GDP)	25.85	67.25	45.90	36.41
GDP (current US$ billions)	5.89	4.98	32.17	65.56
Guinea				
Population, total	6,352,283	8,240,730	10,192,176	12,414,318
Population growth (annual %)	2.95	2.28	2.26	2.83
GDP growth (annual %)	4.32	2.50	4.81	6.16
Inflation, GDP deflator (annual %)	17.28	6.30	16.10	−1.34
Exports of goods and services (% of GDP)	31.08	24.52	30.34	37.60
Imports of goods and services (% of GDP)	33.44	28.96	43.21	53.02
GDP (current US$ billions)	2.67	3.00	6.85	10.91
Guinea–Bissau				
Population, total	975,261	1,201,301	1,522,599	1,874,309
Population growth (annual %)	2.23	2.03	2.57	2.49
GDP growth (annual %)	6.10	5.43	4.61	3.80
Inflation, GDP deflator (annual %)	30.25	80.90	2.97	−0.42
Exports of goods and services (% of GDP)	9.94	21.76	14.91	25.34
Imports of goods and services (% of GDP)	37.03	33.12	35.22	32.46
GDP (current US$ billions)	0.24	0.37	0.85	1.46
Kenya				
Population, total	23,724,579	31,964,557	42,030,676	51,393,010
Population growth (annual %)	3.38	2.75	2.72	2.31
GDP growth (annual %)	4.19	0.60	8.41	6.32
Inflation, GDP deflator (annual %)	10.64	6.08	2.09	2.84
Exports of goods and services (% of GDP)	25.69	21.59	20.66	13.18
Imports of goods and services (% of GDP)	31.33	31.72	33.57	23.01
GDP (current US$ billions)	8.57	12.71	40.00	87.91
Lesotho				
Population, total	1,703,747	2,032,804	1,995,581	2,108,132
Population growth (annual %)	2.21	0.65	0.27	0.80

(continued)

(continued)

	1990	2000	2010	2018
GDP growth (annual %)	6.05	3.88	6.43	1.13
Inflation, GDP deflator (annual %)	11.99	6.30	9.61	4.39
Exports of goods and services (% of GDP)	..	..	39.31	43.83
Imports of goods and services (% of GDP)	..	..	100.77	84.18
GDP (current US$ billions)	0.60	0.89	2.39	2.74
Liberia				
Population, total	2,097,232	2,884,522	3,948,125	4,818,977
Population growth (annual %)	−1.62	5.34	3.52	2.45
GDP growth (annual %)	−51.03	28.62	6.10	1.22
Inflation, GDP deflator (annual %)	−0.17	−6.89	5.47	−1.85
Exports of goods and services (% of GDP)	–	31.38	19.14	26.01
Imports of goods and services (% of GDP)	–	38.94	92.64	94.33
GDP (current US$ billions)	0.38	0.53	1.29	3.26
Libya				
Population, total	4,436,661	5,357,891	6,197,663	6,678,567
Population growth (annual %)	2.46	1.54	1.03	1.48
GDP growth (annual %)	..	3.68	5.02	7.95
Inflation, GDP deflator (annual %)	..	13.31	14.16	15.83
Exports of goods and services (% of GDP)	39.68	31.56	65.60	62.23
Imports of goods and services (% of GDP)	31.12	13.72	42.10	40.12
GDP (current US$ billions)	28.90	38.27	74.77	48.36
Madagascar				
Population, total	11,598,633	15,766,806	21,151,640	26,262,368
Population growth (annual %)	2.89	3.12	2.79	2.67
GDP growth (annual %)	3.13	4.76	0.62	4.56
Inflation, GDP deflator (annual %)	11.46	7.23	10.22	7.58
Exports of goods and services (% of GDP)	16.60	30.68	21.87	28.68
Imports of goods and services (% of GDP)	28.03	38.01	36.00	33.82
GDP (current US$ billions)	3.08	3.88	9.98	13.85
Malawi				
Population, total	9,404,500	11,148,758	14,539,612	18,143,315

(continued)

(continued)

	1990	2000	2010	2018
Population growth (annual %)	3.56	2.68	2.87	2.64
GDP growth (annual %)	5.69	1.58	6.87	3.50
Inflation, GDP deflator (annual %)	10.66	30.53	12.13	8.60
Exports of goods and services (% of GDP)	23.78	25.60	22.79	33.14
Imports of goods and services (% of GDP)	33.42	35.33	34.86	45.04
GDP (current US$ billions)	1.88	1.74	6.96	7.06
Mali				
Population, total	8,449,913	10,946,445	15,049,353	19,077,690
Population growth (annual %)	1.83	2.81	3.16	3.01
GDP growth (annual %)	−2.50	−0.06	5.41	4.90
Inflation, GDP deflator (annual %)	7.60	−0.62	4.37	1.84
Exports of goods and services (% of GDP)	15.65	22.48	22.84	23.60
Imports of goods and services (% of GDP)	30.93	32.94	35.15	34.05
GDP (current US$ billions)	2.68	2.95	10.68	17.16
Mauritania				
Population, total	2,034,346	2,630,219	3,494,195	4,403,319
Population growth (annual %)	2.61	2.64	2.93	2.78
GDP growth (annual %)	−1.77	−0.43	4.77	3.55
Inflation, GDP deflator (annual %)	2.64	5.40	18.88	2.75
Exports of goods and services (% of GDP)	45.64	29.96	50.74	45.09
Imports of goods and services (% of GDP)	60.73	45.30	61.18	76.22
GDP (current US$ billions)	1.02	1.29	4.34	5.23
Mauritius				
Population, total	1,058,775	1,186,873	1,250,400	1,265,303
Population growth (annual %)	0.71	0.98	0.24	0.05
GDP growth (annual %)	7.19	8.20	4.38	3.77
Inflation, GDP deflator (annual %)	10.58	3.41	1.13	1.71
Exports of goods and services (% of GDP)	64.96	61.09	51.24	40.66
Imports of goods and services (% of GDP)	72.16	61.22	62.22	54.19
GDP (current US$ billions)	2.65	4.66	10.00	14.22
Morocco				

(continued)

(continued)

	1990	2000	2010	2018
Population, total	24,807,462	28,793,679	32,343,389	36,029,138
Population growth (annual %)	1.84	1.18	1.29	1.25
GDP growth (annual %)	3.41	1.91	3.82	2.99
Inflation, GDP deflator (annual %)	7.69	−0.74	0.98	1.07
Exports of goods and services (% of GDP)	24.56	26.79	32.23	38.73
Imports of goods and services (% of GDP)	30.07	32.37	43.01	49.26
GDP (current US$ billions)	30.18	38.86	93.22	117.92
Mozambique				
Population, total	12,987,292	17,711,927	23,531,574	29,495,962
Population growth (annual %)	1.41	2.68	2.74	2.91
GDP growth (annual %)	1.00	1.19	6.49	3.43
Inflation, GDP deflator (annual %)	34.06	11.10	7.98	2.12
Exports of goods and services (% of GDP)	8.17	11.43	28.46	47.76
Imports of goods and services (% of GDP)	36.07	35.73	42.33	84.22
GDP (current US$ billions)	2.51	5.55	11.09	14.72
Namibia				
Population, total	1,432,905	1,794,571	2,118,874	2,448,255
Population growth (annual %)	3.33	1.73	1.80	1.88
GDP growth (annual %)	2.05	3.49	6.04	−0.55
Inflation, GDP deflator (annual %)	6.38	10.19	3.56	6.97
Exports of goods and services (% of GDP)	43.63	41.67	47.76	38.73
Imports of goods and services (% of GDP)	50.27	45.42	60.66	44.92
GDP (current US$ billions)	2.79	3.83	11.28	14.52
Niger				
Population, total	8,026,591	11,331,557	16,464,025	22,442,948
Population growth (annual %)	3.12	3.61	3.84	3.82
GDP growth (annual %)	−1.28	−1.41	8.36	6.48
Inflation, GDP deflator (annual %)	−1.60	4.52	3.02	2.59
Exports of goods and services (% of GDP)	14.81	17.80	22.20	15.74
Imports of goods and services (% of GDP)	21.60	25.69	49.09	33.04
GDP (current US$ billions)	2.48	1.80	5.72	9.29

(continued)

(continued)

	1990	2000	2010	2018
Nigeria				
Population, total	95,212,450	122,283,850	158,503,197	195,874,740
Population growth (annual %)	2.58	2.50	2.67	2.59
GDP growth (annual %)	11.78	5.02	8.01	1.94
Inflation, GDP deflator (annual %)	6.67	22.67	16.34	10.23
Exports of goods and services (% of GDP)	20.97	36.02	25.66	15.49
Imports of goods and services (% of GDP)	9.95	12.97	17.66	17.51
GDP (current US$ billions)	54.04	69.45	363.36	397.27
Rwanda				
Population, total	7,288,882	7,933,681	10,039,338	12,301,939
Population growth (annual %)	0.16	5.60	2.59	2.64
GDP growth (annual %)	−2.40	8.37	7.33	8.61
Inflation, GDP deflator (annual %)	13.46	2.78	2.61	−0.79
Exports of goods and services (% of GDP)	5.61	6.32	11.88	17.37
Imports of goods and services (% of GDP)	14.07	24.88	29.60	34.13
GDP (current US$ billions)	2.55	1.73	5.85	9.51
Sao Tome and Principe				
Population, total	113,893	138,606	174,776	211,028
Population growth (annual %)	2.01	1.98	2.29	1.88
GDP growth (annual %)	–	–	6.67	2.66
Inflation, GDP deflator (annual %)	–	–	12.48	4.69
Exports of goods and services (% of GDP)	–	–	–	..
Imports of goods and services (% of GDP)	–	–	–	..
GDP (current US$ billions)	–	–	0.20	0.42
Senegal				
Population, total	7,526,307	9,797,734	12,678,148	15,854,360
Population growth (annual %)	3.00	2.37	2.74	2.78
GDP growth (annual %)	−0.68	3.20	3.56	6.77
Inflation, GDP deflator (annual %)	−0.02	1.94	1.08	2.35
Exports of goods and services (% of GDP)	25.41	27.93	19.83	21.85
Imports of goods and services (% of GDP)	32.19	37.22	32.10	36.09

(continued)

(continued)

	1990	2000	2010	2018
GDP (current US$ billions)	7.24	5.92	16.22	24.13
Seychelles				
Population, total	69,507	81,131	89,770	96,762
Population growth (annual %)	0.49	0.89	2.79	0.95
GDP growth (annual %)	7.00	1.51	5.95	3.63
Inflation, GDP deflator (annual %)	6.83	3.98	−4.21	4.06
Exports of goods and services (% of GDP)	15.33	75.47	93.80	87.03
Imports of goods and services (% of GDP)	50.52	81.90	108.08	102.08
GDP (current US$ billions)	0.37	0.61	0.97	1.59
Sierra Leone				
Population, total	4,319,762	4,584,571	6,415,634	7,650,154
Population growth (annual %)	1.52	2.70	2.25	2.14
GDP growth (annual %)	3.35	6.65	5.35	3.45
Inflation, GDP deflator (annual %)	70.59	3.28	17.18	13.43
Exports of goods and services (% of GDP)	34.69	18.13	16.79	17.47
Imports of goods and services (% of GDP)	34.00	39.40	34.48	39.23
GDP (current US$ billions)	0.65	0.64	2.58	4.09
Somalia				
Population, total	7,225,092	8,872,254	12,043,883	15,008,154
Population growth (annual %)	1.28	3.66	2.75	2.83
GDP growth (annual %)	−1.48	..	..	..
Inflation, GDP deflator (annual %)	215.47	..	..	..
Exports of goods and services (% of GDP)	9.79	..	..	25.93
Imports of goods and services (% of GDP)	37.74	..	..	99.60
GDP (current US$ billions)	0.92			4.72
South Africa				
Population, total	36,800,509	44,967,708	51,216,964	57,779,622
Population growth (annual %)	2.39	1.41	1.46	1.36
GDP growth (annual %)	−0.32	4.20	3.04	0.79
Inflation, GDP deflator (annual %)	15.48	8.80	6.35	3.92
Exports of goods and services (% of GDP)	23.49	27.16	28.62	29.91

(continued)

(continued)

	1990	2000	2010	2018
Imports of goods and services (% of GDP)	18.19	24.28	27.37	29.56
GDP (current US$ billions)	115.55	136.36	375.35	368.29
South Sudan				
Population, total	5,492,623	6,199,394	9,508,364	10,975,920
Population growth (annual %)	−0.34	4.38	3.93	0.60
GDP growth (annual %)	..	..	5.49	..
Inflation, GDP deflator (annual %)	..	..	12.93	..
Exports of goods and services (% of GDP)	..	..	61.43	..
Imports of goods and services (% of GDP)	..	..	29.51	..
GDP (current US$ billions)	..	..	14.60	..
Sudan				
Population, total	20,147,590	27,275,015	34,545,013	41,801,533
Population growth (annual %)	3.39	2.41	2.23	2.39
GDP growth (annual %)	−5.47	6.35	3.47	−2.32
Inflation, GDP deflator (annual %)	66.24	9.85	19.58	23.93
Exports of goods and services (% of GDP)	4.02	15.98	19.74	10.25
Imports of goods and services (% of GDP)	7.07	13.42	17.23	12.35
GDP (current US$ billions)	12.41	12.26	65.63	40.85
Swaziland				
Population, total	822,420	1,005,435	1,064,837	1,136,191
Population growth (annual %)	2.95	1.13	0.69	1.01
GDP growth (annual %)	21.02	1.76	3.79	2.35
Inflation, GDP deflator (annual %)	30.38	25.34	3.20	2.79
Exports of goods and services (% of GDP)	59.02	71.27	46.47	40.50
Imports of goods and services (% of GDP)	68.88	85.13	60.19	43.91
GDP (current US$ billions)	1.11	1.74	4.44	4.71
Tanzania				
Population, total	25,203,845	33,499,180	44,346,525	56,318,348
Population growth (annual %)	3.19	2.47	2.91	2.98
GDP growth (annual %)	7.05	4.52	6.34	5.44
Inflation, GDP deflator (annual %)	22.45	8.20	9.43	4.78

(continued)

(continued)

	1990	2000	2010	2018
Exports of goods and services (% of GDP)	12.62	10.81	19.61	19.48
Imports of goods and services (% of GDP)	37.45	13.17	28.03	22.61
GDP (current US$ billions)	4.26	13.38	32.01	58.00
Togo				
Population, total	3,774,312	4,924,402	6,421,679	7,889,094
Population growth (annual %)	2.57	2.97	2.70	2.45
GDP growth (annual %)	−0.24	−0.78	6.10	4.91
Inflation, GDP deflator (annual %)	2.98	10.05	0.63	1.33
Exports of goods and services (% of GDP)	33.47	28.22	37.84	31.32
Imports of goods and services (% of GDP)	45.34	40.45	53.37	42.29
GDP (current US$ billions)	1.63	1.49	3.43	5.36
Tunisia				
Population, total	8,242,496	9,708,350	10,635,244	11,565,204
Population growth (annual %)	2.24	0.98	1.04	1.15
GDP growth (annual %)	7.95	4.71	3.51	2.48
Inflation, GDP deflator (annual %)	4.48	3.28	3.82	6.91
Exports of goods and services (% of GDP)	43.56	39.55	49.50	48.92
Imports of goods and services (% of GDP)	50.60	42.91	54.65	62.04
GDP (current US$ billions)	12.29	21.47	44.05	39.87
Uganda				
Population, total	17,354,392	23,650,172	32,428,167	42,723,139
Population growth (annual %)	3.47	2.99	3.19	3.72
GDP growth (annual %)	6.47	3.14	5.64	6.15
Inflation, GDP deflator (annual %)	44.38	11.12	10.57	3.20
Exports of goods and services (% of GDP)	7.24	10.65	17.13	19.51
Imports of goods and services (% of GDP)	19.37	22.10	28.59	28.69
GDP (current US$ billions)	4.30	6.19	20.19	27.46
Zambia				
Population, total	8,036,845	10,415,944	13,605,984	17,351,822
Population growth (annual %)	2.73	2.68	2.91	2.91
GDP growth (annual %)	−0.48	3.90	10.30	3.79

(continued)

(continued)

	1990	2000	2010	2018
Inflation, GDP deflator (annual %)	106.39	32.61	13.95	9.33
Exports of goods and services (% of GDP)	..	23.92	37.03	37.42
Imports of goods and services (% of GDP)	..	36.46	30.87	38.24
GDP (current US$ billions)	3.29	3.60	20.27	26.72
Zimbabwe				
Population, total	10,432,421	11,881,477	12,697,723	14,439,018
Population growth (annual %)	2.71	0.50	1.35	1.41
GDP growth (annual %)	6.99	−3.06	19.68	6.16
Inflation, GDP deflator (annual %)	−0.92	0.63	4.10	28.01
Exports of goods and services (% of GDP)	22.87	38.16	29.64	22.92
Imports of goods and services (% of GDP)	22.79	35.91	53.48	25.51
GDP (current US$ billions)	8.78	6.69	12.04	31.00

Appendix 3
Double Taxation Treaties

Botswana

Agreement Between The Government of The People's Republic of China And The Government of The Republic of Botswana for The Avoidance of Double Taxation and The Prevention of Fiscal Evasion With Respect to Taxes On Income

The Government of the People's Republic of China and the Government of the Republic of Botswana,

Desiring to conclude an Agreement for the avoidance of double taxation and the prevention of fiscal evasion with respect to taxes on income,

Have agreed as follows:

Article 1: Persons Covered

This Agreement shall apply to persons who are residents of one or both of the Contracting States.

Article 2: Taxes Covered

1. This Agreement shall apply to taxes on income imposed on behalf of a Contracting State or of its political subdivisions or local authorities, irrespective of the manner in which they are levied.
2. There shall be regarded as taxes on income all taxes imposed on total income, or on elements of income, including taxes on gains from the alienation of movable or immovable property and taxes on the total amounts of wages or salaries paid by enterprises.
3. The existing taxes to which the Agreement shall apply are in particular:

   a. in China:
      i. the individual income tax;
      ii. the enterprise income tax; (hereinafter referred to as "Chinese tax");

L. Riccardi and G. Riccardi, *China in Africa*,
https://doi.org/10.1007/978-981-16-1148-3

b. in Botswana:
   the income tax including taxation of capital gains;
   (hereinafter referred to as "Botswana tax").

4. The Agreement shall apply also to any identical or substantially similar taxes that are imposed after the date of signature of the Agreement in addition to, or in place of, the existing taxes. The competent authorities of the Contracting States shall notify each other of any significant changes which have been made in their taxation laws.

Article 3: General Definitions

1. For the purposes of this Agreement, unless the context otherwise requires:

   a. the term "China" means the People's Republic of China; when used in geographical sense, means all the territory of the People's Republic of China, including its territorial sea, in which the Chinese laws relating to taxation apply, and any area beyond its territorial sea, within which the People's Republic of China has sovereign rights of exploration for and exploitation of resources of the sea-bed and its sub-soil and superjacent water resources in accordance with international law and its internal law;
   b. the term "Botswana" means the Republic of Botswana";
   c. the term "person" includes an individual, a company and any other body of persons;
   d. the term "company" means anybody corporate or any entity that is treated as a body corporate for tax purposes;
   e. the terms "enterprise of a Contracting State" and "enterprise of the other Contracting State" mean, respectively, an enterprise carried on by a resident of a Contracting State and an enterprise carried on by a resident of the other Contracting State;
   f. the term "international traffic" means any transport by a ship or aircraft operated by an enterprise of a Contracting State, except when the ship or aircraft is operated solely between places in the other Contracting State;
   g. the term "competent authority" means, in the case of China, the State Administration of Taxation or its authorized representative, and in the case of Botswana, the Minister of Finance and Development Planning, represented by the Commissioner General of the Botswana Unified Revenue Service or his authorized representative;
   h. the term "national", in relation to a Contracting State, means:
      i. any individual possessing the nationality of a Contracting State; and
      ii. any legal person, partnership or association deriving its status as such from the laws in force in a Contracting State.

2. As regards the application of the Agreement at any time by a Contracting State, any term not defined therein shall, unless the context otherwise requires, have the meaning which it has at that time under the law of that State for the purposes

of the taxes to which the Agreement applies, any meaning under the applicable tax laws of that State prevailing over a meaning given to the term under other laws of that State.

Article 4: Resident

1. For the purposes of this Agreement, the term "resident of a Contracting State" means any person who, under the laws of that State, is liable to tax therein by reason of his domicile, residence, place of incorporation, place of effective management or any other criterion of a similar nature, and also includes that State and any political subdivision or local authority thereof. This term, however, does not include any person who is liable to tax in that State in respect only of income from sources in that State or capital situated therein.
2. Whereby reason of the provisions of paragraph 1 an individual is a resident of both Contracting States, then his status shall be determined as follows:
   a. he shall be deemed to be a resident only of the State in which he has a permanent home available to him; if he has a permanent home available to him in both States, he shall be deemed to be a resident only of the State with which his personal and economic relations are closer (centre of vital interests);
   b. if the State in which he has his centre of vital interests cannot be determined, or if he has not a permanent home available to him in either State, he shall be deemed to be a resident only of the State in which he has an habitual abode;
   c. if he has a habitual abode in both States or in neither of them, he shall be deemed to be a resident only of the State of which he is a national;
   d. if he is a national of both States or of neither of them, the competent authorities of the Contracting States shall settle the question by mutual agreement.
3. Whereby reason of the provisions of paragraph 1 a person other than an individual is a resident of both Contracting States, then it shall be deemed to be a resident only of the State in which its place of effective management is situated.

Article 5: Permanent Establishment

1. For the purposes of this Agreement, the term "permanent establishment" means a fixed place of business through which the business of an enterprise is wholly or partly carried on.
2. The term "permanent establishment" includes especially:
   a. a place of management;
   b. a branch;
   c. an office;
   d. a factory;

e. a workshop; and
f. a mine, an oil or gas well, a quarry or any other place of extraction of natural resources.

3. The term "permanent establishment" likewise encompasses:

a. a building site, or construction, assembly or installation project or supervisory activities in connection therewith, but only if such site, project or activities last more than 12 months;
b. the furnishing of services, including consultancy services, by an enterprise through employees or other personnel engaged for such purpose, but only if activities of that nature continue (for the same or a connected project) within a Contracting State for a period or periods aggregating more than 183 days within any twelve-month period.

4. Notwithstanding the preceding provisions of this Article, the term "permanent establishment" shall be deemed not to include:

a. the use of facilities solely for the purpose of storage, display or delivery of goods or merchandise belonging to the enterprise;
b. the maintenance of a stock of goods or merchandise belonging to the enterprise solely for the purpose of storage, display or delivery;
c. the maintenance of a stock of goods or merchandise belonging to the enterprise solely for the purpose of processing by another enterprise;
d. the maintenance of a fixed place of business solely for the purpose of purchasing goods or merchandise or of collecting information, for the enterprise;
e. the maintenance of a fixed place of business solely for the purpose of carrying on, for the enterprise, any other activity of a preparatory or auxiliary character; and
f. the maintenance of a fixed place of business solely for any combination of activities mentioned in sub-paragraphs a) to e), provided that the overall activity of the fixed place of business resulting from this combination is of a preparatory or auxiliary character.

5. Notwithstanding the provisions of paragraphs 1 and 2, where a person–other than an agent of an independent status to whom paragraph 6 applies–is acting in a Contracting State on behalf of an enterprise of the other Contracting State, and has, and habitually exercises, in that Contracting State an authority to conclude contracts in the name of the enterprise, that enterprise shall be deemed to have a permanent establishment in that Contracting State in respect of any activities which that person undertakes for the enterprise, unless the activities of such person are limited to those mentioned in paragraph 4 which, if exercised through a fixed place of business, would not make this fixed place of business a permanent establishment under the provisions of that paragraph.

6. An enterprise of a Contracting State shall not be deemed to have a permanent establishment in the other Contracting State merely because it carries on business in that other State through a broker, general commission agent or any other agent of an independent status, provided that such persons are acting in the ordinary course of their business. 7. The fact that a company which is a resident of a Contracting State controls or is controlled by a company which is a resident of the other Contracting State, or which carries on business in that other State (whether through a permanent establishment or otherwise), shall not of itself constitute either company a permanent establishment of the other.

Article 6: Income from Immovable Property

1. Income derived by a resident of a Contracting State from immovable property (including income from agriculture or forestry) situated in the other Contracting State may be taxed in that other State.
2. The term "immovable property" shall have the meaning which it has under the law of the Contracting State in which the property in question is situated. The term shall in any case include property accessory to immovable property, livestock and equipment used in agriculture and forestry, rights to which the provisions of general law respecting landed property apply, usufruct of immovable property and rights to variable or fixed payments as consideration for the working of, or the right to work, mineral deposits, sources and other natural resources; ships and aircraft shall not be regarded as immovable property.
3. The provisions of paragraph 1 shall apply to income derived from the direct use, letting, or use in any other form of immovable property.
4. The provisions of paragraphs 1 and 3 shall also apply to the income from immovable property of an enterprise and to income from immovable property used for the performance of independent personal services.

Article 7: Business Profits

1. The profits of an enterprise of a Contracting State shall be taxable only in that State unless the enterprise carries on business in the other Contracting State through a permanent establishment situated therein. If the enterprise carries on business as aforesaid, the profits of the enterprise may be taxed in the other State, but only so much of them as is attributable to that permanent establishment.
2. Subject to the provisions of paragraph 3, where an enterprise of a Contracting State carries on business in the other Contracting State through a permanent establishment situated therein, there shall in each Contracting State be attributed to that permanent establishment the profits which it might be expected to make if it were a distinct and separate enterprise engaged in the same or similar activities under the same or similar conditions and dealing wholly independently with the enterprise of which it is a permanent establishment.

3. In determining the profits of a permanent establishment, there shall be allowed as deductions expenses which are incurred for the purposes of the permanent establishment, including executive and general administrative expenses so incurred, whether in the State in which the permanent establishment is situated or elsewhere.
4. Insofar as it has been customary in a Contracting State to determine the profits to be attributed to a permanent establishment on the basis of an apportionment of the total profits of the enterprise to its various parts, nothing in paragraph 2 shall preclude that Contracting State from determining the profits to be taxed by such an apportionment as may be customary; the method of apportionment adopted shall, however, be such that the result shall be in accordance with the principles contained in this Article.
5. No profits shall be attributed to a permanent establishment by reason of the mere purchase by that permanent establishment of goods or merchandise for the enterprise.
6. For the purposes of the preceding paragraphs, the profits to be attributed to the permanent establishment shall be determined by the same method year by year unless there is good and sufficient reason to the contrary.
7. Where profits include items of income which are dealt with separately in other Articles of this Agreement, then the provisions of those Articles shall not be affected by the provisions of this Article.

Article 8: Shipping and Air Transport

1. Profits from the operation of ships or aircraft in international traffic by an enterprise of a Contracting State shall be taxable only in that Contracting State.
2. The provisions of paragraph 1 shall also apply to profits from the participation in a pool, a joint business or an international operating agency.

Article 9: Associated Enterprises

1. Where

   a. an enterprise of a Contracting State participates directly or indirectly in the management, control or capital of an enterprise of the other Contracting State, or
   b. the same persons participate directly or indirectly in the management, control or capital of an enterprise of a Contracting State and an enterprise of the other Contracting State, and in either case conditions are made or imposed between the two enterprises in their commercial or financial relations which differ from those which would be made between independent enterprises, then any profits which would, but for those conditions, have accrued to one of the enterprises, but, by reason of those conditions, have not so accrued, may be included in the profits of that enterprise and taxed accordingly.

2. Where a Contracting State includes in the profits of an enterprise of that State– and taxes accordingly–profits on which an enterprise of the other Contracting State has been charged to tax in that other State and the profits so included are profits which would have accrued to the enterprise of the first-mentioned State if the conditions made between the two enterprises had been those which would have been made between independent enterprises, then that other State shall make an appropriate adjustment to the amount of the tax charged therein on those profits. In determining such adjustment, due regard shall be had to the other provisions of this Agreement and the competent authorities of the Contracting States shall, if necessary, consult each other.

Article 10: Dividends

1. Dividends paid by a company which is a resident of a Contracting State to a resident of the other Contracting State may be taxed in that other State.
2. However, such dividends may also be taxed in the Contracting State of which the company paying the dividends is a resident and according to the laws of that State, but if the beneficial owner of the dividends is a resident of the other Contracting State, the tax so charged shall not exceed 5 per cent of the gross amount of the dividends.
   The competent authorities of the Contracting States shall by mutual agreement settle the mode of application of these limitations.
   This paragraph shall not affect the taxation of the company in respect of the profits out of which the dividends are paid.
3. The term "dividends" as used in this Article means income from shares, mining shares or other rights, not being debt-claims, participating in profits, as well as income from other corporate rights which is subjected to the same taxation treatment as income from shares by the laws of the State of which the company making the distribution is a resident.
4. The provisions of paragraphs 1 and 2 shall not apply if the beneficial owner of the dividends, being a resident of a Contracting State, carries on business in the other Contracting State of which the company paying the dividends is a resident through a permanent establishment situated therein, or performs in that other State independent personal services from a fixed base situated therein, and the holding in respect of which the dividends are paid is effectively connected with such permanent establishment or fixed base. In such case the provisions of Article 7 or Article 14, as the case may be, shall apply.
5. Where a company which is a resident of a Contracting State derives profits or income from the other Contracting State, that other State may not impose any tax on the dividends paid by the company, except insofar as such dividends are paid to a resident of that other State or insofar as the holding in respect of which the dividends are paid is effectively connected with a permanent establishment or a fixed base situated in that other State, nor subject the company's undistributed profits to a tax on the company's undistributed profits, even if the dividends paid

or the undistributed profits consist wholly or partly of profits or income arising in such other State.

6. The provision of this Article shall not apply if it was the main purpose or one of the main purposes of any person concerned with the creation or assignment of the shares or other rights in respect of which the dividend is paid to take advantage of this Article by means of that creation or assignment.

Article 11: Interest

1. Interest arising in a Contracting State and paid to a resident of the other Contracting State may be taxed in that other State.
2. However, such interest may also be taxed in the Contracting State in which it arises and according to the laws of that State, but if the beneficial owner of the interest is a resident of the other Contracting State, the tax so charged shall not exceed 7.5 per cent of the gross amount of the interest. The competent authorities of the Contracting States shall by mutual agreement settle the mode of application of this limitation.
3. Notwithstanding the provisions of paragraph 2, interest arising in a Contracting State and paid to, or on loans guaranteed or insured by, the Government, a political subdivision or a local authority, the Central Bank or any financial institution wholly owned by the Government of the other Contracting State shall be exempt from tax in the first-mentioned State.
4. The term "interest" as used in this Article means income from debt-claims of every kind, whether or not secured by mortgage and whether or not carrying a right to participate in the debtor's profits, and in particular, income from government securities and income from bonds or debentures, including premiums and prizes attaching to such securities, bonds or debentures. Penalty charges for late payment shall not be regarded as interest for the purpose of this Article.
5. The provisions of paragraphs 1 and 2 shall not apply if the beneficial owner of the interest, being a resident of a Contracting State, carries on business in the other Contracting State in which the interest arises, through a permanent establishment situated therein, or performs in that other State independent personal services from a fixed base situated therein, and the debt-claim in respect of which the interest is paid is effectively connected with such permanent establishment or fixed base. In such case the provisions of Article 7 or Article 14, as the case may be, shall apply.
6. Interest shall be deemed to arise in a Contracting State when the payer is a resident of that State. Where, however, the person paying the interest, whether he is a resident of a Contracting State or not, has in a Contracting State a permanent establishment or a fixed base in connection with which the indebtedness on which the interest is paid was incurred, and such interest is borne by such permanent establishment or fixed base, then such interest shall be deemed to arise in the State in which the permanent establishment or fixed base is situated.
7. Where, by reason of a special relationship between the payer and the beneficial owner or between both of them and some other person, the amount of the interest,

having regard to the debt-claim for which it is paid, exceeds the amount which would have been agreed upon by the payer and the beneficial owner in the absence of such relationship, the provisions of this Article shall apply only to the last-mentioned amount. In such case, the excess part of the payments shall remain taxable according to the laws of each Contracting State, due regard being had to the other provisions of this Agreement.

8. The provision of this Article shall not apply if it was the main purpose or one of the main purposes of any person concerned with the creation or assignment of the debt-claim in respect of which the interest is paid to take advantage of this Article by means of that creation or assignment.

Article 12: Royalties

1. Royalties arising in a Contracting State and beneficially owned by a resident of the other Contracting State may be taxed in that other State.
2. However, such royalties may also be taxed in the Contracting State in which they arise and according to the laws of that State, but if the beneficial owner of the royalties is a resident of the other Contracting State, the tax so charged shall not exceed 5 per cent of the gross amount of the royalties. The competent authorities of the Contracting States shall by mutual agreement settle the mode of application of this limitation.
3. The term "royalties" as used in this Article means payments of any kind received as a consideration for the use of, or the right to use, any copyright of literary, artistic or scientific work including cinematography films, or films or tapes or discs for radio or television broadcasting, any patent, trade mark, design or model, plan, secret formula or process, or for information concerning industrial, commercial or scientific experience, or for technical and consultancy services.
4. The provisions of paragraphs 1 and 2 shall not apply if the beneficial owner of the royalties, being a resident of a Contracting State, carries on business in the other Contracting State in which the royalties arise, through a permanent establishment situated therein, or performs in that other State independent personal services from a fixed base situated therein, and the right or property in respect of which the royalties are paid is effectively connected with such permanent establishment or fixed base. In such case the provisions of Article 7 or Article 14, as the case may be, shall apply.
5. Royalties shall be deemed to arise in a Contracting State when the payer is a resident of that Contracting State. Where, however, the person paying the royalties, whether he is a resident of a Contracting State or not, has in a Contracting State a permanent establishment or a fixed base in connection with which the liability to pay the royalties was incurred, and such royalties are borne by such permanent establishment or fixed base, then such royalties shall be deemed to arise in the State in which the permanent establishment or fixed base is situated.
6. Where, by reason of a special relationship between the payer and the beneficial owner or between both of them and some other person, the amount of the royalties, having regard to the use, right or information for which they are paid,

exceeds the amount which would have been agreed upon by the payer and the beneficial owner in the absence of such relationship, the provisions of this Article shall apply only to the last-mentioned amount. In such case, the excess part of the payments shall remain taxable according to the laws of each Contracting State, due regard being had to the other provisions of this Agreement.

7. The provision of this Article shall not apply if it was the main purpose or one of the main purposes of any person concerned with the creation or assignment of the rights in respect of which the royalties are paid to take advantage of this Article by means of that creation or assignment.

Article 13: Capital Gains

1. Gains derived by a resident of a Contracting State from the alienation of immovable property referred to in Article 6 and situated in the other Contracting State may be taxed in that other State.
2. Gains from the alienation of movable property forming part of the business property of a permanent establishment which an enterprise of a Contracting State has in the other Contracting State or of movable property pertaining to a fixed base available to a resident of a Contracting State in the other Contracting State for the purpose of performing independent personal services, including such gains from the alienation of such a permanent establishment (alone or with the whole enterprise) or of such a fixed base, may be taxed in that other State.
3. Gains from the alienation of ships or aircraft operated in international traffic by an enterprise of a Contracting State, or movable property pertaining to the operation of such ships or aircraft, shall be taxable only in that Contracting State.
4. Gains derived by a resident of a Contracting State from the alienation of shares deriving more than 50 per cent of their value directly or indirectly from immovable property situated in the other Contracting State may be taxed in that other State.
5. Gains from the alienation of any property, other than that referred to in paragraphs 1 to 4, shall be taxable only in the Contracting State of which the alienator is a resident.

Article 14: Independent Personal Services

1. Income derived by a resident of a Contracting State in respect of professional services or other activities of an independent character shall be taxable only in that State except in the following circumstances, when such income may also be taxed in the other Contracting State:

   a. if he has a fixed base regularly available to him in the other Contracting State for the purpose of performing his activities; in that case, only so much of the income as is attributable to that fixed base may be taxed in that other State; or

b. if his stay in the other Contracting State is for a period or periods amounting to or exceeding in the aggregate 183 days in any twelve month period commencing or ending in the fiscal year concerned; in that case, only so much of the income as is derived from his activities performed in that other State may be taxed in that other State.

2. The term "professional services" includes especially independent scientific, literary, artistic, educational or teaching activities as well as the independent activities of physicians, lawyers, engineers, architects, dentists and accountants.

Article 15: Income from Employment

1. Subject to the provisions of Articles 16, 18, and 19, salaries, wages and other similar remuneration derived by a resident of a Contracting State in respect of an employment shall be taxable only in that State unless the employment is exercised in the other Contracting State. If the employment is so exercised, such remuneration as is derived therefrom may be taxed in that other State.
2. Notwithstanding the provisions of paragraph 1, remuneration derived by a resident of a Contracting State in respect of an employment exercised in the other Contracting State shall be taxable only in the first-mentioned State if:

   a. the recipient is present in the other State for a period or periods not exceeding in the aggregate 183 days in any twelve-month period commencing or ending in the fiscal year concerned, and
   b. the remuneration is paid by, or on behalf of, an employer who is not a resident of the other State, and
   c. the remuneration is not borne by a permanent establishment or a fixed base which the employer has in the other State.

3. Notwithstanding the preceding provisions of this Article, remuneration derived in respect of an employment exercised aboard a ship or aircraft operated in international traffic by an enterprise of a Contracting State, may be taxed in that Contracting State.

Article 16: Directors' Fees

Directors' fees and other similar payments derived by a resident of a Contracting State in his capacity as a member of the board of directors of a company which is a resident of the other Contracting State may be taxed in that other State.

Article 17: Artistes and Sportsman

1. Notwithstanding the provisions of Articles 7, 14 and 15, income derived by a resident of a Contracting State as an entertainer, such as a theatre, motion picture, radio or television artiste, or a musician, or as a sportsman, from his personal activities as such exercised in the other Contracting State, may be taxed in that other State.

2. Where income in respect of personal activities exercised by an entertainer or a sportsman in his capacity as such accrues not to the entertainer or sportsman himself but to another person, that income may, notwithstanding the provisions of Articles 7, 14 and 15, be taxed in the Contracting State in which the activities of the entertainer or sportsman are exercised.
3. Notwithstanding the provisions of paragraphs 1 and 2, income derived from such activities as are referred to in paragraph 1 performed under a cultural agreement or arrangement between the Contracting States shall be exempt from tax in the Contracting State in which the activities are exercised if the visit to that State is wholly or substantially supported by public or government funds of either Contracting State.

Article 18: Pensions

1. Subject to the provisions of paragraph 2 of Article 19, pensions and other similar remuneration paid to a resident of a Contracting State in consideration of past employment shall be taxable only in that State.
2. Notwithstanding the provisions of paragraph 1, pensions paid, and other similar payments made by the Government of a Contracting State or a local authority thereof under a public welfare scheme of the social security system of that State shall be taxable only in that State.

Article 19: Government Service

a. Salaries, wages and other similar remuneration, other than a pension, paid by a Contracting State or a political subdivision or a local authority thereof to an individual in respect of services rendered to that State or subdivision or authority, shall be taxable only in that State.
b. However, such salaries, wages and other similar remuneration shall be taxable only in the other Contracting State if the services are rendered in that State and the individual is a resident of that State who:

   i. is a national of that State; or
   ii. did not become a resident of that State solely for the purpose of rendering the services.

c. Pensions and other similar remuneration paid by, or out of funds created by, a Contracting State or a political subdivision or a local authority thereof to an individual in respect of services rendered to that State or subdivision or authority shall be taxable only in that State.
d. However, such pensions and other similar remuneration shall be taxable only in the other Contracting State if the individual is a resident of, and a national of, that State.

e. The provisions of Articles 15, 16, 17, and 18 shall apply to salaries, wages, pensions, and other similar remuneration in respect of services rendered in connection with a business carried on by a Contracting State or a political subdivision or a local authority thereof.

Article 20: Students

Payments which a student who is or was immediately before visiting a Contracting State a resident of the other Contracting State and who is present in the first-mentioned State solely for the purpose of his education receives for the purpose of his maintenance or education shall not be taxed in that State, provided that such payments arise from sources outside that State.

Article 21: Other Income

1. Items of income of a resident of a Contracting State, wherever arising, not dealt with in the foregoing Articles of this Agreement shall be taxable only in that State.
2. The provisions of paragraph 1 shall not apply to income, other than income from immovable property as defined in paragraph 2 of Article 6, if the recipient of such income, being a resident of a Contracting State, carries on business in the other Contracting State through a permanent establishment situated therein, or performs in that other State independent personal services from a fixed base situated therein, and the right or property in respect of which the income is paid is effectively connected with such permanent establishment or fixed base. In such case the provisions of Article 7 or Article 14, as the case may be, shall apply.
3. The provision of this Article shall not apply if it was the main purpose or one of the main purposes of any person concerned with the creation or assignment of the rights in respect of which the income is paid to take advantage of this Article by means of that creation or assignment.

Article 22: Methods for Elimination of Double Taxation

1. In China, in accordance with the provisions of the law of China, double taxation shall be eliminated as follows:
   a. Where a resident of China derives income from Botswana, the amount of tax on that income payable in Botswana in accordance with the provisions of this Agreement may be credited against the Chinese tax imposed on that resident. The amount of the credit, however, shall not exceed the amount of the Chinese tax on that income computed in accordance with the taxation laws and regulations of China.
   b. Where the income derived from Botswana is dividend paid by a company which is a resident of Botswana to a company which is a resident of China and which owns not less than 20 per cent of the shares of the company paying the dividend, the credit shall take into account the tax paid to Botswana by the company paying the dividend in respect of its income.

2. In Botswana, double taxation shall be eliminated as follows: Subject to the provisions of the laws of Botswana regarding the allowance of a credit against Botswana tax of tax payable under the laws of a country outside Botswana, China tax payable under the laws of China and in accordance with this Agreement, whether directly or by deduction, on profits or income liable to tax in China shall be allowed as a credit against any Botswana tax payable in respect of the same profits or income by reference to which the China tax is computed. However, the amount of such credit shall not exceed the amount of the Botswana tax payable on that income in accordance with the laws of Botswana.

Article 23: Miscellaneous Rule

Nothing in this Agreement shall prejudice the right of each Contracting State to apply its domestic laws and measures concerning the prevention of tax avoidance, whether or not described as such, insofar as they do not give rise to taxation contrary to this Agreement.

Article 24: Non-Discrimination

1. Nationals of a Contracting State shall not be subjected in the other Contracting State to any taxation or any requirement connected therewith, which is other or more burdensome than the taxation and connected requirements to which nationals of that other State in the same circumstances, in particular with respect to residence, are or may be subjected. This provision shall, notwithstanding the provisions of Article 1, also apply to persons who are not residents of one or both of the Contracting States.
2. The taxation on a permanent establishment which an enterprise of a Contracting State has in the other Contracting State shall not be less favourably levied in that other State than the taxation levied on enterprises of that other State carrying on the same activities. This provision shall not be construed as obliging a Contracting State to grant to residents of the other Contracting State any personal allowances, reliefs and reductions for taxation purposes on account of civil status or family responsibilities which it grants to its own residents.
3. Except where the provisions of paragraph 1 of Article 9, paragraph 7 of Article 11, or paragraph 6 of Article 12, apply, interest, royalties and other disbursements paid by an enterprise of a Contracting State to a resident of the other Contracting State shall, for the purpose of determining the taxable profits of such enterprise, be deductible under the same conditions as if they had been paid to a resident of the first-mentioned State. Similarly, any debts of an enterprise of a Contracting State to a resident of the other Contracting State shall, for the purpose of determining the taxable capital of such enterprise, be deductible under the same conditions as if they had been contracted to a resident of the first-mentioned State.
4. Enterprises of a Contracting State, the capital of which is wholly or partly owned or controlled, directly or indirectly, by one or more residents of the other Contracting State, shall not be subjected in the first-mentioned State to

any taxation or any requirement connected therewith which is other or more burdensome than the taxation and connected requirements to which other similar enterprises of the first-mentioned State are or may be subjected.

5. The provisions of the Article shall, notwithstanding the provisions of Article 2, apply to taxes of every kind and description.

Article 25: Mutual Agreement Procedure

1. Where a person considers that the actions of one or both of the Contracting States result or will result for him in taxation not in accordance with the provisions of this Agreement, he may, irrespective of the remedies provided by the domestic law of those States, present his case to the competent authority of the Contracting State of which he is a resident or, if his case comes under paragraph 1 of Article 24, to that of the Contracting State of which he is a national. The case must be presented within three years from the first notification of the action resulting in taxation not in accordance with the provisions of the Agreement.
2. The competent authority shall endeavour, if the objection appears to it to be justified and if it is not itself able to arrive at a satisfactory solution, to resolve the case by mutual agreement with the competent authority of the other Contracting State, with a view to the avoidance of taxation which is not in accordance with the Agreement. Any agreement reached shall be implemented notwithstanding any time limits in the domestic law of the Contracting States.
3. The competent authorities of the Contracting States shall endeavour to resolve by mutual agreement any difficulties or doubts arising as to the interpretation or application of the Agreement. They may also consult together for the elimination of double taxation in cases not provided for in the Agreement.
4. The competent authorities of the Contracting States may communicate with each other directly for the purpose of reaching an agreement in the sense of paragraphs 2 and 3. When it seems advisable for reaching an agreement, representatives of the competent authorities of the Contracting States may meet together for an oral exchange of opinions.

Article 26: Exchange of Information

1. The competent authorities of the Contracting States shall exchange such information as is foreseeably relevant for carrying out the provisions of this Agreement or to the administration or enforcement of the domestic laws concerning taxes of every kind and description imposed on behalf of the Contracting States, or of their political subdivisions or local authorities, insofar as the taxation thereunder is not contrary to the Agreement. The exchange of information is not restricted by Articles 1 and 2.
2. Any information received under paragraph 1 by a Contracting State shall be treated as secret in the same manner as information obtained under the domestic laws of that State and shall be disclosed only to persons or authorities (including courts and administrative bodies) concerned with the assessment or collection

of, the enforcement or prosecution in respect of, the determination of appeals in relation to the taxes referred to in paragraph 1, or the oversight of the above. Such persons or authorities shall use the information only for such purposes. They may disclose the information in public court proceedings or in judicial decisions.

3. In no case shall the provisions of paragraphs 1 and 2 be construed so as to impose on a Contracting State the obligation:

   a. to carry out administrative measures at variance with the laws and administrative practice of that or of the other Contracting State;
   b. to supply information which is not obtainable under the laws or in the normal course of the administration of that or of the other Contracting State;
   c. to supply information which would disclose any trade, business, industrial, commercial or professional secret or trade process, or information, the disclosure of which would be contrary to public policy (ordre public).

4. If information is requested by a Contracting State in accordance with this Article, the other Contracting State shall use its information gathering measures to obtain the requested information, even though that other State may not need such information for its own tax purposes. The obligation contained in the preceding sentence is subject to the limitations of paragraph 3 but in no case shall such limitations be construed to permit a Contracting State to decline to supply information solely because it has no domestic interest in such information.
5. In no case shall the provisions of paragraph 3 be construed to permit a Contracting State to decline to supply information solely because the information is held by a bank, other financial institution, nominee or person acting in an agency or a fiduciary capacity or because it relates to ownership interests in a person.

Article 27: Assistance in the Collection of Taxes

1. The Contracting States shall endeavour to lend assistance to each other in the collection of revenue claims. The competent authorities of the Contracting States may by mutual agreement settle the mode of application of this Article.
2. In no case shall the provision of this Article be construed so as to impose on a Contracting State the obligations:

   a. to carry out administrative measures at variance with the law and administrative practice of that or of the other Contracting State;
   b. to carry out measures which would be contrary to public policy (order public).

Article 28: Members of Diplomatic Missions and Consular Posts

Nothing in this Agreement shall affect the fiscal privileges of members of diplomatic missions or consular posts under the general rules of international law or under the provisions of special agreements.

Article 29: Entry into Force

1. Both Contracting States shall notify each other through diplomatic channels that they have completed the internal legal procedures necessary for the entry into force of this Agreement. This Agreement shall enter into force on the date of receipt of the latter notification.
2. The provisions of this Agreement shall apply:

    a. In China, in respect of income derived during the taxable years beginning on or after the first day of January next following that in which this Agreement enters into force; and
    b. In Botswana:
        i. with regard to taxes withheld at source, with respect to amounts credited on or after the thirtieth day following the date upon which the Agreement enters into force; and
        ii. with regard to other taxes, on taxable income derived on or after the first day of July of the year next following that of the entry into force of this Agreement.

Article 30: Termination

1. This Agreement shall continue in effect indefinitely but either of the Contracting States may, after the expiration of a period of five years from the date of its entry into force, give written notice of termination to the other Contracting State through diplomatic channels.
2. In such event, this Agreement shall cease to have effect:

    a. In China, in respect of income derived during the taxable years beginning on or after the first day of January next following that in which the notice of termination is given; and
    b. In Botswana:
        i. with regard to taxes withheld at source, with respect to amounts credited on or after the thirtieth day following the date upon which the notice of termination is given; and
        ii. with regard to other taxes, on taxable income derived on or after the first day of July of the year next following that in which the notice of termination is given.

IN WITNESS whereof the undersigned, duly authorized thereto, have signed this Agreement.

Done at Gaborone on the 11th day of April 2012, in duplicate in the Chinese and English languages, both texts being equally authentic.

For the Government of the People's Republic of China

Xiao Jie
For the Government of The Republic of Botswana
Kenneth Matambo

Mauritius

Agreement Between the Government of the People's Republic of China and the Government of the Republic of Mauritius for the Avoidance of Double Taxation and the Prevention of Fiscal Evasion with Respect to Taxes on Income

The Government of the People's Republic of China and the Government of the Republic of Mauritius;

Desiring to conclude an Agreement for the avoidance of double taxation and the prevention of fiscal evasion with respect to taxes on income;

Have agreed as follows:

Article 1: Personal Scope

This Agreement shall apply to persons who are residents of one or both of the Contracting States.

Article 2: Taxes Covered

1. This Agreement shall apply to taxes on income imposed on behalf of a Contracting State or of its local authorities, irrespective of the manner in which they are levied.
2. There shall be regarded as taxes on income all taxes imposed on total income, or on elements of income, including taxes on gains from the alienation of movable or immovable property, as well as taxes on capital appreciation.
3. The existing taxes to which this Agreement shall apply are:
    a. in the People's Republic of China:
        i. the individual income tax;
        ii. the income tax for enterprises with foreign investment and foreign enterprises;
        iii. the local income tax; (hereinafter referred to as "Chinese tax")
    b. in the Republic of Mauritius:
    the income tax;
    (hereinafter referred to as "Mauritius tax")

L. Riccardi and G. Riccardi, *China in Africa*,
https://doi.org/10.1007/978-981-16-1148-3

4. This Agreement shall also apply to any identical or substantially similar taxes which are imposed after the date of signature of this Agreement in addition to, or in place of, the existing taxes referred to in paragraph 3. The competent authorities of the Contracting States shall notify each other of any substantial changes which have been made in their respective taxation laws within a reasonable period of time after such changes.

Article 3: General Definitions

1. For the purposes of this Agreement, unless the context otherwise requires:

   a. the term "China" means the People's Republic of China; when used in geographical sense, means all the territory of the People's Republic of China, including its territorial sea, in which the Chinese laws relating to taxation apply, and any area beyond its territorial sea, within which the People's Republic of China has sovereign rights of exploration for and exploitation of resources of the seabed and its sub-soil and super jacent water resources in accordance with international law;

   b. the term "Mauritius" means the Republic of Mauritius and includes:

      i. all the territories and islands which, in accordance with the laws of Mauritius, constitute the State of Mauritius;

      ii. the territorial sea of Mauritius; and

      iii. any area outside the territorial sea of Mauritius which in accordance with international law has been or may hereafter be designated, under the laws of Mauritius, as an area, including the Continental Shelf, within which the rights of Mauritius with respect to the sea, the seabed and sub-soil and their natural resources may be exercised;

   c. the terms "a Contracting State" and "the other Contracting State" mean China or Mauritius as the context requires;

   d. the term "tax" means Chinese tax or Mauritius tax, as the context requires;

   e. the term "person" includes an individual, a company, any other body of persons as well as any entity treated as a taxable unit under the taxation laws in force in either Contracting State;

   f. the term "company" means anybody corporate or any entity which is treated as a body corporate for tax purposes;

   g. the terms "enterprise of a Contracting State" and "enterprise of the other Contracting State" mean, respectively, an enterprise carried on by a resident of a Contracting State and an enterprise carried on by a resident of the other Contracting State;

   h. the term "nationals" means:

      i. in relation to China, all individuals possessing the nationality of China and all juridical persons created or organized under the laws of China, as well as organizations without juridical personality treated for tax purposes as juridical persons created or organized under the laws of China;

ii. in relation to Mauritius, all individuals who are citizens of Mauritius and all legal persons, partnerships, associations or other entities deriving their status as such from the laws of Mauritius;

i. the term "international traffic" means any transport by a ship or aircraft operated by an enterprise which is a resident of a Contracting State, except when the ship or aircraft is operated solely between places in the other Contracting State;

j. the term "competent authority" means, in the case of China, the State Administration of Taxation or its authorized representative, and in the case of Mauritius, the Commissioner of Income Tax or his authorized representative.

2. As regards the application of this Agreement by a Contracting State, any term not defined therein shall, unless the context otherwise requires, have the meaning which it has under the laws of that Contracting State concerning the taxes to which this Agreement applies.

Article 4: Resident

1. For the purposes of this Agreement, the term "resident of a Contracting State" means any person who, under the laws of that Contracting State, is liable to tax therein by reason of his domicile, residence, place of head office or place of effective management or any other criterion of a similar nature.
2. Whereby reason of the provisions of paragraph 1 an individual is a resident of both Contracting States, then his status shall be determined as follows:

    a. he shall be deemed to be a resident of the Contracting State in which he has a permanent home available to him; if he has a permanent home available to him in both Contracting States, he shall be deemed to be a resident of the Contracting State with which his personal and economic relations are closer (centre of vital interests);
    b. if the Contracting State in which he has his centre of vital interests cannot be determined, or if he has not a permanent home available to him in either Contracting State, he shall be deemed to be a resident of the State in which he has an habitual abode;
    c. if he has a habitual abode in both Contracting States or in neither of them, he shall be deemed to be a resident of the Contracting State of which he is a national;
    d. if he is a national of both Contracting States or of neither of them, the competent authorities of the Contracting States shall settle the question by mutual agreement.

3. Where by reason of the provisions of paragraph 1 a person other than an individual is a resident of both Contracting States, then it shall be deemed to be a resident of the Contracting State in which its place of head office or place of effective management is situated. However, where such a person has its place

of effective management in a Contracting State and its place of head office in the other Contracting State, the competent authorities of the Contracting States shall by mutual agreement determine the State of which the person in question is a resident.

Article 5: Permanent Establishment

1. For the purposes of this Agreement, the term "permanent establishment" means a fixed place of business through which the business of an enterprise is wholly or partly carried on.
2. The term "permanent establishment" includes especially:

   a. a place of management;
   b. a branch;
   c. an office;
   d. a factory;
   e. a workshop;
   f. a warehouse, in relation to a person providing storage facilities for others;
   g. a mine, an oil or gas well, a quarry or any other place of extraction of natural resources; and
   h. a farm or plantation.

3. The term "permanent establishment" likewise encompasses:

   a. a building site, a construction, assembly or installation project or supervisory activities in connection therewith, but only where such site, project or activities continue for a period of more than 12 months;
   b. the furnishing of services, including consultancy services, by an enterprise of a Contracting State through employees or other personnel engaged in the other Contracting State, provided that such activities continue for the same project or a connected project for a period or periods aggregating more than 12 months within any 24-month period.

4. Notwithstanding the preceding provisions of paragraphs 1 to 3, the term "permanent establishment" shall be deemed not to include:

   a. the use of facilities solely for the purpose of storage, display or delivery of goods or merchandise belonging to the enterprise;
   b. the maintenance of a stock of goods or merchandise belonging to the enterprise solely for the purpose of storage, display or delivery;
   c. the maintenance of a stock of goods or merchandise belonging to the enterprise solely for the purpose of processing by another enterprise;
   d. the maintenance of a fixed place of business solely for the purpose of purchasing goods or merchandise or of collecting information, for the enterprise;
   e. the maintenance of a fixed place of business solely for the purpose of advertising, for the supply of information, for scientific research or for

similar activities which have a preparatory or auxiliary character, for the enterprise;

f. the maintenance of a fixed place of business solely for any combination of activities mentioned in sub-paragraphs (a) to (e), provided that the overall activity of the fixed place of business resulting from this combination is of a preparatory or auxiliary character.

5. Notwithstanding the provisions of paragraphs 1 and 2, where a person—other than an agent of an independent status to whom the provisions of paragraph 6 apply—is acting in a Contracting State on behalf of an enterprise of the other Contracting State, has and habitually exercises an authority to conclude contracts in the name of the enterprise, that enterprise shall be deemed to have a permanent establishment in the first-mentioned Contracting State in respect of any activities which that person undertakes for the enterprise, unless the activities of such person are limited to those mentioned in paragraph 4 which, if exercised through a fixed place of business, would not make this fixed place of business a permanent establishment under the provisions of that paragraph.
6. An enterprise of a Contracting State shall not be deemed to have a permanent establishment in the other Contracting State merely because it carries on business in that other Contracting State through a broker, a general commission agent or any other agent of an independent status, provided that such persons are acting in the ordinary course of their business. However, when the activities of such an agent are devoted wholly or almost wholly on behalf of that enterprise, he will not be considered an agent of an independent status within the meaning of this paragraph.
7. The fact that a company which is a resident of a Contracting State controls or is controlled by a company which is a resident of the other Contracting State, or which carries on business in that other State (whether through a permanent establishment or otherwise), shall not of itself constitute either company a permanent establishment of the other.

Article 6: Income from Immovable Property

1. Income derived by a resident of a Contracting State from immovable property situated in the other Contracting State may be taxed in that other Contracting State.
2. The term "immovable property" shall have the meaning which it has under the law of the Contracting State in which the property in question is situated. The term shall in any case include property accessory to immovable property, livestock and equipment used in agriculture and forestry, rights to which the provisions of general law respecting landed property apply, usufruct of immovable property and rights to variable or fixed payments as consideration for the working of, or the right to work, mineral deposits, sources and other natural resources. Ships and aircraft shall not be regarded as immovable property.

3. The provisions of paragraph 1 shall apply to income derived from the direct use, letting, or use in any other form of immovable property.
4. The provisions of paragraphs 1 and 3 shall also apply to the income from immovable property of an enterprise and to income from immovable property used for the performance of independent personal services.

Article 7: Business Profits

1. The profits of an enterprise of a Contracting State shall be taxable only in that Contracting State unless the enterprise carries on business in the other Contracting State through a permanent establishment situated therein. If the enterprise carries on business as aforesaid, the profits of the enterprise may be taxed in the other Contracting State but only so much of them as is attributable to that permanent establishment.
2. Subject to the provisions of paragraph 3, where an enterprise of a Contracting State carries on business in the other Contracting State through a permanent establishment situated therein, there shall in each Contracting State be attributed to that permanent establishment the profits which it might be expected to make if it were a distinct and separate enterprise engaged in the same or similar activities under the same or similar conditions and dealing wholly independently with the enterprise of which it is a permanent establishment.
3. In determining the profits of a permanent establishment, there shall be allowed as deductions expenses which are incurred for the purposes of the business of the permanent establishment, including executive and general administrative expenses so incurred, whether in the State in which the permanent establishment is situated or elsewhere.
4. Insofar as it has been customary in a Contracting State to determine the profits to be attributed to a permanent establishment on the basis of an apportionment of the total profits of the enterprise to its various parts, nothing in paragraph 2 shall preclude that Contracting State from determining the profits to be taxed by such an apportionment as may be customary. The method of apportionment adopted shall, however, be such that the result shall be in accordance with the principles contained in this Article.
5. No profits shall be attributed to a permanent establishment by reason of the mere purchase by that permanent establishment of goods or merchandise for the enterprise.
6. For the purposes of paragraphs 1 to 5, the profits to be attributed to the permanent establishment shall be determined by the same method year by year unless there is good and sufficient reason to the contrary.
7. Where profits include items of income which are dealt with separately in other Articles of this Agreement, then the provisions of those Articles shall not be affected by the provisions of this Article.

Article 8: Shipping and Air Transport

1. Profits derived by an enterprise which is a resident of a Contracting State from the operation of ships or aircraft in international traffic shall be taxable only in that Contracting State.
2. The provisions of paragraph 1 shall also apply to profits from the participation in a pool, a joint business or an international operating agency.

Article 9: Associated Enterprises

1. Where:
   a. an enterprise of a Contracting State participates directly or indirectly in the management, control or capital of an enterprise of the other Contracting state, or
   b. the same persons participate directly or indirectly in the management, control or capital of an enterprise of a Contracting State and an enterprise of the other Contracting State, and in either case conditions are made or imposed between the two enterprises in their commercial or financial relations which differ from those which would be made between independent enterprises, then any profits which would, but for those conditions, have accrued to one of the enterprises, but, by reason of those conditions, have not so accrued, may be included in the profits of that enterprise and taxed accordingly.
2. Where a Contracting State includes in the profits of an enterprise of that Contracting State and taxes accordingly profits on which an enterprise of the other Contracting State has been charged to tax in that other Contracting State, and the profits so included are profits which would have accrued to the enterprise of the first-mentioned Contracting State if the conditions made between the two enterprises had been those which would have been made between independent enterprises, then that other State shall make an appropriate adjustment to the amount of tax charged therein on those profits. In determining such adjustment, due regard shall be had to the other provisions of this Agreement and the competent authorities of the Contracting States shall, if necessary, consult each other.

Article 10: Dividends

1. Dividends paid by a company which is a resident of a Contracting State to a resident of the other Contracting State may be taxed in that other Contracting State.
2. However, such dividends may also be taxed in the Contracting State of which the company paying the dividends is a resident and according to the laws of that Contracting State, but if the recipient is the beneficial owner of the dividends the tax so charged shall not exceed 5 per cent of the gross amount of the dividends.

The provisions of this paragraph shall not affect the taxation of the company in respect of the profits out of which the dividends are paid.

3. The term "**dividends**" as used in this Article means income from shares, or other rights, not being debt-claims, participating in profits, as well as income from other corporate rights which is subjected to the same taxation treatment as income from shares by the laws of the State of which the company making the distribution is a resident.
4. The provisions of paragraphs 1 and 2 shall not apply if the beneficial owner of the dividends, being a resident of a Contracting State, carries on business in the other Contracting State of which the company paying the dividends is a resident, through a permanent establishment situated therein, or performs in that other Contracting State independent personal services from a fixed base situated therein, and the holding in respect of which the dividends are paid is effectively connected with such permanent establishment or fixed base. In such case the provisions of Article 7 or Article 14, as the case may be, shall apply.
5. Where a company which is a resident of a Contracting State derives profits or income from the other Contracting State, that other Contracting State may not impose any tax on the dividends paid by the company, except insofar as such dividends are paid to a resident of that other Contracting State or insofar as the holding in respect of which the dividends are paid is effectively connected with a permanent establishment or a fixed base situated in that other Contracting State, nor subject the company's undistributed profits to a tax on the company's undistributed profits, even if the dividends paid or the undistributed profits consist wholly or partly of profits or income arising in such other Contracting State.

Article 11: Interest

1. Interest arising in a Contracting State and paid to a resident of the other Contracting State may be taxed in that other Contracting State.
2. However, such interest may also be taxed in the Contracting State in which it arises and according to the laws of that Contracting State, but if the recipient is the beneficial owner of the interest the tax so charged shall not exceed 10 per cent of the gross amount of the interest.
3. Notwithstanding the provisions of paragraph 2, interest arising in a Contracting State and derived by the Government of the other Contracting State, a local authority and the Central Bank thereof or any financial institution wholly owned by that Government, or by any other financial institution agreed upon by that competent authorities of the Contracting States, or by any other resident of that other Contracting State with respect to debt-claims indirectly financed by the Government of that other Contracting State, a local authority, and the Central Bank thereof or any financial institution wholly owned by the Government, or by any other financial institution agreed upon by the competent authorities of the Contracting States shall be exempt from tax in the first-mentioned Contracting State.

4. The term "interest" as used in this Article means income from debt-claims of every kind, whether or not secured by mortgage and whether or not carrying a right to participate in the debtor's profits, and in particular, income from government securities and income from bonds or debentures, including premiums and prizes attaching to such securities, bonds or debentures. Penalty charges for late payment shall not be regarded as interest for the purpose of this Article.
5. The provisions of paragraphs 1, 2 and 3 shall not apply if the beneficial owner of the interest, being a resident of a Contracting State, carries on business in the other Contracting State in which the interest arises, through a permanent establishment situated therein, or performs in that other Contracting State independent personal services from a fixed base situated therein, and the debt-claim in respect of which the interest is paid is effectively connected with such permanent establishment or fixed base. In such case the provisions of Article 7 or Article 14, as the case may be, shall apply.
6. Interest shall be deemed to arise in a Contracting State when the payer is the Government of that Contracting State, a local authority thereof or a resident of that Contracting State. Where, however, the person paying the interest, whether he is a resident of a Contracting State or not, has in a Contracting State a permanent establishment or a fixed base in connection with which the indebtedness on which the interest is paid was incurred, and such interest is borne by such permanent establishment or fixed base, then such interest shall be deemed to arise in the Contracting State in which the permanent establishment or fixed base is situated.
7. Where, by reason of a special relationship between the payer and the beneficial owner or between both of them and some other person, the amount of the interest, having regard to the debt-claim for which it is paid, exceeds the amount which would have been agreed upon by the payer and the beneficial owner in the absence of such relationship, the provisions of this Article shall apply only to the last-mentioned amount. In such case, the excess part of the payments shall remain taxable according to the laws of each Contracting State, due regard being had to the other provisions of this Agreement.

Article 12: Royalties

1. Royalties arising in a Contracting State and paid to a resident of the other Contracting State may be taxed in that other Contracting State.
2. However, such royalties may also be taxed in the Contracting State in which they arise, and according to the laws of that Contracting State, but if the recipient is the beneficial owner of the royalties, the tax so charged shall not exceed 10 per cent of the gross amount of the royalties.
3. The term "royalties" as used in this Article means payments of any kind received as a consideration for the use of, or the right to use, any copyright of literary, artistic or scientific work including cinematograph films and films or tapes for radio or television broadcasting, any patent, trade mark, design or model, plan, secret formula or process, or for the use of, or the right to use, industrial,

commercial or scientific equipment, or for information concerning industrial, commercial or scientific experience.

4. The provisions of paragraphs 1 and 2 shall not apply if the beneficial owner of the royalties, being a resident of a Contracting State, carries on business in the other Contracting State in which the royalties arise, through a permanent establishment situated therein, or performs in that other Contracting State independent personal services from a fixed base situated therein, and the right or property in respect of which the royalties are paid is effectively connected with such permanent establishment or fixed base. In such case the provisions of Article 7 or Article 14, as the case may be, shall apply.
5. Royalties shall be deemed to arise in a Contracting State when the payer is the Government of that Contracting State, a local authority thereof or a resident of that Contracting State. Where, however, the person paying the royalties, whether he is a resident of a Contracting State or not, has in a Contracting State a permanent establishment or a fixed base in connection with which the liability to pay the royalties was incurred, and such royalties are borne by such permanent establishment or fixed base, then such royalties shall be deemed to arise in the Contracting State in which the permanent establishment or fixed base is situated.
6. Where, by reason of a special relationship between the payer and the beneficial owner or between both of them and some other person, the amount of the royalties, having regard to the use, right or information for which they are paid, exceeds the amount which would have been agreed upon by the payer and the beneficial owner in the absence of such relationship, the provisions of this Article shall apply only to the last-mentioned amount. In such case, the excess part of the payments shall remain taxable according to the laws of each Contracting State, due regard being had to the other provisions of this Agreement.

Article 13: Capital Gains

1. Gains derived by a resident of a Contracting State from the alienation of immovable property referred to in Article 6 and situated in the other Contracting State may be taxed in that other Contracting State.
2. Gains from the alienation of movable property forming part of the business property of a permanent establishment which an enterprise of a Contracting State has in the other Contracting State or of movable property pertaining to a fixed base available to a resident of a Contracting State in the other Contracting State for the purpose of performing independent personal services, including such gains from the alienation of such a permanent establishment (alone or together with the whole enterprise) or of such a fixed base, may be taxed in that other Contracting State.
3. Gains derived by an enterprise which is a resident of a Contracting State from the alienation of ships or aircraft operated in international traffic or movable property pertaining to the operation of such ships or aircraft shall be taxable only in that Contracting State.

4. Gains from the alienation of shares of the capital stock of a company the property of which consists directly or indirectly principally of immovable property situated in a Contracting State may be taxed in that Contracting State. 5. Gains from the alienation of any property other than that referred to in paragraphs 1 to 4, shall be taxable only in the Contracting State of which the alienator is a resident.

Article 14: Independent Personal Services

Income derived by a resident of a Contracting State in respect of professional services or other activities of an independent character shall be taxable only in that Contracting State except in one of the following circumstances, when such income may also be taxed in the other Contracting State:

a. if he has a fixed base regularly available to him in the other Contracting State for the purpose of performing his activities; in that case, only so much of the income as is attributable to that fixed base may be taxed in that other Contracting State; or
b. if his stay in the other Contracting State is for a period or periods exceeding in the aggregate 183 days in any 12-month period; in that case, only so much of the income as is derived from his activities performed in that other Contracting State may be taxed in that other Contracting State.

The term "professional services" includes especially independent scientific, literary, artistic, educational or teaching activities as well as the independent activities of physicians, lawyers, engineers, architects, dentists and accountants.

Article 15: Dependent Personal Services

1. Subject to the provisions of Articles 16, 18, 19, 20 and 21, salaries, wages and other similar remuneration derived by a resident of a Contracting State in respect of an employment shall be taxable only in that Contracting State unless the employment is exercised in the other Contracting State. If the employment is so exercised, such remuneration as is derived therefrom may be taxed in that other Contracting State.
2. Notwithstanding the provisions of paragraph 1, remuneration derived by a resident of a Contracting State in respect of an employment exercised in the other Contracting State shall be taxable only in the first-mentioned State if:

    a. the recipient is present in the other Contracting State for a period or periods not exceeding in the aggregate 183 days in any 12-month period; and
    b. the remuneration is paid by, or on behalf of, an employer who is not a resident of the other Contracting State; and
    c. the remuneration is not borne by a permanent establishment or a fixed base which the employer has in the other Contracting State.

3. Notwithstanding the preceding provisions of paragraphs 1 and 2 of this article, remuneration derived in respect of an employment exercised aboard a ship or

aircraft operated by an enterprise which is a resident of a Contracting State in international traffic, shall be taxable only in that Contracting State.

Article 16: Directors' Fees

Directors' fees and other similar payments derived by a resident of a Contracting State in his capacity as a member of the board of directors of a company which is a resident of the other Contracting State may be taxed in that other Contracting State.

Article 17: Artistes and Athletes

1. Notwithstanding the provisions of Articles 14 and 15, income derived by a resident of a Contracting State as an entertainer, such as a theatre, motion picture, radio or television artiste, or a musician, or as an athlete, from his personal activities as such exercised in the other Contracting State, may be taxed in that other Contracting State.
2. Where income in respect of personal activities exercised by an entertainer or an athlete in his capacity as such accrues not to the entertainer or athlete himself but to another person, that income may, notwithstanding the provisions of Articles 7, 14 and 15, be taxed in the Contracting State in which the activities of the entertainer or athlete are exercised.
3. Notwithstanding the provisions of paragraphs 1 and 2, income derived by entertainers or athletes who are residents of a Contracting State from the activities exercised in the other Contracting State under a plan of cultural exchange between the Governments, local authorities or wholly or substantially government-funded bodies of both Contracting States shall be exempt from tax in that other Contracting State.

Article 18: Pensions

1. Subject to the provisions of paragraph 2 of Article 19, pensions and other similar remuneration paid to a resident of a Contracting State in consideration of past employment shall be taxable only in that Contracting State.
2. Notwithstanding the provisions of paragraph 1, pensions paid and other similar payments made by the Government of a Contracting State or a local authority thereof under a public welfare scheme of the social security system of that Contracting State shall be taxable only in that Contracting State.

Article 19: Government Service

a. Remuneration, other than a pension, paid by the Government of a Contracting State or a local authority thereof to an individual in respect of services rendered to the Government of that Contracting State or a local authority thereof, in the discharge of functions of a governmental nature, shall be taxable only in that Contracting State.

b. However, such remuneration shall be taxable only in the other Contracting State if the services are rendered in that other Contracting State and the individual is a resident of that other Contracting State who:

  i. is a national of that other Contracting State; or
  ii. did not become a resident of that other Contracting State solely for the purpose of rendering the services.

c. Any pension paid by, or out of funds to which contributions are made by the Government of a Contracting State or a local authority thereof to an individual in respect of services rendered to the Government of that 16 Contracting State or a local authority thereof shall be taxable only in that Contracting State.
d. However, such pension shall be taxable only in the other Contracting State if the individual is a resident of, and a national of, that other Contracting State.
e. The provisions of Articles 15, 16, 17 and 18 shall apply to remuneration and pensions in respect of services rendered in connection with a business carried on by the Government of a Contracting State or a local authority thereof.

Article 20: Teachers and Researchers

An individual who is, or immediately before visiting a Contracting State was, a resident of the other Contracting State and is present in the first-mentioned Contracting State for the primary purpose of teaching, giving lectures or conducting research at a university, college, school or educational institution or scientific research institution approved by the Government of the first-mentioned Contracting State shall be exempt from tax in the first-mentioned Contracting State, for a period of two years from the date of his first arrival in the first-mentioned Contracting State, in respect of remuneration for such teaching, lectures or research.

Article 21: Students and Trainees

A student, business apprentice or trainee who is or was immediately before visiting a Contracting State a resident of the other Contracting State and who is present in the first-mentioned State solely for the purpose of his education or training shall be exempt from tax in that first-mentioned State on the following payments or income received or derived by him for the purpose of his maintenance, education or training:

a. payments derived from sources outside that Contracting State for the purpose of his maintenance, education, study, research or training;
b. grants, scholarships or awards supplied by the Government, or a scientific, educational, cultural or other tax-exempt organization; and
c. income derived from personal services performed in that Contracting State.

Article 22: Other Income

1. Items of income of a resident of a Contracting State, wherever arising, not dealt with in the foregoing Articles of this Agreement shall be taxable only in that Contracting State.
2. The provisions of paragraph 1 shall not apply to income, other than income from immovable property as defined in paragraph 2 of Article 6, if the recipient of such income, being a resident of a Contracting State, carries on business in the other Contracting State through a permanent establishment situated therein, or performs in that other Contracting State independent personal services from a fixed base situated therein, and the right or property in respect of which the income is paid is effectively connected with such permanent establishment or fixed base. In such case the provisions of Article 7 or Article 14, as the case may be, shall apply.

Article 23: Methods for The Elimination of Double Taxation

1. In China, double taxation shall be eliminated as follows:

   a. Where a resident of China derives income from Mauritius the amount of tax on that income payable in Mauritius in accordance with the provisions of this Agreement, may be credited against the Chinese tax imposed on that resident. The amount of credit, however, shall not exceed the amount of the Chinese tax on that income computed in accordance with the taxation laws and regulations of China.
   b. Where the income derived from Mauritius is a dividend paid by a company which is a resident of Mauritius to a company which is a resident of China and which owns not less than 10 per cent of the shares of the company paying the dividend, the credit shall take into account the tax paid in Mauritius by the company paying the dividend in respect of the profits out of which the dividend is paid.

2. In Mauritius, double taxation shall be eliminated as follows:

   a. Where a resident of Mauritius derives income from China, the amount of tax on that income payable in China in accordance with the provisions of this Agreement, may be credited against the Mauritius tax imposed on that resident. The amount of credit, however, shall not exceed the amount of the Mauritius tax on that income computed in accordance with the taxation laws and regulations of Mauritius.
   b. Where the income derived from China is a dividend paid by a company which is a resident of China to a company which is a resident of Mauritius and which owns not less than 10 per cent of the shares of the company paying the dividend, the credit shall take into account the tax paid in China by the company paying the dividend in respect of the profits out of which the dividend is paid.

3. The tax paid in a Contracting State mentioned in paragraphs 1 and 2 of this Article, shall be deemed to include the tax which would have been payable but for the legal provisions concerning tax reduction, exemption or other tax incentives of the Contracting State for the promotion of economic development.

Article 24: Non-Discrimination

1. Nationals of a Contracting State shall not be subjected in the other Contracting State to any taxation or any requirement connected therewith, which is other or more burdensome than the taxation and connected requirements to which nationals of that other Contracting State in the same circumstances are or may be subjected. The provisions of this paragraph shall, notwithstanding the provisions of Article 1, also apply to persons who are not residents of one or both of the Contracting States.
2. The taxation on a permanent establishment which an enterprise of a Contracting State has in the other Contracting State shall not be less favourably levied in that other Contracting State than the taxation levied on enterprises of that other Contracting State carrying on the same activities. The provisions of this paragraph shall not be construed as obliging a Contracting State to grant to residents of the other Contracting State any personal allowances, reliefs and reductions for taxation purposes on account of civil status or family responsibilities which it grants to its own residents.
3. Except where the provisions of Article 9, paragraph 7 of Article 11, or paragraph 6 of Article 12, apply, interest, royalties and other disbursements paid by an enterprise of a Contracting State to a resident of the other Contracting State shall, for the purpose of determining the taxable profits of such enterprise, be deductible under the same conditions as if they had been paid to a resident of the first-mentioned State.
4. Enterprises of a Contracting State, the capital of which is wholly or partly owned or controlled, directly or indirectly, by one or more residents of the other Contracting State, shall not be subjected in the first-mentioned State to any taxation or any requirement connected therewith which is other or more burdensome than the taxation and connected requirements to which other similar enterprises of the first-mentioned State are or may be subjected.
5. In this Article, the term "taxation" means taxes of every kind and description.

Article 25: Mutual Agreement Procedure

1. Where a person considers that the actions of one or both of the Contracting States result or will result for him in taxation not in accordance with the provisions of this Agreement, he may, irrespective of the remedies provided by the domestic law of those States, present his case to the competent authority of the Contracting State of which he is a resident or, if his case comes under paragraph 1 of Article 24, to that of the Contracting State of which he is a national. The case must be

presented within three years from the first notification of the action resulting in taxation not in accordance with the provisions of the Agreement.

2. The competent authority shall endeavour, if the objection appears to it to be justified and if it is not itself able to arrive at a satisfactory solution, to resolve the case by mutual agreement with the competent authority of the other Contracting State, with a view to the avoidance of taxation which is not in accordance with the provisions of this Agreement. Any agreement reached shall be implemented notwithstanding any time limits in the domestic law of the Contracting States.
3. The competent authorities of the Contracting States shall endeavour to resolve by mutual agreement any difficulties or doubts arising as to the interpretation or application of the Agreement. They may also consult together for the elimination of double taxation in cases not provided for in this Agreement. 4. The competent authorities of the Contracting States may communicate with each other directly for the purpose of reaching an agreement in the sense of the paragraphs 2 and 3. When it seems advisable for reaching agreement, representatives of the competent authorities of the Contracting States may meet together for an oral exchange of opinions.

Article 26: Exchange of Information

1. The competent authorities of the Contracting States shall exchange such information as is necessary for carrying out the provisions of this Agreement or of the domestic laws of the Contracting States concerning taxes covered by the Agreement, insofar as the taxation thereunder is not contrary to this Agreement, in particular for the prevention of evasion of such taxes. The exchange of information is not restricted by Article 1. Any information received by a Contracting State shall be treated as secret and shall be disclosed only to persons or authorities (including courts and administrative bodies) involved in the assessment or collection of, the enforcement or prosecution in respect of, or the determination of appeals in relation to, the taxes covered by the Agreement. Such persons or authorities shall use the information only for such purposes. They may disclose the information in public court proceedings or in judicial decisions.
2. In no case shall the provisions of paragraph 1 be construed so as to impose on a Contracting State the obligation:
    a. to carry out administrative measures at variance with the laws and administrative practice of that or of the other Contracting State;
    b. to supply information which is not obtainable under the laws or in the normal course of the administration of that or of the other Contracting State;
    c. to supply information which would disclose any trade, business, industrial, commercial or professional secret or trade process, or information, the disclosure of which would be contrary to public policy (order public).

Article 27: Diplomatic Agents and Consular Officers

Nothing in this Agreement shall affect the fiscal privileges of diplomatic agents or consular officer under the general rules of international law or under the provisions of special agreements.

Article 28: Entry into Force

This Agreement shall enter into force on the thirtieth day after the date on which diplomatic notes indicating the completion of internal legal procedures necessary in each country for the entry into force of this Agreement have been exchanged. This Agreement shall have effect:

a. in China, as respects income derived during the taxable years beginning on or after the first day of January next following that in which this Agreement enters into force.
b. in Mauritius, as respects income derived during the income years beginning on or after the first day of July next following the date on which the Agreement enters into force.

Article 29: Termination

This Agreement shall continue in effect indefinitely but either of the Contracting State may, on or before the thirtieth day of June in any calendar year beginning after the expiration of a period of five years from the date of its entry into force, give written notice of termination to the other Contracting State through the diplomatic channels. In such event this Agreement shall cease to have effect:

a. in the case of China, as respects income derived during the taxable years beginning on or after the first day of January in the calendar year next following that in which the notice of termination is given;
b. in the case of Mauritius, as respects income derived during the income years beginning on or after the first day of July in the calendar year next following that in which the notice of termination is given.

DONE at Beijing on the first day of August 1994 in duplicate in the Chinese and English languages, both texts being equally authentic.

For the Government of the People's Republic of China
For the Government of the Republic of Mauritius

Nigeria

Agreement Between the Government of the People's Republic of China and the Government of the Federal Republic of Nigeria for the Avoidance of Double Taxation and the Prevention of Fiscal Evasion with Respect to Taxes on Income

The Government of the People's Republic of China and the Government of the Federal Republic of Nigeria,

Desiring to conclude an Agreement for the avoidance of double taxation and the prevention of fiscal evasion with respect to taxes on income and on capital gains,

Have agreed as follows:

Article 1: Persons Covered

This Agreement shall apply to persons who are residents of one or both of the Contracting States.

Article 2: Taxes Covered

1. This Agreement shall apply to taxes on income imposed on behalf of a Contracting State or of its local authorities, irrespective of the manner in which they are levied.
2. There shall be regarded as taxes on income all taxes imposed on total income, or on elements of income, including taxes on gains from the alienation of movable or immovable property, as well as taxes on capital appreciation.
3. The existing taxes to which the Agreement shall apply are in particular:

    a. in Nigeria:

        i. the personal income tax;
        ii. the companies income tax;
        iii. the petroleum profits tax;
        iv. the capital gains tax; and
        v. the education tax.
        (hereinafter referred to as "Nigerian tax")

L. Riccardi and G. Riccardi, *China in Africa*,
https://doi.org/10.1007/978-981-16-1148-3

b. in China:

i. the individual income tax;
ii. the income tax for enterprises with foreign investment and foreign enterprises.
(hereinafter referred to as "Chinese tax")

4. The Agreement shall also apply to any identical or substantially similar taxes which are imposed after the date of signature of the Agreement in addition to, or in place of, the existing taxes. The competent authorities of the Contracting States shall notify each other of any substantial changes which have been made in their respective taxation laws.

Article 3: General Definitions

1. For the purposes of this Agreement, unless the context otherwise requires:
   a. the term "Nigeria" means the Federal Republic of Nigeria including any area outside the territorial waters of the Federal Republic of Nigeria which in accordance with international law has been or may hereafter be designated, under the laws of the Federal Republic of Nigeria concerning the Continental Shelf, as an area within which the rights of the Federal Republic of Nigeria with respect to the sea-bed and sub-soil and their natural resources may be exercised;
   b. the term "China" means the People's Republic of China; when used in geographical sense, means all the territory of the People's Republic of China, including its territorial sea, in which the Chinese laws relating to taxation apply, and any area beyond its territorial sea, within which the People's Republic of China has sovereign rights of exploration for and exploitation of resources of the sea-bed and its sub-soil and superjacent water resources in accordance with international law;
   c. the terms "a Contracting State" and "the other Contracting State" mean Nigeria or China as the context requires;
   d. the term "tax" means Nigerian tax or Chinese tax, as the context requires;
   e. the term "person" includes an individual, a company and any other body of persons;
   f. the term "company" means anybody corporate or any entity which is treated as a body corporate for tax purposes;
   g. the terms "enterprise of a Contracting State" and "enterprise of the other Contracting State" mean, respectively, an enterprise carried on by a resident of a Contracting State and an enterprise carried on by a resident of the other Contracting State;
   h. the term "national" means:
      i. in the case of Nigeria, any individual possessing the citizenship or nationality of Nigeria; in the case of China, any individual possessing the nationality of China;

   ii. any legal person, partnership or association deriving its status as such from the laws in force in a Contracting State;

i. the term "international traffic" means any transport by a ship or aircraft operated by an enterprise of a Contracting State, except when the ship or aircraft is operated solely between places in the other Contracting State;
j. the term "competent authority" means, in the case of Nigeria, the Federal Minister of Finance or his authorized representative, and in the case of China, the State Administration of Taxation or its authorized representative.

2. As regards the application of the Agreement by a Contracting State, any term not defined therein shall, unless the context otherwise requires, have the meaning which it has under the law of that Contracting State concerning the taxes to which the Agreement applies.

Article 4: Resident

1. For the purposes of this Agreement, the term "resident of a Contracting State" means any person who, under the laws of that State, is liable to tax therein by reason of his domicile, residence, place of head office, place of incorporation or any other criterion of a similar nature.
2. Whereby reason of the provisions of paragraph 1 an individual is a resident of both Contracting States, then his status shall be determined as follows:

   a. he shall be deemed to be a resident of the State in which he has a permanent home available to him; if he has a permanent home available to him in both States, he shall be deemed to be a resident of the State with which his personal and economic relations are closer (centre of vital interests);
   b. if the State in which he has his centre of vital interests cannot be determined, or if he has not a permanent home available to him in either State, he shall be deemed to be a resident of the State in which he has an habitual abode;
   c. if he has a habitual abode in both States or in neither of them, he shall be deemed to be a resident of the State of which he is a national;
   d. if he is a national of both States or of neither of them, the competent authorities of the Contracting States shall settle the question by mutual agreement.

3. Whereby reason of the provisions of paragraph 1 a person other than an individual is a resident of both Contracting States, then the competent authorities shall settle the question by mutual agreement.

Article 5: Permanent Establishment

1. For the purposes of this Agreement, the term "permanent establishment" means a fixed place of business through which the business of an enterprise is wholly or partly carried on.
2. The term "permanent establishment" includes especially:

a. a place of management;
b. a branch;
c. an office;
d. a factory;
e. a workshop;
f. a sales outlet; and
g. a mine, an oil or gas well, a quarry or any other place of extraction of natural resources.

3. The term "permanent establishment" likewise encompasses: a building site, a construction, assembly or installation project or supervisory activities in connection therewith, but only where such site, project or activities continue for a period of more than six months.

4. Notwithstanding the preceding provisions of this Article, the term "permanent establishment" shall be deemed not to include:

a. the use of facilities solely for the purpose of storage or display of goods or merchandise belonging to the enterprise;
b. the maintenance of a stock of goods or merchandise belonging to the enterprise solely for the purpose of storage or display;
c. the maintenance of a stock of goods or merchandise belonging to the enterprise solely for the purpose of processing by another enterprise;
d. the maintenance of a fixed place of business solely for the purpose of purchasing goods or merchandise or of collecting information, for the enterprise;
e. the maintenance of a fixed place of business solely for the purpose of carrying on, for the enterprise, any other activity of a preparatory or auxiliary character;
f. the maintenance of a fixed place of business solely for any combination of activities mentioned in sub-paragraphs a) to e), provided that the overall activity of the fixed place of business resulting from this combination is of a preparatory or auxiliary character.

5. Notwithstanding the provisions of paragraphs 1 and 2, where a person—other than an agent of an independent status to whom paragraph 6 applies—is acting in a Contracting State on behalf of an enterprise of the other Contracting State, and has and habitually exercises an authority to conclude contracts on behalf of the enterprise, that enterprise shall be deemed to have a permanent establishment in the first-mentioned Contracting State in respect of any activities which that person undertakes for the enterprise, unless the activities of such person are limited to those mentioned in paragraph 4 which, if exercised through a fixed place of business, would not make this fixed place of business a permanent establishment under the provisions of that paragraph.
6. An enterprise of a Contracting State shall not be deemed to have a permanent establishment in the other Contracting State merely because it carries on

business in that other State through a broker, general commission agent or any other agent of an independent status, provided that such persons are acting in the ordinary course of their business. However, when the activities of such an agent are devoted wholly or almost wholly on behalf of that enterprise, and conditions are made or imposed between that enterprise and the agent in their commercial and financial relations which differ from those which would have been made between independent enterprises, he will not be considered an agent of an independent status within the meaning of this paragraph.

7. The fact that a company which is a resident of a Contracting State controls or is controlled by a company which is a resident of the other Contracting State, or which carries on business in that other State (whether through a permanent establishment or otherwise), shall not of itself constitute either company a permanent establishment of the other.

Article 6: Income from Immovable Property

1. Income derived by a resident of a Contracting State from immovable property (including income from agriculture or forestry) situated in the other Contracting State may be taxed in that other State.
2. The term "immovable property" shall have the meaning which it has under the law of the Contracting State in which the property in question is situated. The term shall in any case include property accessory to immovable property, livestock and equipment used in agriculture and forestry, rights to which the provisions of general law respecting landed property apply, usufruct of immovable property and rights to variable or fixed payments as consideration for the working of, or the right to work, mineral deposits, sources and other natural resources. Ships and aircraft shall not be regarded as immovable property.
3. The provisions of paragraph 1 shall apply to income derived from the direct use, letting, or use in any other form of immovable property.
4. The provisions of paragraphs l and 3 shall also apply to the income from immovable property of an enterprise and to income from immovable property used for the performance of independent personal services.

Article 7: Business Profits

1. The profits of an enterprise of a Contracting State shall be taxable only in that State unless the enterprise carries on business in the other Contracting State through a permanent establishment situated therein. If the enterprise carries on business as aforesaid, the profits of the enterprise may be taxed in the other State, but only so much of them as is attributable to that permanent establishment.
2. Subject to the provisions of paragraph 3, where an enterprise of a Contracting State carries on business in the other Contracting State through a permanent establishment situated therein, there shall in each Contracting State be attributed to that permanent establishment the profits which it might be expected to make if it were a distinct and separate enterprise engaged in the same or similar activities

under the same or similar conditions and dealing wholly independently with the enterprise of which it is a permanent establishment.

3. In determining the profits of a permanent establishment, there shall be allowed as deductions, expenses which are incurred for the purposes of the business of the permanent establishment, including executive and general administrative expenses so incurred, whether in the State in which the permanent establishment is situated or elsewhere. However, no such deduction shall be allowed in respect of amounts, if any, paid (otherwise than towards reimbursement of actual expenses) by the permanent establishment to the head office of the enterprise or any of its other offices, by way of royalties, fees or other similar payments in return for the use of patents or other rights, or by way of commission, for specific services performed or for management, or, except in the case of a banking enterprise, by way of interest on moneys lent to the permanent establishment. Likewise, no account shall be taken, in the determination of the profits of the permanent establishment, for amounts charged (otherwise than towards reimbursement of actual expenses), by the permanent establishment to the head office of the enterprise or any of its other offices, by way of royalties, fees or other similar payments in return for the use of patents or other rights, or by way of commission for specific services performed or for management, or, except in the case of a banking enterprise, by way of interest on moneys lent to the head office of the enterprise or any of its other offices.
4. Insofar as it has been customary in a Contracting State to determine the profits to be attributed to a permanent establishment on the basis of an apportionment of the total profits of the enterprise to its various parts, nothing in paragraph 2 shall preclude that Contracting State from determining the profits to be taxed by such an apportionment as may be customary. The method of apportionment adopted shall, however, be such that the result shall be in accordance with the principles contained in this Article.
5. No profits shall be attributed to a permanent establishment by reason of the mere purchase by that permanent establishment of goods or merchandise for the enterprise.
6. For the purposes of the preceding paragraphs, the profits to be attributed to the permanent establishment shall be determined by the same method year by year unless there is good and sufficient reason to the contrary.
7. Where profits include items of income which are dealt with separately in other Articles of this Agreement, then the provisions of those Articles shall not be affected by the provisions of this Article.

Article 8: Shipping and Air Transport

1. An enterprise of a Contracting State shall be exempt from tax in the other Contracting State in respect of profits or gains from the operation of ships or aircraft in international traffic.
2. The provisions of paragraph 1 shall also apply to profits from the participation in a pool, a joint business or an international operating agency.

Article 9: Associated Enterprises

1. Where

   a. an enterprise of a Contracting State participates directly or indirectly in the management, control or capital of an enterprise of the other Contracting State, or
   b. the same persons participate directly or indirectly in the management, control or capital of an enterprise of a Contracting State and an enterprise of the other Contracting State, and in either case conditions are made or imposed between the two enterprises in their commercial or financial relations which differ from those which would be made between independent enterprises, then any profits which would, but for those conditions, have accrued to one of the enterprises, but, by reason of those conditions, have not so accrued, may be included in the profits of that enterprise and taxed accordingly.

2. Where a Contracting State includes in the profits of an enterprise of that State—and taxes accordingly—profits on which an enterprise of the other Contracting State has been charged to tax in that other State and the profits so included are profits which would have accrued to the enterprise of the first-mentioned State if the conditions made between the two enterprises had been those which would have been made between independent enterprises, then that other State shall make an appropriate adjustment to the amount of the tax charged therein on those profits. In determining such adjustment, due regard shall be had to the other provisions of this Agreement and the competent authorities of the Contracting States shall, if necessary, consult each other.

Article 10: Dividends

1. Dividends paid by a company which is a resident of a Contracting State to a resident of the other Contracting State may be taxed in that other State.
2. However, such dividends may also be taxed in the Contracting State of which the company paying the dividends is a resident and according to the laws of that State, but if the recipient is the beneficial owner of the dividends, the tax so charged shall not exceed 7.5% of the gross amount of the dividends. The competent authorities of the Contracting States shall by mutual agreement settle the mode of application of this limitation. This paragraph shall not affect the taxation of the company in respect of the profits out of which the dividends are paid.
3. The term "dividends" as used in this Article means income from shares, "jouissance" shares or "jouissance" rights, mining shares, founders rights or other rights, not being debt-claims, participating in profits, as well as income from other corporate rights which is subjected to the same taxation treatment as income from shares by the laws of the State of which the company making the distribution is a resident.

4. The provisions of paragraphs 1 and 2 shall not apply if the beneficial owner of the dividends, being a resident of a Contracting State, carries on business in the other Contracting State of which the company paying the dividends is a resident, through a permanent establishment situated therein, or performs in that other State independent personal services from a fixed base situated therein, and the holding in respect of which the dividends are paid is effectively connected with such permanent establishment or fixed base. In such case the provisions of Article 7 or Article 14, as the case may be, shall apply.
5. The provisions of this Article shall not apply if the right giving rise to the dividend was created or assigned mainly for the purpose of taking advantage of this Article and not for bonafide commercial reasons.
6. Where a company which is a resident of a Contracting State derives profits or income from the other Contracting State, that other State may not impose any tax on the dividends paid by the company, except insofar as such dividends are paid to a resident of that other State or insofar as the holding in respect of which the dividends are paid is effectively connected with a permanent establishment or a fixed base situated in that other State, nor subject the company's undistributed profits to a tax on the company's undistributed profits, even if the dividends paid or the undistributed profits consist wholly or partly of profits or income arising in such other State.

Article 11: Interest

1. Interest arising in a Contracting State and paid to a resident of the other Contracting State may be taxed in that other State.
2. However, such interest may also be taxed in the Contracting State in which it arises and according to the laws of that State, but if the recipient is the beneficial owner of the interest, the tax so charged shall not exceed 7.5% of the gross amount of the interest.
3. Notwithstanding the provisions of paragraph 2, interest arising in a Contracting State and derived by the Government of the other Contracting State, a local authority and the Central Bank thereof or any financial institution wholly owned by the Government of that other State shall be exempt from tax in the first-mentioned State.
4. The term "interest" as used in this Article means income from debt-claims of every kind, whether or not secured by mortgage and whether or not carrying a right to participate in the debtor's profits, and in particular, income from government securities and income from bonds or debentures, including premiums and prizes attaching to such securities, bonds or debentures. Penalty charges for late payment shall not be regarded as interest for the purpose of this Article.
5. The provisions of paragraphs 1, 2 and 3 shall not apply if the beneficial owner of the interest, being a resident of a Contracting State, carries on business in the other Contracting State in which the interest arises, through a permanent establishment situated therein, or performs in that other State independent personal services from a fixed base situated therein, and the debt-claim in respect of

which the interest is paid is effectively connected with such permanent establishment or fixed base. In such case the provisions of Article 7 or Article 14, as the case may be, shall apply.

6. Interest shall be deemed to arise in a Contracting State when the payer is the Government of that State, a local authority thereof or a resident of that State. Where, however, the person paying the interest, whether he is a resident of a Contracting State or not, has in a Contracting State a permanent establishment or a fixed base in connection with which the indebtedness on which the interest is paid was incurred, and such interest is borne by such permanent establishment or fixed base, then such interest shall be deemed to arise in the State in which the permanent establishment or fixed base is situated.
7. The provisions of this Article shall not apply if the right giving rise to the interest was created or assigned mainly for the purpose of taking advantage of this Article and not for bonafide commercial reasons.
8. Where, by reason of a special relationship between the payer and the beneficial owner or between both of them and some other person, the amount of the interest, having regard to the debt-claim for which it is paid, exceeds the amount which would have been agreed upon by the payer and the beneficial owner in the absence of such relationship, the provisions of this Article shall apply only to the last-mentioned amount. In such case, the excess part of the payments shall remain taxable according to the laws of each Contracting State, due regard being had to the other provisions of this Agreement.

Article 12: Royalties

1. Royalties arising in a Contracting State and paid to a resident of the other Contracting State may be taxed in that other State.
2. However, such royalties may also be taxed in the Contracting State in which they arise and according to the laws of that State, but if the recipient is the beneficial owner of the royalties, the tax so charged shall not exceed 7.5% of the gross amount of the royalties.
3. The term "royalties" as used in this Article means payments of any kind received as a consideration for the use of, or the right to use, any copyright of literary, artistic or scientific work including cinematography films, or films or tapes for radio or television broadcasting, any patent, trade mark, design or model, plan, secret formula or process, or for the use of, or the right to use, industrial, commercial, or scientific equipment, or for information concerning industrial, commercial or scientific experience.
4. The provisions of paragraphs l and 2 shall not apply if the beneficial owner of the royalties, being a resident of a Contracting State, carries on business in the other Contracting State in which the royalties arise, through a permanent establishment situated therein, or performs in that other State independent personal services from a fixed base situated therein, and the right or property in respect of which the royalties are paid is effectively connected with such permanent

establishment or fixed base. In such case the provisions of Article 7 or Article 14, as the case may be, shall apply.

5. Royalties shall be deemed to arise in a Contracting State when the payer is the Government of that Contracting State, a local authority thereof or a resident of that Contracting State. Where, however, the person paying the royalties, whether he is a resident of a Contracting State or not, has in a Contracting State a permanent establishment or a fixed base in connection with which the liability to pay the royalties was incurred, and such royalties are borne by such permanent establishment or fixed base, then such royalties shall be deemed to arise in the State in which the permanent establishment or fixed base is situated.
6. The provisions of this Article shall not apply if the right giving rise to the royalties was created or assigned mainly for the purpose of taking advantage of this Article and not for bonafide commercial reasons.
7. Where, by reason of a special relationship between the payer and the beneficial owner or between both of them and some other person, the amount of the roya1ties, having regard to the use, right or information for which they are paid, exceeds the amount which would have been agreed upon by the payer and the beneficial owner in the absence of such relationship, the provisions of this Article shall apply only to the last-mentioned amount. In such case, the excess part of the payments shall remain taxable according to the laws of each Contracting State, due regard being had to the other provisions of this Agreement.

Article 13: Capital Gains

1. Gains derived by a resident of a Contracting State from the alienation of immovable property referred to in Article 6 and situated in the other Contracting State may be taxed in that other State.
2. Gains from the alienation of movable property forming part of the business property of a permanent establishment which an enterprise of a Contracting State has in the other Contracting State or of movable property pertaining to a fixed base available to a resident of a Contracting State in the other Contracting State for the purpose of performing independent personal services, including such gains from the alienation of such a permanent establishment (alone or with the whole enterprise) or of such a fixed base, may be taxed in that other State.
3. Gains from the alienation of ships or aircraft operated in international traffic by an enterprise of a Contracting State or movable property pertaining to the operation of such ships or aircraft shall be taxable only in that State.

Article 14: Independent Personal Services

1. Income derived by a resident of a Contracting State in respect of professional services or other activities of an independent character shall be taxable only in that State unless he has a fixed base regularly available to him in the other Contracting State for the purpose of performing his activities. If he has such a fixed base, the income may be taxed in that other State but only so much of it as is attributable to that fixed base.

2. The term “professional services” includes especially independent scientific, literary, artistic, educational or teaching activities as well as the independent activities of physicians, lawyers, engineers, architects, dentists and accountants.

Article 15: Dependent Personal Services

1. Subject to the provisions of Articles 16, 18, 19, 20 and 21, salaries, wages and other similar remuneration derived by a resident of a Contracting State in respect of an employment shall be taxable only in that State unless the employment is exercised in the other Contracting State. If the employment is so exercised, such remuneration as is derived therefrom may be taxed in that other State.
2. Notwithstanding the provisions of paragraph1, remuneration derived by a resident of a Contracting State in respect of an employment exercised in the other Contracting State shall be taxable only in the first-mentioned State if:

   a. the recipient is present in the other State for a period or periods not exceeding in the aggregate 183 days in any twelve-month period commencing or ending in the fiscal year concerned; and
   b. the remuneration is paid by, or on behalf of, an employer who is not a resident of the other State; and
   c. the remuneration is not borne by a permanent establishment or a fixed base which the employer has in the other State.

3. Notwithstanding the preceding provisions of this Article, remuneration derived in respect of an employment exercised aboard a ship or aircraft operated in international traffic by an enterprise of a Contracting State, shall be taxable only in that State.

Article16: Directors' Fees

Directors' fees and other similar payments derived by a resident of a Contracting State in his capacity as a member of the board of directors of a company which is a resident of the other Contracting State may be taxed in that other State.

Article 17: Artistes and Sportsmen

1. Notwithstanding the provisions of Articles 14 and 15, income derived by a resident of a Contracting State as an entertainer, such as a theatre, motion picture, radio or television artiste, or a musician, or as a sportsman, from his personal activities as such exercised in the other Contracting State, may be taxed in that other State.
2. Where income in respect of personal activities exercised by an entertainer or a sportsman in his capacity as such accrues not to the entertainer or sportsman himself but to another person, that income may, notwithstanding the provisions of Articles 7, 14 and 15, be taxed in the Contracting State in which the activities of the entertainer or sportsman are exercised.

3. Notwithstanding the preceding provisions of this Article, income derived by entertainers or sportsmen who are residents of a Contracting State from the activities exercised in the other Contracting State under a plan of cultural exchange between the Governments of both Contracting States shall be exempt from tax in that other State.

Article 18: Pensions

1. Subject to the provisions of paragraph 2 of Article 19, pensions and other similar remuneration paid to a resident of a Contracting State in consideration of past employment shall be taxable only in that State.
2. Notwithstanding the provisions of paragraph 1, pensions paid, and other similar payments made by the Government of a Contracting State or a local authority thereof under a public welfare scheme of the social security system of that State shall be taxable only in that State.

Article 19: Government Service

a. Remuneration, other than a pension, paid by the Government of a Contracting State or a local authority thereof to an individual in respect of services rendered to the Government of that State or a local authority thereof shall be taxable only in that State.
b. However, such remuneration shall be taxable only in the other Contracting State if the services are rendered in that other State and the individual is a resident of that other State who:

    i. is a national of that State; or
    ii. did not become a resident of that State solely for the purpose of rendering the services.

c. Any pension paid by, or out of funds to which contributions are made by the Government of a Contracting State or a local authority thereof to an individual in respect of services rendered to the Government of that State or a local authority thereof shall be taxable only in that State.
d. However, such pension shall be taxable only in the other Contracting State if the individual is a resident of, and a national of, that other State.
e. The provisions of Articles 15, 16, 17 and 18 shall apply to remuneration and pensions in respect of services rendered in connection with a business carried on by the Government of a Contracting State or a local authority thereof.

Article 20: Teachers and Researchers

1. Remuneration which an individual who is or was immediately before visiting a Contracting State, a resident of the other Contracting State and who is present in the first-mentioned State for the primary purpose of teaching, giving lectures or conducting research at a university, college, school or educational institution

or scientific research institution recognized by the Government of the first-mentioned State, derives for the purpose of such teaching, lectures or research shall not be taxed in the first-mentioned State, for a period of two years from the date of his first arrival in the first-mentioned State.

2. The provisions of paragraph 1 of this Article shall not apply to income from research if such research is undertaken not in the public interest but primarily for the private benefit of a specific person or persons.

Article 21: Students and Trainees

1. Payments which a student, business apprentice or trainee who is or was immediately before visiting a Contracting State a resident of the other Contracting State and who is present in the first-mentioned State solely for the purpose of his education or training receives for the purpose of his maintenance, education or training shall not be taxed in that State, provided that such payments arise from sources outside that State.
2. In respect of grants, scholarships and remuneration from employment not covered by paragraph 1, a student, business apprentice or trainee described in paragraph 1 shall, in addition, be entitled during such education or training to the same exemptions, reliefs or reductions in respect of taxes available to residents of the State which he is visiting.

Article 22: Other Income

1. Items of income of a resident of a Contracting State, wherever arising, not dealt with in the foregoing Articles of this Agreement shall be taxable only in that State.
2. The provisions of paragraph 1 shall not apply to income, other than income from immovable property as defined in paragraph 2 of Article 6, if the recipient of such income, being a resident of a Contracting State, carries on business in the other Contracting State through a permanent establishment situated therein, or performs in that other State independent personal services from a fixed base situated therein, and the right or property in respect of which the income is paid is effectively connected with such permanent establishment or fixed base. In such case the provisions of Article 7 or Article 14, as the case may be, shall apply.

Article 23: Methods for the Elimination of Double Taxation

1. In Nigeria, double taxation shall be eliminated as follows:

   a. Chinese tax payable under the laws of China and in accordance with this Agreement, whether directly or by deduction, on profits, income, or chargeable gains from sources within China (excluding in the case of a dividend, tax payable in respect of the profits out of which the dividend is paid) shall be allowed as a credit against any Nigerian tax computed by reference to the same profit, income or chargeable gains by reference to which Chinese tax is computed;

b. in the case of a dividend paid by a company which is a resident of China to a company which is a resident of Nigeria and which controls directly or indirectly at least ten per cent of the voting power in the company paying the dividend, the credit shall take into account (in addition to any Chinese tax for which credit may be allowed under the provisions of sub-paragraph (a) of this paragraph) Chinese tax payable by the company in respect of the profits out of which such dividend is paid.

2. In China, double taxation shall be eliminated as follows:
Where a resident of China derives income from Nigeria the amount of tax on that income payable in Nigeria in accordance with the provisions of this Agreement, may be credited against the Chinese tax imposed on that resident. The amount of the credit, however, shall not exceed the amount of the Chinese tax on that income computed in accordance with the taxation laws and regulations of China.

Article 24: Non-Discrimination

1. Nationals of a Contracting State shall not be subjected in the other Contracting State to any taxation or any requirement connected therewith, which is other or more burdensome than the taxation and connected requirements to which nationals of that other State in the same circumstances are or may be subjected. This provision shall, notwithstanding the provisions of Article 1, also apply to persons who are not residents of one or both of the Contracting States.
2. The taxation on a permanent establishment which an enterprise of a Contracting State has in the other Contracting State shall not be less favourably levied in that other State than the taxation levied on enterprises of that other State carrying on the same activities. This provision shall not be construed as obliging a Contracting State to grant to residents of the other Contracting State any personal allowances, reliefs and reductions for taxation purposes on account of civil status or family responsibilities which it grants to its own residents.
3. Except where the provisions of paragraph l of Article 9, paragraph 7 of Article 11, or paragraph 6 of Article 12, apply, interest, royalties and other disbursements paid by an enterprise of a Contracting State to a resident of the other Contracting State shall, for the purpose of determining the taxable profits of such enterprise, be deductible under the same conditions as if they had been paid to a resident of the first-mentioned State.
4. Enterprises of a Contracting State, the capital of which is wholly or partly owned or controlled, directly or indirectly, by one or more residents of the other Contracting State, shall not be subjected in the first-mentioned State to any taxation or any requirement connected therewith which is other or more burdensome than the taxation and connected requirements to which other similar enterprises of the first-mentioned State are or may be subjected.

5. The provisions of this Article shall, notwithstanding the provisions of Article 2, apply to taxes of every kind and description.

Article 25: Mutual Agreement Procedure

1. Where a person considers that the actions of one or both of the Contracting States result or will result for him in taxation not in accordance with the provisions of this Agreement, he may, irrespective of the remedies provided by the domestic law of those States, present his case to the competent authority of the Contracting State of which he is a resident or, if his case comes under paragraph 1 of Article 24, to that of the Contracting State of which he is a national. The case must be presented within three years from the first notification of the action resulting in taxation not in accordance with the provisions of the Agreement.
2. The competent authority shall endeavour, if the objection appears to it to be justified and if it is not itself able to arrive at a satisfactory solution, to resolve the case by mutual agreement with the competent authority of the other Contracting State, with a view to the avoidance of taxation which is not in accordance with the Agreement. Any agreement reached shall be implemented notwithstanding any time limits in the domestic law of the Contracting States.
3. The competent authorities of the Contracting States shall endeavour to resolve by mutual agreement any difficulties or doubts arising as to the interpretation or application of the Agreement. They may also consult together for the elimination of double taxation in cases not provided for in the Agreement.
4. The competent authorities of the Contracting States may communicate with each other directly for the purpose of reaching an agreement in the sense of paragraphs 2 and 3. When it seems advisable for reaching agreement, representatives of the competent authorities of the Contracting States may meet together for an oral exchange of opinions.

Article 26: Exchange of Information

1. The competent authorities of the Contracting States shall exchange such information as is necessary for carrying out the provisions of this Agreement or of the domestic laws of the Contracting States concerning taxes covered by the Agreement, insofar as the taxation thereunder is not contrary to the Agreement, in particular for the prevention of evasion of such taxes. The exchange of information is not restricted by Article 1. Any information received by a Contracting State shall be treated as secret in the same manner as information obtained under the domestic laws of that State. However, if the information is originally regarded as secret in the transmitting State it shall be disclosed only to persons or authorities (including courts and administrative bodies) concerned with the assessment or collection of, the enforcement or prosecution in respect of, or the determination of appeals in relation to the taxes which are subject of the Agreement. Such persons or authorities shall use the information only for such purposes but may disclose the information in public court proceedings

or in judicial decisions. The competent authorities, shall, through consultation, develop appropriate conditions, methods and techniques, concerning the matters in respect of which such exchanges of information shall be made, including, where appropriate, exchanges of information regarding tax avoidance.

2. In no case shall the provisions of paragraph 1 be construed so as to impose on a Contracting State the obligation:

   a. to carry out administrative measures at variance with the laws and administrative practice of that or of the other Contracting State;
   b. to supply information which is not obtainable under the laws or in the normal course of the administration of that or of the other Contracting State;
   c. to supply information which would disclose any trade, business, industrial, commercial or professional secret or trade process, or information, the disclosure of which would be contrary to public policy (Ordre Public).

Article 27: Members of Diplomatic Missions and Consular Posts

Nothing in this Agreement shall affect the fiscal privileges of members of diplomatic missions or consular posts under the general rules of international law or under the provisions of special agreements.

Article 28: Entry into Force

This Agreement shall enter into force on the thirtieth day after the date on which diplomatic notes indicating the completion of internal legal procedures necessary in each country for the entry into force of this Agreement have been exchanged. This Agreement shall have effect:

1. In Nigeria:

   a. in respect of withholding tax on income and taxes on capital gains derived by a non-resident, in relation to income and capital gains derived on or after 1st January in the calendar year immediately following that in which the Agreement enters into force;
   b. in respect of other taxes, in relation to income of any basis period beginning on or after 1st January in the calendar year immediately following that in which the Agreement enters into force.

2. In China, as respects income derived during the taxable years beginning on or after the first day of January next following that in which this Agreement enters into force.

Article 29: Termination

This Agreement shall continue in effect indefinitely but either of the Contracting States may, on or before the thirtieth day of June in any calendar year beginning after the expiration of a period of five years from the date of its entry into force, give written notice of termination to the other Contracting State through diplomatic channels. In such event this Agreement shall cease to have effect:

1. In Nigeria:
   a. in respect of withholding tax on income and taxes on capital gains derived by a non-resident, in relation to income and capital gains derived on or after 1st January in the calendar year immediately following that in which the notice of termination is given;
   b. in respect of other taxes, in relation to income of any basis period beginning on or after 1st January in the calendar year immediately following that in which the notice of termination is given.
2. In China, as respects income derived during the taxable years beginning on or after the first day of January in the calendar year next following that in which the notice of termination is given.

IN WITNESS whereof the undersigned, duly authorized thereto, have signed this Agreement.

Done in duplicate at Abuja, this 15th day of April 2002, in the Chinese and English languages, both texts being equally authentic. In case of divergence, the English text shall prevail.

For the Government of the People's Republic of China
For the Government of the Federal Republic of Nigeria

Seychelles

Agreement Between the Government of the People's Republic of China and the Government of the Republic of Seychelles for the Avoidance of Double Taxation and the Prevention of Fiscal Evasion with Respect to Taxes on Income

The Government of the People's Republic of China and the Government of the Republic of Seychelles,

Desiring to conclude an Agreement for the avoidance of double taxation and the prevention of fiscal evasion with respect to taxes on income,Have agreed as follows:

Article 1: Personal Scope

This Agreement shall apply to persons who are residents of one or both of the Contracting States.

Article 2: Taxes Covered

1. This Agreement shall apply to taxes on income imposed on behalf of a Contracting State or of its local authorities, irrespective of the manner in which they are levied.
2. There shall be regarded as taxes on income all taxes imposed on total income, or on elements of income, including taxes on gains from the alienation of movable or immovable property.
3. The existing taxes to which the Agreement shall apply are in particular:
   a. in China:
      i. the individual income tax;
      ii. the income tax for enterprises with foreign investment and foreign enterprises; (here in after referred to as "Chinese tax");
   b. in Seychelles:
      i. the business tax;
      ii. the petroleum income tax;
      (hereinafter referred to as "Seychelles tax").

L. Riccardi and G. Riccardi, *China in Africa*,
https://doi.org/10.1007/978-981-16-1148-3

4. The Agreement shall also apply to any identical or substantially similar taxes which are imposed after the date of signature of the Agreement in addition to, or in place of, the existing taxes. The competent authorities of the Contracting States shall notify each other of any substantial changes which have been made in their respective taxation laws within a reasonable period of time after such changes.

Article 3: General Definitions

1. For the purposes of this Agreement, unless the context otherwise requires:

    a. the term "China" means the People′s Republic of China; when used in geographical sense, means all the territory of the People′s Republic of China, including its territorial sea, in which the Chinese laws relating to taxation apply, and any area beyond its territorial sea, within which the People′s Republic of China has sovereign rights of exploration for and exploitation of resources of the sea bed and its subsoil and superjacent water resources in accordance with international law;
    b. the term "Seychelles" means the territory of the Republic of Seychelles including its exclusive economic zone and continental shelf where the Seychelles exercises exclusive jurisdiction with regard to fiscal laws and regulations in conformity with the provisions of the United Nations Convention on the Law of the Sea.
    c. the terms "a Contracting State" and "the other Contracting State" mean China or Seychelles as the context requires;
    d. the term "tax" means Chinese tax or Seychelles tax, as the context requires;
    e. the term "person" includes an individual, a company and any other body of persons;
    f. the term "company" means anybody corporate or any entity which is treated as a body corporate for tax purposes;
    g. the terms "enterprise of a Contracting State" and "enterprise of the other Contracting State" mean, respectively, an enterprise carried on by a resident of a Contracting State and an enterprise carried on by a resident of the other Contracting State;
    h. the term "national" means:
        i. any individual possessing the nationality of a Contracting State;
        ii. any legal person, partnership or association deriving its status as such from the laws in force in a Contracting State;
    i. the term "imitational traffic" means any transport by a ship or aircraft operated by an enterprise of a Contracting State, except when the ship or aircraft is operated solely between places in the other Contracting State;
    j. the term "competent authority" means, in the case of China, the State Administration of Taxation or its authorized representative, and in the case of Seychelles, the Minister of Finance or his authorized representative.

2. As regards the application of the Agreement by a Contracting State, any term not defined therein shall, unless the context otherwise requires, have the meaning which it has under the law of that Contracting State concerning the taxes to which the Agreement applies.

Article 4: Resident

1. For the purposes of this Agreement, the term "resident of a Contracting State" means any person who, under the laws of that State, is liable to tax therein by reason of his domicile, residence, place of head office, place of effective management or any other criterion of a similar nature.
2. Whereby reason of the provisions of paragraph 1 an individual is a resident of both Contracting States, then his status shall be determined as follows:
   a. he shall be deemed to be a resident only of the State in which he has a permanent home available to him; if he has a permanent home available to him in both States, he shall be deemed to be a resident only of the State with which his personal and economic relations are closer (centre of vital interests);
   b. if the State in which he has his centre of vital interests cannot be determined, or if he has not a permanent home available to him in either State, he shall be deemed to be a resident only of the State in which he has a habitual abode;
   c. if he has a habitual abode in both States or in neither of them, he shall be deemed to be a resident only of the State of which he is a national;
   d. if he is a national of both States or of neither of them, the competent authorities of the Contracting States shall settle the question by mutual agreement.
3. Where by reason of the provisions of paragraph 1 of this Article a person other than an individual is a resident of both Contracting States, then it shall be deemed to be a resident only of the Contracting State in which the place of effective management of its business is situated .However, where such a person has the place of effective management of its business in one of the Contracting State and the place of head office of the business in the other Contracting State, then the competent authorities of the Contracting States shall determine by mutual agreement the Contracting State of which the company shall be deemed to be a resident for the purposes of this Agreement.

Article 5: Permanent Establishment

1. For the purposes of this Agreement, the term "permanent establishment" means a fixed place of business through which the business of an enterprise is wholly or partly carried on.
2. The term "permanent establishment" includes especially:

a. a place of management;
b. a branch;
c. an office;
d. a factory;
e. a workshop; and
f. a mine, an oil or gas well, a quarry or any other place of extraction of natural resources.

3. The term "permanent establishment" likewise encompasses:

a. a building site, a construction, assembly or installation project or supervisory activities in connection therewith, but only where such site, project or activities continue for a period of more than 12 months.
b. the furnishing of services, including consultancy services, by an enterprise through employees or other personnel engaged by the enterprise for such purpose, but only where activities of that nature continue (for the same or a connected project) within the country for a period or periods aggregating more than 12 months within any 24-month period.

4. Notwithstanding the preceding provisions of this Article, the term "permanent establishment" shall be deemed not to include:

a. the use of facilities solely for the purpose of storage, display or delivery of goods or merchandise belonging to the enterprise;
b. the maintenance of a stock of goods or merchandise belonging to the enterprise solely for the purpose of storage, display or delivery;
c. the maintenance of a stock of goods or merchandise belonging to the enterprise solely for the purpose of processing by another enterprise;
d. the maintenance of a fixed place, of business solely for the purpose of purchasing goods or merchandise or of collecting information, for the enterprise;
e. the maintenance of a fixed place of business solely for the purpose of carrying on, for the enterprise, any other activity of a preparatory or auxiliary character;
f. the maintenance of a fixed place of business solely for any combination of activities mentioned in sub paragraphs a) to e), provided that the overall activity of the fixed place of business resulting from this combination is of a preparatory or auxiliary character.

5. Notwithstanding the provisions of paragraphs 1 and 2,where a person—other than an agent of an independent status to whom paragraph 6 applies—is acting in a Contracting State on behalf of an enterprise of the other Contracting State, has and habitually exercises an authority to conclude contracts in the name of the enterprise, that enterprise shall be deemed to have a permanent establishment in the first mentioned Contracting State in respect of any activities which that person undertakes for the enterprise, unless the activities of such person are limited to those mentioned in paragraph 4 which, if exercised through a fixed

place of business, would not make this fixed place of business a permanent establishment under the provisions of that paragraph.

6. An enterprise of a Contracting State shall not be deemed to have a permanent establishment in the other Contracting State merely because it carries on business in that other State through a broker, general commission agent or any other agent of an independent status, provided that such persons are acting in the ordinary course of their business. However, when the activities of such an agent are devoted wholly or almost wholly on behalf of that enterprise, he will not be considered an agent of an independent status within the meaning of this paragraph.
7. The fact that a company which is a resident of a Contracting State controls or is controlled by a company which is a resident of the other Contracting State, or which carries on business in that other State (whether through a permanent establishment or otherwise),shall not of itself constitute either company a permanent establishment of the other.

Article 6: Income from Immovable Property

1. Income derived by a resident of a Contracting State from immovable property (including income from agriculture or forestry) situated in the other Contracting State may be taxed in that other State.
2. The term "immovable property" shall have the meaning which it has under the law of the Contracting State in which the property in question is situated. The term shall in any case include property accessory to immovable property, livestock and equipment used in agriculture and forestry, rights to which the provisions of general law respecting landed property apply, usufruct of immovable property and rights to variable or fixed payments as consideration for the working of, or the right to work, mineral deposits, sources and other natural resources. Ships and aircraft shall not be regarded as immovable property.
3. The provisions of paragraph 1 shall apply to income derived from the direct use, letting, or use in any other form of immovable property.
4. The provisions of paragraphs 1 and 3 shall also apply to the income from immovable property of an enterprise and to income from immovable property used for the performance of independent personal services.

Article 7: Business Profits

1. The profits of an enterprise of a Contracting State shall be taxable only in that State unless the enterprise carries on business in the other Contracting State through a permanent establishment situated therein. If the enterprise carries on business as aforesaid, the profits of the enterprise may be taxed in the other State, but only so much of them as is attributable to that permanent establishment.
2. Subject to the provisions of paragraph 3,where an enterprise of a Contracting State carries on business in the other Contracting State through a permanent establishment situated therein, there shall in each Contracting State be attributed

to that permanent establishment the profits which it might be expected to make if it were a distinct and separate enterprise engaged in the same or similar activities under the same or similar conditions and dealing wholly independently with the enterprise of which it is a permanent establishment.

3. In determining the profits of a permanent establishment, there shall be allowed as deductions expenses which are incurred for the purposes of the business of the permanent establishment, including executive and general administrative expenses so incurred, whether in the State in which the permanent establishment is situated or elsewhere.
4. Insofar as it has been customary in a Contracting State to determine the profits to be attributed to a permanent establishment on the basis of an apportionment of the total profits of the enterprise to its various parts, nothing in paragraph 2 shall preclude that Contracting State from determining the profits to be taxed by such an apportionment as may be customary. The method of apportionment adopted shall, however, be such that the result shall be in accordance with the principles contained in this Article.
5. No profits shall be attributed to a permanent establishment by reason of the mere purchase by that permanent establishment of goods or merchandise for the enterprise.
6. For the purposes of the preceding paragraphs, the profits to be attributed to the permanent establishment shall be determined by the same method year by year unless there is good and sufficient reason to the contrary.
7. Where profits include items of income which are dealt with separately in other Articles of this Agreement, then the provisions of those Articles shall not be affected by the provisions of this Article.

Article 8: Shipping and Air Transport

1. Profits from the operation of ships or aircraft in international traffic carried on by an enterprise of a Contracting State shall be taxable only in that Contracting State.
2. The provisions of paragraph 1 shall also apply to profits from the participation in a pool, a joint business or an international operating agency.

Article 9: Associated Enterprises

1. Where

   a. an enterprise of a Contracting State participates directly or indirectly in the management, control or capital of an enterprise of the other Contracting State, or
   b. the same persons participate directly or indirectly in the management, control or capital of an enterprise of a Contracting State and an enterprise of the other Contracting State, and in either case conditions are made or imposed between the two enterprises in their commercial or financial

relations which differ from those which would be made between independent enterprises, then any profits which would, but for those conditions, have accrued to one of the enterprises, but, by reason of those conditions, have not so accrued, may be included in the profits of that enterprise and taxed accordingly.

2. Where a Contracting State includes in the profits of an enterprise of that State—and taxes accordingly—profits on which an enterprise of the other Contracting State has been charged to tax in that other State and the profits so included are profits which would have accrued to the enterprise of the first mentioned State if the conditions made between the two enterprises had been those which would have been made between independent enterprises, then that other State shall make an appropriate adjustment to the amount of the tax charged therein on those profits In determining such adjustment, due regard shall be had to the other provisions of this Agreement and the competent authorities of the Contracting States shall, if necessary, consult each other.

Article 10: Dividends

1. Dividends paid by a company which is a resident of a Contracting State to a resident of the other Contracting State may be taxed in that other State.
2. However, such dividends may also be taxed in the Contracting State of which the company paying the dividends is a resident and according to the laws of that State, but if the recipient is the beneficial owner of the dividends the tax so charged shall not exceed 5 per cent of the gross amount of the dividends. The competent authorities of the Contracting States shall by mutual agreement settle the mode of application of this limitation. This paragraph shall not affect the taxation of the company in respect of the profits out of which the dividends are paid.
3. The term "dividends" as used in this Article means income from shares, or other rights, not being debt claims, participating in profits, as well as income from other corporate rights which is subjected to the same taxation treatment as income from shares by the laws of the State of which the company making the distribution is a resident.
4. The provisions of paragraphs 1 and 2 shall not apply if the beneficial owner of the dividends, being a resident of a Contracting State, carries on business in the other Contracting State of which the company paying the dividends is a resident, through a permanent establishment situated therein, or performs in that other State independent personal services from a fixed base situated therein, and the holding in respect of which the dividends are paid is effectively connected with such permanent establishment or fixed base. In such case the provisions of Article 7 or Article 14, as the case may be, shall apply.
5. Where a company which is a resident of a Contracting State derives profits or income from the other Contracting State, that other State may not impose any tax on the dividends paid by the company, except insofar as such dividends are paid

to a resident of that other State or insofar as the holding in respect of which the dividends are paid is effectively connected with a permanent establishment or a fixed base situated in that other State nor subject the company's undistributed profits to a tax on the company's undistributed profits, even if the dividends paid or the undistributed profits consist wholly or partly of profits or income arising in such other State.

Article 11: Interest

1. Interest arising in a Contracting State and paid to a resident of the other Contracting State may be taxed in that other State.
2. However, such interest may also be taxed in the Contracting State in which it arises and according to the laws of that State, but if the recipient is the beneficial owner of the interest the tax so charged shall not exceed 10 per cent of the gross amount of the interest. The competent authorities of the Contracting States shall by mutual agreement settle the mode of application of this limitation.
3. Notwithstanding the provisions of paragraph 2,interest arising in a Contracting State and derived by the Government of the other Contracting State, a local authority and the Central Bank thereof or any financial institution wholly owned by the Government of that other State, or by any other resident of that other State with respect to debt claims indirectly financed by the Government of that other State, a local authority, and the Central Bank thereof or any financial institution wholly owned by the Government of that other State, shall be exempt from tax in the first mentioned State.
4. The term "interest" as used in this Article means income from debt claims of every kind, whether or not secured by mortgage and whether or not carrying a right to participate in the debtor′s profits, and in particular, income from government securities and income from bonds or debentures, including premiums and prizes attaching to such securities, bonds or debentures. Penalty charges for late payment shall not be regarded as interest for the purpose of this Article.
5. The provisions of paragraphs 1,2 and 3 shall not apply if the beneficial owner of the interest, being a resident of a Contracting State, carries on business in the other Contracting State in which the interest arises, through a permanent establishment situated therein, or performs in that other State independent personal services from a fixed base situated therein, and the debt claim in respect of which the interest is paid is effectively connected with such permanent establishment or fixed base. In such case the provisions of Article 7 or Article 14, as the case may be, shall apply.
6. Interest shall be deemed to arise in a Contracting State when the payer is the Government of that State, a local authority thereof or a resident of that State. Where, however, the person paying the interest, whether he is a resident of a Contracting State or not, has in a Contracting State a permanent establishment or a fixed base in connection with which the indebtedness on which the interest is paid was incurred, and such interest is borne by such permanent establishment

or fixed base, then such interest shall be deemed to arise in the State in which the permanent establishment or fixed base is situated.

7. Where, by reason of a special relationship between: the payer and the beneficial owner or between both of them and some other person, the amount of the interest, having regard to the debt claim for which it is paid, exceeds the amount which would have been agreed upon by the payer and the beneficial owner in the absence of such relationship, the provisions of this Article shall apply only to the last mentioned amount. In such case, the excess part of the payments shall remain taxable according to the laws of each Contracting State, due regard being had to the other provisions of this Agreement.

Article 12: Royalties

1. Royalties arising in a Contracting State and paid to a resident of the other Contracting State may be taxed in that other State.
2. However, such royalties may also be taxed in the Contracting State in which they arise and according to the laws of that State, but if the recipient is the beneficial owner of the royalties, the tax so charged shall not exceed 10 per cent of the gross amount of the royalties. The competent authorities of the Contracting States shall by mutual agreement settle the mode of application of this limitation.
3. The term "royalties" as used in this Article means payments of any kind received as a consideration for the use of, or the right to use, any copyright of literary, artistic or scientific work including cinematography films, or films or tapes for radio or television broadcasting, any patent, trade mark, design or model, plan, secret formula or process, or for the use of, or the right to use, industrial, commercial, or scientific equipment, or for information concerning industrial, commercial or scientific experience.
4. The provisions of paragraphs 1 and 2 shall not apply if the beneficial owner of the royalties, being a resident of a Contracting State, carries on business in the other Contracting State in which the royalties arise, through a permanent establishment situated therein, or performs in that other State independent personal services from a fixed base situated therein, and the right or property in respect of which the royalties are paid is effectively connected with such permanent establishment or fixed base. In such case the provisions of Article 7 or Article 14, as the case may be, shall apply.
5. Royalties shall be deemed to arise in a Contracting State when the payer is the Government of that Contracting State, a local authority thereof or a resident of that Contracting State. Where, however, the person paying the royalties, whether he is a resident of a Contracting State or not, has in a Contracting State a permanent establishment or a fixed base in connection with which the liability to pay the royalties was incurred, and such royalties are borne by such permanent establishment or fixed base, then such royalties shall be deemed to arise in the State in which the permanent establishment or fixed base is situated.

6. Where, by reason of a special relationship between the payer and the beneficial owner or between both of them and some other person, the amount of the royalties, having regard to the use, right or information for which they are paid, exceeds the amount which would have been agreed upon by the payer and the beneficial owner in the absence of such relationship, the provisions of this Article shall apply only to the last mentioned amount. In such case; the excess part of the payments shall remain taxable according to the laws of each Contracting State, due regard being had to the other provisions of this Agreement.

Article 13: Capital Gains

1. Gains derived by a resident of a Contracting State from the alienation of immovable property referred to in Article 6 and situated in the other Contracting State may be taxed in that other State.
2. Gains from the alienation of movable property forming part of the business property of a permanent establishment which an enterprise of a Contracting State has in the other Contracting State or of movable property pertaining to a fixed base available to a resident of a Contracting State in the other Contracting State for the purpose of performing independent personal services, including such gains from the alienation of such a permanent establishment(alone or with the whole enterprise)or of such a fixed base, may be taxed in that other State.
3. Gains from the alienation of ships or aircraft operated in international traffic or movable property pertaining to the operation of such ships or aircraft by an enterprise of a Contracting State shall be taxable only in that Contracting State.
4. Gains from the alienation of shares of the capital stock of a company the property of which consists directly or indirectly principally of immovable property situated in a Contracting State may be taxed in that Contracting State.
5. Gains from the alienation of shares other than those mentioned in paragraph 4 representing a participation of at least 25 per cent in a company which is a resident of a Contracting State may be taxed in that State.
6. Gains from the alienation of any property other than that referred to in paragraphs 1 to 5, shall be taxable only in the Contracting State of which the alienator is a resident.

Article 14: Independent Personal Services

1. Income derived by a resident of a Contracting State in respect of professional services or other activities of an independent character shall be taxable only in that State except in one of the following circumstances, when such income may also be taxed in the other Contracting State:

    a. if he has a fixed base regularly available to him in the other Contracting State for the purpose of performing his activities; in that case, only so much of the income as is attributable to that fixed base may be taxed in that other State;

b. if his stay in the other Contracting State is for a period or periods amounting to or exceeding in the aggregate 183 days in the calendar year concerned; in that case, only so much of the income as is derived from his activities performed in that other State may be taxed in that other State.

2. The term "professional services" includes especially independent scientific, literary, artistic, educational or teaching activities as well as the independent activities of physicians, lawyers, engineers, architects, dentists and accountants.

Article 15: Dependent Personal Services

1. Subject to the provisions of Articles 16,18,19,20 and 21, salaries, wages and other similar remuneration derived by a resident of a Contracting State in respect of an employment shall be taxable only in that State unless the employment is exercised in the other Contracting State. If the employment is so exercised, such remuneration as is derived there from may be taxed in that other State.
2. Notwithstanding the provisions of paragraph 1, remuneration derived by a resident of a Contracting State in respect of an employment exercised in the other Contracting State shall be taxable only in the first mentioned State if:

   a. the recipient is present in the other State for a period or periods not exceeding in the aggregate 183 days in the calendar year concerned; and
   b. the remuneration is paid by, or on behalf of, an employer who is not a resident of the other State; and
   c. the remuneration is not borne by a permanent establishment or a fixed base which the employer has in the other State.

3. Notwithstanding the preceding provisions of this Article, remuneration derived in respect of an employment exercised aboard a ship or aircraft operated by an enterprise of a Contracting State in international traffic, shall be taxable only in that Contracting State.

Article 16: Directors' Fees

Directors′ fees and other similar payments derived by a resident of a Contracting State in his capacity as a member of the board of directors of a company which is a resident of the other Contracting State may be taxed in that other State.

Article 17 Artistes and Sportsmen

1. Notwithstanding the provisions of Articles 14 and 15, income derived by a resident of a Contracting State as an entertainer, such as a theatre, motion picture, radio or television artiste, or a musician, or as a sportsman, from his personal activities as such exercised in the other Contracting State, may be taxed in that other State.
2. Where income in respect of personal activities exercised by an entertainer or a sportsman in his capacity as such accrues not to the entertainer or sportsman

himself but to another person, that income may, notwithstanding the provisions of Articles 7,14 and 15, be taxed in the Contracting State in which the activities of the entertainer or sportsman are exercised.

3. Notwithstanding the preceding provisions of this Article, income derived by entertainers or sportsmen who are residents of a Contracting State from the activities exercised in the other Contracting State under a plan of cultural exchange between the Governments of both Contracting States shall be exempt from tax in that other State.

Article 18: Pensions

1. Subject to the provisions of paragraph 2 of Article 19, pensions and other similar remuneration paid to a resident of a Contracting State in consideration of past employment shall be taxable only in that State.
2. Notwithstanding the provisions of paragraph 1, pensions paid, and other similar payments made by the Government of a Contracting State or a local authority thereof under a public welfare scheme of the social security system of that. State shall be taxable only in that State.

Article 19: Government Service

a. Salaries, wages and other similar remuneration, other than a pension, paid by the Government of a Contracting State or a local authority thereof to an individual in respect of services rendered to the Government of that State or a local authority thereof, in the discharge of functions of a governmental nature, shall be taxable only in that State.
b. However, such salaries, wages and other similar remuneration shall be taxable only in the other Contracting State if the services are rendered in that other State and the individual is a resident of that other State who: (i) is a national of that State; or (ii) did not become a resident of that State solely for the purpose of rendering the services.
c. Any pension paid by, or out of funds to which contributions are made by the Government of a Contracting State or a local authority thereof to an individual in respect of services rendered to the Government of that State or a local authority thereof shall be taxable only in that State.
d. However, such pension shall be taxable only in the other Contracting State if the individual is a resident of, and a national of, that other State.
e. The provisions of Articles 15,16,17 and 18 shall apply to remuneration and pensions in respect of services rendered in connection with a business carried on by the Government of a Contracting State or a local authority thereof.

Article 20: Teachers and Researchers

1. Remuneration which an individual who is or was immediately before visiting a Contracting State, a resident of the other Contracting State and who is present

in the first mentioned State for the primary purpose of teaching, giving lectures or conducting research at a university, college, school or educational institution or scientific research institution recognized by the Government of the first mentioned State derives for the purpose of such teaching, lectures or research shall not be taxed in the first mentioned State, for a period of three years from the date of his first arrival in the first mentioned State.

2. The provisions of paragraph 1 of this Article shall not apply to income from research if such research is undertaken not in the public interest but primarily for the private benefit of a specific person or persons.

Article 21: Students and Trainees

1. Payments which a student, business apprentice or trainee who is or was immediately before visiting a Contracting State a resident of the other Contracting State and who is present in the first mentioned State solely for the purpose of his education or training receives for the purpose of his maintenance, education or training shall not be taxed in that State, provided that such payments arise from sources outside that State.
2. In respect of grants, scholarships and remuneration from employment not covered by paragraph 1, a student, business apprentice or trainee described in paragraph 1 shall, in addition, be entitled during such education or training to the same exemptions, reliefs or reductions in respect of taxes available to residents of the State which he is visiting.

Article 22: Other Income

1. Items of income of a resident of a Contracting State, wherever arising, not dealt with in the foregoing Articles of this Agreement shall be taxable only in that State.
2. The provisions of paragraph 1 shall not apply to income, other than income from immovable property as defined in paragraph 2 of Article 6,if the recipient of such income, being a resident of a Contracting State, carries on business in the other Contracting State through a permanent establishment situated therein, or performs in that other State independent personal services from a fixed base situated therein, and the right or property in respect of which the income is paid is effectively connected with such permanent establishment or fixed base. In such case the provisions of Article 7 or Article 14, as the case may be, shall apply.

Article 23: Methods for Elimination of Double Taxation

1. Double taxation shall be eliminated as follows:

   a. In China, where a resident of China derives income from Seychelles the amount of tax on that income payable in Seychelles in accordance with the provisions of this Agreement, may be credited against the Chinese tax imposed on that resident. The amount of the credit, however, shall not exceed the amount of the Chinese tax on that income computed in accordance with the taxation laws and regulations of China.

b. In Seychelles, Chinese tax paid by residents of Seychelles in respect of income taxable in China, in accordance with the provisions of this Agreement, shall be deducted from the taxes due according to Seychelles fiscal law. Such deductions shall not, however, exceed an amount which bears to the total Seychelles tax payable the same ratio as the income concerned bears to the total income.

2. For the purposes of paragraph 1 of this Article, the terms "Seychelles tax paid" and "Chinese tax paid" shall be deemed to include the amount of tax which would have been paid in Seychelles or China, as the case may be, but for an exemption or reduction granted in accordance with laws designed to promote economic development in that Contracting State.

Article 24: Non-Discrimination

1. Nationals of a Contracting State shall not be subjected in the other Contracting State to any taxation or any requirement connected therewith, which is other or more burdensome than the taxation and connected requirements to which nationals of that other State in the same circumstances are or may be subjected. This provision shall, notwithstanding the provisions of Article 1, also apply to persons who are not residents of one or both of the Contracting States.
2. The taxation on a permanent establishment which an enterprise of a Contracting State has in the other Contracting State shall not be less favourably levied in that other State than the taxation levied on enterprises of that other State carrying on the same activities. This provision shall not be construed as obliging a Contracting State to grant to residents of the other Contracting State any personal allowances reliefs and reductions for taxation purposes on account of civil status or family responsibilities which it grants to its own residents.
3. Except where the provisions of paragraph 1 of Article 9, paragraph 7 of Article 11,or paragraph 6 of Article 12,apply,interest,royalties and other disbursements paid by an enterprise of a Contracting State to a resident of the other Contracting State shall, for the purpose of determining the taxable profits of such enterprise, be deductible under the same conditions as if they had been paid to a resident of the first mentioned State.
4. Enterprises of a Contracting State, the capital of which is wholly or partly owned or controlled, directly or indirectly, by one or more residents of the other Contracting State, shall not be subjected in the first mentioned State to any taxation or any requirement connected therewith which is other or more burdensome than the taxation and connected requirements to which other similar enterprises of the first mentioned State are or may be subjected.

Article 25: Mutual agreement Procedure

1. Where a person considers that the actions of one or both of the Contracting States result or will result for him in taxation not in accordance with the provisions of this Agreement, he may, irrespective of the remedies provided by the domestic law of those States, present his case to the competent authority of the Contracting State of which he is a resident or, if his case comes under paragraph 1 of Article 24,to that of the Contracting State of which he is a national. The case must be presented within three years from the first notification of the action resulting in taxation not in accordance with the provisions of the Agreement.
2. The competent authority shall endeavour, if the objection appears to it to be justified and if it is not itself able to arrive at a satisfactory solution, to resolve the case by mutual agreement with the competent authority of the other Contracting State, with a view to the avoidance of taxation which is not in accordance with the Agreement. Any agreement reached shall be implemented notwithstanding any time limits in the domestic law of the Contracting States.
3. The competent authorities of the Contracting States shall endeavour to resolve by mutual agreement any difficulties or doubts arising as to the interpretation or application of the Agreement. They may also consult together for the elimination of double taxation in cases not provided for in the Agreement.
4. The competent authorities of the Contracting States may communicate with each other directly for the purpose of reaching an agreement in the sense of paragraphs 2 and 3. When it seems advisable for reaching agreement, representatives of the competent authorities of the Contracting States may meet together for an oral exchange of opinions.

Article 26: Exchange of Information

1. The competent authorities of the Contracting States shall exchange such information as is necessary for carrying out the provisions of this Agreement or of the domestic laws of the Contracting States concerning taxes covered by the Agreement, insofar as the taxation there under is not contrary to the Agreement, in particular for the prevention of evasion of such taxes. The exchange of information is not restricted by Article 1. Any information received by a Contracting State shall be treated as secret and shall be disclosed only to persons or authorities (including courts and administrative bodies)involved in the assessment or collection of, the enforcement or prosecution in respect of, or the determination of appeals in relation to, the taxes covered by the Agreement. Such persons or authorities shall use the information only for such purposes. They may disclose the information in public court proceedings or in judicial decisions.
2. In no case shall the provisions of paragraph 1 be construed so as to impose on a Contracting State the obligation:

    a. to carry out administrative measures at variance with the laws and administrative practice of that or of the other Contracting State;

b. to supply information which is not obtainable under the laws or in the normal course of the administration of that or of the other Contracting State;

c. to supply information which would disclose any trade, business, industrial, commercial or professional secret or trade process, or information, the disclosure of which would be contrary to public policy (order public).

Article 27: Diplomatic Agents and Consular Officers

Nothing in this Agreement shall affect the fiscal privileges of diplomatic agents or consular officers under the general rules of international law or under the provisions of special agreements.

Article 28: Entry into Force

This Agreement shall enter into force on the thirtieth day after the date on which diplomatic notes indicating the completion of internal legal procedures necessary in each country for the entry into force of this Agreement have been exchanged. This Agreement shall have effect as respects income derived during the taxable years beginning on or after the first day of January next following that in which this Agreement enters into force.

Article 29: Termination

This Agreement shall continue in effect indefinitely but either of the Contracting States may, on or before the thirtieth day of June in any calendar year beginning after the expiration of a period of five years from the date of its entry into force, give written notice of termination to the other Contracting State through the diplomatic channels. In such event this Agreement shall cease to have effect as respects income derived during the taxable years beginning on or after the first day of January in the calendar year next following that in which the notice of termination is given.IN WITNESS whereof the undersigned, duly authorized thereto, have signed this Agreement.

Done at Beijing on the 26th day of August 1999, in duplicate in the Chinese and English languages, both texts being equally authentic.

For the Government of the People's Republic of China
Cheng Fa Guang
For the Government of the Republic of Seychelles
Zhang Liang

Sudan

Agreement Between the Government of the People's Republic of China and the Government of the Republic of the Sudan for the Avoidance of Double Taxation and the Prevention of Fiscal Evasion with Respect to Taxes on Income

The Government of the People's Republic of China and the Government of The Sudan.

Desiring to conclude an Agreement for the avoidance of double taxation and the prevention of fiscal evasion with respect to taxes on income,

Have agreed as follows:

Article 1: Personal Scope

This Agreement shall apply to persons who are residents of one or both of the Contracting States.

Article 2: Taxes Covered

1. This Agreement shall apply to taxes on income imposed on behalf of a Contracting State or of its local authorities, irrespective of the manner in which they are levied.
2. There shall be regarded as taxes on income all taxes imposed on total income, or on elements of income, including taxes on gains from the alienation of movable or immovable property, as well as taxes on capital appreciation.
3. The existing taxes to which the Agreement shall apply are:
   a. in the People's Republic of China:
      i. the individual income tax;
      ii. the income tax for enterprises with foreign investment and foreign enterprises.
      iii. the local income tax;
      (hereinafter referred to as "Chinese tax")
   b. in the Republic of the Sudan:

L. Riccardi and G. Riccardi, *China in Africa*,
https://doi.org/10.1007/978-981-16-1148-3

i. the income tax;
ii. the capital gains tax;
(hereinafter referred to as "Sudanese tax").

4. This Agreement shall also apply to any identical or substantially similar taxes which are imposed after the date of signature of this Agreement in addition to, or in place of, the existing taxes referred to in paragraph 3. The competent authorities of the Contracting States shall notify each other of any substantial changes which have been made in their respective taxation laws within a reasonable period of time after such changes.

Article 3: General Definitions

1. For the purposes of this Agreement, unless the context otherwise requires:
   a. the term "China" means the People's Republic of China: when used in geographical sense, means all the territory of the People's Republic of China, including its territorial sea, in which the Chinese laws relating to taxation apply, and any area beyond its territorial sea, within which the People's Republic of China has sovereign rights of exploration for and exploitation of resources of the sea-bed and its sub-soil and super jacent water resources in accordance with international law;
   b. the term "The Sudan" means the Republic of the Sudan, including any area outside the territorial sea of the Republic of the Sudan which in accordance with international law has been or may be hereafter be designated, under the laws of the Republic of the Sudan concerning the continental shelf, as 3 an area within which the rights of the Republic of the Sudan with respect to sea bed and sub-soil and their natural resources may be exercised;
   c. the terms "a Contracting State" and "the other Contracting State" mean China or the Sudan as the context requires;
   d. the term "tax" means Chinese tax or Sudanese tax, as the context requires;
   e. the term "person" includes an individual, a company and any other body of persons;
   f. term "company" means anybody corporate or any entity which is treated as a body corporate for tax purposes, place of head office, place of effective management, or any other criterion of a similar nature;
   g. the terms "enterprise of a Contracting State" and "enterprise of the other Contracting State" mean, respectively, an enterprise carried on by a resident of a Contracting State;
   h. the term "nationals" means all individuals possessing the nationality of a Contracting State and all juridical persons created or organised under the laws of that Contracting State, as well as organisations without juridical personality treated for tax purposes as juridical persons created or organised under the laws of that Contracting State;

i. the term "international traffic" means any transport by a ship or aircraft operated by an enterprise which has its head office in a Contracting State, except when the ship or aircraft is operated solely between places in the other Contracting State;

j. the term "competent authority" means, in the case of China, the State Administration of Taxation or its authorized representative, and in the case of the Sudan, the Director of taxation or his authorised representative.

2. As regards the application of this Agreement by a Contracting State, any term not defined therein shall, unless the context otherwise requires, have the meaning which it has under the laws of that Contracting State concerning the taxes to which this Agreement applies.

Article 4: Resident

1. For the purposes of this Agreement, the term "resident of a Contracting State" means any person who, under the laws of that Contracting State, is liable to tax 4 therein by reason of his domicile, residence, place of head office, place of effective management or any other criterion of a similar nature.
2. Whereby reason of the provisions of paragraph 1 an individual is a resident of both Contracting States, then his status shall be determined as follows:

   a. he shall be deemed to be a resident of the Contracting State in which he has a permanent home available to him; if he has a permanent home available to him in both Contracting States he shall be deemed to be a resident of the Contracting State with which his personal and economic relations are closer (centre of vital interests);

   b. if the State in which he has his centre of vital interests cannot be determined, or if he has not a permanent home available to him in either Contracting State, he shall be deemed to be a resident of the State in which he has an habitual abode;

   c. if he has a habitual abode in both Contracting States or in neither of them, he shall be deemed to be a resident of the Contracting State of which he is a national;

   d. if he is a national of both Contracting States or of neither of them, the competent authorities of the Contracting States shall settle the question by mutual agreement.

3. Whereby reason of the provisions of paragraph 1, a person other than an individual is a resident of both Contracting States, then the competent authorities of the Contracting States shall determine his residential status by mutual agreement.

Article 5: Permanent Establishment

1. For the purposes of this Agreement, the term "permanent establishment" means a fixed place of business through which the business of an enterprise is wholly or partly carried on.
2. The term "permanent establishment" includes especially:
   a. a place of management;
   b. a branch;
   c. an office;
   d. a factory;
   e. a workshop; and
   f. a mine, an oil or gas well, a quarry or any other place of extraction of natural resources.
3. The term "permanent establishment" likewise encompasses:
   a. a building site, a construction, assembly or installation project or supervisory activities in connection therewith, but only where such site, project or activities continue for a period of more than 18 months.
   b. the furnishing of services, including consultancy services, by an enterprise of a Contracting State through employees or other engaged personnel in the other Contracting State, provided that such activities continue for the same project or a connected project for a period or periods aggregating more than 12 months within any 24-month period.
4. Notwithstanding the provisions of paragraphs 1 to 3, the term "permanent establishment" shall be deemed not to include:
   a. the use of facilities solely for the purpose of storage, display or delivery of goods or merchandise belonging to the enterprise;
   b. the maintenance of a stock of goods or merchandise belonging to the enterprise solely for the purpose of storage, display or delivery;
   c. the maintenance of a stock of goods or merchandise belonging to the enterprise solely for the purpose of processing by another enterprise;
   d. the maintenance of a fixed place of business solely for the purpose of purchasing goods or merchandise or of collecting information, for the enterprise;
   e. the maintenance of a fixed place of business solely for the purpose of carrying on, for the enterprise, any other activity of a preparatory or auxiliary character;
   f. the maintenance of a fixed place of business solely for any combination of activities mentioned in subparagraphs (a) to (e), provided that the overall activity of the fixed place of business resulting from this combination is of a preparatory or auxiliary character.
5. Notwithstanding the provisions of paragraphs 1 and 2, where a person—other than an agent of an independent status to whom the provisions of paragraph

6 apply—is acting in a Contracting State on behalf of an enterprise of the other Contracting State, has and habitually exercises an authority to conclude contracts in the name of the enterprise, that enterprise shall be deemed to have a permanent establishment in the first mentioned Contracting State in respect of any activities which that person undertakes for the enterprise, unless the activities of such person are limited to those mentioned in paragraph 4 which, if exercised through a fixed place of business, would not make this fixed place of business a permanent establishment under the provisions of that paragraph.

6. An enterprise of a Contracting State shall not be deemed to have a permanent establishment in the other Contracting State merely because it carries on business in that other Contracting State through a broker, general commission agent or any other agent of an independent status, provided that such persons are acting in the ordinary course of their business. However, when the activities of such an agent are devoted wholly or almost wholly on behalf of that enterprise, he will not be considered an agent of an independent status within the meaning of this paragraph.
7. The fact that a company which is a resident of a Contracting State controls or is controlled by a company which is a resident of the other Contracting State, or which carries on business in that other State (whether through a permanent establishment or otherwise), shall not of itself constitute either company a permanent establishment of the other.

Article 6: Income from Immovable Property

1. Income derived by a resident of a Contracting State from immovable property situated in the other Contracting State may be taxed in that other Contracting State.
2. The term "immovable property" shall have the meaning which it has under the law of the Contracting State in which the property in question is situated. The term shall in any case include property accessory to immovable property, livestock and equipment used in agriculture and forestry, rights to which the provisions of general law respecting landed property apply, usufruct of immovable property and rights to variable or fixed payments as consideration for the working of, or the right to work, mineral deposits, sources and other natural resources. Ships and aircraft shall not be regarded as immovable property.
3. The provisions of paragraph 1 shall apply to income derived from the direct use, letting, or use in any other form of immovable property.
4. The provisions of paragraph 1 and 3 shall also apply to the income from immovable property of an enterprise and to income from immovable property used for the performance of independent personal services.

Article 7: Business Profits

1. The profits of an enterprise of a Contracting State shall be taxable only in that Contracting State unless the enterprise carries on business in the other

Contracting State through a permanent establishment situated therein. If the enterprise carries on business as aforesaid, the profits of the enterprise may be taxed in the other Contracting State but only so much of them as is attributable to that permanent establishment.

2. Subject to the provisions of paragraph 3, where an enterprise of a Contracting State carries on business in the other Contracting State through a permanent establishment situated therein, there shall in each Contracting State be attributed to that permanent establishment the profits which it might be expected to make if it were a distinct and separate enterprise engaged in the same or similar activities under the same or similar conditions and dealing wholly independently with the enterprise of which it is a permanent establishment.
3. In determining the profits of a permanent establishment, there shall be allowed as deductions expenses which are incurred for the purposes of the business of the permanent establishment, including executive and general administrative expenses so incurred, whether in the State in which the permanent establishment is situated or elsewhere.
4. Insofar as it has been customary in a Contracting State to determine the profits to be attributed to a permanent establishment on the basis of an apportionment of the total profits of the enterprise to its various parts, nothing in paragraph 2 shall preclude that Contracting State from determining the profits to be taxed by such an apportionment as may be customary. The method of apportionment adopted shall, however, be such that the result shall be in accordance with the principles contained in this Article.
5. No profits shall be attributed to a permanent establishment by reason of the mere purchase by that permanent establishment of goods or merchandise for the enterprise.
6. For the purposes of paragraphs 1 to 5, the profits to be attributed to the permanent establishment shall be determined by the same method year by year unless there is good and sufficient reason to the contrary.
7. Where profits include items of income which are dealt with separately in other Articles of this Agreement, then the provisions of those Articles shall not be affected by the provisions of this Article.

Article 8: Shipping and Air Transport

1. Profits from the operation of ships or aircraft in international traffic shall be taxable only in the Contracting State in which the place of head office of the enterprise is situated.
2. If the place of head office of a shipping enterprise is aboard a ship, then it shall be deemed to be situated in the Contracting State in which the home harbour of the ship is situated, or if there is no such home harbour, in the Contracting State of which the operator of the ship is a resident.
3. The provisions of paragraph 1 shall also apply to profits from the participation in a pool, a joint business or an international operating agency.

Article 9: Associated Enterprises

1. Where
   a. an enterprise of a Contracting State participates directly or indirectly in the management, control or capital of an enterprise of the other Contracting State, or
   b. the same persons participate directly or indirectly in the management, control or capital of an enterprise of a Contracting State and an enterprise of the other Contracting State, and in either conditions are made or imposed between the two enterprise in their commercial or financial relations which differ from those which would be made between independent enterprises, then any profits which would, but for those conditions, have accrued to one of the enterprises, but, by reason of those conditions, have not so accrued, may be included in the profits of that enterprise and taxed accordingly.
2. Where a Contracting State includes in the profits of an enterprise of that Contracting State—and taxes accordingly—profits on which an enterprise of the other Contracting State has been charged to tax in that other Contracting State, and the profits so included are profits which would have accrued to the enterprise of the first-mentioned Contracting State if the conditions made between the two enterprises had been those which would have been made between independent enterprises, then that other State shall make an appropriate adjustment to the amount of the tax charged therein on those profits. In determining such adjustment, due regard shall be had to the other provisions of this Agreement and the competent authorities of the Contracting States shall, if necessary, consult each other.

Article 10: Dividends

1. Dividends paid by a company which is a resident of a Contracting State to a resident of the other Contracting State may be taxed in that other Contracting State.
2. However, such dividends may also be taxed in the Contracting State of which the company paying the dividends is a resident and according to the laws of that Contracting State, but if the recipient is the beneficial owner of the dividends the tax so charged shall not exceed 5 per cent of the gross amount of the dividends. The provisions of this paragraph shall not affect the taxation of the company in respect of the profits out of which the dividends are paid.
3. The term "dividends" as used in this Article means income from shares, or other rights, not being debt-claims, participating in profits, as well as income from other corporate rights which is subjected to the same taxation treatment as income from shares by the laws of the State of which the company making the distribution is a resident.

4. The provision of paragraphs 1 and 2 shall not apply if the beneficial owner of the dividends, being a resident of a Contracting State, carries on business in the other Contracting State of which the company paying the dividends is a resident, through a permanent establishment situated therein, or performs in that Contracting State independent personal services from a fixed base situated therein, and the holding in respect of which the dividends are paid is effectively connected with such permanent establishment or fixed base. In such case the provisions of Article 7 or Article 14, as the case may be, shall apply.
5. Where a company which is a resident of a Contracting State derives profits or income from the other Contracting State, that other Contracting State may not impose any tax on the dividends paid by the company, except insofar as such dividends are paid to a resident of that other Contracting State or insofar as the holding in respect of which the dividends are paid is effectively connected with a permanent establishment or a fixed base situated in the other Contracting State, nor subject the company's undistributed profits to a tax on the company's undistributed profits, even if the dividends paid or the undistributed profits consist wholly or partly of profits or income arising in such other Contracting State.

Article 11: Interest

1. Interest arising in a Contracting State and paid to a resident of the other Contracting State may be taxed in that other Contracting State.
2. However, such interest may also be taxed in the Contracting State in which it arises and according to the laws of that Contracting State, but if the recipient is the beneficial owner of the interest the tax so charged shall not exceed 10 per cent of the gross amount of the interest.
3. Notwithstanding the provisions of paragraph 2, interest arising in a Contracting State and derived by the government of the other Contracting State, a local authority and the Central Bank thereof or any financial institution wholly owned by that Government, or by any other resident of that other Contracting State with respect to debt-claims indirectly financed by the Government of that other Contracting State, a local authority, and the Central Bank thereof or any financial institution wholly owned by that Government, shall be exempt from tax in the first-mentioned State.
4. The term "interest" as used in this Article means income from debt-claims of every kind, whether or not secured by mortgage and whether or not carrying a right to participate in the debtor's profits, and in particular, income from government securities and income from bonds or debentures, income from premiums and prizes attaching to such securities, bonds or debentures. Penalty charges for late payment shall not be regarded as interest for the purpose of this Article.
5. The provisions of paragraphs 1, 2 and 3 shall not apply if the beneficial owner of the interest, being a resident of a Contracting State, carries on business in the other Contracting State in which the interest arises, through a permanent establishment situated therein, or performs in that other Contracting State independent personal services from a fixed base situated therein, and the debt-claim

in respect of which the interest is paid is effectively connected with such permanent establishment or fixed base. In such case the provisions of Article 7 or Article 14, as the case may be, shall apply.

6. Interest shall be deemed to arise in a Contracting State when the payer is the Government of that Contracting State, a local authority thereof or a resident of that Contracting State. Where, however, the person paying the interest, whether he is a resident of a Contracting State or not, has in a Contracting State a permanent establishment or a fixed base in connection with which the indebtedness on which the interest is paid was incurred, and such interest is borne by such permanent establishment or fixed base, then such interest shall be deemed to arise in the Contracting State in which the permanent establishment or fixed base is situated.
7. Where, by reason of a special relationship between the payer and the beneficial owner or between both of them and some other person, the amount of the interest, having regard to the debt-claim for which it is paid, exceeds the amount which would have been agreed upon by the payer and the beneficial owner in the absence of such relationship, the provisions of this Article shall apply only to the last-mentioned amount. In such case, the excess part of the payments shall remain taxable according to the laws of each Contracting State, due regard being had to the other provisions of this Agreement.

Article 12: Royalties

1. Royalties arising in a Contracting State and paid to a resident of the other Contracting State may be taxed in that other Contracting State.
2. However, such royalties may also be taxed in the Contracting State in which they arise, and according to the laws of that Contracting State, but if the recipient is the beneficial owner of the royalties, the tax so charged shall not exceed 10 per cent of the gross amount of the royalties.
3. The term "royalties" as used in this Article means payments of any kind received as consideration for the use of, or the right to use, any copyright of literary, artistic or scientific work including cinematograph films and films or tapes for radio or television broadcasting, any patent, know-how trade mark, design or model, plan, secret formula or process, or for the use of, or the right to use, industrial, commercial or scientific equipment, or for information concerning industrial, commercial or scientific experience.
4. The provisions of paragraphs 1 and 2 shall not apply if the beneficial owner of the royalties, being a resident of a Contracting State, carries on business in the other Contracting State in which the royalties arise, through a permanent establishment situated therein, or performs in that other Contracting State independent personal services from a fixed base situated therein, and the right or property in respect of which the royalties are paid is effectively connected with such permanent establishment or fixed base. In such case the provisions of Article 7 or Article 14, as the case may be, shall apply.

5. Royalties shall be deemed to arise in a Contracting State when the payer is the Government of that Contracting State, a local authority thereof or a resident of that Contracting State. Where, however, the person paying the royalties, whether he is a resident of a Contracting State or not, has in a Contracting State a permanent establishment or a fixed base in connection with which the liability to pay the royalties was incurred, and such royalties are borne by such permanent establishment or fixed base, then such royalties are borne by such permanent establishment of fixed base, then such royalties shall be deemed to arise in the Contracting State in which the permanent establishment or fixed base is situated.
6. Where, by reason of a special relationship between the payer and the beneficial owner or between both of them and some other person, the amount of the royalties, having regard to the use, right or information for which they are paid, exceeds the amount which would have been agreed upon by the payer and the beneficial owner in the absence of such relationship, the provision of this Article shall apply only to the last-mentioned amount. In such case, the excess part of the payments shall remain taxable according to the laws of each Contracting State, due regard being had to the other provisions of this Agreement.

Article 13: Capital Gains

1. Gains derived by a resident of a Contracting State from the alienation of immovable property referred to in Article 6 and situated in the other Contracting State may be taxed in that other Contracting State.
2. Gains from the alienation of movable property forming part of the business property of a permanent establishment which an enterprise of a Contracting State has in the other Contracting State or of movable property pertaining to a fixed base available to a resident of a Contracting State in the other Contracting State for the purpose of performing independent personal services, including such gains from the alienation of such a permanent establishment (alone or together with the whole enterprise) or of such a fixed base, may be taxed in that other Contracting State.
3. Gains from the alienation of ships or aircraft operated in international traffic or movable property pertaining to the operation of such ships or aircraft shall be taxable only in the Contracting State in which the place of head office of the enterprise is situated.
4. Gains from the alienation of shares of the capital stock of a company the property of which consists directly or indirectly principally of immovable property situated in a Contracting State may be taxed in that Contracting State.
5. Gains from the alienation of shares other than those mentioned in paragraph 4 representing a participation of at least 25 per cent in a company which is a resident of a Contracting State may be taxed in that Contracting State.
6. Gains from the alienation of any property other than that referred to in paragraphs 1 to 5, shall be taxable only in the Contracting State of which the alienator is a resident.

Article 14: Independent Personal Services

1. Income derived by a resident of a Contracting State in respect of professional services or other activities of an independent character shall be taxable only in that Contracting State except in one of the following circumstances, when such income may also be taxed in the other Contracting State.
   a. if he has a fixed base regularly available to him in the other Contracting State for the purpose of performing his activities; in that case, only so much of the income as is attributable to that fixed base may be taxed in that other Contracting State;
   b. if his stay in the other Contracting State is for a period or periods exceeding in the aggregate 183 days in the calendar year concerned; in that case, only so much of the income as is derived from his activities performed in that other Contracting State may be taxed in that other Contracting State.
2. The term "professional services" includes especially independent scientific, literary, artistic, educational or teaching activities as well as the independent activities of physicians, lawyers, engineers, architects, dentists and accountants.

Article 15: Dependent Personal Services

1. Subject to the provisions of Articles 16, 18, 19, 20 and 21, salaries, wages and other similar remuneration derived by a resident of a Contracting State in respect of an employment shall be taxable only in that Contracting State unless the employment is exercised in the other Contracting State. If the employment is so exercised, such remuneration as is derived there from may be taxed in that other Contracting State.
2. Notwithstanding the provisions of paragraph 1, remuneration derived by a resident of a Contracting State in respect of an employment exercised in the other Contracting State shall be taxable only in the first-mentioned State if:
   a. the recipient is present in the other Contracting State for a period or periods not exceeding in the aggregate 183 days in the calendar year concerned; and
   b. the remuneration is paid by, or on behalf of, an employer who is not a resident of the other Contracting State; and
   c. the remuneration is not borne by a permanent establishment or a fixed base which the employer has in the other Contracting State.
3. Notwithstanding the provisions of paragraphs 1 and 2 of this Article, remuneration derived in respect of an employment exercised aboard a ship or aircraft operated by an enterprise of a Contracting State in international traffic, shall be taxable only in the Contracting State in which the place of head office of the enterprise is situated.

Article 16: Directors' Fees

Directors' fees and other similar payments derived by a resident of a Contracting State in his capacity as a member of the board of directors of a company which is a resident of the other Contracting State may be taxed in that other Contracting State.

Article 17: Artistes and Athletes

1. Notwithstanding the provisions of Articles 14 and 15, income derived by a resident of a Contracting State as an entertainer, such as a theatre, motion picture, radio or television artists, or a musician, or as an athlete, from his personal activities as such exercised in the other Contracting State, may be taxed in that other Contracting State.
2. Where income in respect of personal activities exercised by an entertainer or an athlete in his capacity as such accrues not to the entertainer or athlete himself but to another person, that income may, notwithstanding the provisions of Articles 7, 14 and 15, be taxed in the Contracting State in which the activities of the entertainer or athlete are exercised.
3. Notwithstanding the provisions of paragraphs 1 and 2, income derived by entertainers or athletes who are residents of a Contracting State from the activities exercised in the other Contracting State under a plan of cultural exchange between the Governments of both Contracting States shall be exempt from tax in that other Contracting State.

Article 18: Pensions

1. Subject to the provisions of paragraph 2 of Article 19, pensions and other similar remuneration paid to a resident of a Contracting State in consideration of past employment shall be taxable only in that Contracting State.
2. Notwithstanding the provisions of paragraph 1, pensions paid, and other similar payments made by the Government of a Contracting State or a local authority thereof under a public welfare scheme of the social security system of that Contracting State shall be taxable only in that Contracting State.

Article 19: Government Service

a. remuneration, other than pension, paid by the Government of a Contracting State or a local authority thereof to an individual in respect of services rendered to the Government of that Contracting State or a local authority thereof, in the discharge of functions of a governmental nature, shall be taxable only in that Contracting State.
b. however, such remuneration shall be taxable only in the other Contracting State if the services are rendered in that other Contracting State and the individual is a resident of that other Contracting State who:

    i. is a national of that other Contracting State; or

ii. did not become a resident of that other Contracting State solely for the purpose of rendering the services.

c. any pension paid by, or out of funds to which contributions are made by the Government of a Contracting State or a local authority thereof to an individual in respect of services rendered to the Government of that Contracting State or a local authority there of shall be taxable only in that Contracting State.
d. however, such pension shall be taxable only in the other Contracting State if the individual is a resident of, and a national of, that other Contracting State.
e. The provisions of Articles 15, 16, 17 and 18 shall apply to remuneration and pensions in respect of services rendered in connection with a business carried on by the Government of a Contracting State or a local authority thereof.

Article 20: Teachers and Researchers

An individual who is, or immediately before visiting a Contracting State was, a resident of the other Contracting State and is present in the first-mentioned Contracting State for the primary purpose of teaching, giving lectures or conducting research at a university, college, school or educational institution accredited by the 16 Government of the first-mentioned Contracting State shall be exempt from tax in the first-mentioned Contracting State, for a period of three years from the date of his first arrival in the first-mentioned Contracting State, in respect of remuneration for such teaching, lectures or research.

Article 21: Students and Trainees

A student, business apprentice or trainee who is or was immediately before visiting a Contracting State a resident of the other Contracting State and who is present in the first-mentioned State solely for the purpose of his education, training shall be exempt from tax in that first-mentioned State on the following payments or income received or derived by him for the purpose of his maintenance, education or training:

a. payments derived from sources outside that Contracting State for the purpose of his maintenance, education, study, research or training;
b. grants, scholarships or awards supplied by the Government, or a scientific, educational, cultural or other tax-exempt organization; and
c. income derived from personal services performed in that Contracting State.

Article 22: Other Income

1. Items of income of a resident of a Contracting State, wherever arising, not dealt with in the foregoing Articles of this Agreement shall be taxable only in that Contracting State.
2. The provisions of paragraph 1 shall not apply to income, other than income from immovable property as defined in paragraph 2 of Article 6, if the recipient of such income, being a resident of a Contracting State, carries on business in the other Contracting State through a permanent establishment situated therein,

or performs in that other Contracting State independent personal services from a fixed base situated therein, and the right or property in respect of which the income is paid is effectively connected with such permanent establishment or fixed base. In such case the provisions of Article 7 or Article 14, as the case may be, shall apply.

Article 23: Methods for Elimination of Double Taxation

1. In China, double taxation shall be eliminated as follows:

   a. where a resident of China derives income from the Sudan the amount of tax on that income payable in the Sudan in accordance with the provisions of this Agreement, may be credited against the Chinese tax imposed on that resident. The amount of the credit, however, shall not exceed the amount of the Chinese tax on that income computed in accordance with the taxation laws and regulations of China.
   b. where the income derived from the Sudan is a dividend paid by a company which is a resident of the Sudan to a company which is a resident of China and which owns not less than 10 per cent of the shares of the company paying the dividend, the credit shall take into account the tax paid to the Sudan by the company paying the dividend in respect of its income.

2. In the Sudan, double taxation shall be eliminated as follows:
   Where a resident of the Sudan derives profits, income, or capital gains from sources within the People's Republic of China in accordance with the provision of this Agreement, the amount of the People's Republic of China tax payable in respect of those profits, income or capital gains shall be allowed as credit against Sudan tax imposed on that resident, provided.

   a. that the amount of credit shall not exceed that part of the Sudan tax which is appropriate to those profits or income or as the case may be.
   b. that in the case of a dividend, tax payable in respect of the profits out of which the dividend is paid to a company which controls directly or indirectly at least 10 per cent of the voting power in the company paying the dividend.

Article 24: Non-Discrimination

1. Nationals of a Contracting State shall not be subjected in the other Contracting State to any taxation or any requirement connected therewith, which is other or more burdensome than the taxation and connected requirements to which nationals of that other Contracting State in the same circumstances are or may be subjected. The provisions of this paragraph shall, notwithstanding the provisions of Article 1, also apply to persons who are not residents of one or both of the Contracting States.

2. The taxation on a permanent establishment which an enterprise of a Contracting State has in the other Contracting State shall not be less favourably levied in that other Contracting State than the taxation levied on enterprises of that other Contracting State carrying on the same activities. The provisions of this paragraph shall not be construed as obliging a Contracting State to grant to residents of the other Contracting 18 State any personal allowances, reliefs and reductions for taxation purposes on account of civil status or family responsibilities which it grants to its own residents.
3. Except where the provisions of Article 9, paragraph 7 of Article 11, or paragraph 6 of Article 12, apply, interest, royalties and other disbursements paid by an enterprise of a Contracting State to a resident of the other Contracting State shall, for the purpose of determining the taxable profits of such enterprise, be deductible under the same conditions as if they had been paid to a resident of the first-mentioned State.
4. Enterprises of a Contracting State, the capital of which is wholly or partly owned or controlled, directly or indirectly, by one or more residents of the other Contracting State, shall not be subjected in the first-mentioned State to any taxation or any requirement connected therewith which is other or more burdensome than the taxation and connected requirements to which other similar enterprises of the first-mentioned State are or may be subjected.

Article 25: Mutual Agreement Procedure

1. Where a person considers that the actions of one or both of the Contracting States result or will result for him in taxation not in accordance with the provisions of this Agreement, he may, irrespective of the remedies provided by the domestic law of those States, present his case to the competent authority of the Contracting State of which he is a resident or, if his case comes under paragraph 1 of Article 24, to that of the Contracting State of which he is a national. The case must be presented within three years from the first notification of the action resulting in taxation not in accordance with the provisions of the Agreement.
2. The competent authority shall endeavour, if the objection appears to it to be justified and if it is not itself able to arrive at a satisfactory solution, to resolve the case by mutual agreement with the competent authority of the other Contracting State, with a view to the avoidance of taxation which is not in accordance with the provisions of this Agreement. Any agreement reached shall be implemented notwithstanding any time limits in the domestic law of the Contracting States.
3. The competent authorities of the Contracting States shall endeavour to resolve by mutual agreement any difficulties or doubts arising as to the interpretation or application of the Agreement. They may also consult together for the elimination of double taxation in cases not provided for in this Agreement.
4. The competent authorities of the Contracting States may communicate with each other directly for the purpose of reaching an agreement in the sense of paragraphs 2 and 3. When it seems advisable for reaching agreement, representatives of the

competent authorities of the Contracting States may meet together for an oral exchange of opinions.

Article 26: Exchange of Information

1. The competent authorities of the Contracting States shall exchange such information as is necessary for carrying out the provisions of this Agreement or of the domestic laws of the Contracting States concerning taxes covered by the Agreement, insofar as the taxation thereunder is not contrary to this Agreement, in particular for the prevention of evasion of such taxes. The exchange of information is not restricted by Article 1. Any information received by a Contracting State shall be treated as secret and shall be disclosed only to persons or authorities (including courts and administrative bodies) involved in the assessment or collection of, the enforcement or prosecution in respect of, or the determination of appeals in relation to, the taxes covered by the Agreement. Such persons or authorities shall use the information only for such purposes. They may disclose the information in public court proceedings or in judicial decisions.
2. In no case shall the provisions of paragraph 1 be construed so as to impose on a Contracting State the obligation:
   a. to carry out administrative measures at variance with the laws and administrative practice of that or of the other Contracting State;
   b. to supply information which is not obtainable under the laws or in the normal course of the administration of that or of the other Contracting State;
   c. to supply information which would disclose any trade, business, industrial, commercial or professional secret or trade process, or information, the disclosure of which would be contrary to public policy (public order).

Article 27: Diplomatic Agents and Consular Officers

Nothing in this Agreement shall affect the fiscal privileges of diplomatic agents or consular officers under the general rules of international law or under the provisions of special agreements.

Article 28: Entry into Force

The Agreement shall enter into force on the thirtieth day after the date on which diplomatic notes indicating the completion of internal legal procedures necessary in each for the entry into force of this Agreement have been exchanged. This Agre ement shall have effect as respects income derived during the taxable years beginning on or after the first day of January next following that in which this Agreement enters into force.

Article 29: Termination

DONE in duplicate at Beijing, this thirtieth day of May 1997, in the Chinese, Arabic and English languages, all three texts being equally authentic. In the case of divergence of interpretation, the English text shall prevail.

For the Government of the People's Republic of China

For the Government of the Republic of the Sudan.

Uganda

Agreement Between the Government of the People's Republic of China and the Government of the Republic of Uganda for the Avoidance of Double Taxation and the Prevention of Fiscal Evasion with Respect to Taxes on Income.

The Government of the People's Republic of China and the Government of the Republic of Uganda,

Desiring to conclude an Agreement for the avoidance of double taxation and the prevention of fiscal evasion with respect to taxes on income,

Have agreed as follows:

Article 1: Persons Covered

This Agreement shall apply to persons who are residents of one or both of the Contracting States.

Article 2: Taxes Covered

1. This Agreement shall apply to taxes on income imposed on behalf of a Contracting State or its local authorities, irrespective of the manner in which they are levied.
2. There shall be regarded as taxes on income all taxes imposed on total income, or on elements of income, including taxes on gains from the alienation of movable or immovable property, as well as taxes on capital appreciation.
3. The existing taxes to which the Agreement shall apply are in particular:
    a. in China:
        i. the individual income tax;
        ii. the enterprise income tax;

    b. in Uganda:
    (hereinafter referred to as "Chinese tax") and
    the income tax;
    (hereinafter referred to as "Ugandan tax").

L. Riccardi and G. Riccardi, *China in Africa*,
https://doi.org/10.1007/978-981-16-1148-3

4. The Agreement shall apply also to any identical or substantially similar taxes that are imposed after the date of signature of the Agreement in addition to, or in place of, the existing taxes. The competent authorities of the Contracting States shall notify each other of any significant changes which have been made in their taxation laws.

Article 3: General Definitions

1. For the purposes of this Agreement, unless the context otherwise requires:

   a. the term "China" means the People's Republic of China; when used in geographical sense, means all the territory of the People's Republic of China, including its territorial sea, in which the Chinese laws relating to taxation apply, and any area beyond its territorial sea, within which the People's Republic of China has sovereign rights of exploration for and exploitation of resources of the seabed and its subsoil and superjacent water resources in accordance with international law and its internal law;
   b. the term "Uganda" means the Republic of Uganda;
   c. the terms "a Contracting State" and "the other Contracting State" mean China or Uganda as the context requires;
   d. the term "person" includes an individual, a company, a partnership and any other body of persons;
   e. the term "company" means anybody corporate or any entity which is treated as a body corporate for tax purposes;
   f. the terms "enterprise of a Contracting State" and "enterprise of the other Contracting State" mean, respectively, an enterprise carried on by a resident of a Contracting State and an enterprise carried on by a resident of the other Contracting State;—3
   g. the term "national" means:
      i. any individual possessing the nationality of a Contracting State;
      ii. any legal person, partnership and association deriving its status as such from the laws in force in a Contracting State;
   h. the term "international traffic" means any transport by a ship or aircraft operated by an enterprise of a Contracting State, except when the ship or aircraft is operated solely between places in the other Contracting State;
   i. the term "competent authority" means, in the case of China, the State Administration of Taxation or its authorized representative, and in the case of Uganda, the Minister responsible for finance or his/her authorized representative.

2. As regards the application of the Agreement at any time by a Contracting State, any term not defined therein shall, unless the context otherwise requires, have the meaning which it has at that time under the law of that State for the purposes of the taxes to which the Agreement applies, any meaning under the applicable tax laws of that State prevailing over a meaning given to the term under other laws of that State.

Article 4: Resident

1. For the purposes of this Agreement, the term "resident of a Contracting State" means any person who, under the laws of that State, is liable to tax therein by reason of his domicile, residence, place of incorporation, place of management, or any other criterion of a similar nature, and also includes that State and any local authority thereof. This term, however, does not include any person who is liable to tax in that State in respect only of income from sources in that State.
2. Whereby reason of the provisions of paragraph 1 an individual is a resident of both Contracting States, then his status shall be determined as follows:

   a. he shall be deemed to be a resident only of the State in which he has a permanent home available to him; if he has a permanent home available to him in both States, he shall be deemed to be a resident only of the State with which his personal and economic relations are closer (centre of vital interests);
   b. if the State in which he has his centre of vital interests cannot be determined, or if he has not a permanent home available to him in either State, he shall be deemed to be a resident only of the State in which he has a habitual abode;
   c. if he has a habitual abode in both States or in neither of them, he shall be deemed to be a resident only of the State of which he is a national;
   d. if he is a national of both States or of neither of them, the competent authorities of the Contracting States shall settle the question by mutual agreement.

3. Whereby reason of the provisions of paragraph 1 a person other than an individual is a resident of both Contracting States, then it shall be deemed to be a resident only of the State in which its place of effective management is situated.

Article 5: Permanent Establishment

1. For the purposes of this Agreement, the term "permanent establishment" means a fixed place of business through which the business of an enterprise is wholly or partly carried on.
2. The term "permanent establishment" includes especially:

   a. a place of management;
   b. a branch;
   c. an office;
   d. a factory;
   e. a workshop;
   f. a sales outlet; and
   g. a mine, an oil or gas well, a quarry or any other place of extraction of natural resources.

3. The term "permanent establishment" likewise encompasses:

a. a building site, a construction, assembly or installation project or supervisory activities in connection therewith, but only where such site, project or activities continue for a period of more than six months; and
b. the furnishing of services, including consultancy services, by an enterprise through employees or other personnel, where activities of that nature continue (for the same or a connected project) within the country for a period or periods aggregating more than 183 days within any twelve-month period.

4. Notwithstanding the preceding provisions of this Article, the term "permanent establishment" shall be deemed not to include:

a. the use of facilities solely for the purpose of storage, display or delivery of goods or merchandise belonging to the enterprise;
b. the maintenance of a stock of goods or merchandise belonging to the enterprise solely for the purpose of storage, display or delivery;
c. the maintenance of a stock of goods or merchandise belonging to the enterprise solely for the purpose of processing by another enterprise;
d. the maintenance of a fixed place of business solely for the purpose of purchasing goods or merchandise or of collecting information, for the enterprise;
e. the maintenance of a fixed place of business solely for the purpose of carrying on, for the enterprise, any other activity of a preparatory or auxiliary character;
f. the maintenance of a fixed place of business solely for any combination of activities mentioned in sub-paragraphs a) to e), provided that the overall activity of the fixed place of business resulting from this combination is of a preparatory or auxiliary character.

5. Notwithstanding the provisions of paragraphs 1 and 2, where a person – other than an agent of an independent status to whom paragraph 6 applies – is acting in a Contracting State on behalf of an enterprise of the other Contracting State, has and habitually exercises an authority to conclude contracts in the name of the enterprise, that enterprise shall be deemed to have a permanent establishment in the first-mentioned Contracting State in respect of any activities which that person undertakes for the enterprise, unless the activities of such person are limited to those mentioned in paragraph 4 which, if exercised through a fixed place of business, would not make this fixed place of business a permanent establishment under the provisions of that paragraph.
6. An enterprise of a Contracting State shall not be deemed to have a permanent establishment in the other Contracting State merely because it carries on business in that other State through a broker, general commission agent or any other agent of an independent status, provided that such persons are acting in the ordinary course of their business. However, when the activities of such an agent are devoted wholly or almost wholly on behalf of that enterprise, he will

not be considered an agent of an independent status within the meaning of this paragraph.

7. The fact that a company which is a resident of a Contracting State controls or is controlled by a company which is a resident of the other Contracting State, or which carries on business in that other State (whether through a permanent establishment or otherwise), shall not of itself constitute either company a permanent establishment of the other.

Article 6: Income from Immovable Property

1. Income derived by a resident of a Contracting State from immovable property (including income from agriculture or forestry) situated in the other Contracting State may be taxed in that other State.
2. The term "immovable property" shall have the meaning which it has under the law of the Contracting State in which the property in question is situated. The term shall in any case include property accessory to immovable property, livestock and equipment used in agriculture and forestry, rights to which the provisions of general law respecting landed property apply, usufruct of immovable property and rights to variable or fixed payments as consideration for the working of, or the right to work, mineral deposits, sources and other natural resources. Ships and aircraft shall not be regarded as immovable property.
3. The provisions of paragraph 1 shall apply to income derived from the direct use, letting, or use in any other form of immovable property.
4. The provisions of paragraphs 1 and 3 shall also apply to the income from immovable property of an enterprise and to income from immovable property used for the performance of independent personal services.

Article 7: Business Profits

1. The profits of an enterprise of a Contracting State shall be taxable only in that State unless the enterprise carries on business in the other Contracting State through a permanent establishment situated therein. If the enterprise carries on business as aforesaid, the profits of the enterprise may be taxed in the other State, but only so much of them as is attributable to that permanent establishment.
2. Subject to the provisions of paragraph 3, where an enterprise of a Contracting State carries on business in the other Contracting State through a permanent establishment situated therein, there shall in each Contracting State be attributed to that permanent establishment the profits which it might be expected to make if it were a distinct and separate enterprise engaged in the same or similar activities under the same or similar conditions and dealing wholly independently with the enterprise of which it is a permanent establishment.
3. In determining the profits of a permanent establishment, there shall be allowed as deductions expenses which are incurred for the purposes of the business of the permanent establishment, including executive and general administrative

expenses so incurred, whether in the State in which the permanent establishment is situated or elsewhere.

4. Insofar as it has been customary in a Contracting State to determine the profits to be attributed to a permanent establishment on the basis of an apportionment of the total profits of the enterprise to its various parts, nothing in paragraph 2 shall preclude that Contracting State from determining the profits to be taxed by such an apportionment as may be customary. The method of apportionment adopted shall, however, be such that the result shall be in accordance with the principles contained in this Article.
5. No profits shall be attributed to a permanent establishment by reason of the mere purchase by that permanent establishment of goods or merchandise for the enterprise.
6. For the purposes of the preceding paragraphs, the profits to be attributed to the permanent establishment shall be determined by the same method year by year unless there is good and sufficient reason to the contrary.
7. Where profits include items of income which are dealt with separately in other Articles of this Agreement, then the provisions of those Articles shall not be affected by the provisions of this Article.

Article 8: Shipping and Air Transport

1. Profits derived by an enterprise of a Contracting State from the operation of ships or aircraft in international traffic shall be taxable only in that State.
2. The provisions of paragraph 1 shall also apply to profits from the participation in a pool, a joint business or an international operating agency.

Article 9: Associated Enterprises

1. Where

   a. an enterprise of a Contracting State participates directly or indirectly in the management, control or capital of an enterprise of the other Contracting State, or
   b. the same persons participate directly or indirectly in the management, control or capital of an enterprise of a Contracting State and an enterprise of the other Contracting State, and in either case conditions are made or imposed between the two enterprises in their commercial or financial relations which differ from those which would be made between independent enterprises, then any profits which would, but for those conditions, have accrued to one of the enterprises, but, by reason of those conditions, have not so accrued, may be included in the profits of that enterprise and taxed accordingly.

2. Where a Contracting State includes in the profits of an enterprise of that State – and taxes accordingly – profits on which an enterprise of the other Contracting State has been charged to tax in that other State and the profits so included

are profits which would have accrued to the enterprise of the first-mentioned State if the conditions made between the two enterprises had been those which would have been made between independent enterprises, then that other State shall make an appropriate adjustment to the amount of the tax charged therein on those profits. In determining such adjustment, due regard shall be had to the other provisions of this Agreement and the competent authorities of the Contracting States shall, if necessary, consult each other.

Article 10: Dividends

1. Dividends paid by a company which is a resident of a Contracting State to a resident of the other Contracting State may be taxed in that other State.
2. However, such dividends may also be taxed in the Contracting State of which the company paying the dividends is a resident and according to the laws of that State, but if the beneficial owner of the dividends is a resident of the other Contracting State, the tax so charged shall not exceed 7.5 per cent of the gross amount of the dividends. The competent authorities of the Contracting States shall by mutual agreement settle the mode of application of this limitation. This paragraph shall not affect the taxation of the company in respect of the profits out of which the dividends are paid.
3. The term "dividends" as used in this Article means income from shares, or other rights, not being debt-claims, participating in profits, as well as income from other corporate rights which is subjected to the same taxation treatment as income from shares by the laws of the State—10—of which the company making the distribution is a resident.
4. The provisions of paragraphs 1 and 2 shall not apply if the beneficial owner of the dividends, being a resident of a Contracting State, carries on business in the other Contracting State of which the company paying the dividends is a resident, through a permanent establishment situated therein, or performs in that other State independent personal services from a fixed base situated therein, and the holding in respect of which the dividends are paid is effectively connected with such permanent establishment or fixed base. In such case the provisions of Article 7 or Article 14, as the case may be, shall apply.
5. Where a company which is a resident of a Contracting State derives profits or income from the other Contracting State, that other State may not impose any tax on the dividends paid by the company, except insofar as such dividends are paid to a resident of that other State or insofar as the holding in respect of which the dividends are paid is effectively connected with a permanent establishment or a fixed base situated in that other State, nor subject the company's undistributed profits to a tax on the company's undistributed profits, even if the dividends paid or the undistributed profits consist wholly or partly of profits or income arising in such other State.

Article 11: Interest

1. Interest arising in a Contracting State and paid to a resident of the other Contracting State may be taxed in that other State.
2. However, such interest may also be taxed in the Contracting State in which it arises and according to the laws of that State, but if the beneficial owner of the dividends is a resident of the other Contracting State, the tax so charged shall not exceed 10 per cent of the gross amount of the interest. The competent authorities of the Contracting States shall by mutual agreement settle the mode of application of this limitation.
3. Notwithstanding the provisions of paragraph 2, interest arising in a Contracting State and derived by the Government of the other Contracting State, a local authority or the Central Bank thereof or any financial institution wholly owned by the Government of that other State, or by any other resident of that other State with respect to debt-claims insured or guaranteed or indirectly financed by the Government of that other State, a local authority or the Central Bank thereof or any financial institution wholly owned by the Government of that other State, shall be exempt from tax in the first-mentioned Contracting State.
4. The term "interest" as used in this Article means income from debt-claims of every kind, whether or not secured by mortgage and whether or not carrying a right to participate in the debtor's profits, and in particular, income from government securities and income from bonds or debentures, including premiums and prizes attaching to such securities, bonds or debentures. Penalty charges for late payment shall not be regarded as interest for the purpose of this Article.
5. The provisions of paragraphs 1 and 2 shall not apply if the beneficial owner of the interest, being a resident of a Contracting State, carries on business in the other Contracting State in which the interest arises, through a permanent establishment situated therein, or performs in that other State independent personal services from a fixed base situated therein, and the debt-claim in respect of which the interest is paid is effectively connected with such permanent establishment or fixed base. In such case the provisions of Article 7 or Article 14, as the case may be, shall apply.
6. Interest shall be deemed to arise in a Contracting State when the payer is the Government of that State, a local authority thereof or a resident of that State. Where, however, the person paying the interest, whether he is a resident of a Contracting State or not, has in a Contracting State a permanent establishment or a fixed base in connection with which the indebtedness on which the interest is paid was incurred, and such interest is borne by such permanent establishment or fixed base, then such interest shall be deemed to arise in the State in which the permanent establishment or fixed base is situated.
7. Where, by reason of a special relationship between the payer and the beneficial owner or between both of them and some other person, the amount of the interest, having regard to the debt-claim for which it is paid, exceeds the amount which would have been agreed upon by the payer and the beneficial owner in the absence of such relationship, the provisions of this Article shall apply only to

the last-mentioned amount. In such case, the excess part of the payments shall remain taxable according to the laws of each Contracting State, due regard being had to the other provisions of this Agreement.

Article 12: Royalties

1. Royalties arising in a Contracting State and paid to a resident of the other Contracting State may be taxed in that other State.
2. However, such royalties may also be taxed in the Contracting State in which they arise and according to the laws of that State, but if the beneficial owner of the dividends is a resident of the other Contracting State, the tax so charged shall not exceed 10 per cent of the gross amount of the royalties. The competent authorities of the Contracting States shall by mutual agreement settle the mode of application of this limitation.
3. The term "royalties" as used in this Article means payments of any kind received as a consideration for the use of, or the right to use, any copyright of literary, artistic or scientific work including cinematography films, or films or tapes for radio or television broadcasting, any patent, trade mark, design or model, plan, secret formula or process, or for the use of, or the right to use, industrial, commercial, or scientific equipment, or for information concerning industrial, commercial or scientific experience.
4. The provisions of paragraphs 1 and 2 shall not apply if the beneficial owner of the royalties, being a resident of a Contracting State, carries on business in the other Contracting State in which the royalties arise, through a permanent establishment situated therein, or performs in that other State independent personal services from a fixed base situated therein, and the right or property in respect of which the royalties are paid is effectively connected with such permanent establishment or fixed base. In such case the provisions of Article 7 or Article 14, as the case may be, shall apply.
5. Royalties shall be deemed to arise in a Contracting State when the payer is the Government of that Contracting State, a local authority thereof or a resident of that Contracting State. Where, however, the person paying the royalties, whether he is a resident of a Contracting State or not, has in a Contracting State a permanent establishment or a fixed base in connection with which the liability to pay the royalties was incurred, and such royalties are borne by such permanent establishment or fixed base, then such royalties shall be deemed to arise in the State in which the permanent establishment or fixed base is situated.
6. Where, by reason of a special relationship between the payer and the beneficial owner or between both of them and some other person, the amount of the royalties, having regard to the use, right or information for which they are paid, exceeds the amount which would have been agreed upon by the payer and the beneficial owner in the absence of such relationship, the provisions of this Article shall apply only to the last-mentioned amount. In such case, the excess part of the payments shall remain taxable according to the laws of each Contracting State, due regard being had to the other provisions of this Agreement.

Article 13: Capital Gains

1. Gains derived by a resident of a Contracting State from the alienation of immovable property referred to in Article 6 and situated in the other Contracting State may be taxed in that other State.
2. Gains from the alienation of movable property forming part of the business property of a permanent establishment which an enterprise of a Contracting State has in the other Contracting State or of movable property pertaining to a fixed base available to a resident of a Contracting State in the other Contracting State for the purpose of performing independent personal services, including such gains from the alienation of such a permanent establishment (alone or with the whole enterprise) or of such a fixed base, may be taxed in that other State.
3. Gains derived by an enterprise of a Contracting State from the alienation of ships or aircraft operated in international traffic or movable property pertaining to the operation of such ships or aircraft shall be taxable only in that Contracting State.
4. Gains derived by a resident of a Contracting State from the alienation of shares deriving more than 50 per cent of their value directly or indirectly from immovable property situated in the other Contracting State may be taxed in that other State.
5. Gains from the alienation of any property other than that referred to in paragraphs 1 to 4 shall be taxable only in the Contracting State of which the alienator is a resident.

Article 14: Independent Personal Services

1. Income derived by a resident of a Contracting State in respect of professional services or other activities of an independent character shall be taxable only in that State except in one of the following circumstances, when such income may also be taxed in the other Contracting State:

   a. if he has a fixed base regularly available to him in the other Contracting State for the purpose of performing his activities; in that case, only so much of the income as is attributable to that fixed base may be taxed in that other State;
   b. if his stay in the other Contracting State is for a period or periods amounting to or exceeding in the aggregate 183 days in any twelve month period commencing or ending in the fiscal year concerned; in that case, only so much of the income as is derived from his activities performed in that other State may be taxed in that other State.

2. The term "professional services" includes especially independent scientific, literary, artistic, educational or teaching activities as well as the independent activities of physicians, lawyers, engineers, architects, dentists and accountants.

Article 15: Dependent Personal Services

1. Subject to the provisions of Articles 16, 18, 19, 20 and 21, salaries, wages and other similar remuneration derived by a resident of a Contracting State in respect of an employment shall be taxable only in that State unless the employment is exercised in the other Contracting State. If the employment is so exercised, such remuneration as is derived therefrom may be taxed in that other State.
2. Notwithstanding the provisions of paragraph 1, remuneration derived by a resident of a Contracting State in respect of an employment exercised in the other Contracting State shall be taxable only in the first-mentioned State if:
   a. the recipient is present in the other State for a period or periods not exceeding in the aggregate 183 days in any twelve-month period commencing or ending in the fiscal year concerned; and
   b. the remuneration is paid by, or on behalf of, an employer who is not a resident of the other State; and
   c. the remuneration is not borne by a permanent establishment or a fixed base which the employer has in the other State.
3. Notwithstanding the preceding provisions of this Article, remuneration derived in respect of an employment exercised aboard a ship or aircraft operated in international traffic by an enterprise of a Contracting State, may be taxed in that State.

Article 16: Directors' Fees

Directors' fees and other similar payments derived by a resident of a Contracting State in his capacity as a member of the board of directors of a company which is a resident of the other Contracting State may be taxed in that other State.

Article 17: Artistes and Sportsmen

1. Notwithstanding the provisions of Articles 14 and 15, income derived by a resident of a Contracting State as an entertainer, such as a theatre, motion picture, radio or television artiste, or a musician, or as a sportsman, from his personal activities as such exercised in the other Contracting State, may be taxed in that other State.
2. Where income in respect of personal activities exercised by an entertainer or a sportsman in his capacity as such accrues not to the entertainer or sportsman himself but to another person, that income may, notwithstanding the provisions of Articles 7, 14 and 15, be taxed in the Contracting State in which the activities of the entertainer or sportsman are exercised.
3. Notwithstanding the preceding provisions of this Article, income derived by entertainers or sportsmen who are residents of a Contracting State from the activities exercised in the other Contracting State under a plan of cultural exchange between the Governments of both Contracting States shall be exempt from tax in that other State.

Article 18: Pensions

1. Subject to the provisions of paragraph 2 of Article 19, pensions and other similar remuneration paid to a resident of a Contracting State in consideration of past employment shall be taxable only in that State.
2. Notwithstanding the provisions of paragraph 1, pensions paid, and other similar payments made by the Government of a Contracting State or a local authority thereof under a public welfare scheme of the social security system of that State shall be taxable only in that State.

Article 19: Government Service

a. Remuneration, other than a pension, paid by the Government of a Contracting State or a local authority thereof to an individual in respect of services rendered to the Government of that State or a local authority thereof, in the discharge of functions of a governmental nature, shall be taxable only in that State.
b. However, such remuneration shall be taxable only in the other Contracting State if the services are rendered in that other State and the individual is a resident of that other State who:

   i. is a national of that State; or
   ii. did not become a resident of that State solely for the purpose of rendering the services.

c. Any pension paid by, or out of funds to which contributions are made by the Government of a Contracting State or a local authority thereof to an individual in respect of services rendered to the Government of that State or a local authority thereof shall be taxable only in that State.
d. However, such pension shall be taxable only in the other Contracting State if the individual is a resident of, and a national of, that other State.
e. The provisions of Articles 15, 16, 17 and 18 shall apply to remuneration and pensions in respect of services rendered in connection with a business carried on by the Government of a Contracting State or a local authority thereof.

Article 20: Teachers and Researchers

1. Remuneration which an individual who is or was immediately before visiting a Contracting State, a resident of the other Contracting State and who is present in the first-mentioned state for the primary purpose of teaching, giving lectures or conducting research at a university, college, school or educational institution or scientific research institution recognized by the Government of the first-mentioned State derives for the purpose of such teaching, lectures or research shall not be taxed in the first-mentioned State for a period of two years from the date of his first arrival in the first-mentioned State.
2. The provisions of paragraph 1 of this Article shall apply only to income from lecturing, teaching or research derived by any individual if such activity is in

public interest and undertaken pursuant to a technical cooperation agreement between the Contracting States.

Article 21: Students and Trainees

1. Payments which a student, business apprentice or trainee who is or was immediately before visiting a Contracting State a resident of the other Contracting State and who is present in the first-mentioned State solely for the purpose of his education or training receives for the purpose of his maintenance, education or training shall not be taxed in that State, provided that such payments arise from sources outside that State.
2. In respect of grants, scholarships and remuneration from employment not covered by paragraph 1, a student, business apprentice or trainee described in paragraph 1 shall, in addition, be entitled during such education or training to the same exemptions, reliefs or reductions in respect of taxes available to residents of the State which he is visiting.

Article 22: Other Income

1. Items of income of a resident of a Contracting State, wherever arising, not dealt with in the foregoing Articles of this Agreement shall be taxable only in that State.
2. The provisions of paragraph 1 shall not apply to income, other than income from immovable property as defined in paragraph 2 of Article 6, if the recipient of such income, being a resident of a Contracting State, carries on business in the other Contracting State through a permanent establishment situated therein, or performs in that other State independent personal services from a fixed base situated therein, and the right or property in respect of which the income is paid is effectively connected with such permanent establishment or fixed base. In such case the provisions of Article 7 or Article 14, as the case may be, shall apply.

Article 23: Methods for The Elimination of Double Taxation

1. In China, double taxation shall be eliminated as follows:
   a. Where a resident of China derives income from Uganda, the amount of tax on that income payable in Uganda in accordance with the provisions of this Agreement, may be credited against the Chinese tax imposed on that resident. The amount of the credit, however, shall not exceed the amount of the Chinese tax on that income computed in accordance with the taxation laws and regulations of China.
   b. Where the income derived from Uganda is dividend paid by a company which is a resident of Uganda to a company which is a resident of China and which owns not less than 20 per cent of the shares of the company paying

the dividend, the credit shall take into account the tax paid to Uganda by the company paying the dividend in respect of its income.

2. In Uganda, double taxation shall be eliminated as follows:
In Uganda, where a resident of Uganda derives income which, in accordance with the provisions of this Agreement, may be taxed in China, Uganda shall allow as a deduction from the tax on the income of that resident an amount equal to the Chinese tax paid. Such deduction shall not, however, exceed that part of the income tax as computed before the deduction is given, which is attributable, as the case may be, to the income which may be taxed in China.

Article 24: Non-Discrimination

1. Nationals of a Contracting State shall not be subjected in the other Contracting State to any taxation or any requirement connected therewith, which is other or more burdensome than the taxation and connected requirements to which nationals of that other State in the same circumstances are or may be subjected. This provision shall, notwithstanding the provisions of Article 1, also apply to persons who are not residents of one or both of the Contracting States.
2. The taxation on a permanent establishment which an enterprise of a Contracting State has in the other Contracting State shall not be less favourably levied in that other State than the taxation levied on enterprises of that other State carrying on the same activities. This provision shall not be construed as obliging a Contracting State to grant to residents of the other Contracting State any personal allowances, reliefs and reductions for taxation purposes on account of civil status or family responsibilities which it grants to its own residents.
3. Except where the provisions of paragraph 1 of Article 9, paragraph 7 of Article 11, or paragraph 6 of Article 12, apply, interest, royalties and other disbursements paid by an enterprise of a Contracting State to a resident of the other Contracting State shall, for the purpose of determining the taxable profits of such enterprise, be deductible under the same conditions as if they had been paid to a resident of the first-mentioned State.
4. Enterprises of a Contracting State, the capital of which is wholly or partly owned or controlled, directly or indirectly, by one or more residents of the other Contracting State, shall not be subjected in the first-mentioned State to any taxation or any requirement connected therewith which is other or more burdensome than the taxation and connected requirements to which other similar enterprises of the first-mentioned State are or may be subjected.

Article 25: Mutual Agreement Procedure

1. Where a person considers that the actions of one or both of the Contracting States result or will result for him in taxation not in accordance with the provisions of this Agreement, he may, irrespective of the remedies provided by the domestic law of those States, present his case to the competent authority of the Contracting

State of which he is a resident or, if his case comes under paragraph 1 of Article 24, to that of the Contracting State of which he is a national. The case must be presented within three years from the first notification of the action resulting in taxation not in accordance with the provisions of the Agreement.

2. The competent authority shall endeavour, if the objection appears to it to be justified and if it is not itself able to arrive at a satisfactory solution, to resolve the case by mutual agreement with the competent authority of the other Contracting State, with a view to the avoidance of taxation which is not in accordance with the Agreement. Any agreement reached shall be implemented notwithstanding any time limits in the domestic law of the Contracting States.
3. The competent authorities of the Contracting States shall endeavour to resolve by mutual agreement any difficulties or doubts arising as to the interpretation or application of the Agreement. They may also consult together for the elimination of double taxation in cases not provided for in the Agreement.
4. The competent authorities of the Contracting States may communicate with each other directly for the purpose of reaching an agreement in the sense of paragraphs 2 and 3. When it seems advisable for reaching agreement, representatives of the competent authorities of the Contracting States may meet together for an oral exchange of opinions.

Article 26: Exchange of Information

1. The competent authorities of the Contracting States shall exchange such information as is foreseeably relevant for carrying out the provisions of this Agreement or to the administration or enforcement of the domestic laws concerning taxes of every kind and description imposed on behalf of the Contracting States, or of their local authorities, insofar as the taxation thereunder is not contrary to the Agreement. The exchange of information is not restricted by Articles 1 and 2.
2. Any information received under paragraph 1 by a Contracting State shall be treated as secret in the same manner as information obtained under the domestic laws of that State and shall be disclosed only to persons or authorities (including courts and administrative bodies) concerned with the assessment or collection of, the enforcement or prosecution in respect of, the determination of appeals in relation to the taxes referred to in paragraph 1, or the oversight of the above. Such persons or authorities shall use the information only for such purposes. They may disclose the information in public court proceedings or in judicial decisions.
3. In no case shall the provisions of paragraphs 1 and 2 be construed so as to impose on a Contracting State the obligation:

    a. to carry out administrative measures at variance with the laws and administrative practice of that or of the other Contracting State;
    b. to supply information which is not obtainable under the laws or in the normal course of the administration of that or of the other Contracting State;

c. to supply information which would disclose any trade, business, industrial, commercial or professional secret or trade process, or information, the disclosure of which would be contrary to public policy (order public).

4. If information is requested by a Contracting State in accordance with this Article, the other Contracting State shall use its information gathering measures to obtain the requested information, even though that other State may not need such information for its own tax purposes. The obligation contained in the preceding sentence is subject to the limitations of paragraph 3 but in no case shall such limitations be construed to permit a Contracting State to decline to supply information solely because it has no domestic interest in such information.
5. In no case shall the provisions of paragraph 3 be construed to permit a Contracting State to decline to supply information solely because the information is held by a bank, other financial institution, nominee or person acting in an agency or a fiduciary capacity or because it relates to ownership interests in a person.

Article 27: Diplomatic Agents and Consular Officers

Nothing in this Agreement shall affect the fiscal privileges of diplomatic agents or consular officers under the general rules of international law or under the provisions of special agreements.

Article 28: Entry into Force

Both Contracting States shall notify each other through diplomatic channels that they have completed the internal legal procedures necessary for the entry into force of this Agreement. This Agreement shall enter into force on the thirtieth day upon the receipt of the latter notification. This Agreement shall be applicable in respect of income derived during the taxable years beginning on or after the first day of January next following that in which this Agreement enters into force.

Article 29: Termination

This Agreement shall continue in effect indefinitely but either of the Contracting States may, on or before the thirtieth day of June in any calendar year beginning after the expiration of a period of five years from the date of its entry into force, give written notice of termination to the other Contracting State through diplomatic channels. In such event this Agreement shall cease to have effect as respects income derived during the taxable years beginning on or after the first day of January in the calendar year next following that in which the notice of termination is given.

IN WITNESS whereof the undersigned, duly authorized thereto, have signed this Agreement.

Done at ___ on the _____ day of ___, ___, in duplicate in the Chinese and English languages, both texts being equally authentic.

For the Government of The People's Republic of China
For the Government of The Republic of Uganda

Protocol

At the signing of the Agreement between the Government of the People's Republic of China and the Government of the Republic of Uganda for the Avoidance of Double Taxation and the Prevention of Fiscal Evasion with respect to Taxes on Income (hereinafter referred to as "the Agreement"), both sides have agreed upon the following provisions which shall form an integral part of the Agreement.

1. With respect to paragraph 3 of Article 7:
   It is understood that the following is in line with the principle stated therein: No deduction shall be allowed in respect of amounts, if any, paid (otherwise than towards reimbursement of actual expenses) by the permanent establishment to the head office of the enterprise or any other offices, by way of royalties, fees or other similar payments in return for the use of patents or other rights, by way of commission, for specific services performed or for management, or except in the case of a banking enterprise, by way of interest on moneys lent to the permanent establishment. Likewise, no account shall be taken, in the determination of the profits of a permanent establishment, of amounts charged (otherwise than towards reimbursement of actual expenses), by the permanent establishment to the head office of the enterprise or any of its other offices, by way of royalties, fees or similar payments in return for the use of patent or other rights, or by way of commission for the specific services or for management, or except in the case of a banking enterprise, by way of interest on moneys lent to the head office of the enterprise or any of its other offices.
2. With respect to paragraph 3 of Article 11:
   a. in the case of China:
      It is understood that "any financial institution wholly owned by the Government" refers to the following:
      i. the China Development Bank;
      ii. the Agricultural Development Bank of China;
      iii. the Export-Import Bank of China;

L. Riccardi and G. Riccardi, *China in Africa*,
https://doi.org/10.1007/978-981-16-1148-3

iv. the National Council for Social Security Fund;
v. the China Export & Credit Insurance Corporation; and
vi. any institution wholly owned by the Government of China as may be agreed upon from time to time between the competent authorities of the Contracting States.

b. in the case of Uganda:
i. the Uganda Development bank;
ii. the National Social Security Fund; and
iii. any institution wholly owned by the Government of Uganda as may be agreed upon from time to time between the competent authorities of the Contracting States.

3. With respect to Article 12:
It is agreed that only 70 per cent of the gross amount of royalties paid for the use of, or the right to use, industrial, commercial, or scientific equipment is liable to tax in the Contracting State in which they arise.

IN WITNESS WHEREOF the undersigned, being duly authorized thereto, have signed this Protocol.

Done at ___ on the day____ of ___, ___, in duplicate in the Chinese and English languages, both texts being equally authentic.

For the Government of The People's Republic of China
For the Government of The Republic of Uganda

Zambia

Agreement Between the Government of the People's Republic of China and the Government of the Republic of Zambia for the Avoidance of Double Taxation and the Prevention of Fiscal Evasion with Respect to Taxes on Income

The Government of the People's Republic of China and the Government of the Republic of Zambia,

Desiring to conclude an Agreement for the Avoidance of Double Taxation and the Prevention of Fiscal Evasion with respect to Taxes on Income (hereinafter referred to as "the Agreement"),

Have agreed as follows:

Article 1: Persons Covered

This Agreement shall apply to persons who are residents of one or both of the Contracting States.

Article 2: Taxes Covered

1. This Agreement shall apply to taxes on income imposed on behalf of a Contracting State or its local authorities, irrespective of the manner in which they are levied.
2. There shall be regarded as taxes on income all taxes imposed on total income, or on elements of income, including taxes on gains from the alienation of movable or immovable property, taxes on the total amounts of wages or salaries paid by enterprises, as well as taxes on capital appreciation.
3. The existing taxes to which the Agreement shall apply are in particular:
    a. in China:
        i. the individual income tax;
        ii. the enterprise income tax. (hereinafter referred to as "Chinese tax")
    b. in Zambia:
        the income tax.
        (hereinafter referred to as "Zambian tax")

L. Riccardi and G. Riccardi, *China in Africa*,
https://doi.org/10.1007/978-981-16-1148-3

4. The Agreement shall apply also to any identical or substantially similar taxes that are imposed after the date of signature of the Agreement in addition to, or in place of, the existing taxes. The competent authorities of the Contracting States shall notify each other of any significant changes which have been made in their taxation laws.

Article 3: General Definitions

1. For the purposes of this Agreement, unless the context otherwise requires:
   a. the term "China" means the People's Republic of China; when used in geographical sense, means all the territory of the People's Republic of China, including its territorial sea, in which the Chinese laws relating to taxation apply, and any area beyond its territorial sea, within which the People's Republic of China has sovereign rights of exploration for and exploitation of resources of the sea-bed and its sub-soil and superjacent water resources in accordance with international law and its internal law;
   b. the term "Zambia" means the Republic of Zambia; or any area within which Zambia, in accordance with International Law, may exercise sovereign right or jurisdiction;
   c. the term "person" includes an individual, a company and any other body of persons;
   d. the term "company" means anybody corporate or any entity that is treated as a body corporate for tax purposes;
   e. the term "enterprise" applies to the carrying on of any business;
   f. the terms "enterprise of a Contracting State" and "enterprise of the other Contracting State" mean, respectively, an enterprise carried on by a resident of a Contracting State and an enterprise carried on by a resident of the other Contracting State;
   g. the term "international traffic" means any transport by a ship or aircraft operated by an enterprise of a Contracting State, except when the ship or aircraft is operated solely between places in the other Contracting State;
   h. the term "competent authority" means, in the case of China, the State Administration of Taxation or its authorized representative, and in the case of Zambia, the Commissioner General of the Zambian Revenue Authority or the authorized representative;
   i. the term "national", in relation to a Contracting State, means:
      i. any individual possessing the nationality of a Contracting State; and
      ii. any legal person, partnership or association deriving its status as such from the laws in force in a Contracting State; and
   j. the term "business" includes the performance of professional services and of other activities of an independent character.

2. As regards the application of the Agreement at any time by a Contracting State, any term not defined therein shall, unless the context otherwise requires, have the meaning which it has at that time under the law of that State for the purposes of the taxes to which the Agreement applies, any meaning under the applicable tax laws of that State prevailing over a meaning given to the term under other laws of that State.

Article 4: Resident

1. For the purposes of this Agreement, the term "resident of a Contracting State" means any person who, under the laws of that State, is liable to tax therein by reason of his domicile, residence, place of incorporation, place of effective management or any other criterion of a similar nature, and also includes that State and any local authority thereof. This term, however, does not include any person who is liable to tax in that State in respect only of income from sources in that State or capital situated therein.
2. Whereby reason of the provisions of paragraph 1 an individual is a resident of both Contracting States, then his status shall be determined as follows:

   a. he shall be deemed to be a resident only of the State in which he has a permanent home available to him; if he has a permanent home available to him in both States, he shall be deemed to be a resident only of the State with which his personal and economic relations are closer (centre of vital interests);
   b. if the State in which he has his centre of vital interests cannot be determined, or if he has not a permanent home available to him in either State, he shall be deemed to be a resident only of the State in which he has a habitual abode;
   c. if he has a habitual abode in both States or in neither of them, he shall be deemed to be a resident only of the State of which he is a national;
   d. if he is a national of both States or of neither of them, the competent authorities of the Contracting States shall settle the question by mutual agreement.
3. Whereby reason of the provisions of paragraph 1 a person other than an individual is a resident of both Contracting States, then it shall be deemed to be a resident only of the State in which its place of effective management is situated.

Article 5: Permanent Establishment

1. For the purposes of this Agreement, the term "permanent establishment" means a fixed place of business through which the business of an enterprise is wholly or partly carried on.
2. The term "permanent establishment" includes especially:

   a. a place of management;

b. a branch;
c. an office;
d. a factory;
e. a workshop; and
f. a mine, an oil or gas well, a quarry or any other place of extraction or exploitation of natural resources.

3. The term "permanent establishment" likewise encompasses:

a. A building site, or construction, assembly or installation project or supervisory activities in connection therewith, but only if such site, project or activities last more than 9 months;
b. The furnishing of services, including consultancy services, by an enterprise through employees or other personnel engaged for such purpose, but only if activities of that nature continue (for the same or a connected project) within a Contracting State for a period or periods aggregating more than 183 days within any twelve-month period.

4. Notwithstanding the preceding provisions of this Article, the term "permanent establishment" shall be deemed not to include:

a. the use of facilities solely for the purpose of storage, display or delivery of goods or merchandise belonging to the enterprise;
b. the maintenance of a stock of goods or merchandise belonging to the enterprise solely for the purpose of storage, display or delivery;
c. the maintenance of a stock of goods or merchandise belonging to the enterprise solely for the purpose of processing by another enterprise;
d. the maintenance of a fixed place of business solely for the purpose of purchasing goods or merchandise or of collecting information, for the enterprise;
e. the maintenance of a fixed place of business solely for the purpose of carrying on, for the enterprise, any other activity of a preparatory or auxiliary character;
f. the maintenance of a fixed place of business solely for any combination of activities mentioned in sub-paragraphs a) to e), provided that the overall activity of the fixed place of business resulting from this combination is of a preparatory or auxiliary character.

5. Notwithstanding the provisions of paragraphs 1 and 2, where a person – other than an agent of an independent status to whom paragraph 6 applies—is acting in a Contracting State on behalf of an enterprise of the other Contracting State, and has, and habitually exercises, in that Contracting State an authority to conclude contracts in the name of the enterprise, that enterprise shall be deemed to have a permanent establishment in that Contracting State in respect of any activities which that person undertakes for the enterprise, unless the activities of such person are limited to those mentioned in paragraph 4 which, if exercised through

a fixed place of business, would not make this fixed place of business a permanent establishment under the provisions of that paragraph.

6. An enterprise of a Contracting State shall not be deemed to have a permanent establishment in the other Contracting State merely because it carries on business in that other State through a broker, general commission agent or any other agent of an independent status, provided that such persons are acting in the ordinary course of their business.
7. The fact that a company which is a resident of a Contracting State controls or is controlled by a company which is a resident of the other Contracting State, or which carries on business in that other State (whether through a permanent establishment or otherwise), shall not of itself constitute either company a permanent establishment of the other.

Article 6: Income from Immovable Property

1. Income derived by a resident of a Contracting State from immovable property (including income from agriculture or forestry) situated in the other Contracting State may be taxed in that other State.
2. The term "immovable property" shall have the meaning which it has under the law of the Contracting State in which the property in question is situated. The term shall in any case include property accessory to immovable property, livestock and equipment used in agriculture and forestry, rights to which the provisions of general law respecting landed property apply, usufruct of immovable property and rights to variable or fixed payments as consideration for the working of, or the right to work, mineral deposits, sources and other natural resources; ships and aircraft shall not be regarded as immovable property.
3. The provisions of paragraph 1 shall apply to income derived from the direct use, letting, or use in any other form of immovable property.
4. The provisions of paragraphs 1 and 3 shall also apply to the income from immovable property of an enterprise.

Article 7: Business Profits

1. The profits of an enterprise of a Contracting State shall be taxable only in that State unless the enterprise carries on business in the other Contracting State through a permanent establishment situated therein. If the enterprise carries on business as aforesaid, the profits of the enterprise may be taxed in the other State, but only so much of them as is attributable to that permanent establishment.
2. Subject to the provisions of paragraph 3, where an enterprise of a Contracting State carries on business in the other Contracting State through a permanent establishment situated therein, there shall in each Contracting State be attributed to that permanent establishment the profits which it might be expected to make if it were a distinct and separate enterprise engaged in the same or similar activities under the same or similar conditions and dealing wholly independently with the enterprise of which it is a permanent establishment.

3. In determining the profits of a permanent establishment, there shall be allowed as deductions expenses which are incurred for the purposes of the permanent establishment, including executive and general administrative expenses so incurred, whether in the State in which the permanent establishment is situated or elsewhere.
4. Insofar as it has been customary in a Contracting State to determine the profits to be attributed to a permanent establishment on the basis of an apportionment of the total profits of the enterprise to its various parts, nothing in paragraph 2 shall preclude that Contracting State from determining the profits to be taxed by such an apportionment as may be customary; the method of apportionment adopted shall, however, be such that the result shall be in accordance with the principles contained in this Article.
5. No profits shall be attributed to a permanent establishment by reason of the mere purchase by that permanent establishment of goods or merchandise for the enterprise.
6. For the purposes of the preceding paragraphs, the profits to be attributed to the permanent establishment shall be determined by the same method year by year unless there is good and sufficient reason to the contrary.
7. Where profits include items of income which are dealt with separately in other Articles of this Agreement, then the provisions of those Articles shall not be affected by the provisions of this Article.

Article 8: Shipping and Air Transport

1. Profits from the operation of ships or aircraft in international traffic shall be taxable only in the Contracting State in which the place of effective management of the enterprise is situated.
2. If the place of effective management of a shipping enterprise is aboard a ship, then it shall be deemed to be situated in the Contracting State in which the home harbour of the ship is situated, or, if there is no such home harbour, in the Contracting State of which the operator of the ship is a resident.
3. For the purposes of this Article, profits from the operation of ships or aircraft in international traffic particularly include:
   a. profits from the rental on a bareboat basis of ships or aircraft; and
   b. profits from the use, maintenance or rental of containers (including trailers and related equipment for the transport of containers) used for the transport of goods or merchandise, where such rental or such use, maintenance or rental, as the case may be, is incidental to the operation of ships or aircraft in international traffic.
4. The provisions of paragraphs 1, 2 and 3 of this Article shall also apply to profits from the participation in a pool, a joint business or an international operating agency.

Article 9: Associated Enterprises

1. Where

   a. an enterprise of a Contracting State participates directly or indirectly in the management, control or capital of an enterprise of the other Contracting State, or
   b. the same persons participate directly or indirectly in the management, control or capital of an enterprise of a Contracting State and an enterprise of the other Contracting State, and in either case conditions are made or imposed between the two enterprises in their commercial or financial relations which differ from those which would be made between independent enterprises, then any profits which would, but for those conditions, have accrued to one of the enterprises, but, by reason of those conditions, have not so accrued, may be included in the profits of that enterprise and taxed accordingly.

2. Where a Contracting State includes in the profits of an enterprise of that State—and taxes accordingly—profits on which an enterprise of the other Contracting State has been charged to tax in that other State and the profits so included are profits which would have accrued to the enterprise of the first-mentioned State if the conditions made between the two enterprises had been those which would have been made between independent enterprises, then that other State shall make an appropriate adjustment to the amount of the tax charged therein on those profits. In determining such adjustment, due regard shall be had to the other provisions of this Agreement and the competent authorities of the Contracting States shall, if necessary, consult each other.

Article 10: Dividends

1. Dividends paid by a company which is a resident of a Contracting State to a resident of the other Contracting State may be taxed in that other State.
2. However, such dividends may also be taxed in the Contracting State of which the company paying the dividends is a resident and according to the laws of that State, but if the beneficial owner of the dividends is a resident of the other Contracting State, the tax so charged shall not exceed 5 per cent of the gross amount of the dividends. The competent authorities of the Contracting States shall by mutual agreement settle the mode of application of this limitation. This paragraph shall not affect the taxation of the company in respect of the profits out of which the dividends are paid.
3. The term "dividends" as used in this Article means income from shares or other rights, not being debt-claims, participating in profits, as well as income from other corporate rights which is subjected to the same taxation treatment

as income from shares by the laws of the State of which the company making the distribution is a resident.

4. The provisions of paragraphs 1 and 2 shall not apply if the beneficial owner of the dividends, being a resident of a Contracting State, carries on business in the other Contracting State of which the company paying the dividends is a resident through a permanent establishment situated therein and the holding in respect of which the dividends are paid is effectively connected with such permanent establishment. In such case the provisions of Article 7 shall apply.
5. Where a company which is a resident of a Contracting State derives profits or income from the other Contracting State, that other State may not impose any tax on the dividends paid by the company, except insofar as such dividends are paid to a resident of that other State or insofar as the holding in respect of which the dividends are paid is effectively connected with a permanent establishment situated in that other State, nor subject the company's undistributed profits to a tax on the company's undistributed profits, even if the dividends paid or the undistributed profits consist wholly or partly of profits or income arising in such other State.

Article 11: Interest

1. Interest arising in a Contracting State and paid to a resident of the other Contracting State may be taxed in that other State.
2. However, such interest may also be taxed in the Contracting State in which it arises and according to the laws of that State, but if the beneficial owner of the interest is a resident of the other Contracting State, the tax so charged shall not exceed 10 per cent of the gross amount of the interest. The competent authorities of the Contracting States shall by mutual agreement settle the mode of application of this limitation.
3. Notwithstanding the provisions of paragraph 2, interest arising in a Contracting State and paid to, or on loans guaranteed or insured by, the Government or a local authority, the Central Bank or any financial institution wholly owned by the Government of the other Contracting State shall be exempt from tax in the first-mentioned State.
4. The term "interest" as used in this Article means income from debt-claims of every kind, whether or not secured by mortgage and whether or not carrying a right to participate in the debtor's profits, and in particular, income from government securities and income from bonds or debentures, including premiums and prizes attaching to such securities, bonds or debentures. Penalty charges for late payment shall not be regarded as interest for the purpose of this Article.
5. The provisions of paragraphs 1 and 2 shall not apply if the beneficial owner of the interest, being a resident of a Contracting State, carries on business in the other Contracting State in which the interest arises, through a permanent establishment situated therein and the debt-claim in respect of which the interest is paid is effectively connected with such permanent establishment. In such case the provisions of Article 7 shall apply.

6. Interest shall be deemed to arise in a Contracting State when the payer is a resident of that State. Where, however, the person paying the interest, whether he is a resident of a Contracting State or not, has in a Contracting State a permanent establishment in connection with which the indebtedness on which the interest is paid was incurred, and such interest is borne by such permanent establishment, then such interest shall be deemed to arise in the State in which the permanent establishment is situated.
7. Where, by reason of a special relationship between the payer and the beneficial owner or between both of them and some other person, the amount of the interest, having regard to the debt-claim for which it is paid, exceeds the amount which would have been agreed upon by the payer and the beneficial owner in the absence of such relationship, the provisions of this Article shall apply only to the last-mentioned amount. In such case, the excess part of the payments shall remain taxable according to the laws of each Contracting State, due regard being had to the other provisions of this Agreement.

Article 12: Royalties

1. Royalties arising in a Contracting State and beneficially owned by a resident of the other Contracting State may be taxed in that other State.
2. However, such royalties may also be taxed in the Contracting State in which they arise and according to the laws of that State, but if the beneficial owner of the royalties is a resident of the other Contracting State, the tax so charged shall not exceed 5 per cent of the gross amount of the royalties. The competent authorities of the Contracting States shall by mutual agreement settle the mode of application of this limitation.
3. The term "royalties" as used in this Article means payments of any kind received as a consideration for the use of, or the right to use, any copyright of literary, artistic or scientific work including cinematography films, or films or tapes for radio or television broadcasting, any patent, trade mark, design or model, plan, secret formula or process, or for information concerning industrial, commercial or scientific experience.
4. The provisions of paragraphs 1 and 2 shall not apply if the beneficial owner of the royalties, being a resident of a Contracting State, carries on business in the other Contracting State in which the royalties arise, through a permanent establishment situated therein and the right or property in respect of which the royalties are paid is effectively connected with such permanent establishment. In such case the provisions of Article 7 shall apply.
5. Royalties shall be deemed to arise in a Contracting State when the payer is a resident of that Contracting State. Where, however, the person paying the royalties, whether he is a resident of a Contracting State or not, has in a Contracting State a permanent establishment in connection with which the liability to pay the royalties was incurred, and such royalties are borne by such permanent establishment, then such royalties shall be deemed to arise in the State in which the permanent establishment is situated.

6. Where, by reason of a special relationship between the payer and the beneficial owner or between both of them and some other person, the amount of the royalties, having regard to the use, right or information for which they are paid, exceeds the amount which would have been agreed upon by the payer and the beneficial owner in the absence of such relationship, the provisions of this Article shall apply only to the last-mentioned amount. In such case, the excess part of the payments shall remain taxable according to the laws of each Contracting State, due regard being had to the other provisions of this Agreement.

Article 13: Capital Gains

1. Gains derived by a resident of a Contracting State from the alienation of immovable property referred to in Article 6 and situated in the other Contracting State may be taxed in that other State.
2. Gains from the alienation of movable property forming part of the business property of a permanent establishment which an enterprise of a Contracting State has in the other Contracting State, including such gains from the alienation of such a permanent establishment (alone or with the whole enterprise), may be taxed in that other State.
3. Gains from the alienation of ships or aircraft operated in international traffic by an enterprise of a Contracting State, or movable property pertaining to the operation of such ships or aircraft, shall be taxable only in that Contracting State.
4. Gains derived by a resident of a Contracting State from the alienation of shares deriving more than 50 per cent of their value directly or indirectly from immovable property situated in the other Contracting State may be taxed in that other State.
5. Gains from the alienation of any property, other than that referred to in paragraphs 1 to 4, shall be taxable only in the Contracting State of which the alienator is a resident.

Article 14: Income from Employment

1. Subject to the provisions of Articles 15, 17, and 18, salaries, wages and other similar remuneration derived by a resident of a Contracting State in respect of an employment shall be taxable only in that State unless the employment is exercised in the other Contracting State. If the employment is so exercised, such remuneration as is derived therefrom may be taxed in that other State.
2. Notwithstanding the provisions of paragraph 1, remuneration derived by a resident of a Contracting State in respect of an employment exercised in the other Contracting State shall be taxable only in the first-mentioned State if:

   a. the recipient is present in the other State for a period or periods not exceeding in the aggregate 183 days in any twelve-month period commencing or ending in the fiscal year concerned, and

b. the remuneration is paid by, or on behalf of, an employer who is not a resident of the other State, and
c. the remuneration is not borne by a permanent establishment which the employer has in the other State.

3. Notwithstanding the preceding provisions of this Article, remuneration derived in respect of an employment exercised aboard a ship or aircraft operated in international traffic by an enterprise of a Contracting State, may be taxed in that Contracting State in which the place of effective management of the enterprise is situated.

Article 15: Directors' Fees

Directors' fees and other similar payments derived by a resident of a Contracting State in his capacity as a member of the board of directors of a company which is a resident of the other Contracting State may be taxed in that other State.

Article 16: Artistes and Sportsmen

1. Notwithstanding the provisions of Articles 7 and 14, income derived by a resident of a Contracting State as an entertainer, such as a theatre, motion picture, radio or television artiste, or a musician, or as a sportsman, from his personal activities as such exercised in the other Contracting State, may be taxed in that other State.
2. Where income in respect of personal activities exercised by an entertainer or a sportsman in his capacity as such accrues not to the entertainer or sportsman himself but to another person, that income may, notwithstanding the provisions of Articles 7 and 14, be taxed in the Contracting State in which the activities of the entertainer or sportsman are exercised.
3. Income derived by a resident of a Contracting State from activities exercised in the other Contracting State as envisaged in paragraphs 1 and 2, shall be exempt from tax in that other State if the visit to that other State is supported wholly or mainly by public funds of the first-mentioned Contracting State or a local authority thereof, or takes place under a cultural agreement or arrangement between the Governments of the Contracting States.

Article 17: Pensions

1. Subject to the provisions of paragraph 2 of Article 18, pensions and other similar remuneration paid to a resident of a Contracting State in consideration of past employment shall be taxable only in that State.
2. Notwithstanding the provisions of paragraph 1, pensions paid, and other similar payments made by the Government of a Contracting State or a local authority thereof under a public welfare scheme of the social security system of that State shall be taxable only in that State.

Article 18: Government Service

a. Salaries, wages and other similar remuneration, other than a pension, paid by a Contracting State or a local authority thereof to an individual in respect of services rendered to that State or authority, shall be taxable only in that State.
b. However, such salaries, wages and other similar remuneration shall be taxable only in the other Contracting State if the services are rendered in that State and the individual is a resident of that State who:

   i. is a national of that State; or
   ii. did not become a resident of that State solely for the purpose of rendering the services.

c. Pensions and other similar remuneration paid by, or out of funds created by, a Contracting State or a local authority thereof to an individual in respect of services rendered to that State or authority shall be taxable only in that State.
d. However, such pensions and other similar remuneration shall be taxable only in the other Contracting State if the individual is a resident of, and a national of, that State.
e. The provisions of Articles 14, 15, 16, and 17 shall apply to salaries, wages, pensions, and other similar remuneration in respect of services rendered in connection with a business carried on by a Contracting State or a local authority thereof.

Article 19: Student, Apprentices and Business Trainees

A student, or business apprentice who is present in a Contracting State solely for the purpose of the student's or business apprentice's education or training and who is, or immediately before being so present was, a resident of the other Contracting State, shall be exempt from tax in the first-mentioned State on payments received from outside that first-mentioned State for the purposes of the student's or business apprentice's maintenance, education or training.

Article 20: Other Income

1. Items of income of a resident of a Contracting State, wherever arising, not dealt with in the foregoing Articles of this Agreement shall be taxable only in that State.
2. The provisions of paragraph 1 shall not apply to income, other than income from immovable property as defined in paragraph 2 of Article 6, if the recipient of such income, being a resident of a Contracting State, carries on business in the other Contracting State through a permanent establishment situated therein and the right or property in respect of which the income is paid is effectively connected with such permanent establishment. In such case the provisions of Article 7 shall apply.

Article 21: Methods for Elimination of Double Taxation

1. In China, in accordance with the provisions of the law of China, double taxation shall be eliminated as follows:
   a. Where a resident of China derives income from Zambia, the amount of tax on that income payable in Zambia in accordance with the provisions of this Agreement may be credited against the Chinese tax imposed on that resident. The amount of the credit, however, shall not exceed the amount of the Chinese tax on that income computed in accordance with the taxation laws and regulations of China.
   b. Where the income derived from Zambia is dividend paid by a company which is a resident of Zambia to a company which is a resident of China and which owns not less than 10 per cent of the shares of the company paying the dividend, the credit shall take into account the tax paid to Zambia by the company paying the dividend in respect of its income.
2. In Zambia, double taxation shall be eliminated as follows:
   In Zambia, where a resident of Zambia derives income from China which may be taxed in China in accordance with the provisions of this Agreement, the amount of the tax payable in respect of that income shall be allowed as a credit against Zambian tax imposed on that resident. The amount of credit, however, shall not exceed that part of Zambian tax which is appropriate to that income.

Article 22: Non-Discrimination

1. Nationals of a Contracting State shall not be subjected in the other Contracting State to any taxation or any requirement connected therewith, which is other or more burdensome than the taxation and connected requirements to which nationals of that other State in the same circumstances, in particular with respect to residence, are or may be subjected. This provision shall, notwithstanding the provisions of Article 1, also apply to persons who are not residents of one or both of the Contracting States.
2. The taxation on a permanent establishment which an enterprise of a Contracting State has in the other Contracting State shall not be less favourably levied in that other State than the taxation levied on enterprises of that other State carrying on the same activities. This provision shall not be construed as obliging a Contracting State to grant to residents of the other Contracting State any personal allowances, reliefs and reductions for taxation purposes on account of civil status or family responsibilities which it grants to its own residents.
3. Except where the provisions of paragraph 1 of Article 9, paragraph 7 of Article 11, or paragraph 6 of Article 12, apply, interest, royalties and other disbursements paid by an enterprise of a Contracting State to a resident of the other Contracting State shall, for the purpose of determining the taxable profits of such enterprise, be deductible under the same conditions as if they had been paid to a resident of the first-mentioned State. Similarly, any debts of an enterprise of a Contracting State to a resident of the other Contracting State shall, for

the purpose of determining the taxable capital of such enterprise, be deductible under the same conditions as if they had been contracted to a resident of the first-mentioned State.

4. Enterprises of a Contracting State, the capital of which is wholly or partly owned or controlled, directly or indirectly, by one or more residents of the other Contracting State, shall not be subjected in the first-mentioned State to any taxation or any requirement connected therewith which is other or more burdensome than the taxation and connected requirements to which other similar enterprises of the first-mentioned State are or may be subjected.
5. The provisions of the Article shall, notwithstanding the provisions of Article 2, apply to taxes of every kind and description.

Article 23: Mutual Agreement Procedure

1. Where a person considers that the actions of one or both of the Contracting States result or will result for him in taxation not in accordance with the provisions of this Agreement, he may, irrespective of the remedies provided by the domestic law of those States, present his case to the competent authority of the Contracting State of which he is a resident or, if his case comes under paragraph 1 of Article 22, to that of the Contracting State of which he is a national. The case must be presented within three years from the first notification of the action resulting in taxation not in accordance with the provisions of the Agreement.
2. The competent authority shall endeavour, if the objection appears to it to be justified and if it is not itself able to arrive at a satisfactory solution, to resolve the case by mutual agreement with the competent authority of the other Contracting State, with a view to the avoidance of taxation which is not in accordance with the Agreement. Any agreement reached shall be implemented notwithstanding any time limits in the domestic law of the Contracting States.
3. The competent authorities of the Contracting States shall endeavour to resolve by mutual agreement any difficulties or doubts arising as to the interpretation or application of the Agreement. They may also consult together for the elimination of double taxation in cases not provided for in the Agreement.
4. The competent authorities of the Contracting States may communicate with each other directly for the purpose of reaching an agreement in the sense of paragraphs 2 and 3. When it seems advisable for reaching an agreement, representatives of the competent authorities of the Contracting States may meet together for an oral exchange of opinions.

Article 24: Exchange of Information

1. The competent authorities of the Contracting States shall exchange such information as is foreseeably relevant for carrying out the provisions of this Agreement or to the administration or enforcement of the domestic laws concerning taxes of every kind and description imposed on behalf of the Contracting States

or their local authorities, insofar as the taxation thereunder is not contrary to the Agreement. The exchange of information is not restricted by Articles 1 and 2.

2. Any information received under paragraph 1 by a Contracting State shall be treated as secret in the same manner as information obtained under the domestic laws of that State and shall be disclosed only to persons or authorities (including courts and administrative bodies) concerned with the assessment or collection of, the enforcement or prosecution in respect of, the determination of appeals in relation to the taxes referred to in paragraph 1, or the oversight of the above. Such persons or authorities shall use the information only for such purposes. They may disclose the information in public court proceedings or in judicial decisions.
3. In no case shall the provisions of paragraphs 1 and 2 be construed so as to impose on a Contracting State the obligation:

   a. to carry out administrative measures at variance with the laws and administrative practice of that or of the other Contracting State;
   b. to supply information which is not obtainable under the laws or in the normal course of the administration of that or of the other Contracting State;
   c. to supply information which would disclose any trade, business, industrial, commercial or professional secret or trade process, or information, the disclosure of which would be contrary to public policy (order public).

4. If information is requested by a Contracting State in accordance with this Article, the other Contracting State shall use its information gathering measures to obtain the requested information, even though that other State may not need such information for its own tax purposes. The obligation contained in the preceding sentence is subject to the limitations of paragraph 3 but in no case shall such limitations be construed to permit a Contracting State to decline to supply information solely because it has no domestic interest in such information.
5. In no case shall the provisions of paragraph 3 be construed to permit a Contracting State to decline to supply information solely because the information is held by a bank, other financial institution, nominee or person acting in an agency or a fiduciary capacity or because it relates to ownership interests in a person.

Article 25: Members of Diplomatic Missions and Consular Posts

Nothing in this Agreement shall affect the fiscal privileges of members of diplomatic missions or consular posts under the general rules of international law or under the provisions of special agreements.

Article 26: Entry into Force

This Agreement shall enter into force on the thirtieth day of the latter of the notification through which the Contracting States shall notify each other that the internal legal procedures for the entry into force of this Agreement have been complied with and its provisions shall have effect with respect to income derived during the taxable years beginning on or after the first day of January next following that in which this Agreement enters into force.

Article 27: Termination

This Agreement shall continue in effect indefinitely but either of the Contracting States may, on or before the thirtieth day of June in any calendar year beginning after the expiration of a period of five years from the date of its entry into force, give written notice of termination to the other Contracting State through the diplomatic channels. In such event this Agreement shall cease to have effect with respect to income derived during the taxable years beginning on or after the first day of January in the calendar year next following that in which the notice of termination is given.

IN WITNESS whereof the undersigned, duly authorized thereto, have signed this Agreement.

Done at ______________ on the ________ day of________, ________, in duplicate in the Chinese and English languages, both texts being equally authentic.

For the Government of the People's Republic of China

For the Government of the Republic of Zambia.

MIX
Papier aus verantwortungsvollen Quellen
Paper from responsible sources
FSC® C105338

If you have any concerns about our products,
you can contact us on
ProductSafety@springernature.com

In case Publisher is established outside the EU,
the EU authorized representative is:
Springer Nature Customer Service Center GmbH
Europaplatz 3, 69115 Heidelberg, Germany

Printed by Libri Plureos GmbH
in Hamburg, Germany